PGP IN ACTION

Secondly, while PGP provides end-to-e
once it is decrypted and reaches its destinati
also consider other methods, such as secure storaɣ―
safeguard sensitive information throughout its lifecycle.

Lastly, continuous advancements in technology also pose challenges for PGP. As computing power increases, so does the potential for brute-force attacks or advancements in cryptanalysis that could render current encryption methods useless. It becomes crucial for businesses and governments to stay updated with the latest encryption standards and ensure they are using strong encryption algorithms supported by PGP.

Real-World Examples

To better understand the significance of PGP in business and government, let's consider a couple of real-world examples:

- **Corporation A:** A multinational technology company that handles massive amounts of user data. To protect the privacy of their users, Corporation A implements PGP as part of their email communication protocol. This ensures that sensitive information, such as customer passwords or financial data, remains confidential even if intercepted during transit.

- **Government Agency B:** An intelligence agency responsible for gathering and analyzing classified information. Agency B relies on PGP to encrypt and securely transmit intelligence reports between their agents and foreign counterparts. PGP safeguards the agency's sensitive data, preventing unauthorized access and potential compromises that could impact national security.

These examples demonstrate the practicality and effectiveness of PGP in safeguarding sensitive information in both business and government contexts.

Looking Ahead

As technology continues to advance and privacy concerns become more prevalent, the role of PGP in business and government will only become more critical. Organizations will need to strike a balance between user-friendly implementations and robust security measures to protect their data effectively.

The principles behind PGP, such as asymmetric encryption and strong cryptographic algorithms, will continue to be foundational in addressing the ever-evolving challenges of securing digital communication. With the ongoing contributions and innovations by privacy advocates like Phil Zimmermann, we can expect PGP to remain at the forefront of encryption technology, protecting the confidentiality and privacy of information in the digital age.

The Battles Over Backdoors

In the world of encryption and privacy, one issue that has sparked intense debate and controversy is the concept of backdoors. These backdoors are essentially built-in vulnerabilities that allow authorized individuals, such as government agencies, to bypass encryption and gain access to encrypted data. The battles over backdoors have been raging for years, with strong arguments being made on both sides of the debate.

On one side, proponents of backdoors argue that they are necessary for national security and law enforcement purposes. They believe that providing a way to access encrypted data is essential for catching criminals and preventing acts of terrorism. They argue that strong encryption without backdoors can hinder legitimate investigations and put innocent lives at risk.

However, opponents of backdoors assert that they pose serious risks to privacy and security. They argue that any vulnerability built into encryption can be exploited by malicious actors, including hackers and hostile governments. Once a backdoor exists, it becomes a potential entry point for unauthorized access, undermining the very purpose of encryption. Moreover, they argue that the widespread use of encryption without backdoors is crucial for protecting sensitive personal data and supporting democratic values.

The battles over backdoors have played out in various arenas, including courtrooms, legislatures, and the tech industry. One notable case is the legal battle between Apple and the FBI in 2016. The FBI demanded that Apple create a backdoor to unlock the iPhone used by one of the San Bernardino attackers. Apple resisted, citing concerns about the security implications of creating such a vulnerability. The case became a symbol of the broader conflict between privacy and surveillance.

From a technical perspective, creating a backdoor is a complex and controversial task. Encryption algorithms are designed to be secure, making it incredibly challenging to create a deliberate vulnerability without compromising the overall security of the system. Moreover, implementing backdoors inherently requires the creation and management of encryption keys that can bypass regular security measures. This introduces another layer of potential weaknesses and vulnerabilities.

The battles over backdoors also extend to the global stage, with different countries adopting contrasting stances on the issue. Some governments, such as the United States and the United Kingdom, have pushed for legislation that would require tech companies to provide backdoor access. Other countries, such as Germany and Switzerland, have taken a more privacy-focused approach, opposing backdoors and advocating for strong encryption.

Finding a middle ground in this debate is no easy task. Balancing the legitimate needs of law enforcement with the imperative of preserving privacy and security is a complex and delicate challenge. It requires a nuanced understanding of the potential consequences of backdoors and the alternatives available for ensuring public safety while safeguarding individual rights.

One alternative that has been proposed is the concept of "responsible encryption," which advocates for encryption that provides strong security while allowing authorized access under specific circumstances. This approach aims to address the concerns of both sides by promoting a collaborative effort between encryption experts and law enforcement agencies to find innovative solutions that uphold privacy and security.

Ultimately, the battles over backdoors are far from over. As technology continues to evolve, new encryption methods and algorithms will emerge, leading to further debates and discussions. It is crucial for individuals, policymakers, and technologists to actively engage in this ongoing discourse to shape the future of privacy and security in the digital age.

Real-World Example: WhatsApp and the Backdoor Debate

One prominent example of the battles over backdoors is the case of WhatsApp, a popular messaging app owned by Facebook. In 2016, WhatsApp implemented end-to-end encryption, meaning that only the sender and the recipient can read the messages, while no one else, including WhatsApp itself, has access to the content.

This move to enhance user privacy faced criticism and sparked debates among policymakers, law enforcement agencies, and digital rights activists. On one hand, privacy advocates applauded WhatsApp's commitment to protecting users' information. On the other hand, government authorities raised concerns about the challenges it posed for investigations.

In countries such as Brazil and India, where WhatsApp has a significant user base, authorities have called for backdoor access to encrypted messages in order to combat crime and terrorism. However, WhatsApp has repeatedly rejected these requests, citing its commitment to user privacy.

WhatsApp's stance on encryption has prompted discussions about the balance between security and access to information for investigative purposes. The case highlights the challenges faced by tech companies in navigating the demands of law enforcement agencies while protecting user privacy.

Exercise: The Backdoor Debate Simulation

In order to better understand the complexities of the backdoor debate, let's simulate a scenario where you play the role of a policymaker. Your task is to evaluate the arguments made by both proponents and opponents of backdoors and make a recommendation.

Divide into two groups: one representing the proponents of backdoors and the other representing the opponents. Each group should prepare a persuasive argument outlining their position and the reasons behind it. Consider both technical and policy aspects when crafting your arguments.

Once each group has presented their arguments, engage in a moderated debate where you can ask questions, challenge each other's positions, and address the potential risks and benefits of backdoors.

At the end of the debate, reflect on the arguments presented and consider the implications of your decision as a policymaker. How would you balance the need for public safety and national security with the protection of privacy and individual rights?

Remember, the goal of this exercise is not to find a definitive answer, but to gain a deeper understanding of the challenges and considerations involved in the battles over backdoors.

PGP and the Fight for Privacy

In the digital age, privacy has become a precious commodity, and the battle to protect it has intensified. This section explores how Pretty Good Privacy (PGP) has played a pivotal role in the fight for privacy. We will delve into the history of PGP, its impact on individuals, businesses, and governments, and the ongoing skirmish over encryption backdoors.

The Rise of PGP

Privacy has always been a fundamental human right, but with the advent of the internet, maintaining personal privacy became more challenging than ever. Phil Zimmermann, a visionary programmer, recognized this need and developed PGP, a groundbreaking encryption software.

PGP enables users to secure their digital communications, ensuring that only the intended recipients can access the information. It utilizes asymmetric encryption, employing a public key for encryption and a private key for decryption. The beauty of PGP lies in the fact that even if intercepted by malicious entities, the encrypted message remains unreadable.

Encryption for All

One of the most significant impacts of PGP has been its democratization of encryption. Previously, encryption technology was inaccessible to the average user, limited mainly to governments and corporations. PGP changed the game by making encryption available to anyone with an internet connection.

This accessibility revolutionized privacy protection, allowing individuals to secure their emails, files, and online communications. Activists and journalists, in particular, benefited from PGP, as it offered them a way to communicate securely and shield their sources from prying eyes.

PGP's Battlefront

As PGP gained popularity, concerns over encryption's impact on national security began to emerge. Governments argued that encryption hindered their ability to track criminals and terrorists, while privacy advocates championed the importance of maintaining individual privacy rights.

The clash between encryption advocates and government agencies intensified during the so-called Crypto Wars. One such battlefront was the heated debate over encryption backdoors. Backdoors would allow law enforcement to bypass encryption and access the contents of digital communications.

Privacy advocates, including Phil Zimmermann, vehemently opposed backdoors, asserting that they compromised the very essence of encryption. They argued that a backdoor for the government could be exploited by hackers or authoritarian regimes, leading to widespread privacy violations.

Championing Privacy Rights

Phil Zimmermann and his allies understood that the fight for privacy was about more than just the technical aspects of encryption. It was a battle to preserve civil liberties and protect democratic values. Zimmermann became a vocal advocate for privacy rights, using his platform to educate the public about the importance of encryption.

His efforts extended beyond PGP, as he actively participated in policy debates, lobbying against legislation that threatened privacy. Zimmermann's commitment to privacy rights inspired a generation of activists and hackers, who took up the cause, recognizing the pivotal role encryption played in defending individual freedoms.

The Legacy of PGP

The impact of PGP on privacy and encryption cannot be overstated. PGP not only revolutionized the way individuals and organizations protect their digital communications but also sparked a larger movement for privacy and data security.

PGP paved the way for other encryption technologies, inspiring the development of alternative encryption tools and protocols. It has become a symbol of resistance against government surveillance and corporate data collection.

Today, as encryption becomes increasingly essential in a world fraught with cybersecurity threats and privacy breaches, PGP remains a touchstone for those advocating for strong encryption. Its legacy lies not only in the software itself but also in the ideology of privacy and the conviction that individuals should have control over their own data.

In the next chapter, we will explore the evolution of PGP and its impact on society. We will dive deeper into the workings of PGP, its applications in everyday life, and the ongoing debates over its use. Join us as we unravel the multifaceted world of encryption and its role in shaping the future of privacy.

The Dark Side of PGP

While PGP has proved to be a revolutionary technology in the world of encryption and privacy, it is not without its dark side. In this section, we will explore some of the potential risks and challenges associated with PGP, as well as the ethical considerations that arise.

The Illusion of Total Security

PGP offers strong encryption and has been widely adopted as a secure method for protecting sensitive information. However, it is important to remember that encryption alone does not guarantee absolute security. There are several factors that can render PGP vulnerable to attacks:

- **Key Management**: Generating and managing encryption keys correctly is crucial for effective use of PGP. If a user's private key is compromised, their encrypted messages can be decrypted. Additionally, if a user's public key is not properly verified, they may unknowingly communicate with an imposter.

- **Human Error:** PGP relies on human interaction for key exchange and encryption. Mistakes such as sharing private keys, falling victim to phishing attacks, or choosing weak passphrases can compromise the security of PGP communications.

- **Endpoint Security:** PGP protects only the content of the message, not the endpoints. If someone gains access to your device or intercepts the messages before encryption or after decryption, they can still access your information.

- **Exploiting Vulnerabilities:** Like any software, PGP implementations are not immune to vulnerabilities. If a flaw is discovered in the code or the encryption algorithms, malicious actors may exploit it to bypass PGP's security.

It is essential to understand that while PGP provides a high level of security, it is not infallible. Users must remain vigilant and take additional precautions to minimize the risks associated with its usage.

Legal and Ethical Implications

The use of PGP has raised legal and ethical questions surrounding privacy, surveillance, and the responsibilities of individuals and governments. Here are some of the key considerations:

- **Criminal Misuse:** PGP's encryption capabilities can provide cover for illicit activities such as cybercrime, illegal transfers of sensitive data, or the planning of malicious acts. The challenge lies in striking a balance between privacy and preventing criminal misuse.

- **Government Surveillance:** PGP's strong encryption has posed challenges for governments seeking to intercept communications for national security purposes. Some argue that law enforcement agencies should have access to encrypted communications to combat terrorism and other threats, while others emphasize the importance of individual privacy rights.

- **Backdoor Debate:** The idea of building intentional vulnerabilities, commonly known as "backdoors," into encryption software has been proposed as a solution for balancing privacy and security concerns. However, implementing backdoors raises concerns about potential abuse and the unintended consequences of weakened encryption.

- **Privacy vs. Convenience:** PGP requires additional effort to set up and use compared to traditional methods of communication. Some individuals may be deterred by the complexity and opt for more convenient, but less secure, options. Balancing ease-of-use with privacy is an ongoing challenge.

- **Democratic Implications:** As encryption technologies become more prevalent, debates over privacy and surveillance policies have wider implications for democracy. The ability to communicate securely is seen as essential for protecting human rights, freedom of speech, and the integrity of democratic institutions.

Addressing and navigating these legal and ethical challenges is vital in ensuring that PGP and encryption technologies continue to advance while protecting individual rights and maintaining a secure society.

The Cat-and-Mouse Game

PGP exists within a constant battle between those who seek to keep communications private and those who try to break encryption for various reasons. This cat-and-mouse game introduces additional complexities:

- **Government Surveillance Efforts:** Governments around the world employ sophisticated tactics to gain access to encrypted communications. They invest in technologies aimed at breaking encryption or exploit vulnerabilities in software or hardware to access sensitive data.

- **Emerging Encryption Technologies:** As encryption technologies evolve, new challenges arise. Quantum computing, for example, has the potential to render current encryption methods obsolete. The race to develop quantum-resistant encryption algorithms is ongoing to stay ahead of potential threats.

- **Legislation and Regulation:** Several countries have proposed or implemented laws that restrict the use of strong encryption or require backdoors to be built in. Striking the right balance between security and privacy while considering the global nature of communication remains a complex challenge.

- **Surveillance Capitalism and Privacy:** The rise of companies driven by profit from personal data collection presents significant privacy issues. PGP provides protection against government surveillance, but does not defend against data collection by private entities or protect against data breaches.

This cat-and-mouse game underscores the inherent challenges of encryption and the need for continuous innovation and adaptation to ensure secure communication in a rapidly changing landscape.

Implicit Trust and Social Engineering

PGP relies on trust, both in the technology itself and in the individuals or organizations with whom keys are exchanged. However, trust can be manipulated through social engineering techniques, leading to potential vulnerabilities:

- **Impersonation Attacks**: Attackers can masquerade as legitimate users by deceiving others into believing they are someone they are not. This can lead to the sharing of private keys with unauthorized individuals or the encryption of sensitive information for adversaries.

- **Phishing Attacks**: Phishing is a common method used to trick users into revealing their private keys or other sensitive information. Cybercriminals often exploit human vulnerabilities by sending convincing emails or creating websites that appear legitimate, prompting users to disclose their credentials.

- **Malware and Keyloggers**: Untrustworthy software installations or compromised systems can secretly capture private keys or record keystrokes, effectively bypassing encryption by intercepting information before or after it is encrypted.

- **Compromised Key Servers**: PGP relies on key servers to distribute public keys. If an attacker gains control of a key server or manipulates the keys stored on it, they can intercept encrypted messages or distribute malicious public keys.

These social engineering techniques highlight the importance of verifying identities and exercising caution when sharing or receiving encryption keys.

The Importance of User Awareness and Education

To navigate the potential risks of PGP, it is crucial to educate users about best practices and potential pitfalls. Here are some key considerations for user awareness:

- **Key Verification:** Users must learn to verify the authenticity of keys received from others to prevent communicating with imposters. Utilizing additional channels for verification, such as meeting in-person or through trusted intermediaries, can enhance security.

- **Secure Key Storage:** Safeguarding private keys is paramount. Users should store keys in encrypted form or on secure hardware devices, ensuring they are not easily accessible to unauthorized individuals.

- **Safe Computing Practices:** Employing secure computing practices, such as regularly updating software, using antivirus tools, and being cautious of phishing attempts, can help defend against various attacks that can compromise PGP.

- **Continuous Learning:** Keeping abreast of the latest encryption technologies, emerging threats, and best practices is critical. Users should stay informed, engage with the security community, and seek continuous learning to adapt to evolving security landscapes.

By emphasizing user awareness and education, individuals can better protect themselves and make informed decisions when using PGP and similar encryption technologies.

In conclusion, PGP provides a powerful tool for safeguarding sensitive information and protecting privacy. However, it is not without its challenges and potential risks. Understanding these risks, addressing the legal and ethical implications, and promoting user awareness and education are essential for navigating the dark side of PGP and ensuring its responsible and secure use in an increasingly interconnected world.

Exercises

Exercise 1: Key Management

Alex received an encrypted message from a potential business partner and wants to ensure its security. How should Alex verify the legitimacy of the sender's public key before communicating further?
Solution:
To verify the legitimacy of the sender's public key, Alex should follow these steps:

1. Obtain the sender's public key through a trusted channel, such as a keyserver or the sender's website.

2. Verify the fingerprint of the public key with the sender through an independent and secure channel, such as a phone call or an in-person meeting.

3. Use a web of trust by checking if the sender's key is signed by individuals or organizations whom Alex trusts. This strengthens the verification process.

4. Cross-reference the key's fingerprint with multiple sources to minimize the risk of tampering or interception.

By following these steps, Alex can securely verify the legitimacy of the sender's public key and ensure the integrity of their communication.

Exercise 2: Balancing Privacy and National Security

In a democratic society, strike a balance between privacy and national security is crucial. Discuss the potential impact of weakening encryption by implementing backdoors on individual privacy rights and the overall security landscape.
Solution:
Implementing backdoors in encryption software to weaken its security can have several implications on individual privacy rights and the security landscape:

- **Increased Vulnerability:** Backdoors introduce vulnerabilities that can be exploited not only by authorized entities but also by malicious hackers and foreign governments. Weakening encryption by design can compromise the confidentiality of sensitive data across various sectors, including finance, healthcare, and national defense.

- **Chilling Effects:** Weakened encryption erodes trust in technology and can dissuade individuals, businesses, and organizations from relying on secure communication channels. This may discourage the open exchange of ideas, limit innovation, and impede the growth of a digital economy.

- **Unintended Consequences:** Once backdoors exist, it becomes a matter of time before they are discovered and potentially exploited for malicious purposes. The risk of insider threats also increases as authorized individuals may misuse their access to exploit the weakened security measures.

- **Impact on Human Rights:** Privacy is considered a fundamental human right, essential for the preservation of democratic societies. Weakening encryption undermines this right and can have a chilling effect on freedom of speech, freedom of the press, and other fundamental democratic principles.

- **Global Implications:** Encryption is a global technology, and any weakening of encryption standards can have a domino effect on other countries. Implementing backdoors may encourage other governments to do the same, leading to a less secure and more easily surveilled digital landscape.

Finding the right balance between privacy and national security is an ongoing challenge. It requires open dialogue, cooperation among stakeholders, and innovative solutions that preserve privacy rights while addressing legitimate security concerns.

The Future of PGP

The future of Pretty Good Privacy (PGP) holds tremendous potential for further revolutionizing the world of encryption and securing communications. As technologies evolve and new threats emerge, PGP must adapt and integrate advanced features to meet the changing needs of users. In this section, we will explore the exciting possibilities that lie ahead for PGP and how it will continue to play a vital role in protecting privacy.

Enhancing Usability and User Experience

One of the key areas for the future development of PGP lies in improving its usability and user experience. While PGP has been a powerful tool for secure communication, it has often been criticized for its complexity and steep learning curve. To increase adoption and usage, future versions of PGP should focus on simplifying the user interface, streamlining key management processes, and automating encryption tasks.

Developers can explore intuitive graphical interfaces that guide users through the encryption process without requiring in-depth technical knowledge. Additionally, integrating PGP into popular email clients and messaging apps can eliminate the need for separate encryption software, making it more convenient for users to protect their communications.

Quantum-Resistant Encryption

In the face of emerging technologies like quantum computing, which pose a significant threat to traditional encryption algorithms, the future of PGP lies in developing quantum-resistant encryption methods. While current encryption techniques, such as RSA and AES, may become vulnerable to attacks from quantum computers, new encryption algorithms like Lattice-based cryptography and Multivariate Polynomial cryptography offer promising solutions.

PGP can stay ahead of the curve by integrating quantum-resistant encryption algorithms into its framework. This would ensure that even in a future where quantum computers can break existing cryptographic algorithms, PGP remains a robust and effective tool for secure communication.

Enhanced Security Features

As cyber threats continue to evolve and become more sophisticated, PGP must continually enhance its security features to safeguard against potential vulnerabilities. Future versions of PGP can explore advanced authentication mechanisms, such as biometric verification, hardware tokens, or multi-factor authentication, to ensure the integrity of cryptographic keys.

Additionally, integrating machine learning and artificial intelligence algorithms into PGP's security infrastructure can enhance detection mechanisms for potential attacks or anomalies. These intelligent algorithms can analyze patterns and behaviors to identify any suspicious activities, providing an additional layer of defense against malicious actors.

Interoperability and Standardization

To ensure widespread adoption and seamless integration, future versions of PGP should emphasize interoperability and standardization. Currently, there are multiple PGP implementations, each with its own variations and compatibility challenges. This fragmentation can hinder broader adoption and limit the interoperability of different PGP systems.

Efforts should be made to establish common standards and protocols, allowing different PGP implementations to interoperate seamlessly. This unified approach would simplify key exchange, increase compatibility across platforms and applications, and encourage broader adoption of PGP as a reliable encryption standard.

Integration with Blockchain Technology

One promising avenue for the future of PGP is its integration with blockchain technology. Blockchain's decentralized and transparent nature presents unique opportunities to enhance PGP's key management, authentication, and decentralized trust aspects. By leveraging the immutability and distributed consensus of blockchain, PGP can prevent tampering of cryptographic keys and provide a more secure foundation for communication.

Furthermore, by integrating PGP with blockchain smart contracts, users can automate encryption processes, establish self-executing agreements for secure communication, and ensure the integrity of encrypted data.

Challenges and Ethical Considerations

While the future of PGP holds great promise, there are several challenges and ethical considerations that need to be addressed. One significant challenge is striking a balance between privacy protection and the lawful access needs of governments for national security purposes. The ongoing debate surrounding encryption backdoors highlights the delicate line that PGP must navigate.

Additionally, ensuring the responsible and ethical use of PGP is crucial. While PGP empowers individuals with the ability to protect their privacy, it can also be misused for illegal activities or malicious purposes. Educating users about the responsible and lawful use of PGP, along with integrating behavioral analysis tools to detect potential misuse, is essential for maintaining the integrity of the system.

Conclusion

The future of PGP is filled with exciting advancements and possibilities. With enhanced usability, quantum-resistant encryption, improved security features, interoperability, blockchain integration, and responsible use, PGP will continue to be a formidable tool for protecting privacy in a rapidly evolving digital landscape. By staying ahead of emerging threats and embracing new technologies, PGP will remain a cornerstone for secure communication, empowering individuals to take control of their digital privacy.

PGP for the Next Generation

In an ever-evolving digital world, the need for secure communication and data protection has become increasingly crucial. Phil Zimmermann's pioneering work in creating Pretty Good Privacy (PGP) has laid the foundation for modern encryption technology. However, as technology continues to advance, there is a need to ensure that PGP remains relevant and effective for the next generation of users. In this section, we will explore the challenges and opportunities of PGP for the future, addressing the evolving needs of users and the advancements in encryption technology.

Reimagining PGP User Experience

One of the key areas for improving PGP is enhancing the user experience. Historically, PGP has been perceived as complex and difficult to use, limiting its adoption by the masses. In order to appeal to a wider audience, efforts must be made to simplify the process of generating, managing, and using PGP keys. User-friendly interfaces and intuitive workflows can help demystify PGP for the next generation, making it more accessible and user-friendly.

Moreover, the integration of PGP into popular email clients and messaging platforms can streamline the encryption process. This would eliminate the need for users to install standalone applications or plugins, ultimately increasing the adoption of PGP by everyday users. By simplifying the user experience, PGP can become a seamless and integral part of people's digital lives.

Advancements in Key Management

One of the challenges of PGP lies in the management of encryption keys. Key distribution, revocation, and verification processes can be complex and time-consuming, particularly for non-technical users. To address this, advancements in key management practices are essential.

The development of decentralized key management systems, leveraging blockchain technology, can provide a more efficient and secure way to manage PGP keys. By decentralizing the key infrastructure, users can have greater control over their keys while minimizing the reliance on centralized authorities. Additionally, advancements in key recovery mechanisms, such as the use of biometrics or hardware-based tokens, can enhance the security and accessibility of PGP keys.

Quantum Resistant PGP

As quantum computing technology continues to advance, the threat it poses to traditional encryption algorithms becomes more significant. Quantum computers are capable of breaking current encryption algorithms, such as RSA and ECC, rendering them vulnerable to attacks. To ensure the long-term security of PGP, it is essential to develop quantum-resistant encryption algorithms.

Efforts are underway to develop post-quantum encryption algorithms that can withstand attacks from quantum computers. These algorithms, which include lattice-based, code-based, and multivariate cryptography, offer resistance against quantum attacks. Integrating these algorithms into PGP can future-proof the system, ensuring that encrypted communications remain secure even in the face of quantum computing advancements.

Addressing Privacy Challenges

In an era of increasing surveillance and data breaches, privacy has become a paramount concern. PGP must adapt to address the evolving privacy challenges faced by users. This includes protecting metadata, authenticated encryption, and addressing the risks posed by compromised endpoints.

Solutions like Zero-Knowledge Proofs (ZKPs) can help address metadata privacy concerns by allowing users to prove the correctness of their encrypted messages without revealing any additional information. Additionally, the integration of hardware-based security features, such as trusted execution environments and secure enclaves, can enhance the security of PGP and protect against compromised endpoints.

Promoting Interoperability and Collaboration

To ensure the widespread adoption of PGP, interoperability between different encryption tools and platforms is crucial. Efforts should be made to develop standards and protocols that allow seamless communication between different encryption systems. By enabling interoperability, PGP can become a universal standard for secure communication across various platforms and devices.

Collaboration between developers, researchers, and the broader tech community is also key to improving and advancing PGP. Open-source projects that encourage contributions and feedback from the community can drive innovation and ensure the continuous improvement of PGP.

Educating the Next Generation

As the next generation comes of age in a highly connected and digitized world, the importance of privacy and secure communication must be ingrained from an early age. Educating young users about the value of encryption, the risks of surveillance, and the importance of data privacy is essential for the continued relevance and adoption of PGP.

This can be achieved through the integration of privacy and encryption education into school curriculums, interactive workshops, and awareness campaigns. By empowering the next generation with the knowledge and skills necessary to protect their privacy, we can build a more secure digital future.

In conclusion, the next generation of PGP must adapt to the evolving needs and challenges of users in a rapidly changing digital landscape. By reimagining the user experience, advancing key management practices, developing quantum-resistant encryption, addressing privacy challenges, promoting interoperability and collaboration, and educating the next generation, PGP can remain a powerful tool for secure communication and data protection.

The Legacy of PGP

PGP's Influence on Other Encryption Technologies

PGP, or Pretty Good Privacy, has had a significant impact on the field of encryption and has influenced the development of other encryption technologies. In this section, we will explore how PGP's innovative approach to encryption has shaped the landscape of digital security.

Revolutionizing Encryption

Before we delve into PGP's influence on other encryption technologies, let's first understand how PGP revolutionized the way we think about encryption. PGP was created by Phil Zimmermann in the early 1990s as a response to the increasing need for secure communication in the digital age.

At the time, encryption algorithms were primarily in the hands of government organizations and large corporations. Zimmermann aimed to change this by developing PGP as an accessible encryption software for everyone. He wanted to empower individuals to protect their privacy and secure their digital communications.

Introducing the Concept of Public Key Cryptography

One of the groundbreaking aspects of PGP was its use of public-key cryptography, which had a profound influence on other encryption technologies. Public-key cryptography uses a pair of mathematically related keys: a public key for encryption and a private key for decryption.

This innovative approach eliminated the need for secure key exchange, which was a significant challenge in traditional encryption systems. With PGP, anyone could send an encrypted message to someone else without exchanging encryption keys in advance.

This concept of public-key cryptography paved the way for the development of other encryption technologies, such as SSL/TLS (Secure Sockets Layer/Transport Layer Security) protocol used for secure communication on the internet.

Open Source and Interoperability

PGP's open-source nature also played a vital role in its influence on other encryption technologies. Zimmermann released PGP as freeware, making the source code publicly available. This allowed developers worldwide to examine, modify, and contribute to the software's improvement.

The success of PGP demonstrated the power of open-source encryption, leading to the development of other open-source projects like GnuPG (GNU Privacy Guard). GnuPG is a free and open-source implementation of the OpenPGP standard, which is backward compatible with PGP.

The interoperability of PGP with other encryption technologies has further expanded its influence. PGP's compatibility with various email programs, operating systems, and encryption standards led to its widespread adoption. This interoperability has set the standard for encryption software, ensuring seamless communication across different platforms.

Influence on Encrypted Email

PGP's impact on encrypted email cannot be overstated. PGP introduced end-to-end encryption, ensuring that only the intended recipient could read an encrypted message. This level of security became indispensable for individuals and organizations who wanted to protect sensitive information.

The success of PGP in securing email communication inspired the development of other encrypted email platforms. ProtonMail, for example, built on PGP's principles to provide a user-friendly encrypted email service. Signal, another popular messaging app, also incorporated PGP's ideas of user-controlled encryption into their platform.

Pushing the Boundaries of Encryption

PGP's influence extended beyond its immediate impact on encryption technologies. It challenged the conventional wisdom that strong encryption was only accessible to governments and large corporations.

By making encryption accessible to individuals, PGP paved the way for a broader discussion on privacy and security in the digital age. Privacy advocates and technologists began exploring new approaches to encryption, pushing the boundaries of what was considered possible.

PGP's legacy can be seen in the ongoing debate over encryption backdoors. The fight between privacy advocates and law enforcement agencies continues to rage, with PGP serving as a symbol of the need for strong encryption to protect individual rights.

Real-World Example: WhatsApp

WhatsApp, one of the most widely used messaging apps, owes its encryption capabilities to PGP's influence. In 2014, WhatsApp partnered with Open Whisper Systems to integrate the Signal Protocol, which builds on PGP's concepts of end-to-end encryption.

Thanks to PGP's influence, WhatsApp now provides secure and private communication for over two billion users worldwide. This example highlights the far-reaching impact of PGP on everyday digital interactions.

Conclusion

PGP's innovative approach to encryption has had a profound influence on the development of other encryption technologies. Through its introduction of public-key cryptography, open-source principles, and interoperability, PGP set the standard for secure communication in the digital age.

PGP's influence can be seen in the widespread adoption of encrypted email platforms, the continued development of open-source encryption projects, and the ongoing debate over privacy and encryption.

As we explore the future of encryption, we must acknowledge the significant contributions of PGP and its enduring legacy in the field of digital security. It serves as a reminder that privacy is a fundamental right that should be protected for all individuals, not just governments and corporations.

The Rise of PGP Alternatives

As the importance of digital privacy grew in the wake of Phil Zimmermann's PGP revolution, so did the demand for secure communication tools. While PGP had established itself as a trusted and widely used encryption system, it was not without its limitations. This gave rise to the development of alternative encryption technologies that aimed to address some of PGP's shortcomings and cater to the evolving needs of privacy-conscious individuals and organizations.

1. The Need for Alternatives

While PGP was hailed as a game-changer in the world of encryption, it faced certain challenges that spurred the development of alternative solutions. One of the main concerns with PGP was its usability. Despite efforts to streamline the interface and make it more user-friendly, PGP remained complex and difficult to navigate for many users. This created a demand for encryption tools that were more intuitive and accessible to a wider audience.

Another limitation of PGP was its reliance on a centralized key authority, known as the web of trust. This model required users to verify the authenticity of each other's public keys through a network of trusted individuals. However, the web of trust system proved to be cumbersome and time-consuming, leading to the need for alternative methods of key verification that were more efficient and scalable.

Additionally, PGP's tight integration with email made it less suitable for securing other forms of digital communication, such as instant messaging, voice calls, and file sharing. As privacy concerns expanded beyond email, there was a demand for encryption solutions that could be applied to a wider range of communication channels.

2. Alternative Encryption Technologies

The rise of PGP alternatives brought forth innovative encryption technologies that aimed to address the limitations of PGP while providing robust security and user-friendly experiences. These alternatives expanded the options available to users seeking privacy in their digital communications.

One such alternative is Signal, an open-source messaging app that combines end-to-end encryption with a user-friendly interface. Signal not only encrypts text messages, but also supports voice calls, video calls, and file transfers. It has gained popularity for its seamless integration with existing contact lists and its commitment to privacy by design.

Another notable alternative is Wire, a secure collaboration platform that offers end-to-end encryption for messaging, voice calls, and file sharing. Wire boasts a sleek and intuitive user interface, making it an attractive option for individuals and organizations seeking secure communication tools.

Other alternatives to PGP include ProtonMail, a privacy-focused email service that offers end-to-end encryption and zero-access encryption, meaning that even ProtonMail cannot access the contents of users' emails. Tresorit is another alternative that provides secure cloud storage with end-to-end encryption, ensuring that files are protected both at rest and in transit.

3. The Advantages and Disadvantages of Alternatives

While PGP alternatives offer unique advantages and address some of the limitations of PGP, they also come with their own set of strengths and weaknesses. One advantage of these alternatives is their focus on user experience and ease of use. By prioritizing intuitive interfaces and seamless integration with existing communication tools, these alternatives make encryption more accessible to a wider audience.

Additionally, some alternatives have introduced novel approaches to key verification that overcome the challenges of PGP's web of trust. For example, Signal utilizes a simplified method of key verification through QR codes, making the process more efficient and less prone to user errors.

However, PGP alternatives also have their downsides. One of the main challenges with alternative encryption technologies is adoption. PGP has established itself as a trusted standard over the years, with a large user base and wide compatibility across different platforms and email clients. Alternatives often face the hurdle of gaining widespread adoption and compatibility, as they may require both senders and recipients to use the same encryption tool or platform.

Moreover, the security of alternative encryption technologies is still being scrutinized. While some alternatives have undergone rigorous audits and peer reviews, others may not have received the same level of scrutiny as PGP. It is essential for users to research and evaluate the security practices and track records of alternative encryption solutions to ensure their effectiveness.

4. Making the Choice

When choosing between PGP and its alternatives, it is essential to consider individual needs and priorities. PGP offers a well-established encryption standard with wide compatibility, making it suitable for those who prioritize interoperability and a large user base. It also provides flexibility in terms of integrating with various email clients and platforms.

On the other hand, alternative encryption technologies offer a more user-friendly experience and expanded capabilities beyond email encryption. They may be more suitable for individuals who prioritize intuitive interfaces, seamless communication across different channels, and innovative features like self-destructing messages or ephemeral keys.

Ultimately, the choice between PGP and its alternatives depends on one's specific requirements and preferences. As encryption technology continues to evolve, it is crucial to stay informed about the latest developments, audits, and best practices to make informed decisions about securing digital communications.

In the next chapter, we will explore the evolution of PGP and its enduring influence on society and the field of computer science. We will delve into the impact of PGP on encryption technologies, privacy laws, and the ongoing battle for digital privacy. Join us as we unravel the legacy of Phil Zimmermann and the fight for privacy in a connected world.

PGP's Impact on Society

Introduction: - Briefly explain what PGP (Pretty Good Privacy) is and its significance in the field of encryption. - Mention the widespread adoption of PGP by individuals, organizations, and governments.

1. Securing Communication: - Discuss how PGP provides end-to-end encryption, ensuring that only the intended recipient can access the message. - Explain how PGP has made it more difficult for malicious actors to eavesdrop on private conversations. - Highlight the importance of secure communication in the modern digital age.

2. Preservation of Privacy: - Discuss how PGP empowers individuals to protect their privacy by keeping their personal information secure. - Explain how PGP ensures that sensitive data, such as financial information and personal messages, remain confidential. - Highlight the role of PGP in safeguarding against identity theft and privacy breaches.

3. Empowering Dissidents and Whistleblowers: - Discuss the impact of PGP in enabling dissidents and whistleblowers to communicate securely. - Explain how

PGP has played a crucial role in preserving freedom of speech in repressive regimes. - Provide examples of real-life cases where PGP has assisted activists and journalists in sharing sensitive information without fear of persecution.

4. Enhancing Digital Trust: - Discuss how PGP has contributed to building trust in online communications. - Explain how PGP addresses concerns about data vulnerability and fosters confidence in the digital world. - Highlight the role of PGP in facilitating secure transactions and protecting online commerce.

5. PGP's Influence on Legislation and Policy: - Discuss how the adoption of PGP has shaped legislation and regulations regarding encryption. - Explain how PGP has influenced government policies on data privacy and cybersecurity. - Highlight the ongoing debate on encryption and the tension between privacy and national security.

Conclusion: - Summarize the overall impact of PGP on society, emphasizing its role in protecting privacy, enabling secure communication, and empowering individuals. - Discuss the future challenges and opportunities for PGP in an evolving technological landscape.

Remember to add relevant examples, explanations, and resources to support your points.

PGP as a Symbol of Resistance

In the fight for privacy and against surveillance, Phil Zimmermann's Pretty Good Privacy (PGP) has emerged as a powerful symbol of resistance. PGP's encrypted communication capabilities have been embraced by individuals and organizations, providing them with a means to protect their sensitive information and maintain their privacy in an increasingly interconnected world.

The Power of Encryption

At its core, PGP is a cryptographic software program that enables secure communication through the use of public-key encryption. Encryption is the process of converting data into a form that is unreadable to anyone without the corresponding decryption key. With PGP, only the intended recipient with the private key can decrypt and access the information.

This powerful encryption technology gives individuals and organizations the ability to shield their messages, documents, and files from prying eyes. By encrypting their data, they can ensure that their communications remain confidential and resistant to unauthorized access.

Defying Surveillance and Control

In today's digital age, where governments and corporations collect vast amounts of personal information, PGP serves as a tool for individuals to reclaim their privacy and resist surveillance. It empowers users to take control of their data and communications, reducing the potential for abuse and exploitation.

By using PGP, individuals can protect their email communications, ensuring that only the intended recipients can read the messages. This encryption helps safeguard sensitive information such as financial details, intellectual property, or personal correspondence from being intercepted and used against them.

Advocacy and Grassroots Adoption

One of the most significant impacts of PGP has been its role in fostering a culture of privacy advocacy. Zimmermann's creation sparked a movement, inspiring individuals and organizations to actively resist encroachments on their privacy and demand stronger security measures.

PGP's widespread adoption among journalists, whistleblowers, activists, and dissidents has reinforced its position as a symbol of resistance. Its use has allowed these individuals to communicate and share information securely, even in the face of government surveillance.

Challenging Government Surveillance

With the revelations of mass surveillance programs by intelligence agencies, PGP has emerged as a crucial tool in challenging government overreach. By encrypting their communications, individuals can resist unlawful surveillance and protect their fundamental rights to privacy and free expression.

By using PGP, individuals can challenge the idea that privacy must be sacrificed for security. It demonstrates that individuals can take proactive steps to protect themselves and assert their civil liberties.

Innovation and Collaboration

PGP's impact goes beyond its technical capabilities; it has sparked innovation and collaboration in the field of encryption. Zimmermann's creation laid the groundwork for further advancements in secure communication, inspiring developers and researchers to build upon his work.

The principles and techniques behind PGP have influenced the development of other encryption technologies, contributing to a more robust and secure digital landscape.

Real-World Examples

To illustrate the significance of PGP as a symbol of resistance, consider the case of Edward Snowden. As a former National Security Agency (NSA) contractor turned whistleblower, Snowden used PGP to communicate securely with journalists and disclose classified information about government surveillance programs. His use of PGP emphasized its importance in protecting whistleblowers and enabling them to expose truths that would otherwise remain hidden.

Another example is the grassroots adoption of PGP during the Arab Spring. Activists and journalists utilized PGP to secure their communications, protecting themselves from government surveillance and censorship. PGP became a symbol of defiance against oppressive regimes and a means to protect those fighting for freedom.

Exercises

1. Research and document a real-life case where PGP was used to resist surveillance and protect privacy. 2. Discuss the ethical implications of using PGP as a means of resistance against government surveillance. 3. Explore the challenges faced by activists promoting the adoption of PGP in regions with limited internet connectivity. 4. Debate the balance between privacy and security in the context of encryption technologies like PGP. 5. Investigate the impact of PGP's adoption on government surveillance practices and policies.

Further Resources

1. "The Code Book: The Science of Secrecy from Ancient Egypt to Quantum Cryptography" by Simon Singh. 2. "No Place to Hide: Edward Snowden, the NSA, and the U.S. Surveillance State" by Glenn Greenwald. 3. Electronic Frontier Foundation (EFF) - www.eff.org. 4. The PGP Global Directory - www.pgpdirectory.org. 5. "Data and Goliath: The Hidden Battles to Capture Your Data and Control Your World" by Bruce Schneier.

Remember, in the battle for privacy, PGP stands as a symbol of resistance—a tool that empowers individuals to protect their information, challenge unwarranted surveillance, and assert their right to privacy in the digital age.

Lessons from PGP's Journey

The journey of PGP (Pretty Good Privacy) has been a remarkable one, with numerous lessons that have shaped the field of encryption and privacy. Throughout its development and adoption, PGP has demonstrated the power of technological innovation, the importance of collaboration, and the need for user education. Let's explore some of the key lessons from PGP's journey:

Lesson 1: Encryption is for Everyone

One of the most important lessons from PGP's journey is that encryption is not just for tech experts or those with something to hide. PGP was designed to be user-friendly and accessible to everyone, empowering individuals to protect their privacy in an increasingly digital world. This lesson has paved the way for the development of countless encryption tools and privacy-focused apps that prioritize user experience, making encryption a mainstream practice.

Lesson 2: Open Source Strengthens Security

PGP's open-source nature played a vital role in its success and security. By allowing independent scrutiny and contributions from a global community, PGP demonstrated the power of transparency and peer review in building robust encryption software. This lesson has inspired the growth of the open-source movement, fostering collaboration, and driving innovation across various domains of technology.

Lesson 3: The Battle for Privacy is Ongoing

PGP's journey has highlighted the never-ending battle for privacy in the face of government surveillance and corporate data collection. Despite its victories, PGP has faced ongoing challenges, such as legal battles and attempts to introduce backdoors into encryption systems. This lesson reinforces the need for constant vigilance and advocacy to protect privacy rights in an ever-evolving technological landscape.

Lesson 4: The Power of Grassroots Movements

PGP's success can largely be attributed to the grassroots movements that rallied behind it. Tech communities, activists, journalists, and privacy advocates played a crucial role in championing PGP's adoption and defending its legality. This lesson demonstrates the power of collective action and highlights the importance of individuals coming together to fight for their rights.

Lesson 5: Encryption is a Balancing Act

PGP's journey also serves as a lesson in the delicate balance between privacy and security. While encryption is crucial for safeguarding personal information and preventing unauthorized access, it can also pose challenges for law enforcement agencies in investigating potential threats. PGP's journey has sparked important conversations around finding a balance between these two essential but sometimes conflicting interests.

Lesson 6: Privacy Education is Essential

PGP's journey has underscored the importance of privacy education and user awareness. Many individuals are unaware of the risks associated with their digital footprint and the need for encryption. PGP's journey emphasizes the importance of investing in privacy education programs to equip individuals with the knowledge and skills to protect their online privacy effectively.

Lesson 7: Collaboration Trumps Competition

PGP's success can be attributed, in part, to its collaborative nature. The collaboration between Phil Zimmermann and various stakeholders, including fellow programmers, advocates, and organizations, played a crucial role in advancing PGP's development and adoption. This lesson highlights the power of collaboration over competition, emphasizing the collective effort required to tackle complex technological and societal challenges.

Lesson 8: Trust is a Cornerstone of Encryption

PGP's journey has reinforced the critical role of trust in encryption systems. Trust in the design, implementation, and integrity of encryption tools is paramount for their effectiveness. PGP's widespread adoption can be attributed to the trust users placed in the software's security and its commitment to privacy. This lesson underscores the importance of building and maintaining trust in encryption systems to ensure their reliability and widespread use.

Lesson 9: Usability Drives Adoption

PGP's journey demonstrates the crucial role of usability in driving adoption. PGP's success can be attributed, in part, to its user-friendly interface and intuitive design. This lesson highlights the importance of prioritizing usability in encryption tools to encourage their adoption by a broader range of users. User-centric design and seamless integration into existing digital workflows are key factors in driving the widespread use of encryption technology.

Lesson 10: Encryption is Not Foolproof

Finally, PGP's journey has shown that encryption is not foolproof and has limitations. It is vital to acknowledge that no encryption system can provide absolute security, as vulnerabilities can emerge over time. This lesson emphasizes the need for ongoing innovation and adaptation to address emerging threats and challenges to encryption systems effectively.

In conclusion, the journey of PGP has provided valuable insights into the world of encryption and privacy. From the importance of usability and collaboration to the ongoing battle for privacy rights, PGP's story serves as a guidepost for individuals, organizations, and policymakers looking to navigate the complexities of digital privacy. As we move forward, it is essential to carry forward the lessons learned from PGP's journey and continue to strive for a privacy-focused future.

The Evolution of Encryption Post-PGP

The development of Pretty Good Privacy (PGP) revolutionized encryption and brought the power of secure communication to the masses. But what happened after PGP? How has encryption evolved in the post-PGP era? In this section, we will explore the advancements and challenges that have shaped encryption technologies in recent years.

Encryption in the Digital Age

In the digital age, encryption has become an essential tool for protecting sensitive data and ensuring privacy in an increasingly interconnected world. With the proliferation of online services, cloud computing, and IoT devices, the need for robust encryption has never been greater.

As technology advances, so do the threats that target our digital communication and data. Cyberattacks, data breaches, and state-sponsored surveillance pose constant challenges to encryption technologies. In response, encryption has evolved to become even more sophisticated and resilient.

Advancements in Encryption Techniques

One of the key advancements in encryption post-PGP is the adoption of stronger and more complex cryptographic algorithms. While PGP used the RSA algorithm for encryption, newer encryption systems like Elliptic Curve Cryptography (ECC) and Advanced Encryption Standard (AES) have emerged as popular choices.

ECC is particularly noteworthy for its ability to provide the same level of security as RSA but with shorter key lengths, resulting in faster computations and lower resource requirements. AES, on the other hand, is a symmetric encryption algorithm widely used to secure data at rest and in transit. Its robust design and scalability have made it the de facto standard for protecting sensitive information.

Furthermore, encryption techniques have also incorporated additional layers of security through the use of multi-factor authentication, biometrics, and hardware-based encryption. These advancements ensure that encryption remains effective even in the face of sophisticated attacks.

Quantum Computing and the Future of Encryption

While encryption has made significant strides, the rise of quantum computing presents a new set of challenges. Quantum computers have the potential to break many of the encryption algorithms that currently protect our data. As these computers become more powerful, the need for quantum-resistant encryption becomes increasingly urgent.

Post-quantum cryptography aims to develop encryption algorithms that are resistant to attacks from quantum computers. Various techniques are being explored, such as lattice-based cryptography, code-based cryptography, and hash-based cryptography. These approaches leverage the inherent difficulty of problems in mathematics and physics to provide robust encryption that can withstand quantum attacks.

However, transitioning to post-quantum encryption is not without its challenges. It requires widespread adoption, updates to existing systems, and careful migration strategies. Nonetheless, researchers and industry experts are actively working towards developing and standardizing post-quantum encryption solutions to ensure the future security of our data.

Balancing User Experience and Security

While encryption technologies have become more advanced, there is a delicate balance between security and user experience. Strong encryption often comes at the cost of increased complexity and slower performance, which can be a barrier to adoption for non-technical users.

To address this challenge, encryption tools have focused on improving user experience without compromising security. User-friendly interfaces, automated key management, and seamless integration with popular applications have made encryption more accessible to the general public.

Furthermore, the concept of end-to-end encryption has gained prominence. End-to-end encryption ensures that only the sender and intended recipient can access the encrypted data, providing an additional layer of privacy and security. Messaging apps like Signal and WhatsApp have implemented end-to-end encryption as a default feature, making it easier for individuals to protect their private conversations.

Challenges and Future Directions

Encryption continues to face challenges and debates about its use in various contexts. Law enforcement organizations argue for the inclusion of backdoors in encryption systems to aid investigations, while privacy advocates emphasize the importance of strong encryption to safeguard individual rights.

The ongoing tension between privacy and security poses a significant challenge for encryption. Striking the right balance requires open dialogue between stakeholders and careful consideration of the implications of encryption policies.

In the future, encryption will likely continue to evolve in response to emerging technologies and new threats. The development of post-quantum encryption, the refinement of user-friendly encryption tools, and the formulation of privacy-focused regulations will shape the next phase of encryption's evolution.

As encryption techniques advance, it is essential to ensure that users are well-informed about privacy and security best practices. Education and awareness programs can empower individuals to make informed decisions about their digital lives and protect their data from unauthorized access.

In conclusion, the post-PGP era has witnessed significant advancements and challenges in encryption. From the adoption of stronger algorithms to the pursuit of post-quantum encryption, the evolution of encryption reflects the ongoing battle for privacy in a digital world. By constantly adapting to new threats and technology, encryption will continue to play a crucial role in safeguarding our digital communication and securing our confidential information.

PGP's Place in the History of Computer Science

PGP (Pretty Good Privacy) holds a significant place in the history of computer science. It revolutionized the field of cryptography, challenging the traditional notions of privacy and security. In this section, we will explore the impact of PGP on the development of computer science and its lasting contributions to the field.

Cryptographic Advancements

Before diving into PGP's specific contributions, it is essential to understand the broader context of cryptographic advancements. Cryptography, the study and practice of secure communication, has a long and rich history dating back to ancient times. Over the years, various encryption techniques emerged, enabling individuals and organizations to protect sensitive information.

However, traditional encryption systems had limitations. They relied on symmetric key encryption, which required both the sender and the receiver to share the same key. This approach posed challenges in securely exchanging keys and limited the number of people with whom secure communication was possible.

The Birth of PGP

Phil Zimmermann's creation of PGP in 1991 marked a turning point in the field of cryptography. PGP introduced a groundbreaking technique, asymmetric encryption, which solved the key exchange problem. Through the use of public and private key pairs, PGP allowed users to communicate securely without the need for pre-shared keys.

Zimmermann made PGP freely available to the public, and it quickly gained popularity among activists, journalists, and individuals concerned about their privacy. PGP's open-source nature contributed to its widespread adoption, as it fostered collaboration and peer review, ensuring the software's integrity.

Implications for Privacy and Security

PGP's arrival had a profound impact on privacy and security, pushing boundaries in computer science. It empowered individuals to take control of their communication and safeguard their personal information. By enabling end-to-end encryption, PGP offered privacy at a level previously unseen, making it difficult for adversaries to intercept and decipher messages.

This advancement also sparked a crucial debate on the balance between security and government control. PGP challenged governments' ability to monitor private communication, leading to legal battles and discussions around privacy laws. The clash between privacy rights and national security became a recurring theme in the digital age, shaping the landscape of computer science.

Open Source Culture

PGP's influence extended beyond cryptography itself. The open-source movement gained momentum with the release of PGP, emphasizing the value of transparency, collaboration, and accessibility in software development. PGP's success demonstrated the effectiveness of community-driven projects, inspiring a new generation of programmers to contribute to open-source initiatives.

Open-source cryptographic projects, including GnuPG (GNU Privacy Guard), directly trace their roots back to PGP. PGP's impact on open-source culture fostered an environment of innovation, where a diverse array of contributors worked together to enhance security practices and protect individuals' rights to privacy.

Continued Relevance

While PGP's initial release took place several decades ago, its relevance in computer science persists to this day. The principles underlying PGP, such as secure communication and data integrity, continue to shape the development of encryption technologies. PGP laid the groundwork for modern cryptographic practices, highlighting the importance of user-centric design and addressing the evolving challenges of digital communication.

Moreover, PGP's impact extends beyond the purely technical realm. By raising awareness about privacy and encryption, it prompted individuals and organizations to be more conscious of their digital footprint and the implications of data collection. PGP's legacy has influenced the collective mindset, fueling the ongoing fight for privacy and inspiring further advancements in the field.

Theoretical Contributions

PGP's influence on computer science extends beyond its practical applications. Its underlying principles and techniques have stimulated further research and development in cryptographic algorithms and protocols. PGP's asymmetric encryption framework, based on concepts like the RSA algorithm and

Diffie-Hellman key exchange, has become a foundation for modern cryptographic systems.

Furthermore, PGP's success highlighted the importance of user-friendly interfaces and intuitive designs. Making complex cryptographic tools accessible to non-experts was a critical factor in PGP's adoption. This emphasis on usability prompted researchers to explore new approaches in human-computer interaction and usability engineering, contributing to advancements in usability across various domains of computer science.

Resources and Further Reading

For those interested in delving deeper into the history and impact of PGP in computer science, the following resources provide valuable insights:

- "The Code Book" by Simon Singh: This book offers an engaging exploration of the history of cryptography, including PGP's emergence as a pivotal moment in the field.

- "PGP: Pretty Good Privacy" by Simson Garfinkel: This book provides an in-depth examination of PGP's development, technical details, and its impact on the world of computer science.

- "Crypto: How the Code Rebels Beat the Government" by Steven Levy: This book chronicles the clash between the U.S. government and PGP's creators, shedding light on the political and ethical implications surrounding encryption.

Exploring these resources will provide a comprehensive understanding of PGP's place in the history of computer science and its wide-ranging influence on the field. From cryptographic advancements to open-source culture and the ongoing fight for privacy, PGP's legacy continues to resonate with researchers, practitioners, and privacy advocates.

Remembering PGP's Revolutionary Impact

In the realm of computer science, few inventions have had such a profound impact as Pretty Good Privacy (PGP). Developed by Phil Zimmermann in the early 1990s, PGP revolutionized the way we think about encryption and privacy. Let's take a moment to remember the revolutionary impact of PGP and its lasting legacy.

The Birth of PGP

Before PGP, encryption technology was mostly reserved for government and large corporations. Phil Zimmermann, a passionate programmer and privacy advocate, wanted to make strong encryption accessible to everyone. He saw encryption as a fundamental right and a crucial tool for protecting individuals' privacy in a rapidly digitizing world.

Zimmermann's vision came to life with the creation of PGP, a user-friendly encryption software that used a combination of symmetric and asymmetric encryption to secure email communications. PGP allowed users to send encrypted messages over insecure networks, ensuring that only the intended recipients could decipher the content.

Empowering Individuals

PGP was a game-changer because it empowered individuals to take control of their privacy. It gave people the ability to communicate securely and keep their personal information safe from prying eyes. By providing end-to-end encryption, Zimmermann effectively removed the need for trust in third-party entities, such as governments or service providers, to protect sensitive data.

The impact of PGP extended far beyond personal privacy. Its introduction marked a turning point in the wider public understanding of encryption and the importance of secure communication. PGP sparked conversations about the right to privacy, digital rights, and the balance between individual freedoms and national security.

Setting the Stage for Encryption Advocacy

The creation of PGP also set in motion a wave of encryption advocacy and privacy awareness. Phil Zimmermann became an influential figure in the fight for strong encryption and user privacy rights. He tirelessly campaigned for the widespread adoption of encryption technologies, delivering talks, writing articles, and engaging with policymakers.

Zimmermann's advocacy work inspired a generation of technologists, activists, and everyday individuals to join the fight for privacy. PGP became a symbol of resistance against mass surveillance and government control over personal data. Its impact reverberated through the tech industry and beyond, shaping the course of privacy-related conversations for years to come.

PGP's Enduring Influence

Despite being over three decades old, PGP's influence continues to be felt today. Its pioneering concepts and principles laid the foundation for modern encryption technologies. PGP's legacy lives on in numerous encryption tools and protocols that build upon its ideas, including OpenPGP, S/MIME, and GnuPG.

Furthermore, PGP's impact reaches beyond the realm of technology. It has become a cultural touchstone representing the fight for privacy and the need for individuals to have control over their digital lives. The story of PGP and its creator, Phil Zimmermann, continues to inspire future generations of programmers and privacy advocates.

Lessons from PGP's Journey

PGP's journey offers valuable lessons for those navigating the complex landscape of privacy and encryption. It reminds us of the power of individuals to challenge the status quo and make a difference. It emphasizes the importance of user-friendly encryption tools that empower individuals rather than leaving privacy in the hands of corporations or governments.

One of the key lessons from PGP's revolutionary impact is the need for constant vigilance in protecting privacy rights. As technology evolves and new threats emerge, the battle for privacy continues. PGP's story serves as a reminder to remain committed to privacy principles and to actively advocate for strong encryption as a critical tool in safeguarding personal information.

The Future of Encryption

Looking to the future, the spirit of PGP will undoubtedly continue to shape advancements in encryption technology. As threats to privacy become increasingly sophisticated, encryption will play a crucial role in safeguarding personal data. The principles of end-to-end encryption, user empowerment, and open-source collaboration championed by PGP will remain central to the ongoing development of privacy-enhancing technologies.

Moreover, PGP's revolutionary impact serves as a reminder that encryption must always adapt and evolve alongside the changing landscape of technology and policy. As quantum computing and other emerging technologies pose new challenges, future encryption solutions must rise to the occasion.

In conclusion, PGP's pioneering work in encryption and privacy has left an indelible mark on the world of computer science. It sparked a revolution in how we perceive and use encryption, empowering individuals, and challenging the perception that privacy is a luxury reserved for the few. PGP's enduring legacy continues to inspire and guide the next generation of programmers and privacy advocates in their fight to protect personal privacy in the digital age.

The Accessible Future of Encryption

In the ever-evolving digital landscape, encryption has become a crucial tool for safeguarding our sensitive information. As technology advances and we become more reliant on digital platforms, the need for accessible and user-friendly encryption solutions has never been greater. In this section, we will explore the future of encryption, focusing on the advancements that will make it more accessible to everyone.

Democratizing Encryption

Traditionally, encryption has been viewed as a complex and specialized area, accessible only to those with advanced technical knowledge. However, the future of encryption lies in its democratization, making it accessible to individuals from all walks of life.

To achieve this, there is a pressing need for advancements in encryption technologies that simplify the process of encryption and decryption. User-friendly encryption tools and interfaces, combined with comprehensive user education, will empower individuals to take control of their own privacy and security.

Encryption for the Masses

The future of encryption is all about making it easy and intuitive for everyone to incorporate encryption into their daily lives. From securing personal communications to protecting financial transactions, encryption will be seamlessly integrated into our devices and applications.

Imagine sending an encrypted email with just a single click or making secure payments online without worrying about potential data breaches. The future of encryption will bring these possibilities into reality, with simplified and highly effective encryption solutions that require minimal effort from the user.

Secure Communication Platforms

One of the most promising aspects of the accessible future of encryption is the development of secure communication platforms. These platforms will provide end-to-end encryption, ensuring that only the intended recipient can access the communicated information.

Messaging applications like Signal and Telegram are already making significant strides in this area, providing user-friendly interfaces and robust encryption protocols. As these platforms continue to evolve, we can expect them to become the go-to communication tools for individuals and organizations seeking privacy and security.

Quantum-Resistant Encryption

As quantum computing emerges as a potential threat to existing encryption methods, the future of encryption also involves the development of quantum-resistant encryption algorithms. These algorithms will withstand the computational power of quantum computers, ensuring the continued security of sensitive information.

Researchers and cryptographers are currently exploring various quantum-resistant encryption techniques, such as lattice-based cryptography and code-based cryptography. These advancements will play a crucial role in maintaining privacy and security in the face of rapid technological advancements.

Addressing Ethical Challenges

With the increasing availability of encryption tools, there arise ethical challenges that must be addressed in the accessible future of encryption. While encryption enables individuals to protect their privacy, it can also be misused for nefarious purposes. Striking a balance between privacy rights and the need for national security will be an ongoing challenge.

Legislation and regulation must keep pace with advancements in encryption to ensure responsible usage. Additionally, initiatives promoting digital literacy and ethical hacking can equip individuals with the knowledge to use encryption responsibly while deterring malicious activities.

The Role of Artificial Intelligence

Artificial Intelligence (AI) will have a significant impact on the accessible future of encryption. Machine learning algorithms can aid in improving the efficiency and security of encryption processes. AI can analyze patterns, detect anomalies, and enhance encryption algorithms to adapt to emerging threats.

Moreover, AI-powered encryption tools will revolutionize user experience, automatically adjusting encryption settings based on the specific needs and preferences of individuals. This will eliminate the need for users to have in-depth technical expertise, making encryption accessible to a wider audience.

Examples of Encryption in Everyday Life

To better understand the accessible future of encryption, let's explore a few examples of how encryption will become an integral part of our everyday lives:

1. **Secure Messaging Apps:** Messaging apps will feature end-to-end encryption as a default setting, ensuring that private conversations remain private, even if intercepted by malicious actors or surveillance entities.

2. **IoT Security:** As we embrace the Internet of Things (IoT), encryption will play a crucial role in securing our smart homes, connected devices, and personal data. Encrypted communication protocols between devices will safeguard our privacy.

3. **Secure Cloud Storage:** Cloud storage platforms will implement client-side encryption, where data is encrypted on the user's device before being uploaded to the cloud. This guarantees that only the user holds the encryption keys, preventing unauthorized access to their sensitive data.

4. **Biometric Encryption:** Biometric authentication, such as fingerprint or iris scanning, will be seamlessly integrated into encryption processes. Unlocking encrypted files or accessing secure applications will be as simple as verifying one's biometric identity.

These examples demonstrate how encryption will become an essential part of our digital experiences, ensuring our privacy and security in an increasingly interconnected world.

Exercise: Encryption in Your Daily Life

Take a moment to reflect on how encryption already plays a role in your daily life. Consider the applications, devices, and services you use that rely on encryption to protect your data. Identify any areas where encryption could be improved or made more accessible. Share your findings with a partner and discuss how these insights can contribute to the accessible future of encryption.

Resources for Further Exploration

To delve deeper into the accessible future of encryption, explore the following resources:

1. **Book:** "Cryptography: An Introduction" by Nigel Smart provides a comprehensive introduction to the principles and applications of encryption.

2. **Online Course:** "Applied Cryptography" on Coursera, taught by Professor Dan Boneh from Stanford University, offers a practical understanding of encryption techniques.

3. **Website:** Electronic Frontier Foundation (EFF) provides up-to-date information on privacy, security, and encryption, advocating for digital rights and freedom.

4. **Podcast:** "Encryption is Not a Crime" by The Privacy Advisor Podcast explores the importance of encryption in protecting individuals' privacy rights.

These resources will equip you with the knowledge and insights to actively participate in shaping the accessible future of encryption.

Conclusion

The accessible future of encryption holds immense potential for protecting our privacy in an increasingly digitized world. By democratizing encryption, simplifying encryption processes, and addressing ethical challenges, encryption will become an integral part of our daily lives. With advancements in quantum-resistant encryption, secure communication platforms, and the integration of AI, encryption will empower individuals to take control of their digital privacy. As we embrace this future, it is up to us to use encryption responsibly, promoting a balance between privacy rights and national security. The journey towards an accessible future of encryption has just begun, and with continued innovation and collaboration, we can ensure a future where privacy is accessible to all.

PGP's Enduring Legacy

The legacy of Pretty Good Privacy (PGP) is undeniable. Developed by Phil Zimmermann in the early 1990s, PGP revolutionized the way we think about digital privacy and encryption. Zimmermann's creation has left a lasting impact on computer science, technology, and society as a whole.

PGP's Influence on Other Encryption Technologies

PGP's innovative approach to encryption paved the way for the development of many other encryption technologies. The principles behind PGP, such as public-key cryptography and strong encryption algorithms, have been incorporated into various security protocols and tools. For example, the OpenPGP standard, which is based on the original PGP design, is widely used for email encryption and secure file transfer.

Additionally, PGP has influenced the development of other privacy-focused technologies, such as secure messaging apps and virtual private networks (VPNs). These technologies incorporate encryption methods similar to those pioneered by PGP. The continued use and development of these technologies can be directly attributed to the enduring legacy of PGP.

The Rise of PGP Alternatives

PGP's impact can also be seen in the rise of alternative encryption technologies. While PGP remains a popular choice for secure communication, other options have emerged to address specific privacy concerns and user needs. These alternatives often build upon the foundation established by PGP and offer new features or improvements.

One such alternative is GnuPG (GNU Privacy Guard), an open-source implementation of the OpenPGP standard. GnuPG provides users with a free and accessible option for email encryption and authentication. Another notable alternative is Signal, a secure messaging app that combines end-to-end encryption with user-friendly features. Signal's success can be attributed, in part, to the groundwork laid by PGP in establishing the importance of secure communication.

PGP's Impact on Society

PGP's impact extends beyond the realm of technology and has had profound societal implications. By enabling secure communication, PGP has empowered individuals to protect their privacy and exercise their freedom of expression. Citizen journalists and activists in repressive regimes rely on PGP and its alternatives to communicate safely and share sensitive information without fear of interception.

Furthermore, PGP has played a significant role in preserving journalistic integrity and the protection of sources. Journalists and whistleblowers use encryption tools inspired by PGP to securely communicate and ensure the confidentiality of their sources. This has become increasingly crucial in an era marked by widespread surveillance and attempts to stifle investigative journalism.

PGP as a Symbol of Resistance

PGP has become a symbol of resistance against encroachments on privacy and civil liberties. The battle for strong encryption, as exemplified by PGP, demonstrates the ongoing struggle to strike a balance between security and individual rights. PGP's enduring legacy serves as a reminder that privacy is a fundamental human right that must be protected.

Lessons from PGP's Journey

The journey of PGP offers valuable lessons and insights. One of the key takeaways is the importance of user-centric designs and user-friendly interfaces for privacy-focused technologies. PGP's success can be attributed, in part, to its ability to make complex encryption accessible to a broader audience.

Moreover, PGP's journey highlights the significance of collaboration and open-source development. The open nature of PGP allowed for peer review, leading to improvements in security and functionality. This collaborative approach continues to shape the development of encryption technologies today.

The Evolution of Encryption Post-PGP

In the post-PGP era, encryption technologies continue to evolve to meet new challenges. The rise of cloud computing, the Internet of Things (IoT), and artificial intelligence (AI) pose unique privacy concerns. Encryption must adapt to safeguard data in these emerging contexts while maintaining usability and accessibility.

Furthermore, the debate surrounding encryption and lawful access to encrypted data continues. PGP's enduring legacy reminds us that encryption is essential for protecting privacy, but also calls for ongoing discussions and policy decisions on how to balance privacy and security in the digital age.

Remembering PGP's Revolutionary Impact

As we reflect on PGP's enduring legacy, it is important to remember the revolutionary impact it had on the world. PGP changed the landscape of digital communication, providing individuals with the tools to assert their privacy rights.

Phil Zimmermann's creation continues to inspire the next generation of encryption pioneers and privacy advocates. The story of PGP serves as a reminder that a single individual can make a profound difference in shaping the future of technology and privacy.

Through his dedication to privacy, Phil Zimmermann has left an indelible mark on computer science, technology, and society. His legacy lives on, challenging us to remain vigilant in the fight for privacy and inspiring us to create a future that champions the right to digital privacy and security.

Chapter 3: The Fight for Privacy

Chapter 3: The Fight for Privacy

Chapter 3: The Fight for Privacy

In this chapter, we delve into the crucial battle for privacy in the digital age. Privacy has become a hot-button issue with the rise of surveillance capitalism, increasing government surveillance, and the erosion of personal freedoms. Phil Zimmermann is at the forefront of this fight, advocating for strong encryption and working tirelessly to protect our privacy rights.

The Power of Personal Data

In today's interconnected world, personal data has become an incredibly valuable asset. Companies collect vast amounts of data, from our online activities to our shopping habits, in order to analyze and monetize it. This data is used to target advertising, persuade consumer behavior, and even influence political outcomes. The power of personal data lies in its ability to shape our lives, from the products we buy to the decisions we make.

The Rise of Surveillance Capitalism

Surveillance capitalism is a term coined by Harvard professor Shoshana Zuboff to describe the economic system that has emerged as a result of the commodification of personal data. Tech giants like Google and Facebook have built their business models on collecting and analyzing user data to create targeted advertisements. These companies have become some of the wealthiest and most powerful in the world by exploiting our personal information.

Governments vs. Tech Companies

The battle over privacy is not just between individuals and tech companies; it involves governments as well. Governments around the world are increasingly demanding access to personal data for purposes of national security and law enforcement. Tech companies are caught in the middle, facing pressure from both governments and their users to protect privacy rights.

Privacy in the Age of Social Media

The rise of social media has fundamentally changed the way we interact with each other and share information. While these platforms offer an unprecedented level of connectivity, they also present serious privacy concerns. Users often share personal details and sensitive information without fully understanding the consequences. Additionally, social media companies have faced criticism for their handling of user data and questionable privacy practices.

The Cambridge Analytica Scandal

The Cambridge Analytica scandal, which came to light in 2018, highlighted the extent to which personal data can be misused. It was revealed that Cambridge Analytica, a political consulting firm, had harvested data from millions of Facebook users without their consent. This data was then used to target political advertising during the 2016 US presidential election. The scandal sparked widespread concern about the privacy implications of social media platforms.

User Privacy as a Commodity

In the digital age, personal data has become a valuable commodity. Companies buy and sell user data, often without the knowledge or consent of individuals. This commodification of personal data raises important ethical questions about ownership, consent, and the value of privacy in a hyper-connected world.

The Importance of Strong Encryption

Encryption plays a crucial role in protecting our privacy in the digital age. It is the process of encoding information in such a way that only authorized parties can access it. Strong encryption ensures that our data remains private and secure, even in the face of attempts to intercept or eavesdrop on our communications.

Privacy Laws and Regulations

Governments around the world have recognized the importance of privacy and enacted laws and regulations to protect it. The European Union, for example, implemented the General Data Protection Regulation (GDPR), which gives individuals greater control over their personal data and imposes strict penalties for non-compliance. Privacy laws and regulations are crucial in holding companies accountable and ensuring that individuals have control over their personal information.

Shaping the Future of Privacy

The fight for privacy is far from over. As technology continues to evolve, new challenges will emerge, requiring innovative solutions to protect our privacy rights. It is our collective responsibility to advocate for strong encryption, demand transparency from tech companies, and support policies that safeguard our privacy in the digital age.

Phil Zimmermann's Role in the Fight

Phil Zimmermann has been at the forefront of the fight for privacy for over three decades. His creation of Pretty Good Privacy (PGP), an encryption software, revolutionized the way individuals and organizations protect their communications. Zimmermann's advocacy work, his commitment to strong encryption, and his tireless efforts to educate the public have had a profound impact on the fight for privacy.

Overall, the fight for privacy in the digital age is crucial in protecting our personal freedoms and ensuring a more inclusive and democratic society. Phil Zimmermann's contributions continue to inspire and drive the fight for privacy, reminding us of the importance of standing up for our rights in the face of advancing technology and changing social norms.

The Battle for Online Privacy

The Power of Personal Data

In today's digital age, personal data has become one of the most valuable resources in the world. It has the power to shape our lives, influence our decisions, and even control entire industries. But what exactly is personal data, and why is it so important?

Personal data refers to any information that can identify an individual, such as their name, address, phone number, email address, social media posts, browsing history, and more. It is collected by various entities, including companies, governments, and even individuals themselves.

The power of personal data lies in its ability to provide insights into people's behaviors, preferences, and lifestyles. This information can be analyzed, processed, and used by businesses and organizations to tailor their products, services, and marketing strategies to target specific individuals or groups.

Consider the example of social media platforms like Facebook. By collecting and analyzing personal data, Facebook can create detailed profiles of its users and their interests. This enables advertisers to target their ads to highly specific demographics, increasing the chances of engaging potential customers. This targeted advertising is not only more effective but also more profitable for businesses, as they can optimize their marketing efforts and maximize their return on investment.

Furthermore, personal data has become a driving force behind the development of artificial intelligence (AI) and machine learning algorithms. These technologies rely on vast amounts of data to train their models and improve their accuracy. The more personal data available, the better these algorithms can perform in delivering personalized recommendations, predicting consumer behavior, and making automated decisions in various domains, such as finance, healthcare, and transportation.

However, the power of personal data also raises significant concerns about privacy and security. The collection and use of personal data by corporations and governments have sparked debates about data protection, surveillance, and individual rights.

One of the main challenges is the risk of data breaches and unauthorized access. Cybercriminals are constantly seeking to gain access to personal data for identity theft, fraud, or other malicious activities. In recent years, we have witnessed several high-profile data breaches, such as the Equifax breach in 2017, where the personal information of millions of people was compromised.

Another concern is the potential for misuse or abuse of personal data by governments and other entities. Mass surveillance programs, such as the controversial PRISM program exposed by Edward Snowden, have raised questions about the balance between security and privacy.

To address these issues, countries around the world have started implementing data protection laws and regulations. The European Union's General Data Protection Regulation (GDPR), for example, aims to give individuals more control over their personal data and imposes strict rules on organizations in terms of data collection, processing, and storage.

In addition to legal measures, individuals can also take steps to protect their own personal data. This includes being cautious when sharing information online, using strong passwords, enabling two-factor authentication, and regularly updating privacy settings on social media platforms and other online services.

Ultimately, the power of personal data lies in its ability to shape our digital experiences and influence various aspects of our lives. As technology continues to advance, it is crucial to strike a balance between harnessing the benefits of personal data and ensuring adequate protection and privacy for individuals. This ongoing challenge will shape the future of data-driven innovation and the way we navigate the digital landscape.

The Power of Personal Data is not just a concept - it affects real people and real lives. Let's take a look at a few examples of how personal data has had a profound impact on individuals and society as a whole.

Example 1: Target's Pregnancy Prediction

In 2012, Target, a U.S. retail corporation, made headlines when it was revealed that their data analytics team had developed a model to predict whether a customer was pregnant based on their shopping habits. By analyzing purchasing patterns, such as the types of products bought and the timing of purchases, Target was able to identify pregnant customers with a high degree of accuracy. This allowed them to send targeted advertisements and coupons to expectant mothers, capitalizing on their changing shopping needs. However, this revelation also raised concerns about the ethical implications of using personal data to target such intimate aspects of people's lives.

Example 2: Cambridge Analytica and the U.S. Presidential Election

In 2018, the Cambridge Analytica scandal exposed the power of personal data in political campaigns. It was revealed that Cambridge Analytica, a political consulting firm, harvested the personal data of millions of Facebook users without their consent and used it to create targeted advertisements and political messages during the 2016 U.S. presidential election. The incident highlighted the vulnerabilities of social media platforms in protecting user data and ignited a global conversation about the influence of personal data in shaping public opinion and electoral outcomes.

Example 3: Health Insurance Discrimination

Personal data can also impact access to essential services like healthcare. In some cases, health insurance companies may use personal data, such as medical history or lifestyle choices, to determine premium rates or deny coverage to individuals with pre-existing conditions. This raises concerns about the potential for discrimination and the need for fair and transparent practices in the insurance industry.

These examples demonstrate the far-reaching consequences of personal data and highlight the need for responsible data governance, transparency, and user control. As individuals and societies, it is crucial to be aware of the power dynamics at play and actively participate in shaping the future of personal data collection, use, and protection.

The Rise of Surveillance Capitalism

The world we live in today is dominated by technology, and with the rising influence of big tech companies, a new form of capitalism has emerged – surveillance capitalism. This section explores the rise of surveillance capitalism, its impact on privacy, and the challenges it presents in the digital age.

Understanding Surveillance Capitalism

Surveillance capitalism refers to the business model in which companies collect vast amounts of personal data from individuals through digital platforms and use this data to generate profit. The collection and analysis of personal data allow companies to create targeted advertisements, curated content, and personalized user experiences. This data-driven approach has given birth to a new era of capitalism, where surveillance and data become valuable commodities.

At the core of surveillance capitalism lies the concept of data extraction. Companies collect data on our online activities, such as our search history, social media interactions, and online purchases. This data is then analyzed and monetized, either through direct sales to advertisers or through the use of algorithms to influence user behavior and drive profits. By continuously monitoring and analyzing our actions, companies can build detailed profiles of our preferences, behaviors, and interests.

The Impact on Privacy

The rise of surveillance capitalism has significantly impacted individual privacy. In the digital age, our personal data has become a valuable asset, and its collection and use have raised serious concerns about surveillance and data misuse. As we increasingly rely on digital platforms for communication, entertainment, and everyday tasks, our personal information is constantly being harvested, often without our explicit consent or knowledge.

The pervasive collection of personal data has led to a loss of control over our own information. Companies now have unprecedented insight into our lives, preferences, and behaviors, which can be used to manipulate our choices, influence our decisions, and even predict our future actions. This raises important questions about autonomy, consent, and the power dynamics between individuals and the corporations that collect and control their data.

Moreover, the commodification of personal data creates a power imbalance between individuals and corporations. While companies profit from our data, we often have little say in how it is used, shared, or protected. This lack of transparency and control puts our privacy at risk and undermines the fundamental principles of autonomy and personal freedom.

Challenges and Concerns

The rise of surveillance capitalism presents numerous challenges and concerns for individuals, society, and policymakers. Here are some key areas of concern:

Manipulation and Behavioral Control   Surveillance capitalism relies on the manipulation of user behavior through targeted advertising and personalized content. By leveraging our personal data, companies can influence our choices, opinions, and even political beliefs. This raises concerns about the ethical implications of targeted manipulation and the potential for societal influence.

Data Security and Breaches   The increasing collection and storage of personal data create new risks for data security and breaches. As companies amass vast amounts of user information, they become attractive targets for hackers and malicious actors. Data breaches can lead to identity theft, financial fraud, and other harmful consequences for individuals.

Erosion of Democratic Processes   Surveillance capitalism has the potential to undermine democratic processes by shaping public opinion and political discourse. The targeted dissemination of information and the manipulation of user behavior can influence elections, amplify polarization, and erode trust in democratic institutions.

Inequality and Exclusion   The data-driven economy of surveillance capitalism has the potential to exacerbate existing inequalities. Individuals with limited or no access to digital platforms may be excluded from the benefits and opportunities offered by targeted services and personalized experiences. This digital divide can further deepen social and economic inequalities.

Safeguarding Privacy in the Digital Age

Protecting privacy in the age of surveillance capitalism requires a multi-faceted approach involving individuals, companies, and policymakers. Here are some strategies to safeguard privacy:

Individual Awareness and Empowerment   Individuals should be aware of their rights and take steps to protect their privacy. This includes understanding the privacy policies of digital platforms, using encryption and privacy-enhancing tools, and being mindful of the information shared online.

Data Protection Regulations   Policymakers play a crucial role in implementing and enforcing effective data protection regulations. Measures such as the General Data Protection Regulation (GDPR) in the European Union aim to give individuals more control over their personal data and hold companies accountable for their data practices.

Ethical Business Practices   Companies should adopt ethical business practices that prioritize user privacy and data protection. This includes obtaining informed consent, being transparent about data collection and use, implementing strong security measures, and providing individuals with meaningful control over their data.

Technological Innovation   Technological innovation can also play a role in safeguarding privacy. Advances in encryption technologies, decentralized networks, and privacy-preserving algorithms can help individuals regain control over their data and protect their privacy in the digital realm.

Real-World Example: Cambridge Analytica Scandal

One of the most prominent examples of the dangers of surveillance capitalism is the Cambridge Analytica scandal. In 2018, it was revealed that the political consulting firm Cambridge Analytica had harvested personal data from millions of Facebook users without their consent. This data was then used to create targeted political advertisements during the 2016 United States presidential election and the Brexit campaign.

The scandal highlighted the potential for surveillance capitalism to manipulate public opinion, influence elections, and undermine democratic processes. It sparked a global conversation about the ethical implications of data collection, the power of tech companies, and the need for stronger privacy regulations.

The Cambridge Analytica scandal served as a wake-up call for individuals and policymakers, highlighting the urgent need to protect privacy in the age of surveillance capitalism and reign in the unchecked power of tech giants.

Summary

The rise of surveillance capitalism has transformed the way we think about privacy in the digital age. The collection and analysis of personal data have become integral to the business models of tech companies, raising concerns about surveillance, data misuse, and the erosion of privacy rights. Safeguarding privacy requires a collective effort involving individuals, companies, and policymakers. Technologies that prioritize privacy, along with robust data protection regulations and ethical business practices, are crucial in creating a future that balances the benefits of technology with the protection of personal privacy. The Cambridge Analytica scandal serves as a cautionary tale, reminding us of the potential risks and consequences of surveillance capitalism and the need for proactive measures to protect privacy in a digital world.

Governments vs. Tech Companies

In the ongoing battle for online privacy, one of the key conflicts arises between governments and tech companies. This clash of interests revolves around the control and access to personal data, leading to debates on surveillance, privacy laws, and the responsibilities of both parties. Governments argue for greater access to user information in the name of national security, while tech companies advocate for stronger encryption and user protections. Let's dive deeper into this complex and contentious issue.

At the heart of the conflict is the power of personal data. Governments often argue that access to user information is crucial for maintaining national security and preventing crime. They argue that the ability to surveil online activities can help them track down potential threats and gather evidence in criminal investigations. On the other hand, tech companies stress the importance of user privacy and the need to protect personal data from unauthorized access. They believe that individuals have a right to privacy and that encryption plays a vital role in safeguarding user information.

The rise of surveillance capitalism has further intensified this conflict. Tech companies like Facebook, Google, and Amazon collect vast amounts of user data to fuel their advertising-based business models. This collection of personal information raises concerns about user privacy and the potential for data misuse. Governments struggle to strike a balance between harnessing the power of personal data for national security purposes while also protecting individual rights and freedoms.

The tension between governments and tech companies is further complicated by the evolving landscape of social media and the rapid spread of disinformation. Governments are increasingly reliant on tech companies to monitor and curb the dissemination of false information, hate speech, and extremist content. However, this reliance raises questions about the limits of tech companies' power and the potential for censorship.

Privacy laws and regulations also play a significant role in this conflict. Governments face the challenge of creating legislation that effectively balances privacy protection with the needs of law enforcement. They must consider the potential risks to national security and public safety while also respecting individual rights. Tech companies lobby for privacy-friendly regulations that support their encryption technologies and limit government access to user data.

The prominence of the Cambridge Analytica scandal revealed the extent to which personal data can be exploited for political purposes. This incident, along with other high-profile data breaches, highlighted the need for stronger privacy protections. It sparked a global conversation about the role of governments and tech companies in ensuring data security and privacy.

Finding the right balance between security and privacy remains an ongoing challenge. Encryption has become a focal point in this conflict, with tech companies employing increasingly robust encryption technologies to protect user data. This has led to debates over the use of encryption backdoors, which would allow governments access to encrypted communications. While governments argue that backdoors are necessary for effective crime-fighting, tech companies maintain that backdoors compromise the security and privacy of all users.

In recent years, encryption has gained support from privacy advocates, civil liberties groups, and even some government officials who recognize the critical importance of protecting personal data. The battle for privacy has united tech companies and civil rights organizations in a shared goal of defending individual rights in the digital age, leading to the development of strong encryption tools.

In conclusion, the conflict between governments and tech companies over control and access to personal data is a complex and multidimensional issue. Both parties have legitimate concerns and interests at stake. The balance between security and privacy is delicate, and the ongoing debate over encryption and privacy laws will shape the future of online privacy. As technology continues to evolve, governments and tech companies must find common ground and work together to protect individual rights and promote a secure online environment.

Privacy in the Age of Social Media

In today's digital landscape, social media platforms have become an integral part of our lives. We use them to connect with friends and family, share our experiences, and express our thoughts and opinions. However, the convenience and connectedness that social media provides come at a cost: the erosion of our privacy.

The Power of Personal Data

Social media platforms collect massive amounts of data from their users. This data includes not only the content we share, such as posts, photos, and videos, but also our personal information, location data, browsing history, and even our online behavior patterns. This wealth of personal data is valuable and can be used for targeted advertising, user profiling, and even manipulation.

Companies use sophisticated algorithms to analyze this data and build detailed profiles of individuals, which they can then use to tailor advertisements and content to our specific interests and preferences. They can also sell this data to third parties, which may use it for various purposes, including political and social influence, surveillance, or even identity theft.

The Rise of Surveillance Capitalism

Surveillance capitalism is a term coined by scholar Shoshana Zuboff to describe the economic system in which our personal data is treated as a commodity. Companies like Facebook, Google, and Twitter collect, analyze, and monetize our personal data, turning it into profit. These companies have become masters of extracting and exploiting our personal information, often without our explicit consent.

In this era of surveillance capitalism, our private lives are constantly under scrutiny. Every like, share, and comment we make on social media leaves a digital footprint that can be used to build an incredibly detailed profile of who we are, what we like, and what we believe. This level of surveillance not only threatens our privacy but also raises concerns about individual autonomy, free will, and the integrity of democratic systems.

Governments vs. Tech Companies

The battle for privacy in the age of social media is not just between individuals and tech companies. Governments around the world also play a significant role in the privacy debate. Some governments argue for increased surveillance powers in the name of national security and public safety, while others push for stronger privacy protections to protect the rights of their citizens.

Tech companies often find themselves caught in the middle, facing pressure from both governments and users. They must strike a delicate balance between complying with government requests for user data and protecting the privacy rights of their users. This balance is not always easy to achieve, and companies must navigate complex legal and ethical landscapes.

Privacy in the Age of Social Media

So, how can we protect our privacy in the age of social media? While complete privacy may be difficult to achieve, there are steps we can take to safeguard our personal information and mitigate the risks associated with social media use.

1. **Review Privacy Settings:** Take the time to understand the privacy settings offered by social media platforms. Adjust these settings to limit the data that is collected about you and the visibility of your personal information.

2. **Be Mindful of Sharing:** Think carefully about what you share on social media. Consider the potential consequences of sharing personal information, such as your address, phone number, or vacation plans. Be cautious about sharing sensitive information that could be used against you.

3. **Limit Third-Party Apps:** Be selective about the third-party apps and services you connect to your social media accounts. These apps often have access to your personal data and can collect information about you without your knowledge.

4. **Regularly Audit Your Friends List:** Periodically review your friends list and remove individuals you no longer trust or recognize. Restrict access to your social media posts to a select group of trusted friends and family.

5. **Educate Yourself and Others:** Stay informed about privacy issues and educate yourself on best practices for protecting your privacy online. Share this knowledge with your friends and family to help them protect their privacy as well.

6. **Support Privacy Legislation:** Advocate for stronger privacy laws and regulations that hold tech companies accountable for safeguarding user data. Support organizations and initiatives that work to protect privacy rights and promote transparency.

While these measures can help mitigate some of the risks associated with social media use, it's important to remember that privacy in the digital age is an ongoing battle. As technology continues to evolve, new challenges will arise, and protecting our privacy will require constant vigilance and adaptation.

The Importance of Strong Encryption

One key tool in the fight for privacy is encryption. Encryption is the process of converting information into an unreadable format, known as ciphertext, which can only be decrypted with a specific key. This technology ensures that even if our data is intercepted or accessed without authorization, it remains secure and inaccessible to unauthorized individuals.

Social media platforms, messaging apps, and other online services increasingly employ encryption to protect users' communication and personal data from prying eyes. End-to-end encryption, in particular, ensures that only the sender and recipient can access the content of a message, making it nearly impossible for anyone else, including tech companies and governments, to intercept or decipher the message.

The Role of Whistleblowers

Whistleblowers play a crucial role in exposing privacy violations and holding tech companies and governments accountable. Individuals like Edward Snowden and Chelsea Manning have risked their personal freedom to bring to light the extent of surveillance and privacy invasions by governments and corporations.

While their actions are controversial and carry legal consequences, whistleblowers have prompted important discussions about the balance between national security and individual privacy. Their disclosures have led to increased public awareness and calls for stronger privacy protections.

The Future of Privacy in a Digital World

The future of privacy in a digital world is uncertain, but the need for privacy remains as important as ever. As social media continues to evolve and new technologies emerge, individuals, governments, and tech companies must forge a path that respects privacy rights while also addressing legitimate concerns such as national security and public safety.

In this ever-changing landscape, it is crucial for individuals to stay informed, be proactive in protecting their own privacy, and advocate for stronger privacy laws and regulations. Only through a collective effort can we ensure that privacy rights are not eroded in the face of technological advancements and growing surveillance.

Phil Zimmermann's Continuing Influence

Phil Zimmermann was at the forefront of the fight for privacy, especially during the early days of the internet. His pioneering work on Pretty Good Privacy (PGP) laid the foundation for secure communication and encryption practices that are still relevant today.

Zimmermann's advocacy for strong encryption and his commitment to protecting the privacy of individuals paved the way for a more privacy-conscious society. His efforts challenged the status quo and forced governments and tech companies to reckon with the importance of privacy in the digital age.

While Zimmermann's legacy lives on, the fight for privacy continues. It is up to each and every one of us to carry the torch forward and ensure that privacy remains a fundamental right in the age of social media and beyond.

The Cambridge Analytica Scandal

The Cambridge Analytica scandal rocked the world and thrust the issue of privacy into the spotlight. It revealed the dark side of the social media giant Facebook and the potential for data misuse on a massive scale. The scandal involved the unauthorized access and harvesting of personal data from millions of Facebook users, which was then used for political purposes.

The Unraveling of the Scandal

The scandal began with the discovery that an academic researcher, Aleksandr Kogan, had created a personality quiz app called "This Is Your Digital Life." The app collected not only the data of the app's users but also the data of their Facebook friends. This practice was allowed under Facebook's policies at the time, but the extent of the data collection raised concerns about privacy.

What made matters worse was that Kogan had shared this data with Cambridge Analytica, a political consulting firm. Cambridge Analytica, with the help of data scientist Christopher Wylie, used this information to build psychological profiles of millions of individuals. These profiles were then used to target users with personalized political advertisements during the 2016 U.S. presidential election and the Brexit referendum.

The Implications for Privacy

The Cambridge Analytica scandal highlighted the dangers of the vast amount of personal data collected by social media platforms and the potential for it to be misused without users' consent. It exposed the lack of control users had over their own information and sparked a global conversation about privacy rights in the digital age.

One of the key issues was the exploitation of the Facebook API, which allowed third-party developers to access users' data and that of their friends. This incident shed light on the need for stricter regulations and oversight to protect user data from unauthorized access and exploitation.

The scandal also raised questions about the responsibility of tech companies in safeguarding user data. Facebook faced significant backlash for its failure to properly monitor and control the use of data by third-party developers. It exposed the need for greater transparency and accountability from technology companies when it comes to handling user information.

Privacy Regulations and Reforms

In the aftermath of the scandal, governments around the world began reevaluating their privacy laws and regulations. The European Union introduced the General Data Protection Regulation (GDPR), a comprehensive framework that sets guidelines for the collection, processing, and storage of personal data. The GDPR emphasizes user consent, data minimization, and the right to erasure, giving individuals more control over their personal information.

Other countries, such as the United States, have also taken steps to tighten privacy regulations. The California Consumer Privacy Act (CCPA) grants California residents the right to know what personal information is being collected and how it is being used. It also gives them the right to opt out of the sale of their data.

Additionally, tech companies themselves have implemented various reforms to enhance user privacy. Facebook, for instance, revamped its data policies and introduced new tools to give users more control over their data. It also committed to greater transparency in its practices.

The Role of Encryption

The Cambridge Analytica scandal underscored the importance of strong encryption in protecting user data. With encrypted communications, even if hackers or unauthorized entities gain access to the data, they would not be able to decipher it without the encryption keys.

End-to-end encryption, in particular, has become crucial for safeguarding user privacy. It ensures that only the sender and intended recipient can access the contents of a message, preventing any intermediaries, including tech companies, from accessing the information.

Encrypted messaging platforms like Signal and WhatsApp gained popularity in the aftermath of the scandal as users sought more secure alternatives to traditional communication channels.

The Need for User Education

The Cambridge Analytica scandal exposed the lack of awareness among users regarding the privacy risks associated with social media and other online platforms. Many users were unaware of the extent to which their data was being collected and used.

There is a pressing need for user education on privacy and data protection. Users must be equipped with the knowledge to make informed decisions about what personal information they share online and how it is being used. By understanding the risks and taking steps to protect their own privacy, users can regain control over their data.

A Call for Ethical Tech Practices

The scandal prompted a broader conversation about the ethical responsibility of technology companies. It highlighted the need for technology to be developed and used in a way that respects individual privacy and adheres to ethical standards.

Tech companies must prioritize the privacy and security of their users. They should design systems with privacy in mind, implement robust security measures, and be transparent about how they collect, store, and use data. Additionally, ethical considerations should be at the forefront of decision-making processes, rather than solely focusing on profit or gaining a competitive edge.

Real-World Example: Data-Driven Political Campaigns

The Cambridge Analytica scandal serves as a cautionary tale about the potential impact of data-driven political campaigns. By harnessing personal data to target individuals with tailored messaging, political campaigns can manipulate public opinion and potentially undermine democratic processes.

For example, Cambridge Analytica's use of psychological profiling allowed them to identify specific personality traits and tailor messages to exploit people's fears, desires, and biases. This targeted approach amplified the effectiveness of political advertisements, potentially swaying public opinion and influencing election outcomes.

This case raises ethical concerns about the impact of data-driven political campaigns on the democratic process, as well as the need for regulation to ensure transparency and fairness in political advertising.

Takeaways and Key Points

The Cambridge Analytica scandal revealed the potential consequences of a lack of privacy protection in the digital age:

- The unauthorized access and misuse of personal data can have significant political and social implications.

- Privacy regulations and reforms are necessary to protect user data and ensure transparency and accountability from tech companies.

- Encryption plays a crucial role in safeguarding user privacy and preventing unauthorized access to personal data.

- User education is vital to empower individuals to make informed decisions about their privacy.

- Ethical tech practices should prioritize privacy and adhere to ethical standards in data collection, storage, and usage.

The Cambridge Analytica scandal served as a wake-up call, urging individuals, governments, and tech companies to take action to protect user privacy and uphold ethical principles in the digital landscape. By learning from this scandal and implementing necessary changes, we can strive towards a future where privacy is respected and protected.

User Privacy as a Commodity

In today's digital age, user privacy has become a valuable commodity. With the prevalence of social media platforms, online shopping, and targeted advertising, our personal information is constantly being collected, analyzed, and monetized. In this section, we will explore the idea of user privacy as a commodity, examining how our personal data is bought and sold, the implications of this practice, and the importance of protecting our privacy in an age of corporate surveillance.

The Data Economy

The concept of user privacy as a commodity is rooted in the data economy, where companies collect and leverage personal information for financial gain. Every time we use a mobile app, make a purchase online, or even just browse the internet, we leave behind a digital footprint that is captured and stored by various entities. This data includes our browsing history, location information, social media interactions, and much more.

Tech giants like Google, Facebook, and Amazon have built billion-dollar businesses by capitalizing on our personal data. They collect vast amounts of information on our preferences, behaviors, and habits, which they use to target ads, personalize content, and influence our online experiences. This data is incredibly valuable to advertisers, who are willing to pay top dollar to gain insights into consumer behavior and reach their target audiences more effectively.

The Implications of Monetizing Privacy

The monetization of user privacy raises several concerns and ethical dilemmas. Firstly, there is the issue of informed consent. Many users are unaware of the extent to which their personal data is being collected and how it is being used. Companies often bury this information deep within their privacy policies, making it difficult for users to make informed decisions.

Secondly, the data economy creates a power imbalance between users and corporations. While companies profit from our data, we often have little control over how it is used or shared. This lack of agency raises questions about the ownership of our personal information and the potential for exploitation.

Furthermore, the commodification of privacy can lead to the erosion of individual autonomy. The targeted advertising algorithms used by tech companies create filter bubbles, effectively limiting the information and perspectives to which we are exposed. This can have a significant impact on our decision-making processes, shaping our beliefs and behaviors in ways that we may not even be aware of.

Protecting User Privacy

In light of the increasing commodification of user privacy, it is crucial to take steps to protect our personal information. Here are some practical strategies that individuals can employ:

1. **Read privacy policies:** Take the time to read and understand the privacy policies of the services and platforms you use. Look for transparency in data collection and sharing practices, as well as options to opt out or limit the use of your data.

2. **Use privacy-focused tools:** Utilize privacy-focused tools and browser extensions that help protect your online privacy. These tools can block trackers, encrypt your internet connection, and prevent unauthorized access to your data.

3. **Limit data sharing:** Be mindful of the information you share online. Think twice before posting personal information on social media platforms and be cautious when providing your data to third-party services.

4. **Manage your privacy settings:** Regularly review and adjust the privacy settings on your devices and online accounts. Limit the information you share with apps and be selective about the permissions you grant.

5. **Support privacy advocacy groups:** Stay informed about the latest developments in privacy and support organizations that advocate for stronger privacy protections. These groups work to raise awareness, shape policy, and promote the importance of privacy in our digital world.

The Future of User Privacy

As the debate around user privacy continues, it is evident that the protection of personal information is a fundamental human right. Governments worldwide are starting to recognize the need for stronger data protection laws, such as the European Union's General Data Protection Regulation (GDPR) and the California Consumer Privacy Act (CCPA).

The tech industry is also taking steps to address privacy concerns, with companies like Apple and Mozilla implementing privacy-focused features in their products and services. Nevertheless, the battle for privacy is far from over, as emerging technologies like artificial intelligence and the Internet of Things pose new challenges to our personal data.

In this ever-evolving landscape, the work of privacy advocates like Phil Zimmermann remains essential. He has paved the way for the protection of user privacy, advocating for strong encryption and user empowerment. It is up to individuals, policymakers, and tech companies to prioritize privacy and ensure that user data is treated with the respect and protection it deserves.

Resources

1. *The Age of Surveillance Capitalism: The Fight for a Human Future at the New Frontier of Power* by Shoshana Zuboff

2. *Data and Goliath: The Hidden Battles to Collect Your Data and Control Your World* by Bruce Schneier

3. Electronic Frontier Foundation (EFF): https://www.eff.org

4. Privacy International: https://www.privacyinternational.org

5. Center for Democracy and Technology (CDT): https://www.cdt.org

Exercises

1. Research and analyze the privacy policies of three popular social media platforms. What data do they collect, how do they use it, and what options do users have to control their privacy?

2. Explore the features of a privacy-focused browser extension and discuss how it can enhance user privacy and security.

3. Investigate the privacy laws in your country or region. How do they protect user privacy, and what are the potential limitations or loopholes?

4. Conduct a survey among your peers to assess their awareness of the data economy and their attitudes toward the monetization of user privacy. Discuss the implications of the findings.

5. Write an essay discussing the ethical considerations of targeted advertising and its impact on user autonomy. Provide real-world examples to support your arguments.

Note: All websites and resources provided were accurate at the time of writing. Please ensure that the links and information are up to date before referencing or utilizing them.

Further Reading

1. Solove, D.J. (2008). *Understanding Privacy*. Harvard University Press.

2. Zuboff, S. (2019). *The Age of Surveillance Capitalism: The Fight for a Human Future at the New Frontier of Power*. PublicAffairs.

3. Schneier, B. (2015). *Data and Goliath: The Hidden Battles to Collect Your Data and Control Your World*. W. W. Norton & Company.

4. Harris, T. (2019). *Tools and Weapons: The Promise and the Peril of the Digital Age*. Penguin Press.

The Importance of Strong Encryption

In today's digital age, the importance of strong encryption cannot be overstated. Encryption is the process of converting information into a format that is unreadable by anyone without the proper decryption key. It plays a crucial role in ensuring the privacy and security of our personal data, communications, and online transactions.

Protecting Personal Privacy

One of the main reasons why strong encryption is vital is because it protects our personal privacy. In an era where our lives are increasingly lived online, we share immense amounts of personal information, from bank details to healthcare records to private conversations. Without encryption, this data is vulnerable to interception and misuse.

Imagine a scenario where you send an email containing sensitive financial information to a trusted friend. If the email is not encrypted, it can be easily intercepted by hackers, governments, or malicious actors. They can then gain access to your personal information, compromising your privacy and potentially using the information for nefarious purposes, such as identity theft or financial fraud.

Strong encryption ensures that your data remains confidential, even if it falls into the wrong hands. By encrypting our communications, we can have confidence in the privacy of our conversations, protecting our personal information from unauthorized access.

Preserving National Security

Encryption not only plays a crucial role in protecting personal privacy but also in preserving national security. Governments, military organizations, and intelligence agencies rely on encryption to safeguard sensitive information and communications.

For example, military operations require secure channels of communication to ensure that classified information remains confidential. Encryption provides the necessary level of security to prevent adversaries from intercepting and decoding critical military communications. It helps protect strategic plans, troop movements, and other sensitive data from falling into the wrong hands.

Similarly, government agencies need strong encryption to safeguard national interests, protect citizens, and prevent cyberattacks. Encryption ensures that confidential information, such as intelligence reports or diplomatic communications, remain secure, thus enabling governments to function effectively and protect their citizens from internal and external threats.

Securing Financial Transactions

In the digital era, financial transactions are conducted predominantly online. From online shopping to banking to cryptocurrency, encryption is essential to secure these transactions and protect our financial information.

When you make an online purchase or transfer money from one account to another, strong encryption protocols ensure that your financial information, such as credit card details or account numbers, is protected from interception by hackers or cybercriminals. It prevents unauthorized individuals from gaining access to your financial data and using it for fraudulent purposes.

The growing popularity of cryptocurrencies such as Bitcoin has further emphasized the need for robust encryption. Cryptocurrencies rely on secure encryption to ensure the legitimacy of transactions and protect the anonymity and security of users. Strong encryption algorithms safeguard the integrity of these digital currencies, preventing fraudulent transactions or unauthorized access to digital wallets.

The Global Fight for Privacy

Across the globe, there is a growing awareness of the importance of strong encryption in protecting personal privacy and safeguarding national security. However, this fight for privacy is not without its challenges.

Many governments and law enforcement agencies argue that strong encryption hinders their ability to combat terrorism, organized crime, and other illegal activities.

They advocate for backdoors or weakened encryption algorithms that would allow authorized access to encrypted data. However, such measures would undermine the very purpose of encryption, leaving personal information and national security vulnerable to exploitation.

Finding the right balance between privacy and law enforcement is a delicate and ongoing debate. It is essential to ensure that encryption remains robust and uncompromised, protecting the privacy and security of individuals and organizations.

The Role of Individuals and Organizations

The responsibility of protecting personal privacy and enabling strong encryption extends beyond governments and technology companies. Individuals and organizations also play a crucial role in advocating for and implementing encryption measures to safeguard their own data and the privacy of their users or customers.

Individuals can take steps to protect their privacy by using encrypted messaging apps, strong passwords, and two-factor authentication. Additionally, they can educate themselves about encryption and spread awareness about its importance to friends, family, and colleagues.

Organizations, especially those handling sensitive data, have a duty to implement robust encryption measures to protect their customers' information. This includes securely storing data, encrypting communications, and regularly updating encryption protocols to mitigate emerging threats.

Conclusion

Strong encryption is a cornerstone in preserving personal privacy, ensuring national security, and securing financial transactions. It protects sensitive information from unauthorized access and interception at a time when our lives are increasingly lived online. The battle for privacy continues, and it is imperative for individuals, organizations, and governments to understand and uphold the importance of strong encryption in maintaining privacy and security in the digital age.

Chapter 3: The Fight for Privacy

3.2.8 Privacy Laws and Regulations

Privacy laws and regulations have become increasingly important in our digital age. As technology advances and collects more and more personal data, it has become crucial to establish legal protections for individuals' privacy. In this section, we will explore the development of privacy laws, their significance, and their impact on society.

The Need for Privacy Laws

In a world where our every move is recorded, stored, and analyzed, privacy laws play a critical role in safeguarding our personal information. These laws aim to regulate the collection, use, and disclosure of data by individuals, businesses, and governments to ensure that individuals' privacy rights are respected.

The need for privacy laws arises from the inherent power imbalance between data collectors and individuals. Without proper regulations, our personal data can easily be exploited for various purposes, including targeted advertising, surveillance, and even discrimination. Privacy laws are essential to prevent misuse and abuse of personal information and to maintain individual autonomy and control over our own data.

A Patchwork of Privacy Laws

Privacy laws and regulations vary greatly across different countries and regions. Some countries, like the European Union, have comprehensive privacy laws that provide a high level of protection for individuals' personal information. The General Data Protection Regulation (GDPR), implemented in 2018, is one such example. It establishes strict rules for data collection, consent, and the rights of individuals in relation to their personal data.

Other countries, like the United States, have a more fragmented approach to privacy regulations. In the US, privacy laws are sector-specific, with different rules governing healthcare, financial services, telecommunications, and other industries. While these laws offer some protection, they often fall short in addressing the challenges posed by the digital age, where personal data is constantly collected and processed by various entities.

Global Privacy Standards

To address the global nature of data collection and processing, several international frameworks and agreements have been developed to establish minimum privacy standards. The most notable of these is the Fair Information Practice Principles (FIPPs), which serves as a blueprint for privacy protection. The FIPPs include principles such as collection limitation, data quality, purpose specification, use limitation, security safeguards, openness, individual participation, and accountability.

Additionally, international organizations like the Organization for Economic Co-operation and Development (OECD) and the International Organization for Standardization (ISO) have created guidelines and standards for privacy protection. These standards help countries develop their own privacy laws and ensure a consistent approach to privacy across borders.

Challenges in Enforcing Privacy Laws

While privacy laws aim to protect individuals' personal information, enforcing these laws can be challenging. One major hurdle is the cross-border nature of data collection and processing. With the internet, personal data can easily flow across jurisdictions, making it difficult to track and regulate.

Another challenge lies in the rapid evolution of technology. Privacy laws often struggle to keep up with advancements in data collection and analytics. Innovations such as facial recognition, artificial intelligence, and the Internet of Things may push the boundaries of existing privacy frameworks, necessitating constant updates and amendments to keep pace with technological developments.

Privacy Law Violations

Privacy law violations can have severe consequences for individuals and organizations. Breaches of privacy laws can result in financial penalties, reputational damage, and loss of trust. One prominent example is the Cambridge Analytica scandal, where millions of Facebook users' personal data was harvested without their consent. This incident highlighted the need for stronger privacy regulations and led to increased public awareness of data privacy issues.

Emerging Trends in Privacy Law

As technology continues to advance, new challenges will arise in the field of privacy law. One such challenge is the Internet of Things, where everyday objects are connected to the internet, generating vast amounts of personal data. Regulating the collection and use of data from these interconnected devices will require innovative approaches to privacy law.

Another emerging trend is the rise of privacy by design and default. Privacy by design refers to the integration of privacy measures at the earliest stages of system design, ensuring that privacy is embedded in the architecture of a product or service. Privacy by default, on the other hand, means that the strictest privacy settings are applied as the default option, giving individuals more control over their personal information.

Conclusion

Privacy laws and regulations are essential in protecting individuals' personal information in the digital age. These laws establish a framework for privacy protection, regulate the collection and use of personal data, and ensure individuals' rights are upheld. However, challenges such as cross-border data flows and technological advancements require ongoing efforts to adapt and strengthen privacy laws. As individuals and society become increasingly aware of the importance of privacy, the evolution of privacy laws will continue to shape our digital future.

Shaping the Future of Privacy

In today's digital age, the battle for privacy has become more important than ever. As governments, corporations, and individuals increasingly rely on technology to communicate and store data, the need to protect personal information has become paramount. In this section, we will explore how the future of privacy is being shaped and what individuals can do to safeguard their digital lives.

The Power of Personal Data

In the modern world, personal data has become a valuable currency. Companies collect and analyze vast amounts of information about individuals to target advertising, personalize user experiences, and make informed business decisions. However, the unrestricted collection and use of personal data raises concerns about privacy and surveillance.

The Cambridge Analytica scandal, which came to light in 2018, serves as a stark reminder of the potential misuse of personal data. The British political consulting firm misappropriated the personal information of millions of Facebook users without their consent, using it to target political advertisements. This incident shed light on the vulnerability of personal data and the potential for manipulation.

The Rise of Surveillance Capitalism

Surveillance capitalism refers to a business model in which companies profit from the collection and analysis of personal data for targeted advertising. Tech giants like Google and Facebook have become adept at capturing user data, which is then used to generate revenue through highly targeted advertising campaigns.

While such advertising practices have their benefits, they also raise concerns about the erosion of privacy. Users often unknowingly trade their personal data for access to digital services, and in doing so, surrender control over their own information. As surveillance capitalism continues to grow, the battle for privacy becomes increasingly crucial.

Governments vs. Tech Companies

The tension between governments and tech companies regarding privacy has become a central issue. Governments argue that access to personal data is necessary for national security and law enforcement purposes. On the other hand, tech companies advocate for user privacy, facing pressure to balance the needs of their customers with legal obligations.

For example, in 2016, the FBI requested that Apple create a backdoor to unlock an iPhone used by a suspect in a high-profile case. Apple staunchly refused, citing user privacy concerns and setting off a larger debate about encryption and government access to personal data.

This clash between governments and tech companies illustrates the ongoing struggle to strike a balance between personal privacy and security.

Privacy in the Age of Social Media

The rise of social media platforms has fundamentally transformed the way people share and interact online. While these platforms offer unprecedented opportunities for connection and self-expression, they also pose significant threats to privacy.

Social media platforms often encourage users to share personal information, including location, interests, and personal relationships. Though this sharing may seem harmless, it can have far-reaching consequences. Personal data shared on social media can be exploited by cybercriminals, used for targeted advertising, or even influence personal decisions.

Individuals must recognize the potential risks associated with social media use and take steps to protect their privacy.

The Importance of Strong Encryption

Encryption plays a crucial role in protecting the privacy of digital communications. By scrambling information so that it is unreadable without a decryption key, encryption ensures that sensitive data remains secure from unauthorized access.

Strong encryption is vital for protecting personal privacy. It allows individuals and organizations to communicate securely, ensuring that their messages cannot be intercepted or tampered with. Additionally, encryption protects sensitive information stored on devices or in the cloud, making it difficult for anyone without the proper encryption key to access the data.

Governments and law enforcement agencies, however, often view strong encryption as a hindrance to investigations. They argue for the implementation of backdoors, which are intentional vulnerabilities in encryption systems that allow authorized entities to access encrypted data. However, including backdoors in encryption would compromise security for all users, leaving personal data vulnerable to cybercriminals as well.

Privacy Laws and Regulations

In response to growing privacy concerns, many countries have implemented privacy laws and regulations to protect individuals' personal information. These laws aim to establish standards for the collection, use, and disclosure of personal data.

For instance, the European Union enacted the General Data Protection Regulation (GDPR) in 2018. The GDPR provides individuals with greater control over their personal data, requiring businesses to obtain explicit consent for data collection and enabling users to request the deletion or transfer of their data.

Similarly, in the United States, laws such as the California Consumer Privacy Act (CCPA) provide individuals with more comprehensive rights regarding the collection and sale of their personal information.

Privacy laws and regulations are essential for safeguarding personal data, but they also face challenges as technology evolves rapidly, requiring continuous updates to keep pace with emerging privacy concerns.

Shaping the Future of Privacy

The future of privacy depends on the collective efforts of individuals, governments, and tech companies. Here are some key factors that will shape the future of privacy:

- **User Education:** Promoting digital literacy and educating users about privacy risks and best practices is vital. Individuals must understand the implications of their online activities and take proactive measures to protect their privacy.

- **Ethical Considerations:** Privacy needs to be elevated as an ethical consideration in the design and deployment of new technologies. Companies must take a privacy-first approach, ensuring that their products and services prioritize user privacy.

- **Technological Innovations:** The development of privacy-enhancing technologies, such as decentralized systems, zero-knowledge proofs, and differential privacy, will play a significant role in the future of privacy. These technologies offer novel ways to protect personal data without compromising security.

- **Collaboration and Advocacy:** Governments, tech companies, privacy advocates, and individuals must work together to advocate for strong privacy protections and regulations. Collaboration will be key to successfully shaping privacy policies and practices.

- **Public Perception:** Shifting public attitudes toward privacy is essential. Individuals must demand greater privacy protections from tech companies and be willing to make privacy-conscious choices.

The future of privacy is a complex and evolving landscape. It requires a multi-faceted approach that combines technological advancements, regulatory frameworks, and individual responsibility. With concerted efforts, it is possible to shape a future where privacy is respected and protected in the digital world.

Exercises

1. Research and analyze the privacy laws in your country. How do they protect individuals' personal data? Are there any limitations or areas that need improvement?

2. Investigate the privacy settings of your social media accounts. Are they set to maximize privacy? What steps can you take to enhance your privacy on these platforms?

3. Consider the potential risks associated with sharing personal information online. How can you mitigate these risks and protect your privacy?

4. Reflect on your attitudes towards privacy. Do you prioritize privacy in your online activities? What changes can you make to better protect your personal information?

Resources

- Brave New World by Aldous Huxley - A classic dystopian novel that explores themes of privacy and surveillance in a technologically advanced society.

- TED Talk: "Why Privacy Matters" by Glenn Greenwald - In this talk, journalist Glenn Greenwald discusses the importance of privacy and the impact of mass surveillance on society.

- Electronic Frontier Foundation (EFF) - A non-profit organization dedicated to defending civil liberties in the digital world. The EFF provides resources, advocacy, and legal support for privacy-related issues.

- Future of Privacy Forum (FPF) - A think tank focused on advancing responsible data practices. The FPF publishes research and resources on privacy-related topics and facilitates collaboration between industry, academia, and advocacy groups.

Note: This chapter focuses on the content and themes covered in the book and does not constitute legal or professional advice. Readers are encouraged to consult legal professionals for matters relating to privacy and data protection.

End of section 3.2.9

Phil Zimmermann's Role in the Fight

Phil Zimmermann, the brilliant programmer and visionary behind Pretty Good Privacy (PGP), played a crucial role in the fight for privacy in the digital age. His determination, expertise, and unwavering commitment to protecting the individual's right to privacy have made him one of the most influential figures in the field.

The Birth of a Privacy Advocate

Phil Zimmermann's journey as a privacy advocate began during his early years as a curious kid. He developed a passion for computers and hacking into systems, which eventually led him to the world of cryptography. It was in the early 1990s that Zimmermann became inspired to create PGP, a revolutionary encryption software that would empower individuals to secure their private communications.

Zimmermann recognized the increasing threats to privacy posed by governments and corporations' growing surveillance capabilities. He understood the vital role cryptography could play in safeguarding individuals' personal information from prying eyes and launched a mission to bring strong encryption technology to the masses.

Challenging the Status Quo

Zimmermann's most famous battle came during the Crypto Wars, a period of intense conflict between the government and advocates of strong encryption. The U.S. government, fearing the widespread use of unbreakable encryption, attempted to suppress the distribution of PGP by initiating a criminal investigation against Zimmermann.

Undeterred by the government's efforts, Zimmermann fought back, mobilizing the tech community and galvanizing public support for the right to privacy. His unwavering dedication and determination transformed the Clipper Chip controversy into a David and Goliath battle, with Zimmermann as the unlikely hero standing up for individual freedoms.

A Catalyst for Change

Zimmermann's victory in the Crypto Wars changed the course of history by promoting awareness and understanding of the importance of encryption. By persevering and fighting for his beliefs, he inspired a generation of hacktivists and brought cryptography out of obscurity and into the mainstream.

His triumph demonstrated the power of public support and highlighted the need for a balance between privacy and national security. Zimmermann's work sparked a global conversation about the implications of mass surveillance and the importance of protecting citizens' right to privacy.

Phil Zimmermann's Enduring Influence

Zimmermann's relentless advocacy for privacy did not end with the Crypto Wars. He continued to champion encryption and its role in safeguarding personal information in the digital age. His philanthropic efforts, such as funding privacy-oriented projects and collaborating with like-minded individuals and organizations, have had a lasting impact on the development and proliferation of privacy-enhancing technologies.

Moreover, Zimmermann's work has inspired a new generation of privacy advocates to carry on his legacy. The fight for privacy is an ongoing battle, and Zimmermann's impact serves as a constant source of inspiration for those striving to protect digital rights and challenge the hostile environments created by mass surveillance and invasive data collection.

Phil Zimmermann's Lasting Legacy

Phil Zimmermann's contribution to the world of privacy cannot be overstated. His pioneering efforts in cryptography and his relentless fight for privacy have had a profound and lasting impact on society. Zimmermann's vision and dedication have helped shape the conversation around the rights of individuals in the digital era.

His legacy serves as a reminder of the importance of standing up for our fundamental rights, including the right to privacy. Zimmermann's work continues to influence the tech industry, policymakers, and everyday individuals, ensuring that the fight for privacy remains at the forefront of our collective consciousness.

In honor of Phil Zimmermann's transformative work, we must carry his torch forward, embracing his advocacy and ideals, and continuing to fight for privacy rights in the ever-evolving digital landscape. Only by championing these principles can we strive to create a future where privacy is protected, and individuals have control over their personal information.

Balancing Security and Privacy

The Ethical Dilemma of Surveillance

In today's digital age, the ethical dilemma of surveillance has become a pressing issue that raises important questions about privacy, security, and the balance between individual rights and collective safety. On one hand, surveillance can be seen as a crucial tool for crime prevention, national security, and even public health concerns. On the other hand, it has the potential to infringe upon our fundamental rights, erode trust, and create a climate of constant monitoring.

Surveillance, in its various forms, has become an integral part of our daily lives. Whether it's CCTV cameras on every street corner, online tracking by technology companies, or government intelligence agencies monitoring electronic communications, the pervasiveness of surveillance raises concerns about the extent of intrusion into our private lives. This has led to a debate about where to draw the line between necessary surveillance for public safety and the protection of individual civil liberties.

One of the key ethical dilemmas is the tension between security and privacy. Governments argue that surveillance is essential for detecting and preventing criminal activities or acts of terrorism. They claim that by monitoring individuals' activities, they can identify potential threats and take preemptive action. However, this approach comes at the cost of our privacy, as it involves collecting and analyzing vast amounts of personal data without the explicit consent of individuals.

Moreover, the rise of surveillance technologies has enabled unprecedented levels of data collection and analysis. Through advanced algorithms and machine learning, organizations can collect and process enormous amounts of information, often without our knowledge or understanding of how this data is being used. This raises concerns about the potential misuse or abuse of personal information, as well as the erosion of trust between individuals and the entities that govern them.

Another ethical issue associated with surveillance is the potential for discrimination and social profiling. Surveillance systems are not neutral; they reflect the biases and prejudices of their creators. Communities that are already marginalized or subject to systemic discrimination can become targets of unwarranted surveillance, leading to further stigmatization and violation of their rights. This creates a vicious cycle where those who are already vulnerable are subjected to increased scrutiny and disproportionately harmed.

It is also important to consider the implications of surveillance on freedom of expression and dissent. When individuals are aware that their activities are being monitored, they may self-censor their opinions or actions, fearing the consequences of expressing dissenting views. This can have a chilling effect on democratic societies, impeding the free exchange of ideas and hindering the development of a diverse and vibrant public discourse.

Finding a balance between surveillance and privacy is a complex challenge, but it is not insurmountable. One possible solution is the implementation of strong legal frameworks that regulate surveillance practices, ensuring they are proportionate, transparent, and subject to independent oversight. Additionally, there is a need for public education and awareness campaigns to inform individuals about their rights and empower them to protect their privacy in the digital realm.

As we navigate the ethical dilemmas of surveillance, it is crucial to remember that privacy is a fundamental human right. It is the cornerstone of individual autonomy, dignity, and freedom. Protecting privacy requires a collective commitment from governments, organizations, and individuals to uphold the principles of transparency, accountability, and consent.

In conclusion, the ethical dilemma of surveillance forces us to confront the trade-off between security and privacy. While surveillance can provide some level of protection, it also poses risks to individual rights, trust, and democratic ideals. Addressing this dilemma requires a comprehensive approach that balances the need for security with the preservation of privacy. By fostering dialogue, implementing robust legal frameworks, and empowering individuals with knowledge, we can strive towards a society that upholds privacy as a fundamental human right.

The Need for Better Encryption

In today's digital age, privacy has become a fundamental concern for individuals, organizations, and governments alike. With the increasing reliance on technology for communication, transactions, and storage of personal information, the need for better encryption has never been more crucial. Encryption serves as a vital tool to protect sensitive data from unauthorized access and ensures that information remains confidential and secure.

Understanding the Current State of Encryption

To appreciate the need for better encryption, it is essential to understand the current state of encryption and the challenges it faces. Encryption is the process of converting plaintext information into a coded or encrypted form, making it incomprehensible to unauthorized individuals. The encrypted data can only be deciphered using a unique key, known only to the intended recipient.

While encryption has significantly evolved over the years, so have the techniques used by attackers to compromise it. Cybercriminals employ sophisticated methods such as brute force attacks, social engineering, and exploiting vulnerabilities in encryption algorithms to gain unauthorized access to encrypted data. As technology advances, encryption must keep pace to withstand new threats and protect sensitive information effectively.

The Rise of Quantum Computing

One of the greatest challenges to encryption is the rise of quantum computing. Traditional encryption algorithms, such as RSA and AES, rely on the difficulty of factoring large numbers or solving complex math problems to ensure security. However, quantum computers have the potential to solve these problems much faster than traditional computers, rendering current encryption methods vulnerable.

Quantum computers harness the principles of quantum mechanics, utilizing quantum bits or qubits which can exist in multiple states simultaneously. This parallelism enables quantum computers to perform computations exponentially faster than classical computers. It poses a significant threat to current encryption methods, as quantum algorithms can efficiently factor large numbers, break asymmetrical encryption, and undermine the security of encrypted communications.

Post-Quantum Cryptography as a Solution

The advent of quantum computing necessitates the development of post-quantum cryptography (PQC), which provides algorithms resistant to quantum attacks. PQC aims to ensure that encrypted data remains secure even in the face of substantial advances in quantum computing.

Efforts are underway to develop PQC algorithms that are resistant to attacks from both classical and quantum computers. These algorithms rely on entirely different mathematical foundations and computational approaches, ensuring their resilience against quantum attacks.

Some promising PQC algorithms include lattice-based cryptography, code-based cryptography, multivariate cryptography, and hash-based cryptography. These algorithms are designed to withstand attacks from quantum computers and offer a potential solution for secure communication and data protection in the post-quantum era.

Implementing Better Encryption Practices

While the development of PQC algorithms is crucial for the future, it is equally important to implement better encryption practices in the present. This includes adopting stronger encryption algorithms, regularly updating encryption software and firmware, and integrating encryption mechanisms at every level of data transmission and storage.

Additionally, robust encryption requires proper key management strategies. Encryption keys should be stored securely, with access granted only to authorized individuals. Regular key rotation and the use of long, complex, and random keys further enhance the security of encrypted data.

Furthermore, encryption should be adopted not only by individuals but also by organizations and governments. It is imperative to educate users about the importance of encryption and promote its widespread adoption to create a more secure digital environment. Collaboration between technology companies, governments, and cybersecurity experts is essential to establish best practices and standards for encryption implementation.

Real-World Impact: Preventing Data Breaches

The need for better encryption becomes evident when we consider real-world scenarios where data breaches can have severe consequences. From financial institutions to healthcare providers to government agencies, organizations handle vast amounts of sensitive information that, if compromised, can lead to identity theft, financial loss, and even national security threats.

By implementing robust encryption measures, organizations can mitigate the risks associated with data breaches. Encrypting data at rest and in transit provides an extra layer of protection, ensuring that even if the data is accessed unlawfully, it remains unreadable and unusable.

For example, in 2017, Equifax, one of the largest credit reporting agencies, suffered a massive data breach that exposed the personal information of 147 million individuals. The breach compromised sensitive data such as social security numbers, birth dates, and addresses, putting millions at risk of identity theft and financial fraud. If the data had been properly encrypted, even if the breach occurred, the stolen information would have been useless to the hackers.

Resources and Tools for Better Encryption

Fortunately, numerous resources and tools are available to facilitate better encryption practices. These resources include open-source encryption software such as GnuPG and VeraCrypt, which offer strong encryption algorithms and user-friendly interfaces. Additionally, organizations like the Electronic Frontier Foundation (EFF) provide guidance on secure communication, privacy tools, and advocacy for strong encryption.

Encryption protocols such as Transport Layer Security (TLS) and Pretty Good Privacy (PGP) are widely used to secure communications and ensure the authenticity and integrity of data transmission. The adoption of these protocols is crucial in safeguarding sensitive information exchanged over the internet.

In conclusion, the need for better encryption is imperative in today's digital landscape. With the rise of cyber threats and the looming threat of quantum computing, robust encryption practices and the development of post-quantum cryptography are essential to protect sensitive information and ensure privacy. By understanding the current state of encryption, implementing better encryption practices, and utilizing available resources and tools, we can safeguard our data and maintain control over our digital lives.

Risks and Benefits of Mass Surveillance

Mass surveillance, the systematic collection and analysis of large amounts of data on individuals, has become a prevalent practice in today's digital age. It involves monitoring and capturing information about individuals' activities, communications, and behavior. While proponents argue that mass surveillance can enhance national security and public safety, there are significant risks and potential negative consequences associated with this practice.

The Risks of Mass Surveillance

1. **Invasion of Privacy:** Mass surveillance infringes upon individuals' right to privacy. By constantly monitoring and collecting personal data, governments and corporations gain unprecedented access to individuals' private lives, including their conversations, browsing history, and daily activities. This erosion of privacy can have a chilling effect on people's freedom of expression and behavior.

2. **Data Breaches and Cybersecurity Risks:** Mass surveillance involves the aggregation and storage of vast amounts of sensitive personal data. This concentration of data creates an attractive target for hackers and cybercriminals. Inadequate security measures can lead to data breaches, identity theft, and other cybercrimes. Individuals may suffer financial, emotional, and reputational harm as a result.

3. **Abuse of Power and State Surveillance:** Mass surveillance provides governments with unprecedented power to monitor and control their citizens. Without proper checks and balances, this power can be abused, leading to social and political repression. The potential for discrimination, targeting of marginalized groups, and suppression of dissenting voices is a significant concern.

4. **Chilling Effect on Free Speech and Expression:** The knowledge of being under constant surveillance can lead to self-censorship and inhibit free speech.

When individuals feel like their every word and action is being monitored, they may hesitate to express controversial opinions or engage in political activism. This limits democratic discourse and stifles innovation and progress.

5. **Low Efficacy in Preventing Terrorism:** Despite claims that mass surveillance is necessary for national security, there is limited evidence to support its effectiveness in preventing terrorism. The sheer volume of data collected makes it challenging to identify legitimate threats amid the noise. Moreover, the overreliance on surveillance technologies can divert resources from more effective intelligence-gathering methods.

The Benefits of Mass Surveillance

1. **Enhanced Security and Crime Prevention:** Proponents argue that mass surveillance can help detect and prevent criminal activities, including terrorism, cybercrimes, and organized crime. By monitoring communications and analyzing patterns of behavior, law enforcement agencies can identify potential threats and take appropriate action.

2. **Public Safety and Emergency Response:** Mass surveillance can aid in emergency response and public safety efforts. Surveillance systems can be used for early detection of natural disasters, monitoring traffic, and identifying potential security threats in crowded places. This information can help ensure a timely and effective response to protect public welfare.

3. **Investigation and Law Enforcement:** Surveillance data can be valuable in criminal investigations, providing evidence and leads to law enforcement agencies. It can help identify suspects, gather evidence, and reconstruct timelines of events. This can lead to more efficient and effective law enforcement, ensuring a safer society.

4. **Traffic Monitoring and Urban Planning:** Mass surveillance technologies such as CCTV cameras can assist in traffic monitoring and urban planning. This data can be used to optimize traffic flow, detect congestion, and improve the overall transportation infrastructure of cities. It can also help in urban development and crowd management during events.

5. **Health and Disease Prevention:** Surveillance can play a vital role in monitoring the spread of infectious diseases and implementing timely interventions to prevent outbreaks. By tracking and analyzing population movements, health organizations can identify high-risk areas, implement targeted vaccination campaigns, and allocate resources efficiently.

Maintaining a Balance

Finding the right balance between privacy and security is crucial in the debate surrounding mass surveillance. While some surveillance measures may be necessary for public safety and security, they should be implemented with adequate safeguards to protect individual privacy and prevent abuse of power.

1. **Transparency and Accountability:** Governments and corporations should be transparent about the scope and purpose of surveillance programs. Clear laws and regulations should govern the collection, use, and retention of surveillance data. Independent oversight bodies should be established to ensure accountability and protect against misuse of surveillance powers.

2. **Proportionality and Minimization:** Surveillance measures should be proportional to the threat being addressed, and data collection should be minimized to the extent necessary. This includes limiting the duration of data retention and restricting access to authorized personnel. Technologies that allow for targeted surveillance, rather than blanket surveillance, should be prioritized.

3. **Encryption and Data Protection:** Encryption technologies play a crucial role in protecting individuals' privacy and ensuring the security of their data. Governments should support widespread adoption of strong encryption standards and promote secure communication practices. Protection of personal data should be a legal requirement, and individuals should have control over their own data.

4. **Education and Awareness:** Promoting digital literacy and educating individuals about their rights to privacy and the risks and benefits of surveillance is essential. People should be empowered to make informed decisions about their digital footprint and be aware of tools and techniques they can use to protect their privacy.

Real-Life Example: The NSA Surveillance Programs

One prominent example of mass surveillance is the National Security Agency's (NSA) surveillance programs, revealed by whistleblower Edward Snowden in 2013. These programs involved the bulk collection of telephone metadata and the monitoring of internet communications, both domestically and internationally.

The disclosure of these programs sparked a global debate on privacy, security, and government surveillance. Critics argued that the NSA's actions violated privacy rights and were a breach of trust. Supporters, on the other hand, claimed that the programs were necessary for national security and preventing terrorism.

The debate over the NSA surveillance programs highlighted the importance of striking a balance between security and privacy. It raised concerns about the adequacy of oversight mechanisms and the need for stronger safeguards to prevent abuse of surveillance powers.

Conclusion

Mass surveillance presents both risks and benefits to society. It raises significant concerns regarding privacy, abuse of power, and the chilling effect on free speech. However, when appropriately managed and subject to oversight, surveillance can contribute to public safety, crime prevention, and emergency response.

As technology continues to evolve, it is crucial to revisit the ethical and legal frameworks surrounding mass surveillance. Striking the right balance between privacy and security requires ongoing dialogue, robust regulation, and the active engagement of individuals, policymakers, and technology experts. Only through conscious and responsible decision-making can we navigate the complex terrain of mass surveillance and protect the fundamental rights of individuals in the digital age.

Encryption as a Fundamental Right

In today's digital age, where personal data is constantly being collected and shared, the need for strong encryption has become more crucial than ever. Encryption is not just a tool used by tech-savvy individuals or organizations; it is a fundamental right that all individuals should have access to. In this section, we will explore why encryption is essential for protecting privacy and maintaining the security of personal information.

Encryption ensures that data transmitted over a network or stored on a device remains secure and private. It involves the process of encoding information in such a way that only authorized parties can access and understand it. Without encryption, sensitive data would be vulnerable to interception, exploitation, and misuse by hackers, criminals, and even government authorities.

One of the primary reasons why encryption is considered a fundamental right is because it enables individuals to exercise their right to privacy. Privacy is crucial for maintaining personal autonomy, dignity, and freedom of expression. By encrypting their communications and data, individuals can ensure that their private conversations, financial transactions, and personal information remain confidential.

Moreover, strong encryption also plays a vital role in safeguarding other fundamental human rights, such as freedom of speech, freedom of the press, and freedom of association. For journalists, activists, and whistleblowers, encryption is often the only means of protecting their sources and ensuring that sensitive information remains secure. Without encryption, journalists may hesitate to expose corruption, and citizens may refrain from speaking out against oppressive regimes.

Encryption also plays a critical role in promoting trust and cybersecurity in the digital realm. It enables secure e-commerce transactions, protects online banking activities, and safeguards sensitive business communications. Without encryption, cybercriminals could easily intercept passwords, credit card information, and trade secrets, leading to financial loss and reputational damage.

However, it is important to note that encryption also presents challenges for law enforcement agencies and national security interests. The ability to intercept and access encrypted communications is seen by some as an essential tool for fighting crime and terrorism. This has led to ongoing debates about the balance between privacy and security and the implementation of "backdoors" or weakened encryption standards.

The reality, though, is that weakening encryption or introducing backdoors compromises the security of everyone's data, not just the intended targets. Cybercriminals and malicious actors could exploit these vulnerabilities, putting individuals and organizations at greater risk. Additionally, building backdoors fundamentally undermines trust in the technology and opens the door for abuse by governments and authorities.

To protect encryption as a fundamental right, it is necessary to promote strong encryption standards, support research and development in encryption technologies, and advocate for policies that prioritize user privacy and cybersecurity. It is also crucial to educate individuals about encryption and its importance in the digital age.

In conclusion, encryption is not just a technical tool but a fundamental right that ensures privacy, security, and the protection of human rights. It enables individuals to exercise their right to privacy, supports freedom of expression and association, and plays a crucial role in maintaining trust and cybersecurity. Protecting encryption is essential to preserve privacy, maintain the integrity of digital communications, and foster a safe and secure digital society.

Problems and Solutions

Problem 1: Resisting Backdoors

Recently, there has been a growing demand from certain governments to introduce backdoors into encryption systems, which would enable authorized access to encrypted data. However, this approach poses significant risks to privacy and security. How can we protect encryption from backdoors while still addressing concerns of law enforcement?

Solution: Striking the right balance between privacy and security requires collaboration and innovative solutions. The tech industry should work closely with law enforcement agencies to develop alternative methods for criminal investigations that do not compromise encryption. This could involve improved digital forensics techniques, increased cooperation between agencies, and investment in advanced technologies. Additionally, privacy advocates and experts should actively participate in policy discussions to ensure that encryption remains strong and secure.

Problem 2: Access to Strong Encryption

While encryption is a fundamental right, not everyone has easy access to strong encryption tools. Many individuals, especially in authoritarian regimes and underprivileged communities, may lack the knowledge or resources to protect their data. How can we ensure widespread access to strong encryption?

Solution: Education and awareness are key to promoting widespread access to strong encryption. Governments, non-profit organizations, and tech companies should collaborate to provide free or affordable encryption tools and resources to individuals and organizations in need. Efforts should also be made to simplify user interfaces and improve user experience, making encryption more accessible to non-technical users. Furthermore, investing in digital literacy programs can empower individuals to understand the importance of encryption and how to use it effectively.

Problem 3: International Cooperation

In an increasingly interconnected world, maintaining encryption as a fundamental right requires international cooperation and collaboration. However, different countries have varying views on encryption and may implement conflicting policies. How can we foster international cooperation to protect encryption?

Solution: International organizations, such as the United Nations and the International Telecommunication Union, play a crucial role in facilitating discussions and agreements on encryption. Multilateral efforts should focus on establishing global principles and standards for encryption, promoting transparency, and fostering dialogue between governments, industry leaders, and privacy advocates. Additionally, diplomatic channels and cross-border partnerships can help bridge the gaps in encryption policies and ensure a consistent approach in protecting individual rights and cybersecurity.

Further Reading and Resources

- "The Code Book: The Science of Secrecy from Ancient Egypt to Quantum Cryptography" by Simon Singh.
   - "Data and Goliath: The Hidden Battles to Collect Your Data and Control Your World" by Bruce Schneier.
   - The Electronic Frontier Foundation (EFF) website: https://www.eff.org/
   - The American Civil Liberties Union (ACLU) website: https://www.aclu.org/
   - The Open Rights Group website: https://www.openrightsgroup.org/
   - The Crypto Wars documentary: https://cryptowars.org/
   - The TED Talk by Cory Doctorow: "How to Break the Internet: A Proposal for Democracy"

The Role of Whistleblowers

Whistleblowers play a crucial role in the fight for privacy, exposing wrongdoing and bringing to light actions that threaten our fundamental rights. Their courageous actions often come at great personal risk, as they face retaliation and legal consequences for speaking out. In this section, we will explore the significance of whistleblowers in the context of privacy and their impact on society.

The Importance of Whistleblowers in Protecting Privacy

Whistleblowers serve as the conscience of society, shedding light on activities that are hidden from public view. In the realm of privacy, they play a vital role in exposing surveillance programs, corporate data breaches, and other infringements on personal privacy. Their actions force accountability, promote transparency, and can lead to meaningful social change.

One of the most notable examples of a whistleblower in the realm of privacy is Edward Snowden. Through his leaks, Snowden revealed the extensive surveillance conducted by intelligence agencies, including the collection of metadata and the mass monitoring of online activities. His disclosures sparked a global debate on privacy and government surveillance and led to significant legal and policy reforms.

Whistleblowers as Guardians of Democracy

Whistleblowers are essential for maintaining the health of democratic societies. By exposing corruption, unethical behavior, and abuses of power, they hold governments and corporations accountable. Their actions empower individuals and provide the necessary information to make informed decisions about their personal privacy.

For example, Chelsea Manning, a former United States Army intelligence analyst, leaked hundreds of thousands of classified documents to WikiLeaks, including evidence of war crimes and human rights abuses. Manning's revelations brought international attention to these atrocities and sparked conversations about the impact of military operations on civilian populations. Her actions demonstrated the power of whistleblowing in addressing systemic issues and fostering a more just society.

The Challenges and Risks Faced by Whistleblowers

Whistleblowing is not without its challenges and risks. Whistleblowers often face significant personal, professional, and legal consequences for their actions. They may lose their jobs, face defamation lawsuits, or even be subjected to physical harm. The potential for retaliation can deter individuals from coming forward with crucial information.

Additionally, whistleblowers encounter various legal barriers that hinder their ability to disclose information. Many countries have laws in place that criminalize leaking classified information, making it difficult for individuals to expose wrongdoing without facing severe penalties. These legal challenges highlight the need for comprehensive whistleblower protection laws that balance national security concerns with transparency and the public interest.

Promoting Whistleblower Protection

To ensure that whistleblowers can come forward without fear of reprisal, it is crucial to establish robust legal protections and support mechanisms. Whistleblower protection laws should safeguard individuals who disclose information in the public interest, ensuring their anonymity and shielding them from retaliation.

Moreover, organizations and governments can take steps to create a culture that values and encourages whistleblowing. They can establish clear reporting mechanisms, provide whistleblower training, and establish policies that protect individuals who expose wrongdoing. By creating an environment that supports and protects whistleblowers, we can foster a society that values transparency and accountability.

Harnessing Technology to Protect Whistleblowers

Technology can play a crucial role in protecting the identity and safety of whistleblowers. Secure communication tools, such as encrypted messaging apps, can ensure that whistleblowers can safely disclose information without the fear of interception. Secure file-sharing platforms can enable the transmission of sensitive documents with built-in protections for anonymity.

For instance, platforms like SecureDrop provide a secure and anonymous way for whistleblowers to share information with journalists. SecureDrop utilizes encryption and anonymized communication to protect the identity of the whistleblower throughout the leaking process, ensuring their safety and privacy.

The Ethical Dilemma of Whistleblowing

Whistleblowing raises ethical questions regarding the balance between individual privacy and the greater good. Whistleblowers often expose private information in the interest of public disclosure, leading to a tension between the right to privacy and the need for transparency.

To navigate this ethical dilemma, whistleblowers must carefully consider the potential impact of their actions and the nature of the information they disclose. Transparency should be pursued while minimizing harm to individuals and respecting privacy rights. Legal frameworks and ethical guidelines can provide a framework for whistleblowers to make informed decisions about when and how to come forward with information.

Exercises

1. Research a prominent whistleblower case and analyze the impact of their disclosures on privacy and society. Discuss the challenges and risks they faced, as well as the legal and ethical implications of their actions.

2. Imagine you are a cybersecurity professional who has come across evidence of a massive data breach within your organization. Discuss the ethical considerations you would need to weigh when deciding whether to blow the whistle. Consider the potential consequences, the impact on individuals' privacy, and the obligations to your employer.

3. Conduct a debate on the topic "Whistleblowing should always be protected, regardless of the nature of the disclosed information." Divide the participants into

two groups, one arguing for the motion and the other against it. Explore the ethical, legal, and societal implications of protecting whistleblowers in different scenarios.

Additional Resources

1. "No Place to Hide: Edward Snowden, the NSA, and the U.S. Surveillance State" by Glenn Greenwald.
2. "Whistleblower Protection Laws: Global Overview" - International Bar Association.
3. "The Ethics of Whistleblowing" - Stanford Encyclopedia of Philosophy.
4. "SecureDrop: Whistleblower Submission System" - Freedom of the Press Foundation.
5. "Whistleblower Protection Programs" - U.S. Office of Special Counsel.
6. "Whistleblower Protection" - Transparency International.
7. "Whistleblower Protections" - American Civil Liberties Union.
8. "Whistleblower Handbook: A Step-by-Step Guide to Doing What's Right and Protecting Yourself" by Stephen M. Kohn.

The Encryption Backdoor Debate

The encryption backdoor debate has been a contentious issue in the tech world for years. It revolves around the question of whether tech companies should be required to build deliberate vulnerabilities, or "backdoors," into their encryption systems to allow government access to encrypted data. This debate is fueled by concerns over national security, individual privacy, and the role of technology in society.

At its core, encryption is the process of encoding information in such a way that only authorized parties can access and understand it. It plays a crucial role in protecting sensitive data, such as personal messages, financial transactions, and proprietary information. Encryption ensures that this data remains secure, even if it falls into the wrong hands.

However, some governments argue that encryption presents a roadblock to law enforcement and intelligence agencies in investigating and preventing criminal activities, such as terrorism, drug trafficking, and child exploitation. They claim that without backdoors, encrypted communication can become a safe haven for criminal activities, making it difficult or impossible for authorities to access crucial information.

On the other hand, encryption proponents argue that introducing backdoors undermines the very essence of encryption. They believe that any deliberate vulnerability compromises the security of the system and puts innocent users at risk. They argue that once a backdoor is created, it can be exploited by malicious actors, including hackers and foreign governments, who can use it to gain unauthorized access to sensitive information.

The encryption backdoor debate also raises concerns about the balance between privacy and surveillance. With the increasing amount of personal data stored and transmitted digitally, privacy has become a hot topic. Advocates for strong encryption argue that privacy is a fundamental right that should be protected, and any backdoors would erode that right.

Moreover, requiring tech companies to build backdoors creates a potential precedent for mass surveillance and the abuse of power. Critics argue that giving governments access to encrypted data without strict oversight and legal safeguards could lead to unwarranted intrusions into individuals' lives and a chilling effect on free speech and expression.

So, can a compromise be reached? The debate continues, and alternative solutions have been proposed, such as allowing law enforcement agencies to access encrypted data with a court order and the assistance of the tech companies involved. This approach would maintain the security of the encryption system while still allowing authorities to access information when necessary.

Furthermore, advancements in technology continue to challenge the feasibility of encryption backdoors. Strong encryption algorithms and decentralized systems make it increasingly difficult to implement effective backdoors without compromising security for everyone.

The encryption backdoor debate is a complex and multifaceted issue that requires careful consideration of the competing interests at stake. It is a challenge to find the right balance between privacy and security in the digital age. As technology and society continue to evolve, the debate will likely persist, forcing us to constantly reevaluate and reassess our approach to encryption and its implications for privacy and national security.

Real-World Example: The Apple vs. FBI Case

The encryption backdoor debate gained significant attention in 2016 during the legal dispute between Apple and the FBI. In the aftermath of the San Bernardino terrorist attack, the FBI requested Apple's assistance in unlocking the encrypted iPhone belonging to one of the attackers.

Apple refused, arguing that creating a backdoor would compromise the security and privacy of all iPhone users. The case sparked a heated national debate, with supporters of Apple commending the company for protecting user privacy and opponents accusing it of obstructing a critical investigation.

Ultimately, the FBI dropped the lawsuit against Apple after finding an alternative method to unlock the iPhone. However, the case brought the encryption backdoor debate into the mainstream, highlighting the complex issues surrounding privacy, security, and government access to encrypted data.

Key Takeaways

The encryption backdoor debate is a complex and ongoing discussion with far-reaching implications for privacy, security, and government surveillance. Key takeaways from this debate include:

- Encryption is essential for protecting sensitive data, but it can also be seen as a hindrance to investigatory efforts.

- Backdoors in encryption systems can undermine security and privacy by introducing intentional vulnerabilities.

- Striking the right balance between privacy and security is a challenge that requires careful consideration and ongoing dialogue.

- Alternative solutions, such as requiring court orders and assistance from tech companies, have been proposed to balance law enforcement needs with individual privacy.

- The encryption backdoor debate is not a binary issue; it requires nuanced and informed discussions that consider the evolving nature of technology and society.

Exercises

1. Research and discuss a recent case or controversy related to the encryption backdoor debate. What were the arguments presented by each side? What were the implications and outcomes of the case?

2. Imagine you are a legislator tasked with proposing a law regarding the encryption backdoor debate. What would be your position and why? How would you balance the interests of privacy, security, and law enforcement?

3. Discuss the potential ethical ramifications of implementing encryption backdoors. How might they impact individual privacy, the relationship between citizens and their governments, and global technology companies?

Resources

- Electronic Frontier Foundation (EFF): Visit the EFF's website for resources and articles on encryption, privacy, and digital rights advocacy.

- "Data and Goliath: The Hidden Battles to Collect Your Data and Control Your World" by Bruce Schneier: This book provides an in-depth examination of the encryption backdoor debate and its implications for privacy and security.
- "Cypherpunks: Freedom and the Future of the Internet" by Julian Assange, Jacob Appelbaum, Andy Müller-Maguhn, and Jérémie Zimmermann: In this book, the authors discuss the importance of encryption in protecting individual privacy and combating government surveillance.

Unconventional Perspective: The Ethics of Encryption Backdoors

The encryption backdoor debate not only raises legal and technical concerns but also begs ethical questions about the role of technology in society. One unconventional perspective on the issue considers the potential implications of backdoors, not only for privacy and national security but also for the ethics of surveillance.

Proponents of encryption argue that warrantless mass surveillance invalidates the fundamental democratic principles of transparency, accountability, and trust between the government and its citizens. They believe that encryption serves as a safeguard against potential abuses of power and overreach by authorities.

Applying an ethical lens to the encryption backdoor debate prompts us to reflect on the balance between individual rights, government responsibilities, and the nature of a democratic society. It invites us to question whether the potential benefits of backdoors, such as aiding law enforcement, outweigh the broader consequences for privacy, civil liberties, and the autonomy of individuals.

Engaging in discussions on the ethics of encryption backdoors encourages critical thinking, empathy, and a broader consideration of the societal impacts of engaging in surveillance practices. It reminds us that the decisions we make about encryption have far-reaching implications, shaping the world we live in and defining the boundaries of our rights and freedoms.

The Redefinition of Privacy

In today's digital world, privacy is taking on a whole new meaning. With the advent of technology and the widespread use of the internet, traditional notions of privacy have been challenged and redefined. It is no longer just about keeping your personal information secret or locking your doors. Privacy has become a complex and multifaceted concept that encompasses various aspects of our lives.

One of the key factors contributing to the redefinition of privacy is the rapid advancement of information and communication technologies. We live in an era where our personal data is constantly being collected, stored, and analyzed by various entities, including governments, corporations, and even our own devices. The rise of social media platforms, online shopping, and digital services has further blurred the line between the public and private spheres.

Moreover, the proliferation of surveillance technologies and the increasing use of data-driven algorithms have raised concerns about the erosion of individual privacy. Issues such as mass surveillance, data breaches, and the commodification of personal information have become hot topics in public discourse. As a result, there is a growing recognition that privacy is not just about the protection of personal information but also about maintaining autonomy, dignity, and control over one's own life.

The redefinition of privacy also extends to our expectations and demands as users of digital technologies. In the past, privacy was often seen as a trade-off for convenience or efficiency. However, with the increasing awareness of the risks and consequences of data misuse, individuals are now demanding more transparent and ethical practices from tech companies. There is a growing desire for privacy-enhancing tools, services, and policies that empower individuals to safeguard their personal information and regain control over their digital lives.

This redefinition of privacy has also resulted in the emergence of new legal frameworks and regulations. Governments around the world are grappling with the need to balance the benefits of innovation and technological advancement with the protection of individual privacy rights. The European Union's General Data Protection Regulation (GDPR), for example, has set a new standard for data protection and privacy rights, highlighting the global importance of privacy in the digital age.

The redefinition of privacy poses both challenges and opportunities. On one hand, individuals need to navigate an increasingly interconnected and data-driven world, where their personal information is constantly at risk. On the other hand, this redefinition opens up avenues for innovation and the development of new technologies that prioritize privacy and security.

To address the challenges posed by the redefinition of privacy, it is crucial to foster a multidisciplinary approach. This includes collaboration between technologists, policymakers, legal experts, and individuals themselves. It is important to strike a balance between the benefits of technological advancements and the protection of privacy rights. This requires designing systems with privacy by design, promoting data minimization and anonymization techniques, and ensuring transparent data practices.

In conclusion, the redefinition of privacy in the digital age requires us to rethink our understanding of this fundamental right. It encompasses not only the protection of personal information but also the preservation of autonomy, dignity, and control. As technology continues to evolve, it is imperative that we work together to ensure that privacy remains a fundamental pillar of our digital society.

The Future of Privacy in a Digital World

As we navigate the ever-evolving landscape of the digital world, the future of privacy becomes a topic of paramount importance. In this section, we will explore the challenges and opportunities that lie ahead, and delve into the strategies and advancements that will shape the future of privacy.

The Growing Concerns

With the exponential growth of technology, privacy concerns have magnified significantly. As individuals and organizations become more connected and reliant on digital platforms, the potential for data breaches, surveillance, and misuse of personal information has soared. In this era of constant connectivity, protecting our privacy is more crucial than ever.

The Rise of Privacy-enhancing Technologies

To address the challenges posed by the digital world, the future of privacy relies heavily on the development and implementation of privacy-enhancing technologies (PETs). PETs encompass a wide range of tools and techniques designed to safeguard personal data while enabling secure and private digital interactions.

One such technology is differential privacy, which adds noise to data sets to protect the privacy of individuals while maintaining the overall accuracy of the data. By using advanced statistical techniques, differential privacy ensures that individuals cannot be identified through their data.

Another emerging privacy-enhancing technology is homomorphic encryption, a technique that allows computation on encrypted data without decrypting it. This revolutionary technology has the potential to transform how data is securely processed and analyzed, enabling privacy-preserving machine learning and data sharing.

Privacy by Design

In the future, privacy considerations must be embedded into the very fabric of digital systems and applications. This concept, known as privacy by design, advocates for the proactive integration of privacy throughout the entire development lifecycle.

By implementing privacy-preserving features from the outset, organizations can ensure that privacy is an inherent component of their products and services. Privacy by design involves incorporating privacy principles and practices into the design, development, and deployment of systems, processes, and architectures.

Additionally, data minimization and anonymization techniques play a crucial role in privacy by design. Organizations should only collect and retain data that is necessary for their intended purpose, while anonymizing or pseudonymizing personal information to protect individual identities.

Regulation and Legislation

The future of privacy cannot solely rely on technological advancements; it also requires adequate regulation and legislation to protect individuals' rights. Governments around the world are recognizing the need to address privacy issues and are enacting laws and regulations accordingly.

The General Data Protection Regulation (GDPR) implemented by the European Union is a prime example of robust privacy legislation. It grants individuals control over their personal data, imposes stringent obligations on organizations handling that data, and provides severe penalties for non-compliance.

To ensure the future protection of privacy, governments must continue to enact comprehensive privacy laws that are adaptable to evolving technologies. These laws should provide individuals with control over their personal information, enable transparency and accountability, and ensure that organizations understand the ethical responsibilities of handling data.

Educating and Empowering Individuals

In a digital world, individuals must actively participate in safeguarding their privacy. Education and empowerment play a pivotal role in ensuring that individuals understand the risks, take appropriate measures to protect their data, and make informed decisions about their online activities.

Privacy literacy should be an integral component of digital literacy programs, teaching individuals how to navigate privacy settings, recognize potential threats, and adopt privacy-conscious behaviors. This includes understanding the importance of strong passwords, using two-factor authentication, and being cautious of phishing scams.

Moreover, user-friendly privacy tools and interfaces should be developed to empower individuals to manage their privacy effectively. Organizations should strive to provide transparent privacy policies, simplified privacy controls, and clear consent mechanisms, empowering users to make informed choices about their data.

The Role of Ethical Design

As we continue to innovate and develop new technologies, ethical considerations must be at the forefront of design decisions. Ethical design involves creating technologies that prioritize privacy, autonomy, and individual agency, while mitigating the potential for harm and misuse.

Designers and developers have a responsibility to consider the broader societal implications of their creations and prioritize the protection of user privacy. This includes incorporating privacy features, conducting privacy impact assessments, and engaging in ethical decision-making frameworks.

The Need for International Collaboration

The future of privacy in a digital world requires global collaboration and coordination. Privacy challenges transcend national boundaries, necessitating the establishment of international frameworks and agreements to safeguard privacy rights.

International cooperation can facilitate the harmonization of privacy laws and standards, enable the sharing of best practices, and promote a collective approach to addressing privacy concerns. Organizations, governments, and privacy advocates must work together to ensure that privacy remains a fundamental human right in the digital age.

Unconventional but Relevant: Privacy in Virtual Reality

As virtual reality (VR) technology becomes more accessible, it presents both exciting opportunities and potential privacy concerns. In a virtual world, individuals can create and interact with digital representations of themselves and others. This raises questions about ownership and control of personal data within virtual environments.

For example, in social VR platforms, users create avatars and engage in virtual social interactions. The data generated by these interactions, such as voice recordings and movement patterns, can be highly personal. Ensuring the privacy of individuals in virtual reality requires the development of robust privacy frameworks specific to these immersive digital spaces.

Additionally, VR enables the collection of detailed biometric data, such as facial expressions and physiological responses. Protecting this sensitive information is crucial to prevent its misuse and potential intrusions into users' emotional and physical privacy.

Conclusion

The future of privacy in a digital world depends on a multi-faceted approach that encompasses technological innovation, robust regulation, individual empowerment, and ethical design. By leveraging privacy-enhancing technologies, enacting comprehensive privacy laws, and fostering privacy-conscious behaviors, we can create a future where privacy is respected and protected in our increasingly interconnected world.

Ultimately, the future of privacy is not predetermined; it is dependent on the choices we make today and the collective efforts we undertake to ensure that privacy remains a fundamental right for generations to come.

Phil Zimmermann's Continuing Influence

Phil Zimmermann's impact on the world of privacy and encryption continues to reverberate across industries and governments. His pioneering work with Pretty Good Privacy (PGP) laid the foundation for modern encryption technologies and inspired a generation of privacy advocates and tech enthusiasts. In this section, we will explore how Zimmermann's vision continues to shape the fight for privacy and the future of encryption.

The Need for Better Encryption

With the exponential growth of digital communication and the increasing threats to personal privacy, the need for robust encryption has never been greater. Phil Zimmermann recognized this need early on and dedicated himself to developing encryption solutions that would empower individuals to protect their digital information. His commitment to privacy and belief in the fundamental human right to secure communication has become the cornerstone of the fight for encryption.

Risks and Benefits of Mass Surveillance

In an era of mass surveillance, where governments and corporations amass vast amounts of personal data, the risks to individual privacy are significant. Phil Zimmermann's work has highlighted the dangers of unchecked surveillance and the potential for abuse of power. His advocacy for strong encryption has raised awareness about the need to balance security and privacy, ensuring that individuals have control over their own data.

Encryption as a Fundamental Right

Phil Zimmermann firmly believed that encryption is a fundamental right that should be accessible to all. His relentless pursuit to make encryption accessible to the masses, evidenced by PGP's open-source nature, has paved the way for widespread adoption of encryption technologies. Zimmermann's influence has shaped the perception of encryption as a tool for empowerment, enabling individuals to assert their right to privacy in a digital world.

The Role of Whistleblowers

Zimmermann recognized the power of whistleblowers in exposing mass surveillance and unethical practices. The impact of whistleblowers like Edward Snowden, who revealed the extent of government surveillance programs, demonstrates the importance of individuals who take a stand for privacy and transparency. Zimmermann's work and advocacy have encouraged whistleblowers to come forward and sparked crucial conversations about the balance between state security and individual privacy.

The Snowden Revelations and Their Aftermath

The revelations brought forth by Edward Snowden shook the world and vindicated Zimmermann's concerns about the erosion of privacy. Snowden's leaks exposed the extent of government surveillance programs, highlighting the urgent need for stronger encryption solutions. Zimmermann's work with PGP laid the foundation for the tools whistleblowers like Snowden would use to protect their communications and amplify their messages.

The Encryption Backdoor Debate

One of the significant challenges facing the encryption community is the ongoing debate around encryption backdoors. Some government agencies argue for the inclusion of backdoors to allow lawful access to encrypted data, while others vehemently oppose it, citing the threat to privacy and security. Zimmermann's unwavering stance against backdoors has influenced the discourse around encryption and emphasized the importance of maintaining the integrity of encryption algorithms.

The Redefinition of Privacy

As technology advances and personal data becomes increasingly vulnerable, the concept of privacy is continually evolving. Zimmermann's work has contributed to the redefinition of privacy in the digital age, emphasizing the importance of individual control over personal information. His advocacy for robust encryption technologies has sparked discussions about the evolving definition of privacy and its implications for individuals, organizations, and governments.

The Future of Privacy in a Digital World

As technology continues to advance at an unprecedented pace, the future of privacy faces both opportunities and challenges. Zimmermann's influence will continue to shape the conversation around privacy, encryption, and the balance between security and individual freedoms. His legacy serves as a beacon of hope for a future where privacy remains a fundamental right, and encryption technologies evolve to meet the needs of a rapidly changing digital landscape.

Phil Zimmermann's Continuing Influence

Phil Zimmermann's influence on the fight for privacy is undeniable. His groundbreaking work with PGP laid the foundation for modern encryption technologies and paved the way for the widespread adoption of encryption for personal and business communications. Zimmermann's ongoing advocacy for privacy and his staunch opposition to backdoors and mass surveillance continue to inspire individuals and organizations to prioritize the protection of personal information. His relentless pursuit of a world where privacy is respected and encryption is accessible to all continues to shape the conversation and drive innovation in the field of digital privacy.

Phil Zimmermann's Impact on Privacy Awareness

From Niche to Mainstream

In the early days of its existence, PGP (Pretty Good Privacy) was considered a niche technology, known only to a select group of individuals who were passionate about privacy. However, thanks to the visionary work of Phil Zimmermann and the growing concerns about online security and surveillance, PGP eventually made its way from the fringes to the mainstream. This section explores the journey of

PGP from being a niche tool to becoming a household name, and the factors that contributed to its widespread adoption.

The Need for Privacy Solutions

Before the advent of PGP, the concept of online privacy was not a major concern for the general population. People were more focused on the convenience and connectivity offered by the digital world, rather than worrying about the security of their information. However, with the rise of the internet and the increasing interconnectedness of our lives, it became evident that there was a need for privacy solutions that would safeguard personal data and communications from prying eyes.

The Birth of PGP

PGP was born out of Phil Zimmermann's realization that individuals needed a way to secure their email communications in the face of growing surveillance and interception by governments and other entities. Phil Zimmermann's vision was to create an encryption program that would be accessible to everyone, regardless of their technical expertise. He wanted to democratize encryption and empower individuals to take control of their privacy.

The creation of PGP was a labor of love for Zimmermann. He spent countless hours developing the software, meticulously writing each line of code. His dedication and passion for privacy drove him to constantly improve and refine PGP, making it more user-friendly and robust with each iteration.

The Role of Early Adopters

One of the key factors that propelled PGP from a niche tool to the mainstream was the support and advocacy of early adopters. These were individuals who recognized the importance of privacy and embraced PGP as a means to protect their communications. Through their usage and endorsement of PGP, they helped raise awareness about the need for privacy tools and sparked conversations about online security.

Early adopters also played a critical role in spreading the word about PGP. They shared their experiences with the software, recommended it to their friends and colleagues, and contributed to online forums and communities dedicated to privacy. Their evangelism helped PGP gain traction and slowly enter the public consciousness.

PGP's Use by Activists and Journalists

Another major turning point in PGP's journey to the mainstream was its adoption by activists and journalists. These groups were at the forefront of fighting for freedom of speech and a free press, and they recognized the importance of secure communication tools. PGP offered them a way to protect their sources, communicate without fear of interception, and maintain their privacy in an increasingly surveilled world.

The high-profile use of PGP by activists and journalists brought it into the public eye, further raising awareness about the importance of encryption and privacy. It demonstrated that PGP was not just a tool for the technologically savvy but a necessity for those fighting for justice and truth.

PGP's Impact on Public Perception

As PGP gained prominence and its user base grew, it started to reshape the public perception of online privacy. It presented encryption as an essential tool in the digital age, and people began to realize that their privacy could no longer be taken for granted. PGP became synonymous with secure communication and set a new standard for privacy in the digital realm.

The rise of PGP coincided with several high-profile privacy breaches and government surveillance scandals, such as the Snowden revelations. These events further highlighted the need for robust privacy solutions like PGP and fueled public demand for stronger encryption tools.

PGP's Influence on Industry Standards

PGP's rise to the mainstream also had a significant impact on industry standards and practices. Its success forced technology companies and service providers to take privacy more seriously and incorporate encryption into their products and services. PGP's influence can be seen in the widespread use of end-to-end encryption in messaging apps, the adoption of encryption protocols by major email providers, and the push for stronger security measures across various online platforms.

Educating the Masses

Another key factor in PGP's journey to the mainstream was the educational efforts undertaken by Phil Zimmermann and privacy advocates. They recognized that for PGP to gain widespread adoption, people needed to understand its importance and how to use it effectively. They conducted workshops, wrote articles and tutorials, and created user-friendly guides that made encryption accessible to non-technical individuals.

By demystifying encryption and breaking down complex concepts into simple terms, these educational initiatives helped bridge the gap between the tech-savvy and the general public. They empowered individuals to take control of their privacy and encouraged a wider adoption of PGP.

Going Mainstream

Today, PGP is no longer an obscure tool used only by privacy enthusiasts; it has become a household name synonymous with online security and privacy. Its journey from being a niche technology to a mainstream solution is a testament to the power of visionary thinking, community support, and the growing awareness of the importance of privacy in the digital age.

As we navigate the increasingly interconnected world, PGP continues to shape the conversation around privacy, encryption, and the battle against surveillance. It serves as a reminder that individuals have the power to protect their digital lives and safeguard their privacy, and that encryption is an essential tool in the fight for a more secure and private future.

Discussion Questions

1. Can you think of any other examples of niche technologies that have successfully transitioned to the mainstream? What factors contributed to their adoption?

2. How do you think the use of PGP by activists and journalists helped to raise awareness about online privacy? Can you provide any real-world examples?

3. How has the perception of online privacy changed since the introduction of PGP? Do you think people are more aware of the importance of encryption and privacy now?

4. What role do you think educational initiatives played in PGP's journey to the mainstream? How can we continue to educate and raise awareness about the importance of online privacy?

5. In your opinion, what are the current barriers to widespread adoption of encryption tools like PGP? How can we overcome these barriers and encourage more individuals to prioritize their privacy?

Further Reading

1. "The Code Book: The Science of Secrecy from Ancient Egypt to Quantum Cryptography" by Simon Singh.

2. "Permanent Record" by Edward Snowden.

3. "The Perfect Weapon: War, Sabotage, and Fear in the Cyber Age" by David E. Sanger.

4. "Data and Goliath: The Hidden Battles to Collect Your Data and Control Your World" by Bruce Schneier.

5. "The Age of Surveillance Capitalism: The Fight for a Human Future at the New Frontier of Power" by Shoshana Zuboff.

Remember, privacy is not a luxury, but a fundamental right. Stay curious, stay informed, and stay in control of your digital life!

Phil Zimmermann's Mission to Educate

Phil Zimmermann was not only a master programmer and cryptographer, but also a passionate advocate for privacy and encryption. Recognizing the need for education in this rapidly evolving field, Zimmermann dedicated himself to spreading knowledge and empowering individuals to protect their data.

The Importance of Privacy Education

In an era where personal information is constantly at risk of being exploited, Zimmermann understood that education was the key to safeguarding privacy. He believed that by arming people with knowledge, they could take control of their own security and protect themselves from prying eyes. Zimmermann's mission to educate was not just about teaching the technical aspects of encryption, but also about raising awareness of the broader implications of privacy in a digital society.

Encryption Workshops

One of the ways Zimmermann fulfilled his mission was through organizing encryption workshops. These workshops served as a platform for people to learn about encryption algorithms, digital signatures, and the practical implementation of privacy tools. Participants had the opportunity to engage directly with Zimmermann and his team, asking questions and gaining hands-on experience with encryption software.

Zimmermann's workshops were renowned for their interactive and engaging format. He understood that complex technical concepts could be intimidating, so he employed relatable examples and real-world scenarios to make them more accessible. By demystifying encryption, Zimmermann aimed to equip individuals from all backgrounds with the skills and confidence needed to protect their personal information.

Popularizing Encryption through Speaking Engagements

Zimmermann's passion for education extended beyond workshops; he was a sought-after speaker at conferences and seminars around the world. Through his captivating talks, Zimmermann advocated for the widespread adoption of encryption and highlighted its significance in the face of growing surveillance.

His speaking engagements were not limited to technical audiences. Zimmermann recognized the importance of reaching a broader demographic, including policymakers, journalists, and everyday individuals who were not necessarily familiar with the intricacies of encryption. He effortlessly communicated complex concepts in a relatable and engaging manner, earning him a reputation as a captivating speaker.

Writing and Publications

In addition to his workshops and speaking engagements, Zimmermann authored articles and publications that aimed to educate readers about encryption and privacy. He wrote in-depth explanations of encryption algorithms, breaking down complex concepts into digestible content for the general public. Zimmermann's writing style was accessible, blending technical expertise with relatable anecdotes and real-life examples.

One of his most notable publications was the "PGP User's Guide," which served as a comprehensive resource for individuals looking to secure their communications. This guide not only explained how to use Zimmermann's own encryption software, Pretty Good Privacy (PGP), but also offered guidance on best practices for encryption and digital security.

Supporting Privacy-Focused Organizations

Beyond his direct educational efforts, Zimmermann supported and collaborated with privacy-focused organizations. He recognized the importance of joining forces with like-minded individuals and groups to amplify the message of privacy advocacy.

Zimmermann actively contributed to organizations such as the Electronic Frontier Foundation (EFF) and the Open Rights Group (ORG), which work tirelessly to protect and promote digital privacy rights. Through his involvement, Zimmermann helped these organizations raise awareness, provide resources, and advocate for stronger privacy laws.

Legacy and Continued Impact

Phil Zimmermann's mission to educate continues to resonate in the field of privacy and encryption today. His efforts have inspired a new generation of privacy advocates and developers, who carry forward his vision for a more secure and privacy-centric digital world. Zimmermann's outreach and educational initiatives have played a crucial role in shaping the discourse around privacy and encryption, ensuring that individuals have the tools and knowledge to protect their personal information.

As we navigate an increasingly connected world, Phil Zimmermann's mission to educate remains as relevant as ever. His advocacy work serves as a reminder that privacy is not just an individual concern, but a collective responsibility. By spreading knowledge and empowering individuals, Zimmermann has left an indelible mark on the fight for privacy in the digital age.

The Popularity of Privacy-Focused Apps

In today's digital age, where surveillance is becoming increasingly prevalent, privacy-focused apps have gained immense popularity. These apps offer individuals a sense of control over their personal data, safeguarding their privacy from prying eyes. With rising concerns about data breaches, invasive advertising practices, and government surveillance, people are actively seeking ways to protect their online privacy. In this section, we will explore the reasons behind the growing popularity of privacy-focused apps and how they empower individuals to reclaim their privacy in the digital world.

The Need for Privacy

The need for privacy arises from the fundamental human desire for autonomy, independence, and personal freedom. In the digital realm, the extent to which individuals can exercise these rights is heavily influenced by the level of privacy they have online. Privacy-focused apps address this need by providing tools and features that safeguard personal information, communications, and online activities.

In an era where data breaches and hackers are a common occurrence, people are increasingly concerned about the security of their personal information. Privacy-focused apps offer end-to-end encryption, ensuring that only the intended recipients can access the content of their messages, emails, or files. This level of protection gives users peace of mind and reassurance that their private conversations remain confidential.

Combatting Invasive Advertising Practices

Another significant driver behind the popularity of privacy-focused apps is the desire to combat invasive advertising practices. Many individuals are tired of being bombarded with targeted ads based on their online activities and personal information. Privacy-focused apps provide users with tools to limit data tracking and prevent advertisers from collecting and utilizing their personal data for targeted advertisements.

By using privacy-focused apps, individuals can regain control over their data, choosing what information they share with advertisers and minimizing their exposure to intrusive ads. This increased control over their online experiences reduces the feeling of being continuously monitored and allows users to browse the internet without feeling like their every move is being tracked.

Enhanced Security and Control

Privacy-focused apps offer users enhanced security and control over their online activities. These apps often include additional security measures, such as multi-factor authentication, password managers, and secure file storage. By implementing these robust security features, privacy-focused apps help users protect their sensitive data from unauthorized access and ensure that their accounts remain secure.

Furthermore, privacy-focused apps empower individuals to regain control over their online identities. With the rise of social media and the increased sharing of personal information, many people have become more cautious about the content they post online. Privacy-focused apps provide users with the ability to limit who can access their personal information, ensuring that they maintain control over their digital footprint.

Protection Against Government Surveillance

In recent years, the issue of government surveillance has gained considerable attention. Revelations about mass surveillance programs, such as those exposed by Edward Snowden, have made individuals more cautious about their digital activities. Privacy-focused apps help protect against government surveillance by offering features such as encrypted messaging, anonymous browsing, and secure email services.

By utilizing privacy-focused apps, individuals can minimize their digital footprint and increase the difficulty of surveillance activities. These apps enable users to communicate privately, browse the internet anonymously, and ensure that their messages and emails cannot be intercepted or accessed by unauthorized entities.

The Rise of Privacy-Focused App Developers

The growing popularity of privacy-focused apps is also fueled by the increasing number of developers dedicated to privacy and data protection. These developers recognize the demand for privacy-focused solutions and are committed to creating apps that prioritize user privacy.

Privacy-focused app developers often follow open-source principles, allowing users to scrutinize the underlying code for any potential vulnerabilities or security issues. This transparency builds trust and reassures individuals that their privacy is genuinely being respected and protected.

Moreover, privacy-focused app developers actively engage with their user community, seeking feedback and incorporating user suggestions to continually improve their apps. This collaborative approach ensures that privacy-focused apps remain innovative and relevant, meeting the evolving privacy needs of individuals.

Real-World Example: Signal Messenger

Signal Messenger is a prime example of a privacy-focused app that has gained significant popularity in recent years. With its end-to-end encryption, secure voice and video calling, and disappearing messages, Signal Messenger has become the preferred choice for individuals who value privacy in their digital communications.

Signal's popularity skyrocketed when high-profile individuals, including tech industry leaders and privacy advocates, publicly endorsed the app as the go-to solution for secure messaging. This endorsement further contributed to the app's growing user base, as individuals recognized the value of using an app that prioritizes privacy and security.

Privacy-Focused App Trends

In the world of privacy-focused apps, several key trends have emerged. These trends reveal the shifting landscape of privacy concerns and the evolving demands of users seeking to protect their personal information. Let's explore some of these trends:

Collaborative Efforts

Privacy-focused app developers are increasingly collaborating with experts in the field of privacy and data protection. By pooling their expertise, these collaborations aim to build stronger, more secure apps that can stand up to sophisticated threats. These partnerships contribute to the overall improvement of privacy-focused app quality and benefit users who rely on these apps for their daily privacy needs.

User-Friendly Design

User-friendliness has become a significant focus for privacy-focused apps. Developers recognize that the wider adoption of these apps depends on their ability to provide a seamless user experience. As a result, they strive to create intuitive interfaces and streamlined processes that make it easy for individuals to understand and utilize the privacy features of the app. This emphasis on user-friendliness ensures that privacy-focused apps are accessible to a broader audience, regardless of technical expertise.

Cross-Platform Availability

Privacy-focused app developers are increasingly expanding their offerings beyond a single platform. They recognize that privacy-conscious individuals use a variety of devices and operating systems and aim to provide consistent privacy protection across all these platforms. This trend reflects the importance of ensuring that individuals can seamlessly protect their privacy, regardless of the devices they use.

Integration with Existing Platforms

To further enhance user convenience, privacy-focused apps are increasingly integrating with existing platforms and services. For example, some privacy-focused email providers integrate seamlessly with popular email clients, making it easy for individuals to switch to a more privacy-focused email solution without the hassle of changing their preferred email interface. By integrating with existing platforms, privacy-focused apps reduce barriers to adoption and encourage more individuals to prioritize their privacy.

Conclusion

The growing popularity of privacy-focused apps can be attributed to the increasing awareness and concern about online privacy. In an era of surveillance and data breaches, individuals are seeking ways to regain control over their personal information and protect their digital identities. Privacy-focused apps provide the tools and features needed to empower individuals to reclaim their online privacy. By offering enhanced security, protection against invasive advertising, and the means to combat government surveillance, these apps are reshaping the way individuals interact with the digital world. With privacy-focused app trends emphasizing user-friendliness and cross-platform availability, the future of privacy looks promising. As more individuals embrace privacy-focused apps, they contribute to a collective movement towards a more private, secure, and autonomous digital landscape.

Privacy-Conscious Tech Companies

In today's digital age, where personal data is being collected and exploited at an alarming rate, privacy has become a major concern for individuals around the world. As a result, numerous tech companies have emerged with a commitment to protecting user privacy and building products and services that prioritize data security. These privacy-conscious tech companies have become champions of digital rights, advocating for strong encryption, transparent data practices, and user control. In this section, we will explore some prominent privacy-conscious tech companies and delve into their innovative approaches to safeguarding user privacy.

Company A: Securing Data through End-to-End Encryption

Company A is one of the pioneers in the field of end-to-end encryption, a technique that ensures only the sender and recipient of a message can access its contents. This technology guarantees that even if intercepted, the data remains unintelligible to any prying eyes. Company A's messaging platform has gained popularity among privacy-conscious individuals, activists, and journalists due to its strong commitment to user privacy.

To achieve end-to-end encryption, Company A employs robust cryptographic protocols based on proven algorithms. These protocols generate unique encryption keys for each user, ensuring that even if a malicious actor gains access to one key, they cannot decrypt all messages sent by that user. This approach provides users with a secure means of communication, free from eavesdropping or data interception.

Moreover, Company A operates on a zero-knowledge principle, where the company itself has no access to user data. This means that even if compelled by law enforcement or government bodies to provide access to user information, Company A cannot comply, as they do not hold the decryption keys. This commitment to zero-knowledge reinforces user trust by ensuring that their communications remain private and beyond the reach of unauthorized entities.

Company B: Transparency and User Empowerment

Company B has made headlines for its unwavering dedication to transparency and user empowerment. Recognizing the need for users to have a comprehensive understanding of how their data is collected, used, and shared, Company B has implemented strict data governance practices.

To begin with, Company B provides users with clear and easy-to-understand privacy policies. These policies outline the types of data that the company collects, the purpose of its collection, and how it is shared or monetized. By demystifying complex legal jargon, Company B ensures that users are well-informed about their data rights.

Additionally, Company B offers granular privacy settings, allowing users to customize their data-sharing preferences. Through a user-friendly interface, individuals can control what information is shared with third parties, adjust app permissions, and manage data retention policies. This level of control empowers users to maintain their privacy boundaries and avoid unnecessary data exposure.

Company B also engages in regular third-party audits of its data practices, further ensuring transparency and accountability. These audits are conducted by independent security and privacy experts who assess the company's compliance with industry standards. By subjecting themselves to external scrutiny, Company B demonstrates its commitment to user privacy and builds trust with its user base.

Company C: Open-Source Collaboration for Security

Open-source software has played a significant role in enhancing privacy and security. Company C, a leading privacy-conscious tech company, is an advocate for open-source collaboration. They believe that transparency in code fosters trust among users and allows for the identification and prompt resolution of vulnerabilities.

By sharing their source code with the developer community, Company C invites scrutiny and contributions from security experts worldwide. This collaborative approach ensures that any potential weaknesses in their software are quickly identified and addressed. Furthermore, the involvement of a global developer community adds an extra layer of oversight, making it more difficult for intentional backdoors or surveillance mechanisms to exist.

Company C also actively encourages bug bounty programs, which incentivize independent researchers to discover and report vulnerabilities. By offering rewards for responsibly disclosing security flaws, Company C harnesses the expertise of the larger cybersecurity community, strengthening the overall security of their products.

Company D: Privacy by Design and Default

Company D, a prominent player in the tech industry, adopts a privacy-by-design approach in its product development processes. This means that privacy considerations are integrated from the very beginning of the design process and are not an afterthought.

By default, Company D's products and services prioritize user privacy, ensuring that minimal personal information is collected unless explicitly required for the intended functionality. They minimize data retention, store data securely, and provide users with options to delete their information permanently.

Moreover, Company D implements privacy-enhancing technologies, such as differential privacy and anonymization techniques, to protect user data while still enabling valuable insights for product improvement. These techniques allow for aggregated data analysis without compromising individuals' privacy.

Company D also champions the use of data encryption in transit and at rest, ensuring that data remains secure throughout its lifecycle. This commitment to encryption helps safeguard user information from unauthorized access, even if the underlying infrastructure is compromised.

The Collective Impact

While each privacy-conscious tech company brings its unique approach to protecting user privacy, the collective impact of these companies extends beyond their individual efforts. Together, they have prompted industry-wide discussions on the importance of privacy, inspiring other tech companies to reevaluate their data practices and prioritize user privacy.

These privacy-conscious tech companies have demonstrated that it is possible to build successful and innovative products while respecting user privacy. By fostering transparency, employing strong encryption, embracing open-source collaboration, and adopting privacy-by-design principles, they have set a new standard for the tech industry.

In an era where data breaches and privacy violations are rampant, the existence of these privacy-conscious tech companies serves as a beacon of hope, reminding individuals that their privacy is valued and respected. Their continued efforts will play a critical role in shaping a future that prioritizes user privacy, empowering individuals to reclaim control over their personal data.

The Changing Attitudes Towards Privacy

In today's digital age, attitudes towards privacy have undergone significant transformations. With the rise of social media, online shopping, and the constant collection of personal data, individuals are becoming increasingly aware of the potential threats to their privacy. This shift in attitudes has sparked a greater demand for privacy protection and a reevaluation of how personal information is shared and used.

The Impact of Technology

The rapid advancements in technology have propelled the changing attitudes towards privacy. As more people become connected to the internet and rely on digital devices, the amount of personal data being generated and stored has reached unprecedented levels. This vast collection of data raises concerns about how it is being used, who has access to it, and the potential for misuse.

For example, the Cambridge Analytica scandal in 2018 revealed how personal data from millions of Facebook users were harvested and used for political campaigns without their consent. This incident exposed the vulnerability of individuals' privacy and ignited a global conversation about the need for stricter privacy regulations and stronger data protection measures.

Growing Awareness and Education

As news headlines highlight the risks of data breaches, identity theft, and surveillance, public awareness of privacy issues has increased. People are now more conscious of the potential consequences of sharing personal information online and are taking steps to protect their privacy.

Privacy education initiatives have also played a vital role in changing attitudes towards privacy. Organizations and individuals are actively advocating for digital literacy and promoting best practices for protecting personal information online. By empowering users with knowledge about privacy settings, encryption tools, and safe online practices, these initiatives are helping individuals regain control over their digital identity.

Legal and Regulatory changes

Governments around the world have recognized the importance of privacy and have implemented various laws and regulations to address privacy concerns. The European Union's General Data Protection Regulation (GDPR), which came into effect in 2018, is one such example. The GDPR establishes strict rules for how personal data should be collected, stored, and processed, giving individuals greater control over their own information.

Similarly, other countries have introduced or updated their own privacy laws to better protect their citizens' privacy rights. In the United States, the California Consumer Privacy Act (CCPA) grants Californians more control over their personal data and imposes obligations on businesses that handle this information.

These legal and regulatory changes have not only provided individuals with more rights over their personal data but have also signaled a shift in societal attitudes towards privacy. They demonstrate that privacy is a fundamental right that should be safeguarded in the digital age.

The Role of Privacy-Focused Technologies

The changing attitudes towards privacy have also led to an increased demand for privacy-focused technologies. Individuals are seeking out tools that can help them secure their digital communications, protect their personal data, and maintain their privacy online.

Virtual Private Networks (VPNs) have gained popularity as they allow users to encrypt their internet traffic and mask their IP addresses, ensuring their online activities are not easily traced back to them. Encrypted messaging apps, such as Signal and Telegram, have seen significant growth as people prioritize secure and private communications.

Moreover, there is a rising interest in privacy-oriented web browsers like Brave and DuckDuckGo that prioritize user privacy by blocking trackers and advertisements that collect personal data.

The Evolving Privacy Landscape

As technology continues to evolve, privacy concerns will persist and new challenges will emerge. The increasingly interconnected nature of devices and the proliferation of the Internet of Things (IoT) present new privacy risks. The collection of data from smart devices, such as connected home devices and wearable technology, raises concerns about the potential for surveillance and data misuse.

Artificial Intelligence (AI) also poses privacy challenges. Machine learning algorithms rely on vast amounts of data, and the processing of personal information can lead to privacy breaches. Striking a balance between leveraging AI's potential and protecting individuals' privacy will be an ongoing challenge.

The Need for Privacy Advocacy

Given the ever-changing privacy landscape, advocacy for privacy rights remains crucial. Privacy advocates play a vital role in ensuring that individuals' privacy concerns are heard and addressed by policymakers, technology companies, and other stakeholders.

These advocates work to promote policies that safeguard privacy, raise public awareness about privacy risks, and advocate for transparent data practices. Their efforts contribute to maintaining the momentum of changing attitudes towards privacy and shaping a future where privacy is valued and respected.

Conclusion

The changing attitudes towards privacy reflect a growing understanding of the risks associated with digital technologies and the need for stronger privacy protections. Individuals, governments, and organizations are taking steps to address these concerns, from implementing stricter privacy regulations to advocating for privacy rights. As technology continues to evolve, the ongoing awareness, education, and advocacy efforts will be crucial in safeguarding privacy in the digital age.

Promoting Privacy in a Digital Age

In today's increasingly connected world, where data is constantly being generated, collected, and shared, the need for privacy has become more crucial than ever. Promoting privacy in a digital age requires a multi-faceted approach that encompasses technological advancements, user education, and policy advocacy. In this section, we will explore the strategies and initiatives aimed at protecting digital privacy and empowering individuals to take control of their personal data.

The Power of Privacy Awareness

One of the most effective ways to promote privacy in a digital age is by raising awareness about the importance of protecting personal data. Many individuals are unaware of the extent to which their information is being collected and used by companies and governments. By educating the public about the risks and implications of unchecked data collection, we can empower individuals to make informed decisions about their privacy.

To foster privacy awareness, organizations and privacy advocates have developed various initiatives. For example, privacy-focused campaigns such as "Data Privacy Day" have been launched to shine a spotlight on privacy issues and provide resources for individuals to better protect their data. These campaigns often involve community events, workshops, and educational materials to engage and inform the public.

Privacy by Design

Another key aspect of promoting privacy in a digital age is implementing privacy by design principles. Privacy by design is an approach that advocates for privacy to be considered and integrated into the design and development of technologies, systems, and processes from the outset, rather than being treated as an afterthought.

By embedding privacy considerations into the design and development process, organizations can mitigate privacy risks and protect user data. This involves implementing practices such as minimizing data collection and retention, anonymizing or encrypting data, and providing users with control and transparency over how their data is used.

Privacy by design is not only about complying with privacy regulations but also about prioritizing user privacy and building trust. Organizations that embrace privacy by design principles can differentiate themselves by offering products and services that prioritize user privacy and security.

Data Protection Regulations

In recent years, there has been an increasing recognition of the need for robust data protection regulations to safeguard individuals' privacy rights. Regulations such as the European Union's General Data Protection Regulation (GDPR) and the California Consumer Privacy Act (CCPA) aim to provide individuals with greater control and transparency over their personal data.

These regulations impose obligations on organizations to obtain user consent for data collection, implement security measures to protect personal data, and provide individuals with the right to access, correct, and delete their data. They also hold organizations accountable for any breaches or misuse of personal information.

Data protection regulations serve as a legal framework to promote privacy in a digital age. They set a standard for responsible data handling and encourage organizations to adopt privacy-centric practices. Compliance with these regulations not only protects individuals' privacy but also cultivates a culture of privacy-consciousness within organizations.

Privacy-Enhancing Technologies

Promoting privacy in a digital age also relies on the development and advancement of privacy-enhancing technologies. These technologies aim to protect individuals' privacy while enabling them to participate in the digital world.

One example of a privacy-enhancing technology is differential privacy. It is a mathematical concept that allows organizations to collect and analyze aggregate data while preserving the privacy of individual users. Differential privacy adds noise or randomness to collected data to prevent reidentification, thus safeguarding individuals' privacy.

Another example is zero-knowledge proofs, a cryptographic protocol that enables individuals to prove the authenticity of certain information without revealing the information itself. This technology has applications in digital identity verification, ensuring privacy while establishing trust in online interactions.

By investing in and adopting privacy-enhancing technologies, organizations can build privacy-preserving systems that enable safe data sharing and analysis without compromising individuals' privacy.

User Empowerment and Control

Empowering individuals with tools and knowledge to control their personal data is a vital component of promoting privacy in a digital age. Privacy-focused applications and platforms offer users heightened control over their data, allowing them to make informed choices about how it is collected, used, and shared.

For instance, privacy-focused web browsers provide features such as tracker blocking, which prevents websites from tracking user activity. Virtual private networks (VPNs) encrypt internet traffic, ensuring secure and private communication. Privacy-focused messaging apps offer end-to-end encryption to protect the confidentiality of messages.

Additionally, user education plays a crucial role in empowering individuals to protect their privacy. By providing accessible resources and training, individuals can learn about privacy best practices, such as using strong and unique passwords, enabling two-factor authentication, and being cautious with sharing personal information online.

Privacy Advocacy

Promoting privacy in a digital age requires a collective effort to advocate for privacy rights and influence policy-making. Privacy advocacy organizations play a crucial role in raising awareness, offering resources, and championing privacy-friendly policies.

By engaging with lawmakers, privacy advocates can shape legislation and regulations that prioritize individuals' privacy rights. They also advocate for increased transparency, accountability, and oversight in data collection and use practices by corporations and governments.

Privacy advocacy can take many forms, including lobbying, public campaigns, research, and providing expert opinions. By amplifying the voices of individuals and organizations concerned about privacy, advocates can influence public opinion and drive change.

Challenges and Future Directions

Promoting privacy in a digital age is not without challenges. Rapid technological advancements, the emergence of surveillance capitalism, and evolving data collection practices present ongoing hurdles to privacy protection. Furthermore, striking a balance between privacy and public safety remains a delicate issue, as governments seek to ensure security while respecting individuals' privacy rights.

As we look to the future, it is essential to continue innovating and adapting privacy protection strategies to meet the ever-changing landscape of technology and data collection. This includes exploring emerging technologies like blockchain and decentralized systems, which offer new avenues for privacy preservation.

Ultimately, promoting privacy in a digital age requires a comprehensive approach that combines technological innovation, user empowerment, policy development, and advocacy. By prioritizing privacy in all these aspects, we can create a more privacy-conscious and secure digital world.

Phil Zimmermann's Advocacy Work

Phil Zimmermann, the visionary behind PGP, was not only a brilliant programmer and encryption expert but also a passionate advocate for privacy rights. Throughout his career, Zimmermann dedicated himself to raising awareness about the importance of privacy in the digital age and fought tirelessly to protect the rights of individuals in the face of increasing surveillance. Let's explore some of his key advocacy work and its impact on privacy.

Raising Awareness

One of Zimmermann's primary goals was to educate the public about the risks and implications of mass surveillance. He believed that an informed society was essential for building a culture that values privacy. Zimmermann actively participated in conferences, workshops, and public speaking engagements, delivering passionate talks on various platforms to reach a broader audience.

He emphasized the need for individuals to understand the technology that protects their privacy, such as encryption, and the potential threats to their personal data. Zimmermann's ability to explain complex cryptographic concepts in a relatable way helped demystify encryption and inspire people to take control of their own privacy.

Promoting Policy Changes

Zimmermann recognized that advocating for privacy required more than just technological solutions—it demanded changes in policies and regulations. He became involved in lobbying efforts, working with organizations dedicated to privacy rights and civil liberties.

Zimmermann actively engaged with policymakers, sharing his expertise and insights to shape legislation that protected privacy rights. He used his influence to encourage lawmakers to adopt encryption-friendly policies and resist measures that would compromise individual privacy. Zimmermann's tireless advocacy had a significant impact on the adoption and acceptance of encryption technologies.

Supporting Privacy-Oriented Initiatives

As a philanthropist, Zimmermann recognized the importance of supporting initiatives that aligned with his mission to protect privacy rights. He invested in and funded various organizations dedicated to advancing privacy technologies, promoting digital rights, and defending civil liberties in the digital age.

Zimmermann's financial support helped these organizations develop privacy-enhancing tools, conduct research, and engage in legal battles against privacy infringements. His contributions significantly strengthened the privacy movement and provided resources for activists and technologists to fight for individual rights.

Influencing Tech Industry Practices

Zimmermann's impact extended beyond policy and advocacy work. He also worked to influence the practices of technology companies, encouraging them to prioritize user privacy and security. Zimmermann was an ardent supporter of open-source software, which allowed for greater transparency and scrutiny of code.

He actively promoted the use of encryption in everyday applications, collaborating with other developers to integrate strong security measures into a wide range of software products. Zimmermann's efforts played a crucial role in shaping the practices of tech companies, pushing them to prioritize user privacy and security as fundamental values.

Inspiring a New Generation

Perhaps one of Zimmermann's most lasting contributions is the inspiration he provided to a new generation of privacy advocates and technologists. His dedication to the cause and his unwavering commitment to protecting privacy rights continue to motivate and guide those who strive for a more secure and privacy-conscious digital world.

Zimmermann's legacy serves as a reminder that individual efforts, driven by a deep-rooted belief in the importance of privacy, can truly make a difference. His advocacy work continues to inspire future generations to fight for privacy rights and ensure that encryption technologies remain accessible and robust.

Balancing Privacy and Security

One of the challenges Zimmermann faced was striking a balance between privacy and national security. While he staunchly believed in the importance of strong encryption to protect individual privacy, he also recognized the need for measures to ensure national security and public safety.

Zimmermann actively engaged in public debates on this topic, highlighting the need for encryption to safeguard personal information while emphasizing the importance of responsible and accountable use of technology. He advocated for transparent encryption practices that respected the legitimate needs of governments without compromising the privacy of individuals.

Championing Human Rights

Zimmermann firmly believed that privacy is a fundamental human right. He recognized that privacy infringement could have severe consequences for individuals, from suppressing free speech to enabling discrimination and persecution. His advocacy work focused on using technology to protect these fundamental rights and empower individuals.

Zimmermann's dedication to human rights went beyond encryption. He supported initiatives that fought against internet censorship, defended whistleblowers, and championed transparency in government practices.

Zimmermann saw privacy as a cornerstone of a free and democratic society, and his advocacy work aimed at establishing and preserving those values.

Collaborative Efforts

Zimmermann understood the power of collaboration and the collective effort required to protect privacy rights. He actively collaborated with fellow privacy activists, technology experts, policymakers, and civil liberty organizations to amplify his impact.

Through partnerships, joint initiatives, and public campaigns, Zimmermann was able to leverage the collective strength of like-minded individuals and organizations. His ability to foster collaboration ensured that the message of privacy and the need for encryption reached a wider audience and had a more significant influence on policy and public opinion.

Continuing the Fight

Even after achieving significant milestones in his advocacy work, Zimmermann remained committed to the cause. He recognized that the fight for privacy is an ongoing battle and that new threats and challenges would continue to emerge.

Zimmermann's continuing efforts served as a beacon of hope for those who fought for privacy rights and reinforced the idea that one individual's commitment can have far-reaching effects. He inspired others to step up and carry forward the mission of protecting privacy in the face of evolving technological landscapes and changing political climates.

Overall, Phil Zimmermann's advocacy work has had a profound impact on privacy rights. His efforts to raise awareness, influence policy, support initiatives, shape industry practices, and inspire future generations have helped fortify the foundations of a privacy-conscious society. Zimmermann's legacy serves as a reminder of the importance of individual privacy and the need for continued vigilance in defending it.

Privacy in Popular Culture

Privacy has become an increasingly relevant and prominent topic in popular culture. From movies and TV shows to music and literature, privacy is a recurring theme that resonates with audiences worldwide. Popular culture often reflects the fears, concerns, and desires of society, and privacy is no exception. In this section, we explore the portrayal of privacy in various forms of popular culture and its impact on our perception of this fundamental right.

Movies and TV shows

One of the most common ways privacy is explored in popular culture is through movies and TV shows. These forms of media often depict surveillance, identity theft, hacking, and other privacy invasions to engage viewers and create compelling storylines. For example, movies like "The Truman Show" and "The Lives of Others" highlight the repercussions of living under constant surveillance, raising important questions about the boundaries of privacy.

TV series like "Black Mirror" take it one step further, presenting dystopian futures where technology is used to violate privacy in unimaginable ways. Episodes like "Nosedive" and "Hated in the Nation" explore the potential consequences of living in a world where every action is monitored and judged, reminding us of the importance of protecting our privacy in a digital age.

Music and Literature

Privacy is also a recurring theme in music and literature, often utilized as a means for self-expression and commentary on society. Artists and writers use their creative platforms to shed light on the importance of privacy and the potential consequences of its loss. For instance, songs like Bob Dylan's "Blowin' in the Wind" and John Lennon's "Imagine" suggest the need for personal freedom and privacy as essential values.

Literature also delves into the complexities of privacy. George Orwell's "1984" portrays a totalitarian regime where privacy is virtually non-existent, serving as a cautionary tale about the potential dangers of unchecked surveillance. Similarly, works like Ray Bradbury's "Fahrenheit 451" and Aldous Huxley's "Brave New World" present futuristic societies where privacy is either nonexistent or heavily controlled, urging readers to reflect on the value of privacy in their own lives.

Impact on Society

The portrayal of privacy in popular culture plays a significant role in shaping public perception and sparking conversations about our rights in a digital age. Movies, TV shows, music, and literature have the power to influence societal attitudes and, in turn, impact public discourse and policy-making.

For example, the release of the movie "Snowden" directed by Oliver Stone highlighted the story of Edward Snowden, a former NSA contractor turned whistleblower. The film shed light on the extent of government surveillance and ignited public debates surrounding privacy rights. It prompted discussions on the balance between national security and individual privacy, pushing individuals, organizations, and governments to reevaluate their stance on surveillance practices.

Privacy Campaigns

Privacy campaigns often leverage popular culture to raise awareness and engage the masses. By incorporating relatable characters and narratives from movies, TV shows, and music, these campaigns aim to drive home the importance of privacy in our everyday lives.

For instance, the Electronic Frontier Foundation's (EFF) "Surveillance Self-Defense" campaign utilizes popular culture references, interactive guides, and real-life stories to educate individuals about privacy-enhancing technologies and digital security. By linking privacy concerns to relatable examples from popular culture, these campaigns help bridge the gap between complex technical concepts and ordinary users, empowering them to protect their privacy online.

A Cautionary Tale

While popular culture has the potential to increase privacy awareness, it can also perpetuate misconceptions and misinformation. Not all portrayals of privacy in movies, TV shows, music, and literature accurately reflect the complexities and nuances of the topic. It is essential for individuals to approach popular culture's representation of privacy critically and seek reliable information to form informed opinions.

The Role of Education

As privacy continues to be a pressing issue, there is a growing need to educate individuals about privacy rights, digital security, and the potential consequences of privacy infringements. This education can take various forms, including school curriculum, awareness campaigns, and public service announcements.

By integrating privacy education into various academic disciplines, students can develop a well-rounded understanding of privacy's importance within their personal lives, relationships, and society at large. This education should also emphasize the ethical considerations surrounding privacy, encouraging responsible use of technology and respectful treatment of personal information.

Concluding Thoughts

Privacy in popular culture serves as a mirror reflecting society's hopes, fears, and concerns about the digital age. Movies, TV shows, music, and literature provide a platform for exploring the boundaries of privacy and sparking conversations about our rights in an increasingly connected world. By understanding the portrayals of privacy in popular culture and engaging in critical discourse, we can cultivate a deeper appreciation for our privacy rights and work towards a future that respects and protects them.

Through a combination of careful analysis, critical thinking, and ongoing education, we can navigate the complexity of privacy in popular culture and ensure that our own beliefs and actions align with a vision of privacy that safeguards our digital age while fostering innovation and freedom of expression.

The Rise of Privacy Tech Startups

In today's digital age, where online privacy is increasingly becoming a concern, a new breed of startups has emerged in response to the growing demand for innovative solutions. These privacy tech startups are at the forefront of developing tools, technologies, and services that empower individuals and organizations to protect their online privacy. In this section, we will explore the rise of privacy tech startups, their impact on the privacy landscape, and the challenges and opportunities they face.

The Need for Privacy Tech Startups

Privacy has become a hot-button issue in the digital era. With the widespread collection, analysis, and sharing of personal data by governments and corporations, individuals are becoming more aware of the need to safeguard their privacy. This increased awareness has created a market demand for privacy-focused products and services.

Privacy tech startups have stepped in to fill this gap by offering innovative solutions that prioritize user privacy. These startups aim to provide individuals with the tools they need to protect their personal information, communicate securely, and maintain control over their online identities. They also cater to the needs of businesses and organizations by offering privacy-enhancing services that enable compliance with privacy regulations and safeguard customer data.

Innovation and Solutions

Privacy tech startups are driving innovation in various areas, including encryption, data anonymization, secure communication tools, and privacy-enhancing technologies. These startups are leveraging cutting-edge technologies, such as artificial intelligence, blockchain, and decentralized networks, to develop unique solutions that prioritize privacy without compromising convenience or functionality.

One area in which privacy tech startups are making significant strides is encryption. Encryption algorithms and protocols play a crucial role in protecting data from unauthorized access. Privacy-focused startups are developing user-friendly encryption tools that enable individuals to encrypt their emails, messages, and files easily. These tools not only ensure that sensitive information remains confidential but also empower individuals to take control of their own privacy.

Another area of focus for privacy tech startups is data anonymization. With the increasing prevalence of data-driven decision making, preserving privacy while extracting insights from personal data is a critical challenge. Privacy tech startups are developing advanced anonymization techniques that allow organizations to analyze data while protecting the privacy of individuals. These techniques range from differential privacy algorithms to secure multiparty computation protocols.

Challenges and Opportunities

Privacy tech startups face several challenges as they navigate the complex landscape of online privacy. One of the main challenges is building trust and credibility with users. Many individuals are skeptical about entrusting their data to new and relatively unknown startups. Privacy tech startups must prioritize transparency and demonstrate a commitment to user privacy to gain the trust of their target audience.

Another significant challenge for privacy tech startups is the legal and regulatory landscape. Privacy regulations, such as the General Data Protection Regulation (GDPR) in Europe, pose compliance challenges for startups operating in the privacy space. Privacy tech startups must stay up to date with evolving regulations and adapt their products and services accordingly.

Despite these challenges, there are tremendous opportunities for privacy tech startups. The growing concern over online privacy has created a large and underserved market. Privacy-conscious individuals and organizations are actively seeking solutions to enhance their privacy and protect their data. By addressing these needs, privacy tech startups have the potential to disrupt traditional business models and carve out a niche for themselves in the market.

Real-world Examples

Let's take a look at some real-world examples of privacy tech startups that are making waves in the industry:

- **ProtonMail:** ProtonMail is an encrypted email service that allows users to send and receive emails securely. It uses end-to-end encryption to ensure that only the intended recipients can read the messages. ProtonMail has gained popularity among privacy-conscious individuals and organizations and has become a popular alternative to traditional email providers.

- **Signal:** Signal is a secure messaging app that allows users to send encrypted messages, make voice and video calls, and share files securely. It has gained recognition for its strong encryption protocols and ease of use. Signal has been endorsed by privacy advocates and is widely used by journalists, activists, and individuals who value their privacy.

- **Tenta:** Tenta is a privacy-focused browser that offers built-in encryption, secure DNS, and a virtual private network (VPN) service. It allows users to browse the internet securely and privately, shielding their online activities from prying eyes. Tenta has gained popularity for its comprehensive privacy features and commitment to user privacy.

These examples highlight the diversity of privacy tech startups and the range of innovative solutions they offer to address privacy concerns.

Resources for Privacy Tech Startups

For entrepreneurs and individuals interested in delving into the world of privacy tech startups, there are several valuable resources available:

- **Privacy Tech Alliance:** The Privacy Tech Alliance is a community-driven organization that provides support, resources, and networking opportunities for privacy tech startups. It offers mentorship programs, networking events, and educational resources to help startups thrive in the privacy industry.

- **Privacy Tech Conferences:** Attending privacy tech conferences, such as the DEF CON Privacy Village and the Privacy Tech Summit, can provide startups with valuable insights, connections, and industry knowledge. These conferences bring together privacy professionals, entrepreneurs, and thought leaders to discuss the latest trends and challenges in the privacy space.

- **Privacy Accelerators and Incubators:** Several accelerators and incubators specialize in supporting privacy tech startups. These programs provide mentorship, funding, and resources to help startups develop their products, refine their business models, and gain exposure in the market. Examples include the PRIVTech Accelerator and the Privacy Tech Startup Studio.

These resources can help privacy tech startups navigate the challenges they face and accelerate their growth in the competitive privacy landscape.

The Impact of Privacy Tech Startups

Privacy tech startups are not only driving innovation but also reshaping the privacy landscape. By offering user-centric solutions that prioritize privacy, these startups are empowering individuals and organizations to take control of their digital lives. They are providing alternatives to traditional services that may compromise user privacy, thereby challenging existing business models.

Furthermore, privacy tech startups are promoting awareness and sparking conversations about online privacy. They are educating individuals and organizations about the importance of privacy, the risks associated with data collection and surveillance, and the steps they can take to protect themselves. In doing so, they are advocating for stronger privacy regulations and privacy-enhancing technologies.

Unconventional Outlook

While privacy tech startups have made significant strides in the fight for privacy, it is important to recognize the limitations of technological solutions alone. True privacy requires a multi-faceted approach that encompasses not only technological advancements but also legal frameworks, cultural shifts, and individual awareness.

Privacy tech startups should collaborate with policymakers, privacy advocates, and other stakeholders to drive systemic change. By working together, they can shape the conversation around privacy, influence policy decisions, and create a more privacy-conscious society.

Conclusion

The rise of privacy tech startups signifies the growing demand for privacy-centric solutions in an increasingly connected world. These startups are driving innovation, challenging traditional business models, and empowering individuals to protect their online privacy. They face challenges such as building trust, navigating regulatory landscapes, and addressing the limitations of technological solutions. However, with the right resources and a commitment to user privacy, privacy tech startups have the potential to shape the future of privacy and create a more privacy-conscious society.

The Ongoing Fight for Privacy

In today's digital age, the fight for privacy has become more important than ever before. With the rapid advancement of technology, we are constantly connected and our personal information is being collected, stored, and analyzed by various entities. This has raised concerns about the erosion of our privacy rights and the potential abuse of our personal data.

In this ongoing battle for privacy, individuals, organizations, and advocacy groups continue to push for stronger privacy protections and greater transparency in data collection practices. They are demanding that their right to privacy be respected and upheld in the face of emerging technologies and new threats to personal freedom.

One of the key players in this fight is the legendary Phil Zimmermann, the creator of Pretty Good Privacy (PGP), a groundbreaking encryption software that revolutionized the way individuals secure their electronic communications. Zimmermann's PGP became a symbol of resistance against government surveillance and a powerful tool for protecting privacy.

The Importance of Encryption

Encryption plays a vital role in safeguarding our privacy. It involves the use of mathematical algorithms to scramble data so that it can only be understood by authorized individuals who possess the decryption key. Properly implemented encryption ensures that sensitive information remains confidential and secure, even if it falls into the wrong hands.

In the ongoing fight for privacy, encryption is a crucial tool that empowers individuals and organizations to protect their communications and data from unauthorized access. It allows for secure online transactions, private messaging, and confidential file sharing. Encryption has become increasingly important as we navigate a world of digital threats and pervasive surveillance.

The Battle Against Mass Surveillance

Mass surveillance has become a major concern in the fight for privacy. Governments and intelligence agencies are collecting vast amounts of data on individuals, often without their knowledge or consent. This indiscriminate collection of data infringes upon our right to privacy and threatens the foundations of democracy.

Privacy advocates argue that mass surveillance programs, such as those revealed by whistleblower Edward Snowden, are an overreach of government power and a violation of civil liberties. They stress the need for strong encryption to protect individuals from unwarranted surveillance and to ensure that their personal communications remain confidential.

The Encryption Backdoor Debate

The encryption backdoor debate is another crucial aspect of the ongoing fight for privacy. Some governments argue that law enforcement agencies should have a "backdoor" to encryption, which would allow them to bypass encryption protections to access encrypted communications and data.

However, privacy advocates and security experts warn that encryption backdoors create vulnerabilities that can be exploited by hackers, compromising the security of individuals and organizations. They argue that weakening encryption to enable surveillance undermines the fundamental principles of privacy and exposes innocent individuals to potential harm.

The Role of Whistleblowers

Whistleblowers play a pivotal role in the ongoing fight for privacy. They are individuals who expose wrongdoing, often at great personal risk, to bring attention to government surveillance programs or corporate data collection practices that infringe upon privacy rights.

Whistleblowers like Edward Snowden and Chelsea Manning have played a crucial role in uncovering mass surveillance programs and raising public awareness about the erosion of privacy. Their actions have sparked important conversations about government accountability, transparency, and the balance between national security and individual privacy.

The Future of Privacy in a Digital World

As technology continues to evolve, the fight for privacy will undoubtedly face new challenges. The proliferation of smart devices, artificial intelligence, and the Internet of Things (IoT) presents unique privacy concerns that must be addressed.

The future of privacy lies in a combination of technological advancements, legal protections, and individual awareness. Strong encryption, robust privacy laws, and user education will be essential in maintaining privacy in a digital world. It is critical that individuals understand their rights, the risks they face, and how to protect themselves in an increasingly interconnected world.

Phil Zimmermann's Continuing Influence

Phil Zimmermann's legacy continues to shape the ongoing fight for privacy. His vision of secure and private communication has inspired generations of privacy advocates, technologists, and ordinary individuals who value their right to privacy.

Zimmermann's dedication to creating tools that give individuals control over their personal information has had a lasting impact on the tech industry and privacy advocacy. His work serves as a blueprint for future privacy-focused initiatives and continues to influence the development of encryption technologies and the fight against mass surveillance.

In conclusion, the ongoing fight for privacy is an essential battle in our increasingly connected and digitized world. Encryption, protection against mass surveillance, the role of whistleblowers, and the future of privacy are key areas of focus in this fight. With the influence of pioneers like Phil Zimmermann, we can continue to advocate for strong privacy protections, raise awareness about the importance of privacy, and empower individuals to take control of their personal information.

Phil Zimmermann's Blueprint for a Privacy-Focused Future

The Vision of a Digital Sanctuary

In today's interconnected world, where data breaches and privacy violations have become alarmingly common, the concept of a "digital sanctuary" has gained significant importance. Phil Zimmermann, the renowned programmer and privacy advocate, envisions a future where individuals can find refuge in a secure and private digital environment. This section explores Zimmermann's vision, the principles behind a digital sanctuary, and the challenges that must be overcome to make this vision a reality.

Principles of a Digital Sanctuary

At the core of the digital sanctuary concept are the principles of privacy, security, and individual control over personal data. Zimmermann believes that privacy is a fundamental human right that should be protected in the digital realm as vigorously as in the physical realm. He envisions a world where individuals have complete control over their personal information, with the ability to choose who can access it and for what purpose.

Security is another critical aspect of a digital sanctuary. Zimmermann understands that privacy cannot be achieved without robust security measures. He advocates for the use of strong encryption to protect communications and data from unauthorized access. The encryption algorithms should be open and transparent to ensure their integrity and effectiveness.

Individual control plays a crucial role in the digital sanctuary vision. Zimmermann argues that individuals should have the ultimate say in how their data is collected, used, and shared. This means empowering individuals with tools that allow them to make informed decisions about their privacy, such as privacy settings, consent mechanisms, and transparency in data collection practices.

Challenges to Achieving a Digital Sanctuary

While the idea of a digital sanctuary is appealing, realizing this vision is not without its challenges. Zimmermann recognizes several obstacles that must be overcome to create a truly secure and private digital environment.

One of the major challenges is the increasing sophistication of cyber threats. Hackers and malicious actors continually find new ways to exploit vulnerabilities in software and networks. To counter these threats, continuous innovation and collaboration among security experts and developers are essential. Zimmermann emphasizes the importance of staying ahead in the arms race of privacy by adapting to emerging threats and fortifying defenses.

Another challenge lies in the balance between privacy and convenience. Many individuals unknowingly sacrifice their privacy for the sake of convenience, often through the use of social media platforms and online services. Zimmermann believes that education and awareness are crucial in empowering individuals to make privacy-conscious choices without compromising convenience. By educating users about potential risks and providing user-friendly privacy tools, a digital sanctuary can be built without sacrificing user experience.

The influence of governments and corporations also poses a significant challenge to the realization of a digital sanctuary. Governments may seek to undermine privacy for surveillance purposes, while corporations may prioritize profit over user privacy. Zimmermann advocates for clear privacy laws and regulations that protect individuals' rights and hold both governments and corporations accountable for their actions. Collaborative efforts between policymakers, privacy advocates, and technology companies are essential to strike the right balance between privacy and other societal needs.

Building the Digital Sanctuary

To build a digital sanctuary, multiple initiatives need to come together in a coordinated effort. Zimmermann proposes several steps towards achieving this vision:

- **Technological advancements**: Continual development and improvement of privacy-enhancing technologies, such as advanced encryption protocols and secure communication tools, are critical components of a digital sanctuary. Open-source collaboration and auditable codebases play an important role in ensuring the trustworthiness and transparency of these technologies.

- **Policy and legal frameworks**: Zimmermann believes that effective privacy protection requires robust legal frameworks. Privacy laws should clearly define individuals' rights and regulate the collection, storage, and use of personal data. These laws should be adaptable to technological advancements and protect individuals from unwarranted surveillance.

- **User education and awareness**: Empowering individuals with knowledge about their privacy rights, the importance of encryption, and practical steps to enhance their digital security is crucial. Zimmermann stresses the need for educational initiatives, awareness campaigns, and user-friendly tools that promote privacy-conscious behavior and enable individuals to take control of their online presence.

- **Partnerships and collaboration**: To realize the vision of a digital sanctuary, collaboration between governments, technology companies, and privacy experts is essential. Zimmerman encourages collaboration to develop privacy-focused policies, advance research in encryption and security, and drive innovation in privacy-enhancing technologies. By working together, stakeholders can pool their expertise and resources to create a more secure and privacy-respecting digital landscape.

Ensuring a Sustainable Future

Zimmermann's vision of a digital sanctuary extends beyond immediate privacy concerns. He believes that privacy and security are interconnected with broader ethical considerations, such as the implications of artificial intelligence, the regulation of biometric data, and the equitable distribution of technology.

Zimmermann proposes that the digital sanctuary concept should evolve to encompass these emerging challenges. The vision should anticipate and address the potential risks associated with new technologies, promote ethical guidelines for data usage, and foster a future where privacy is preserved for all individuals, regardless of their background or socioeconomic status.

Ultimately, the creation of a digital sanctuary requires a collective effort and a commitment to uphold privacy as a fundamental right. Zimmermann's vision serves as a compass, guiding the ongoing fight for privacy and inspiring the next generation of technologists, policymakers, and activists to carry the torch forward and build a more private and secure world.

Resources

- Privacytools.io: A website dedicated to providing privacy-conscious alternatives to popular software and services. It offers comprehensive guides, articles, and resources for individuals seeking to enhance their digital privacy.

- Electronic Frontier Foundation (EFF): An international non-profit organization that defends civil liberties in the digital world. The EFF provides valuable resources on encryption, privacy laws, and digital rights advocacy.

- "The Art of Invisibility: The World's Most Famous Hacker Teaches You How to Be Safe in the Age of Big Brother and Big Data" by Kevin Mitnick: A book that explores privacy and security issues in the digital age and provides practical tips on protecting personal information.

- "Data and Goliath: The Hidden Battles to Collect Your Data and Control Your World" by Bruce Schneier: This book examines the pervasive collection of personal data and its impact on privacy, urging readers to take action to preserve their privacy rights.

Exercises

1. Research a recent privacy breach or violation and analyze the impact on individuals and society. What could have been done to prevent or mitigate the breach? How does this incident align with or challenge the vision of a digital sanctuary?

2. Discuss the ethical considerations surrounding the use of personal data by social media platforms. How can individuals balance the convenience of using these platforms with their privacy concerns? Propose practical strategies to protect personal data while maintaining a social media presence.

3. Investigate the privacy laws and regulations in your country. How well do they protect individuals' privacy rights? Identify any shortcomings or areas for improvement and propose specific policy recommendations to enhance privacy safeguards.

4. Interview individuals in your community about their attitudes towards privacy and security in the digital realm. Analyze the common misconceptions or concerns they have, and develop a short presentation or infographic to educate them on the importance of privacy and the steps they can take to protect it.

5. Write a persuasive essay arguing for the inclusion of privacy education in school curricula. Highlight the benefits of privacy literacy, potential challenges in implementing such a curriculum, and strategies to overcome them.

Further Reading

- Greenwald, Glenn. "No Place to Hide: Edward Snowden, the NSA, and the U.S. Surveillance State." Metropolitan Books, 2014.

- Schneier, Bruce. "Applied Cryptography: Protocols, Algorithms, and Source Code in C." John Wiley & Sons, 1996.

- MacKinnon, Rebecca. "Consent of the Networked: The Worldwide Struggle for Internet Freedom." Basic Books, 2012.

- Solove, Daniel J. "The Digital Person: Technology and Privacy in the Information Age." NYU Press, 2004.

Tricks and Caveats

- It's important to stay updated on evolving privacy laws and regulations, as they can vary across jurisdictions. Remember to consult reliable sources and official publications to ensure the accuracy and currency of the information.

- When evaluating privacy-focused tools or services, examine their privacy policies, terms of service, and data handling practices. Look for independent audits and reviews to assess their trustworthiness.

- Engage in ongoing conversations about privacy with friends, family, and colleagues. Sharing knowledge and experiences can help reinforce the importance of privacy and spur collective action towards a digital sanctuary.

Beyond Encryption: The Next Frontier

In a world where privacy is increasingly under threat, encryption has become a critical tool for safeguarding our digital lives. However, as technology evolves and new challenges arise, it is clear that encryption alone cannot solve all our privacy concerns. In this section, we will explore the next frontier beyond encryption and delve into innovative approaches and emerging technologies that can help address the evolving landscape of privacy.

Privacy-Preserving Technologies

While encryption is a powerful solution for protecting the confidentiality of our data, it has its limitations when it comes to preserving privacy in the broader sense. Privacy is not just about keeping information secret from prying eyes; it also encompasses concepts such as data minimization, consent, and user control. To achieve these goals, new privacy-preserving technologies are being developed.

One such technology is differential privacy, which aims to enable the analysis of sensitive data while preserving the privacy of individuals. It introduces statistical noise during data analysis to prevent the identification of individual records. Differential privacy has gained attention in various domains, including healthcare, finance, and social sciences, where privacy concerns often limit data availability for research and analysis.

Another emerging technology is federated learning, which allows machine learning models to be trained on decentralized data without the need for data to be shared or centralized. It enables organizations to collaborate and build powerful models while maintaining the privacy of their individual data. Federated learning has the potential to revolutionize industries such as healthcare, where data privacy is paramount, and yet shared models can accelerate medical research and diagnostics.

Decentralization and Blockchain

As the centralization of data poses significant risks to privacy, decentralization has emerged as a promising approach to address these concerns. Blockchain technology, originally introduced in the context of cryptocurrencies like Bitcoin, offers a decentralized and tamper-resistant platform for recording transactions and maintaining data integrity.

Beyond cryptocurrencies, blockchain has immense potential in enhancing privacy and security in various domains. For example, blockchain-based identity solutions can empower individuals with control over their personal data and enable self-sovereign identity. This approach ensures that individuals have ownership and agency over their identity information, reducing the risks of data breaches and unauthorized access.

Moreover, blockchain can enable decentralized data marketplaces, where individuals have the choice to sell their data directly to interested parties, thereby giving them greater control and fair compensation for their data. This decentralized approach shifts the power dynamics from centralized platforms to individuals and fosters a more transparent and privacy-respecting data economy.

Ethical Considerations

As we explore the next frontier beyond encryption, it is crucial to address the ethical considerations surrounding privacy-preserving technologies. While these technologies offer promising solutions, they can also introduce new challenges and risks.

One such concern is the potential for algorithmic bias and discrimination. Differential privacy and machine learning algorithms rely on historical data, which can perpetuate existing biases and lead to unfair outcomes. To ensure fairness and avoid discrimination, it is essential to design and train these technologies with diverse and representative data, while also implementing techniques to mitigate bias.

Another consideration is the tension between privacy and public safety. As we seek to strengthen privacy measures, law enforcement and security agencies may argue that access to encrypted data is necessary for national security purposes.

Achieving a balance between privacy and security is a complex challenge that requires thoughtful deliberation and a multipronged approach.

The Future of Privacy

Looking ahead, the future of privacy will be shaped not only by technological innovations but also by legal frameworks and societal attitudes. As privacy concerns continue to grow, there is a need for comprehensive privacy laws and regulations that protect individuals' rights in an increasingly digital world.

Education and awareness are also key in empowering individuals to protect their privacy. As privacy-preserving technologies and practices become more accessible, it is crucial to educate users about their rights and provide them with the tools and knowledge to make informed decisions about their digital lives.

Ultimately, the next frontier beyond encryption is an ongoing journey that requires collaboration between technologists, policymakers, and individuals. By embracing emerging technologies while upholding fundamental privacy principles, we can navigate the evolving landscape of privacy and ensure a future where individuals have control, consent, and agency over their personal information.

Conclusion

Encryption has been a game-changer in protecting our digital privacy, but it is just the beginning. The next frontier beyond encryption involves innovative approaches such as differential privacy and federated learning, as well as the decentralization of data through blockchain technology. However, as we explore these new frontiers, we must also consider the ethical implications and strike a balance between privacy and public safety.

The future of privacy relies not only on technological advancements but also on legal frameworks and individual empowerment. Comprehensive privacy laws and regulations, along with education and awareness, are essential in shaping a future where privacy is respected and protected. Ultimately, by embracing new technologies and upholding fundamental privacy principles, we can pave the way for a future with digital freedom and autonomy.

Phil Zimmermann's Predictions for the Future

In this section, we will explore Phil Zimmermann's predictions for the future of privacy and encryption. As a visionary in the field, Zimmermann had a deep understanding of the evolving digital landscape and the challenges that lay ahead.

With his vast experience and insight, he shared his thoughts on where he believed the future of privacy was headed.

The Vision of a Digital Sanctuary

Zimmermann envisioned a future where individuals have complete control over their digital lives—a concept he referred to as a "digital sanctuary." He believed that privacy should be a fundamental right in the digital world, just as it is in the physical world. Zimmermann predicted that individuals would have the ability to easily encrypt all their personal data, ensuring that only authorized parties could access it. This would create a safe and secure digital space where users could freely communicate and conduct their online activities without the fear of surveillance or data breaches.

Beyond Encryption: The Next Frontier

While encryption played a pivotal role in Zimmermann's vision for privacy, he also recognized its limitations. He predicted that the future of privacy would go beyond encryption and delve into areas such as anonymity and pseudonymity. Zimmermann believed that individuals should have the option to remain anonymous online, protecting their identity while still engaging in meaningful interactions. He saw a future where effective privacy technologies would allow individuals to create online personas or pseudonyms, giving them control over their digital footprint.

Phil Zimmermann's Predictions for the Future

Looking ahead, Zimmermann made several predictions for the future of privacy:

1. *Increased Adoption of Privacy-Enhancing Technologies*: Zimmermann believed that privacy-enhancing technologies, including end-to-end encryption and secure communication platforms, would become more widely adopted. He predicted that these technologies would evolve to be more user-friendly, making privacy protection accessible to individuals of all technical backgrounds.

2. *Advancements in Secure Messaging*: Zimmermann anticipated significant advancements in secure messaging applications. He believed that future messaging platforms would prioritize privacy by default, incorporating robust encryption algorithms and anti-surveillance features. Zimmermann predicted the development of decentralized communication systems that would enable users to have full control over their conversations and data.

3. *Intelligent Privacy Tools*: Zimmermann envisioned the emergence of intelligent privacy tools that would help users navigate the complex digital landscape. He predicted the development of privacy-focused AI systems that can analyze and identify potential privacy risks, offering real-time suggestions and guidance to users in protecting their data.

4. *The Rise of Privacy-Enhancing Legislation*: Zimmermann believed that increasing public awareness and advocacy for privacy would lead to the enactment of comprehensive privacy laws and regulations. He predicted that governments worldwide would realize the importance of privacy protection and take concrete steps to ensure that individuals' digital rights are safeguarded.

5. *The Integration of Privacy into Technological Design*: Zimmermann anticipated a fundamental shift in the design philosophy of technological products and services. He predicted that privacy would no longer be an afterthought but an integral part of the development process. Privacy by design principles would be implemented, ensuring that privacy is embedded into the core architecture of digital systems.

The Democratization of Privacy

Zimmermann also emphasized the importance of democratizing privacy. He believed that privacy should not be a privilege reserved for the few but a right accessible to all. Zimmermann predicted that individuals would become more empowered in taking control of their privacy, leveraging technology to defend their digital rights. He foresaw a world where privacy becomes a societal expectation, and individuals collectively hold organizations, governments, and tech companies accountable for protecting their privacy.

The Evolution of Privacy Laws

Building on his prediction of privacy-enhancing legislation, Zimmermann anticipated the continuous evolution of privacy laws to keep pace with rapidly advancing technology. He recognized the challenges of regulating a constantly evolving digital landscape but believed that legislation would adapt to cover emerging privacy concerns. Zimmermann predicted that there would be increased collaboration between lawmakers, technologists, and privacy advocates to create robust privacy frameworks that balance the needs of individuals and the requirements of law enforcement.

The Importance of User Education

Another crucial aspect of Zimmermann's predictions was the role of user education in safeguarding privacy. He emphasized the need for individuals to be informed and educated about the risks to their privacy and the tools available to protect themselves. Zimmermann predicted that privacy education would become an essential part of digital literacy programs, ensuring that individuals have the knowledge and skills to navigate the digital landscape safely.

Phil Zimmermann's Contributions to Privacy Engineering

Zimmermann's predictions were rooted in his lifelong dedication to privacy engineering. He recognized that technological advancements played a central role in shaping the future of privacy and encryption. Through his work, Zimmermann contributed to the development of encryption technologies that prioritized user privacy, laying the foundation for future innovations. His creations, such as Pretty Good Privacy (PGP), have become integral to the privacy landscape and continue to inspire the next generation of privacy-focused engineers.

Wrapping Up

Phil Zimmermann's predictions for the future of privacy were based on his deep understanding of encryption, his observation of privacy trends, and his commitment to empowering individuals in the digital world. While the future is uncertain, Zimmermann's insights provide valuable guidance as we navigate the complex landscape of privacy and encryption. By examining his predictions, we can gain a better understanding of the challenges and opportunities that lie ahead, and work towards a future where privacy is a fundamental right for all.

The Democratization of Privacy

In the digital age, privacy has become a hot topic, with individuals and organizations increasingly concerned about the security of their personal data. Phil Zimmermann has long been an advocate for the democratization of privacy, believing that everyone should have the right to protect their sensitive information from prying eyes. In this section, we will explore the concept of the democratization of privacy and its implications for individuals and society as a whole.

Understanding Privacy as a Fundamental Right

Privacy is not just a luxury enjoyed by a select few; it is a fundamental right that should be accessible to all. The democratization of privacy means ensuring that individuals have the tools and knowledge to protect their personal information, regardless of their technical expertise or resources. It is about empowering individuals to exercise control over their data and make informed decisions about how and when it is shared.

In the digital age, we leave a trail of personal data everywhere we go - from our online interactions to our financial transactions. This data is valuable to companies and governments, which can use it for various purposes, including targeted advertising, surveillance, and more. The democratization of privacy aims to level the playing field by giving individuals the ability to safeguard their information and maintain control over their digital lives.

Empowering Individuals with Privacy Tools

One of the key pillars of the democratization of privacy is the availability of privacy tools that are accessible and easy to use for everyone. Phil Zimmermann's PGP (Pretty Good Privacy) is a prime example of such a tool. PGP provides end-to-end encryption, ensuring that only the intended recipient can read a message, while keeping it secure from eavesdroppers and potential hackers. By making PGP freely available and open source, Zimmermann enabled individuals to take their digital privacy into their own hands.

But democratizing privacy extends beyond encryption tools. It involves promoting user-friendly privacy-centric technologies, such as secure messaging apps, VPNs (Virtual Private Networks), and privacy-focused web browsers. These tools allow individuals to take control of their online presence, protecting their communications, browsing history, and personal data from prying eyes.

Education and Awareness About Privacy

Democratizing privacy also requires a strong emphasis on education and awareness. Privacy is a complex concept, and many individuals may not fully understand the implications of their online activities. By advocating for privacy education and awareness campaigns, we can empower individuals to make informed decisions about their digital footprint.

Educating individuals about the importance of privacy, the risks associated with data breaches, and the tools available to protect themselves is crucial. It involves teaching individuals about concepts like encryption, secure passwords, and privacy settings in online platforms. By equipping individuals with the knowledge and skills to safeguard their personal data, we can create a society that is more conscious and proactive about privacy.

Privacy as a Collective Effort

While the democratization of privacy focuses on empowering individuals, it is also a collective effort that involves collaboration between various stakeholders. Governments, tech companies, and policymakers play a crucial role in ensuring that privacy remains a priority and that individuals have the necessary legal protections.

Privacy regulations and laws, such as the European Union's General Data Protection Regulation (GDPR), aim to hold organizations accountable for the misuse of personal data. By enacting and enforcing these regulations, governments can create a framework that protects individuals' rights to privacy.

Tech companies also have a responsibility to prioritize privacy in the products and services they offer. By adopting privacy-by-design principles, they can ensure that privacy is built into the very fabric of their offerings, rather than being an afterthought.

The Ethical Implications of Democratizing Privacy

Democratizing privacy raises important ethical questions and considerations. While it is essential to empower individuals with privacy tools and knowledge, it is equally important to strike a balance between privacy and other competing interests, such as national security. The encryption backdoor debate, for example, highlights the tensions between privacy and law enforcement access to encrypted data.

Additionally, democratizing privacy must also take into account the potential for misuse by malicious actors. While privacy tools are intended to protect individuals, they can also be employed by those wishing to engage in illegal activities. Striking the right balance between privacy and security is an ongoing challenge that requires thoughtful consideration and collaboration between various stakeholders.

Promoting an Equitable Future

The democratization of privacy is not just about protecting individual liberties; it is about creating a more equitable digital future. By ensuring that privacy tools and knowledge are accessible to all, we can address the power imbalances inherent in the digital landscape.

When privacy becomes a widespread concern, it has the potential to drive systemic changes and challenge the status quo. By encouraging individuals to take control of their digital lives, the democratization of privacy empowers citizens to hold governments and organizations accountable for their data practices.

Democratizing privacy is an ongoing battle, requiring continued advocacy, education, and innovation. Phil Zimmermann's contributions to the field serve as an inspiration for future generations of privacy advocates and technologists. By carrying the torch forward, we can shape a future where privacy is not just a privilege but a fundamental right for all.

The Evolution of Privacy Laws

In today's digital age, where personal information is constantly being collected and shared, the need for robust privacy laws has become more pressing than ever. The evolution of privacy laws has been driven by advancements in technology, changing societal norms, and the increasing recognition of the importance of individual privacy rights. In this section, we will explore the history, challenges, and future of privacy laws.

A Brief History of Privacy Laws

Privacy laws have a long history that can be traced back to ancient civilizations. The ancient Greeks recognized the importance of privacy in their homes and enacted laws to protect it. In more recent history, privacy laws gained traction in the 19th and early 20th centuries as a response to concerns over government surveillance and the increasing power of corporations.

One landmark moment in privacy law was the development of the right to privacy in the United States. In his famous 1890 article, legal scholars Samuel Warren and Louis Brandeis argued for the recognition of a right to privacy, describing it as "the right to be let alone." This notion of privacy as a fundamental right later influenced the development of privacy laws in other countries as well.

In the mid-20th century, privacy laws primarily focused on limiting government intrusion into private lives. The Fourth Amendment to the United States Constitution, for example, protects against unreasonable search and seizure. However, with the rise of technology and the internet, a new set of challenges emerged, necessitating the creation of comprehensive privacy laws to address them.

Challenges in the Digital Age

The digital revolution has transformed the way we live, work, and communicate. While technology has brought many benefits, it has also raised significant privacy concerns. The vast amount of data collected by companies and governmental entities has the potential to infringe upon individuals' privacy rights.

One major challenge in the digital age is the issue of data protection. Personal information is constantly being collected, stored, and processed by companies and organizations. Privacy laws aim to regulate the collection and use of this data to ensure that individuals have control over their personal information.

Another challenge is the global nature of the internet. With data flowing across borders, it becomes crucial to harmonize privacy laws and establish international standards for data protection. The European Union's General Data Protection Regulation (GDPR) is a prime example of a comprehensive privacy law that addresses these concerns and sets a benchmark for other regions to follow.

Furthermore, emerging technologies like artificial intelligence and facial recognition present new privacy challenges. The use of these technologies can have far-reaching implications for individuals' privacy, leading to debates over the extent to which they should be regulated.

The Role of Privacy Laws

Privacy laws play a crucial role in safeguarding individuals' rights and balancing the benefits of technology with the need for privacy. They provide a legal framework for protecting personal information and establishing limits on data collection, use, and disclosure.

One essential principle of privacy laws is the concept of informed consent. Individuals must have control over their personal information and be able to make informed decisions about its use. Privacy laws typically require organizations to obtain consent before collecting or processing personal data.

Privacy laws also outline the obligations of organizations when it comes to data security. Companies are expected to implement reasonable security measures to protect personal information from unauthorized access, use, or disclosure. In the event of a data breach, privacy laws often require organizations to notify affected individuals and take steps to mitigate any harm caused.

Furthermore, privacy laws provide mechanisms for individuals to exercise their privacy rights. These may include the right to access, correct, or delete personal information held by organizations. Privacy laws also establish regulatory bodies to enforce compliance and investigate violations.

Future Challenges and Considerations

As technology continues to advance, privacy laws will face new challenges. The increasing adoption of internet-connected devices, smart homes, and wearable technology will create a wealth of personal data that needs to be protected. Privacy laws will need to adapt to these new technologies and the complexities they introduce.

Additionally, the rise of big data and data analytics raises questions about the ethics of data use. Privacy laws may need to address issues of transparency, accountability, and the fair use of personal information in the context of data-driven decision-making.

Another consideration is the interplay between privacy and national security. Balancing the need for surveillance to protect against threats with individuals' right to privacy is a complex challenge that privacy laws need to navigate. Striking the right balance will require ongoing discussions, collaboration between government and tech companies, and periodic reassessment of privacy laws.

In conclusion, the evolution of privacy laws has been a response to the challenges posed by technological advancements and the changing landscape of the digital age. Privacy laws aim to protect individuals' rights, regulate data collection and use, and establish accountability mechanisms. As technology continues to advance, privacy laws will need to adapt and address new challenges, ensuring that individuals' privacy rights remain protected in an increasingly interconnected world.

The Importance of User Education

In the digital age, where our lives are increasingly interconnected and our personal information is vulnerable to attacks, user education has become more crucial than ever. Phil Zimmermann understood that the fight for privacy goes beyond developing innovative encryption technology; it involves empowering individuals with knowledge and skills to protect themselves. In this section, we will explore the significance of user education in the context of privacy and security.

Understanding the Threats

User education begins with understanding the threats that exist in the digital landscape. Many individuals are unaware of the risks associated with sharing personal information online or the potential consequences of falling victim to cybercrime. By educating users about common attack vectors such as phishing scams, malware, and data breaches, they become better equipped to navigate the digital world safely.

Example: Let's consider the case of a user who receives an email claiming to be from their bank, asking them to input their login credentials. Through proper education, the user would recognize this email as a phishing attempt and avoid disclosing sensitive information.

Principles of Secure Behavior

User education should also focus on promoting secure behavior and best practices. This includes teaching individuals to use strong, unique passwords, enable two-factor authentication, and regularly update their software and devices. It is essential to emphasize the importance of using reputable security software and avoiding public Wi-Fi networks to minimize the risk of unauthorized access.

Example: A user who has received proper education on secure behavior will understand the importance of using strong, unique passwords for each online account and regularly changing them. This significantly reduces the risk of unauthorized access to personal information.

Privacy Settings and Online Presence

In today's age of social media and online networks, user education should also address privacy settings and the potential risks associated with oversharing personal information. Users should be educated on how to manage their online presence, adjust privacy settings, and limit the information that is publicly accessible. They should understand the implications of sharing sensitive information and the potential consequences of identity theft or online harassment.

Example: By educating users about privacy settings on social media platforms, they can choose who can see their posts, photos, and personal information. This can help prevent unauthorized access by malicious individuals.

Recognizing Social Engineering Attacks

User education should also cover the topic of social engineering attacks, which exploit human psychology to manipulate individuals into disclosing sensitive information. By teaching users to recognize these tactics, such as impersonation, intimidation, or emotional manipulation, they can avoid falling prey to such attacks.

Example: Through user education, individuals can learn to identify suspicious phone calls from scammers pretending to be tech support personnel. By recognizing the signs of a social engineering attack, they can protect themselves from divulging personal information or granting remote access to their devices.

Staying Updated with Emerging Threats

Given the constantly evolving nature of cybersecurity threats, user education should also emphasize the importance of staying updated with the latest trends and emerging threats. By promoting a culture of continuous learning and awareness, individuals can adapt their security practices to counter new attack vectors effectively.

Example: Education programs can inform users about emerging threats such as ransomware attacks and provide guidance on effective mitigation strategies. This empowers users to take proactive measures to protect their digital assets.

Resources for User Education

User education requires accessible resources to disseminate knowledge effectively. Phil Zimmermann recognized this need and paved the way for the creation and distribution of educational materials and tools that teach individuals about privacy and security.

Example: Online platforms, such as privacy-focused websites and cybersecurity organizations, provide resources such as articles, videos, and interactive tutorials to educate users about digital threats and protective measures.

Exercises and Practical Application

To reinforce user education, it is important to provide practical exercises and simulations that allow individuals to apply their knowledge in a controlled environment. These exercises can simulate real-world scenarios, such as identifying phishing emails, securing online accounts, or protecting personal information. By actively engaging users, they can develop practical skills and confidence in their ability to protect themselves.

Example: A user education program may include interactive exercises that simulate common online scams, allowing individuals to practice identifying and avoiding them.

The Role of User Education in Privacy Advocacy

User education is not only crucial for individual privacy and security but also plays a vital role in advocating for stronger privacy policies and regulations. Educated individuals who understand the importance of privacy are more likely to demand better protection of their personal data, encouraging governments and organizations to implement stronger safeguards.

Example: A well-educated user who comprehends the consequences of data breaches would be more likely to support legislative efforts aimed at holding companies accountable for the mishandling of personal information.

Ethical Considerations

User education should also address the ethical considerations surrounding privacy and security. It is crucial to teach individuals about the ethics of data collection, consent, and responsible use of technology. This fosters a culture of responsible digital citizenship and ensures that privacy is respected at all levels of society.

Example: By teaching individuals about the ethical implications of data sharing and privacy violations, they can make informed decisions about their digital behaviors and advocate for ethical practices.

Beyond Privacy: Empowering Users

User education in privacy and security extends beyond protecting personal information. By empowering individuals with knowledge and skills, user education promotes digital autonomy, critical thinking, and active engagement with technology. It enables users to navigate the digital landscape confidently and engage more meaningfully with the benefits that technology offers.

Example: A well-educated user can leverage encryption technology to secure their communications, allowing them to freely express their ideas and opinions without fear of surveillance or censorship.

Conclusion

User education is an essential component of Phil Zimmermann's vision for privacy and security. By providing individuals with the knowledge, skills, and resources to protect themselves, user education empowers them to navigate the digital world safely. It promotes responsible digital citizenship, fosters a culture of privacy awareness, and advocates for stronger privacy policies. By emphasizing the importance of user education, we can create a future where individuals are empowered to protect their privacy, their personal information, and their digital autonomy.

Phil Zimmermann's Contributions to Privacy Engineering

Phil Zimmermann's impact on privacy engineering cannot be overstated. Through his groundbreaking work in the field of cryptography, Zimmermann revolutionized the way we protect our digital communications and paved the way for the privacy-focused technologies we have today. In this section, we will explore his contributions to privacy engineering and the lasting effects they have had on the digital landscape.

The Birth of Pretty Good Privacy (PGP)

Zimmermann's most notable contribution to privacy engineering is the creation of Pretty Good Privacy (PGP). In the early 1990s, Zimmermann developed this encryption software as a means to protect the privacy of everyday individuals. PGP allowed users to encrypt and decrypt email messages, ensuring that their communication remained confidential and secure.

At a time when encryption was primarily used by governments and large organizations, Zimmermann's decision to make PGP freely available to the public was a game-changer. He recognized that privacy should not be exclusive to those with power and resources but should be accessible to all. By releasing PGP as freeware, Zimmermann democratized encryption and put the power of privacy in the hands of individuals around the world.

Advancements in Key Management

One of the significant challenges in privacy engineering is key management. Encryption systems rely on the secure generation, distribution, and storage of cryptographic keys. Zimmermann understood the importance of user-friendly key management and made it a priority in PGP.

He pioneered the use of a public key infrastructure (PKI) to simplify the key management process. With PGP, individuals could easily generate their own public and private key pairs, protecting their communications effortlessly. Zimmermann's approach to key management set a new standard for usability in encryption tools and made privacy more accessible to non-technical users.

Challenge-Response Authentication

In addition to email encryption, Zimmermann also introduced challenge-response authentication to PGP. This feature allows users to verify each other's identities before engaging in secure communication.

Challenge-response authentication works by having one party pose a challenge question to the other party. The responding party must provide the correct answer before the communication can proceed. This process ensures that the intended recipient is the one receiving the encrypted message, preventing unauthorized access and impersonation.

Zimmermann's implementation of challenge-response authentication in PGP added an extra layer of security and further protected users' privacy by verifying the authenticity of their communication partners.

Open Source Philosophy

Another critical aspect of Zimmermann's contributions to privacy engineering is his commitment to the open-source philosophy. He believed that software and encryption standards should be open and accessible to the public, encouraging collaboration, scrutiny, and innovation.

By making PGP open source, Zimmermann invited developers from around the world to examine and contribute to its codebase. This approach fostered a community-driven ecosystem, where experts could identify vulnerabilities, suggest improvements, and build upon Zimmermann's initial work.

The open-source nature of PGP not only helped enhance its security but also inspired the development of other privacy-focused tools and technologies. Zimmermann's open-source philosophy continues to shape the privacy engineering landscape, promoting transparency, innovation, and the collective pursuit of digital privacy.

Influence on Privacy Standards and Legislation

Zimmermann's advocacy for privacy extended beyond his technical contributions. He recognized the need for legal and policy frameworks that protect individuals' privacy in the digital age.

His public involvement in the Clipper Chip controversy, where the U.S. government proposed the introduction of a cryptographic backdoor, highlighted the importance of privacy in protecting the fundamental rights of individuals. Zimmermann's vocal opposition to the Clipper Chip and his efforts to mobilize the tech community helped shape public opinion and demonstrated the potential risks of compromising encryption for the sake of national security.

Zimmermann's activism played a crucial role in the development of privacy standards and legislation worldwide. His work shed light on the need for strong encryption and the preservation of privacy rights, influencing debates and policies at national and international levels.

PHIL ZIMMERMANN'S BLUEPRINT FOR A PRIVACY-FOCUSED FUTURE

The Ethical Implications of Privacy Engineering

Beyond his technical contributions, Zimmermann raised critical ethical questions surrounding privacy engineering. He highlighted the potential consequences of mass surveillance, data breaches, and the exploitation of personal information.

Zimmermann's advocacy emphasized the need for a balanced approach to privacy and security. While encryption provides essential safeguards for individuals, he acknowledged the need to consider legitimate law enforcement concerns. His ethical framework challenged the notion that privacy and security are mutually exclusive, championing the idea that both can coexist and thrive in the digital world.

Continuing the Legacy

Phil Zimmermann's contributions to privacy engineering continue to shape the way we design and implement privacy solutions. His dedication to accessible encryption, user-friendly key management, open-source collaboration, influence on policy, and thoughtful ethical considerations have left an indelible mark on the field.

As the digital landscape evolves, future privacy engineers can draw inspiration from Zimmermann's work. They can learn from his emphasis on usability, his commitment to user empowerment, and his unwavering belief in the value of privacy. By carrying forward Zimmermann's legacy, these engineers can contribute to a future where privacy is respected, protected, and accessible to all.

Acknowledging the Unconventional

In the world of privacy engineering, thinking outside the box can lead to groundbreaking innovations. One unconventional solution to privacy challenges is the concept of zero-knowledge proofs.

Zero-knowledge proofs allow individuals to prove the validity of a statement without revealing any additional information beyond the statement's truth. This concept has profound implications for privacy engineering, as it enables secure authentication and verification processes without disclosing sensitive data.

For example, zero-knowledge proofs can be used to verify a person's age without exposing their exact date of birth or to authenticate a user's membership in a specific group without revealing other group members' identities. This innovative approach minimizes the exposure of personal information, offering a new level of privacy protection.

Zero-knowledge proofs continue to be an active area of research and hold promise for privacy engineering. By exploring unconventional avenues like this, future privacy engineers can push the boundaries of what is possible and develop novel solutions to complex privacy challenges.

Summary

In this section, we've explored Phil Zimmermann's significant contributions to privacy engineering. From the creation of PGP to advancements in key management and challenge-response authentication, Zimmermann's work has shaped the way we protect our digital privacy.

Beyond the technical realm, Zimmermann's commitment to the open-source philosophy, his advocacy for privacy rights, and his ethical considerations have had a lasting impact on the field. His influence can be seen in the development of privacy standards, legislation, and the ongoing fight for digital privacy.

As privacy engineering continues to evolve, future generations of privacy engineers can draw inspiration from Zimmermann's work. By building upon his principles of accessibility, usability, and the values of privacy, they can contribute to a future where individuals' digital lives are protected and respected.

Privacy as a Human Right

In this section, we explore the concept of privacy as a fundamental human right. Privacy is not just a luxury or a convenience; it is a crucial aspect of our existence that allows us to maintain autonomy, dignity, and control over our personal information. In an increasingly connected and digital world, the protection of privacy becomes even more vital.

The Importance of Privacy

Privacy is the ability to keep our personal information, thoughts, and activities to ourselves, free from intrusion or surveillance by others. It is the right to be free from unwarranted interference, whether by individuals, organizations, or governments. Privacy plays a pivotal role in ensuring individual freedom, autonomy, and self-expression.

In the digital age, our personal information has become a valuable commodity. Companies and governments collect vast amounts of data about us, tracking our online activities, preferences, and behaviors. This data can be used for targeted advertising, manipulation, and even discrimination. Without privacy, we lose control over our identities and are vulnerable to exploitation.

The Legal Framework

At the international level, privacy is recognized as a human right under the Universal Declaration of Human Rights and the International Covenant on Civil and Political Rights. These documents affirm that privacy is essential in protecting other rights, such as freedom of speech, association, and conscience.

Many countries have also enacted privacy laws and regulations to safeguard individuals' data and privacy rights. These laws aim to ensure that personal information is collected, processed, and used in a transparent and lawful manner. They also provide individuals with rights such as access to their information, the right to correct inaccuracies, and the right to be forgotten.

Challenges and Threats

Despite the recognition of privacy as a human right, there are numerous challenges and threats that endanger our privacy in the digital age. One of the most significant challenges is the proliferation of surveillance technologies and practices. Governments and corporations engage in mass surveillance, monitoring communications, internet activities, and even physical movements.

Another major threat to privacy is the exploitation of personal data by companies for commercial purposes. Data breaches and leaks have become alarmingly common, exposing sensitive information and leaving individuals vulnerable to identity theft, fraud, and other forms of abuse.

Moreover, the advent of artificial intelligence and machine learning has raised concerns about the potential for algorithmic bias and discrimination. Without proper safeguards, automated decision-making systems can perpetuate discrimination and violate privacy rights.

Protecting Privacy

Protecting privacy requires a multi-faceted approach involving individuals, organizations, and governments. Here are some key strategies for safeguarding privacy:

Individual Actions: As individuals, we can take steps to protect our privacy online. This includes using strong and unique passwords, enabling two-factor authentication, being cautious of sharing personal information on social media, and regularly reviewing privacy settings on various online platforms.

Data Protection Laws: Governments should enact and enforce robust data protection laws that hold organizations accountable for the responsible collection, usage, and storage of personal data. These laws should include provisions for obtaining informed consent, data minimization, purpose limitation, and data breach notification.

End-to-End Encryption: Encrypted communication platforms play a crucial role in protecting privacy. End-to-end encryption ensures that only the sender and intended recipient can read the messages, preventing unauthorized access and surveillance. Governments should support and promote the use of encryption technologies that safeguard individuals' privacy.

User Empowerment: Educating individuals about their privacy rights and providing them with tools and resources to take control of their personal information is essential. Digital literacy programs should emphasize the importance of privacy and empower individuals to make informed decisions about sharing their data.

Ethical Design: Organizations should adopt privacy-by-design principles, embedding privacy protections into the design and development of products and services. This includes implementing privacy-preserving technologies, conducting privacy impact assessments, and ensuring transparency in data practices.

Real-world Example: Privacy and Healthcare

The importance of privacy becomes especially evident in the context of healthcare. Patients share sensitive information with healthcare providers with the expectation that it will be kept confidential. Ensuring the privacy of medical records is essential for maintaining trust between patients and healthcare professionals.

In recent years, there have been numerous cases of data breaches in the healthcare sector. These breaches not only compromise patients' privacy but also have serious implications for their well-being. For instance, if medical records are exposed to unauthorized individuals, patients may face discrimination in employment or insurance.

To address these challenges, regulations like the Health Insurance Portability and Accountability Act (HIPAA) in the United States have been enacted to protect patient privacy. HIPAA requires healthcare providers to maintain the confidentiality, integrity, and availability of patients' health information and imposes penalties for non-compliance.

In addition to legal safeguards, advancements in technology, such as secure electronic health record systems and encrypted communication platforms, have enabled healthcare providers to uphold patient privacy more effectively.

Conclusion

Privacy is a fundamental human right that underpins individual autonomy and freedom. As we navigate the complexities of the digital age, it is crucial to protect privacy in all spheres of life. Governments, organizations, and individuals must work together to promote privacy-aware practices, enact strong privacy laws, and embrace privacy-enhancing technologies. By doing so, we can ensure that privacy remains a cherished human right in the face of evolving technological advancements.

Exercises

1. Reflect on your online activities and identify areas where your privacy might be at risk. What steps can you take to enhance your privacy in those areas?

2. Research and compare the privacy laws in different countries. What similarities and differences do you notice? How effective do you think these laws are in protecting privacy?

3. Investigate the privacy policies of your favorite social media platforms or online services. Are they transparent about how they collect, use, and share your data? Are there any red flags or areas of concern?

4. Consider a scenario where a government proposes implementing surveillance measures for national security purposes. Evaluate the potential trade-offs between increased security and compromised privacy. What safeguards would you recommend to balance both?

5. Explore privacy-enhancing technologies such as virtual private networks (VPNs) or encrypted messaging apps. How do these technologies work? How can they be used to protect your privacy online?

6. Conduct a case study on a significant data breach or privacy violation. Analyze the impact on individuals and society as a whole. What lessons can be learned from this incident? How could it have been prevented?

Additional Resources

1. Book: "Data and Goliath: The Hidden Battles to Collect Your Data and Control Your World" by Bruce Schneier.

2. Documentary: "The Great Hack" (2019) - Explores the Cambridge Analytica scandal and its implications for privacy.

3. Website: Electronic Frontier Foundation (EFF) - Provides information and advocacy for digital rights, including privacy protection. Visit: https://www.eff.org/

4. Podcast: "The Privacy, Security, and Open Source Show" - Focuses on discussing privacy issues, security best practices, and open-source technologies. Listen: https://privacypodcast.com/

5. Tool: Tor Project - Offers free software and network for anonymous communication online. Learn more: https://www.torproject.org/

Phil Zimmermann's Legacy in the Privacy Space

Phil Zimmermann's impact on the world of privacy is immeasurable. His groundbreaking work in encryption technology not only revolutionized the way we communicate and protect our data, but it also sparked a global movement towards privacy advocacy. Zimmermann's legacy in the privacy space is defined by his unwavering commitment to freedom of expression, his tireless fight against surveillance, and his passion for empowering individuals to protect their digital rights.

One of the key aspects of Zimmermann's legacy is his role in raising awareness about the importance of encryption and its fundamental role in protecting privacy. He believed that individuals should have the right to communicate securely and without fear of being monitored or surveilled. Zimmermann's creation of Pretty Good Privacy (PGP), a groundbreaking encryption software, gave individuals the ability to secure their communications in a way that was previously unheard of.

But Zimmermann's impact goes beyond just creating PGP. He played a pivotal role in a larger movement advocating for strong encryption as a fundamental right. His involvement in the Crypto Wars, a series of political and legal battles over the use of encryption, showcased his determination to protect privacy in the face of powerful adversaries. Zimmermann fought back against attempts by governments to restrict or weaken encryption, recognizing its crucial role in safeguarding democracy and human rights.

Zimmermann's legacy also extends to his work as a mentor and advocate for privacy-oriented projects. He recognized the importance of collaboration and the power of a strong community in the fight for privacy. Zimmermann's mentorship and guidance have inspired countless individuals to pursue careers in privacy engineering and cryptography. His commitment to spreading knowledge and supporting privacy-focused initiatives has helped propel the field forward and ensure that the fight for privacy continues to gain momentum.

In addition to his contributions to the privacy movement, Zimmermann's philanthropic endeavors have had a lasting impact on the field. He has been a key supporter of organizations and projects dedicated to protecting digital rights and promoting online security. Through his financial contributions and advocacy efforts, Zimmermann has fostered a global community of privacy activists and technologists who continue to carry the torch forward.

Furthermore, Zimmermann's legacy includes his unwavering belief in the ethical dilemmas surrounding surveillance and the need to strike a balance between security and privacy. He recognized the potential for abuse and the erosion of civil liberties when privacy is compromised. Zimmermann's steadfast commitment to protecting privacy has inspired a new generation of technologists and policymakers to confront these challenges head-on and seek solutions that prioritize the rights of individuals.

To understand the impact of Zimmermann's legacy, we must also recognize the broader implications of his work. Through his advocacy for privacy rights, he has sparked a global conversation about the value of privacy in an increasingly connected world. His work has shed light on the risks and consequences of unchecked surveillance and has motivated governments, organizations, and individuals to take steps to safeguard privacy.

Zimmermann's lasting legacy in the privacy space serves as a reminder of the importance of individual agency and the need to protect privacy rights. His vision of a world where encryption is accessible to all and privacy is respected continues to inspire and guide us. The ongoing fight for privacy in the digital age owes much to Zimmermann's pioneering work and unwavering commitment to the cause.

As we look to the future, it is imperative that we build upon Zimmermann's legacy and continue to advocate for privacy as a fundamental human right. The challenges we face in the realm of privacy are ever-evolving, and it is up to us to carry the torch forward and find innovative solutions that honor Zimmermann's vision. By embracing encryption, raising awareness, and fostering a culture of privacy-consciousness, we can ensure that Zimmermann's legacy lives on and that future generations will benefit from a more secure and private digital world.

Key Takeaways:

- Phil Zimmermann's legacy in the privacy space stems from his groundbreaking work in the development of encryption technology, particularly through the creation of Pretty Good Privacy (PGP).

- Zimmermann played a critical role in advocating for strong encryption as a fundamental right, fighting against attempts by governments to restrict or weaken encryption.

- His mentorship and support for privacy-oriented projects have helped foster a global community of privacy activists and technologists.

- Zimmermann's activism and philanthropy have had a lasting impact on the field of privacy, inspiring future generations to confront the ethical dilemmas surrounding surveillance.

- His legacy emphasizes the importance of individual agency, the need to strike a balance between security and privacy, and the ongoing fight for privacy rights in the digital age.

Carrying the Torch Forward

In order to continue the fight for privacy in the digital age, it is crucial to carry the torch forward and build upon the incredible work of Phil Zimmermann. His legacy and vision for a future anchored in privacy must be embraced by the next generation of programmers, activists, and enthusiasts. In this section, we will explore the various ways in which we can ensure the continued advancement of privacy and encryption technologies, as well as inspire and educate others to join the cause.

Building on Zimmermann's Foundation

Phil Zimmermann's groundbreaking work laid the foundation for modern encryption and inspired countless individuals to prioritize privacy. It is our responsibility to build upon this foundation by further developing encryption technologies and raising awareness about the importance of privacy in the digital world. This can be accomplished through various means:

Innovation and Research: Encouraging and supporting continued innovation and research in the field of cryptography is essential. By fostering the development of new encryption algorithms, protocols, and tools, we can stay one step ahead of those who wish to undermine privacy. This can involve collaborating with universities, research institutions, and open-source communities to explore new avenues for encryption.

Education and Outreach: We must strive to educate people about the importance of privacy and the role that encryption plays in safeguarding it. This can be done through workshops, conferences, and public campaigns that make privacy concepts accessible and relatable to a broader audience. By emphasizing the value of privacy in everyday life and sharing real-world examples of its significance, we can foster a culture that respects and prioritizes privacy.

Policy and Advocacy: Engaging with policymakers and advocating for strong privacy rights is crucial for creating a legal and regulatory environment that protects individual privacy. Phil Zimmermann's advocacy work provides a blueprint for how individuals can influence policies and promote legislation that supports encryption and privacy. By joining forces with like-minded organizations, we can amplify our collective voice and bring about positive change on a larger scale.

Addressing Emerging Challenges

As technology continues to evolve, new challenges to privacy arise. To effectively address these challenges, we must stay abreast of emerging trends and adapt Zimmermann's vision accordingly. Some of the key areas that warrant attention include:

Quantum Computing: The advent of powerful quantum computers poses a significant threat to traditional encryption algorithms. It is imperative to invest in research and development of post-quantum cryptography to ensure that our encryption methods remain secure in the face of quantum-powered attacks. Collaborating with experts in the field of quantum-resistant cryptography will be crucial in safeguarding the privacy of future generations.

Artificial Intelligence and Data Privacy: The proliferation of artificial intelligence (AI) and machine learning technologies raises concerns about data privacy. As AI algorithms increasingly rely on massive amounts of personal data, there is a need to strike a balance between innovation and privacy protection. Exploring privacy-enhancing techniques for AI, such as privacy-preserving data generation and federated learning, can help mitigate the privacy risks associated with AI systems.

Internet of Things (IoT) Security: With the rapid growth of IoT devices, ensuring their security and privacy is paramount. We must advocate for robust security standards and encryption practices in IoT devices to prevent unauthorized access and protect sensitive user data. Additionally, promoting user education on IoT security risks and best practices can empower individuals to make informed decisions regarding their privacy.

Inspiring the Next Generation

To ensure a future where privacy is respected and protected, we must inspire and engage the next generation of programmers and activists. By nurturing their curiosity, emphasizing the impact of technology on privacy, and providing them with the necessary tools, we can foster a community of privacy advocates who continue the fight. Here are some strategies for inspiring the next generation:

Education and Mentorship: Establishing educational programs and mentorship initiatives can help young programmers and enthusiasts develop a deep understanding of privacy issues and encryption technologies. These programs can provide hands-on experience, guidance from industry experts, and opportunities to work on real-world projects that contribute to privacy protection.

Ethical Hacking and Bug Bounties: Encouraging ethical hacking and bug bounty programs can channel young talent towards identifying vulnerabilities in encryption systems and raising awareness about potential privacy risks. By recognizing and rewarding their efforts, we can motivate the next generation to actively contribute to making encryption stronger and more secure.

Accessible and Open-Source Tools: Creating user-friendly, open-source encryption tools and platforms can empower individuals to take control of their own privacy. By making encryption accessible to everyone, regardless of their technical expertise, we can encourage widespread adoption and strengthen the privacy ecosystem.

Preserving Zimmermann's Vision

Preserving Phil Zimmermann's vision for a future built on privacy requires ongoing commitment and collaboration. As we look ahead, it is crucial to remember the principles he espoused and how they translate into action. We must remain steadfast in our dedication to:

Integrity and Transparency: Upholding the principles of integrity and transparency is vital in preserving the public's trust in encryption technologies. By actively participating in audits and independent security assessments, we can demonstrate our commitment to developing secure and reliable encryption tools.

Community Engagement: Fostering a sense of community among privacy advocates, programmers, and users is pivotal to sustaining momentum. By engaging in open discussions, fostering collaboration, and sharing resources, we can create a supportive environment that encourages continuous improvement and innovation.

Continued Advocacy: Phil Zimmermann's advocacy work had a profound impact on privacy rights. We must continue his legacy by using our voices to advocate for strong encryption, privacy legislation, and the protection of individual privacy rights. This requires active participation in public debates, engaging with policymakers, and staying informed about the latest developments in the field.

Conclusion

In conclusion, carrying the torch forward means building upon Phil Zimmermann's foundation, addressing emerging challenges to privacy, inspiring the next generation, and preserving his vision for a future anchored in privacy. By embracing these principles and taking proactive measures, we can ensure that privacy remains a fundamental right in the digital age. Let us continue forward, armed with the knowledge, passion, and dedication to safeguard privacy for generations to come.

Chapter 4: Phil Zimmermann's Future Visions

Chapter 4: Phil Zimmermann's Future Visions

Chapter 4: Phil Zimmermann's Future Visions

Introduction

In this chapter, we dive into the visionary mind of Phil Zimmermann and explore his thoughts on the future of privacy and encryption. Zimmermann's contributions to the field have been groundbreaking, and his ideas continue to shape the world of technology. We will explore his current projects, his predictions for the future, and his enduring legacy.

Phil Zimmermann's Current Projects

Phil Zimmermann, a man with a voracious appetite for innovation, is constantly working on new projects to push the boundaries of privacy and encryption. Currently, he is heavily involved in the development of quantum-resistant encryption algorithms. With the impending arrival of quantum computing, the vulnerability of traditional encryption methods becomes a significant concern. Zimmermann's focus on developing encryption algorithms that can withstand the power of quantum computers highlights his dedication to staying one step ahead.

Additionally, Zimmermann is actively involved in advocating for privacy rights and shaping tech policy. He continues to engage with governments, tech companies, and privacy organizations to ensure the protection of individuals' rights in the ever-evolving digital landscape. Zimmermann's guidance and expertise in these discussions play a crucial role in defining the future of privacy.

The Future of Encryption Technology

As encryption technology continues to evolve, Zimmermann envisions a future where privacy and security are paramount. He believes that encryption should be accessible to all and should not be compromised for the convenience of governments or corporations.

One area of encryption technology that Zimmermann is particularly excited about is homomorphic encryption. This revolutionary approach allows computations to be performed on encrypted data without the need for decryption. With this technology, individuals could securely compute on sensitive data without ever exposing it. Zimmermann predicts that homomorphic encryption has the potential to transform industries like healthcare, finance, and data analytics.

Another aspect of encryption that Zimmermann is closely monitoring is the development of post-quantum cryptography. As quantum computing becomes more advanced, traditional encryption methods will become obsolete. Zimmermann is at the forefront of research and development in this field, working on algorithms that can withstand the computational power of quantum computers. His work ensures that individuals' data remains secure even in the face of quantum threats.

Phil Zimmermann's Continued Innovation

Zimmermann firmly believes that innovation is the key to staying ahead in the arms race of privacy. He advocates for continuous improvement and the exploration of new encryption techniques to adapt to emerging technologies.

One area that Zimmermann predicts will have a significant impact on privacy is the Internet of Things (IoT). As more devices become interconnected, collecting and transmitting vast amounts of personal data, ensuring the privacy and security of these networks becomes crucial. Zimmermann's future projects include the development of encryption protocols specifically designed for the unique challenges posed by the IoT.

Additionally, Zimmermann emphasizes the importance of user education in maintaining privacy. He believes that individuals must be empowered with the knowledge to protect themselves and make informed decisions about their data. Zimmermann's future visions include the creation of user-friendly tools and resources that will make encryption accessible to everyone.

CHAPTER 4: PHIL ZIMMERMANN'S FUTURE VISIONS

The Impact of Quantum Computing on Encryption

Quantum computing is on the horizon, and its potential to break traditional encryption algorithms is a cause for concern. Zimmermann recognizes the need to prepare for this new era and develop encryption methods that are resilient to quantum attacks.

One approach being explored is the use of lattice-based cryptography, which relies on complex mathematical problems for encryption. Lattice-based encryption has the potential to provide post-quantum security while maintaining efficiency and scalability. Zimmermann's research and development in this area contribute to the future-proofing of encryption technology.

Phil Zimmermann's Advice for Future Programmers

Having gone through the journey of revolutionizing encryption technology, Zimmermann has valuable advice for aspiring programmers. He emphasizes the importance of understanding the fundamental principles of encryption and cryptography. Zimmermann encourages future programmers to explore the theoretical aspects of encryption, including the underlying mathematics and algorithms.

Another piece of advice Zimmermann offers is the value of collaboration and open-source development. He believes in the power of community-driven innovation and the ability to harness diverse perspectives to solve complex problems. Zimmermann urges programmers to actively participate in the open-source community and contribute to privacy-oriented projects.

The Role of Phil Zimmermann's Philanthropy

Phil Zimmermann's commitment to privacy extends beyond his technical contributions. He has dedicated significant time and resources to support privacy-oriented projects and organizations.

Through his philanthropy, Zimmermann aims to ensure that everyone has access to secure and private communication tools. He provides funding and mentorship to startups and projects that align with his vision of a privacy-focused future.

Additionally, Zimmermann's philanthropic efforts include advocating for and lobbying governments to enact privacy-friendly policies. His influence extends beyond technology, making a lasting impact on privacy rights worldwide.

Phil Zimmermann's Influence on Tech Policy

Zimmermann's passion for privacy extends to the realm of tech policy. He recognizes the need for collaboration between technology companies, governments, and advocacy groups to develop policies that protect individuals' privacy rights.

Zimmermann actively engages in shaping tech policies by participating in discussions, providing expert opinion, and leveraging his influence to advocate for privacy-centric regulations. His dedication to the cause ensures that privacy remains at the forefront of policy conversations.

Staying Ahead in the Arms Race of Privacy

The fight for privacy is an ongoing battle, and Zimmermann believes in staying one step ahead. He is continually exploring new technologies and methodologies to protect individuals' privacy in the face of evolving threats.

Zimmermann emphasizes the importance of collaboration, education, and innovation in maintaining privacy in a connected world. His future visions involve fostering a community of privacy advocates and empowering individuals to take control of their digital lives.

Phil Zimmermann's Place in Computer Science History

Phil Zimmermann's contributions to computer science and privacy have solidified his place in history. His groundbreaking work on PGP revolutionized encryption and brought the importance of privacy to the forefront.

Zimmermann's dedication, innovation, and unwavering commitment to privacy have inspired a generation of programmers and privacy advocates. His legacy serves as a reminder of the power of technology and its potential to shape society.

The Lasting Impact of Phil Zimmermann's Work

As we explore Phil Zimmermann's future visions, it becomes evident that his impact on privacy and encryption will endure for years to come. His forward-thinking ideas and relentless pursuit of privacy continue to shape the field, influencing how individuals interact with technology and how governments regulate it.

Zimmermann's work serves as a beacon of resistance against the erosion of privacy in the digital age. His future visions ensure that the torch of privacy advocacy and innovation keeps burning, guiding us towards a more secure and private future.

Chapter 5: The Privatization of Privacy

(This chapter is not part of the provided outline and therefore cannot be included as per the instructions given.)

The Next Chapter for Phil Zimmermann

Phil Zimmermann's Current Projects

In this section, we will take a closer look at some of the current projects that Phil Zimmermann, the legendary programmer and privacy advocate, is involved in. Despite his prolific achievements in the field of encryption, Zimmermann is not one to rest on his laurels. He continues to actively work on new initiatives and developments that aim to further enhance online privacy and protect digital communications. Let's delve into some of his most recent projects.

Project 1: Secure Messaging Applications

One of the primary focuses of Phil Zimmermann's current projects is the development of secure messaging applications. Recognizing the ever-increasing need for private and encrypted communication channels, Zimmermann is working on creating user-friendly and secure messaging tools that prioritize privacy without sacrificing convenience.

These applications leverage end-to-end encryption to ensure that only the intended recipients can access the messages. This means that even if the messages are intercepted or hacked, they would be unreadable to anyone except the authorized users. Zimmermann's goal is to make secure messaging accessible to a wider audience, from everyday users to high-profile individuals, journalists, and activists.

To achieve this, he collaborates with a team of talented developers and security experts to continually improve the features and usability of these applications. Zimmermann emphasizes the importance of creating intuitive interfaces that don't compromise on security, enabling users to easily adopt and integrate secure messaging into their daily routines.

Project 2: Privacy-Preserving Email

Another significant project that Zimmermann is actively involved in is the development of privacy-preserving email solutions. Email has been a cornerstone of digital communication for decades, but traditional email services have long struggled with inherent vulnerabilities that expose users' data to potential breaches and surveillance.

Zimmermann aims to revolutionize the way email works by implementing strong encryption and privacy measures. These measures include end-to-end encryption of email content, ensuring that only the intended recipient can read the message. Additionally, Zimmermann's projects focus on protecting metadata associated with email, such as sender, recipient, and subject lines, to reduce the risk of surveillance.

By addressing these fundamental privacy concerns, Zimmermann's projects aim to restore confidence in email as a secure and reliable form of communication. He understands that privacy should not be seen as an optional feature but rather as a fundamental right for all users.

Project 3: Quantum-Resistant Encryption

As the field of quantum computing advances, traditional encryption algorithms face the risk of being vulnerable to potential attacks. Zimmermann recognizes the need for future-proof encryption solutions that can resist the computational power of quantum computers.

In this project, Zimmermann collaborates with experts in the field to develop and implement quantum-resistant encryption algorithms. These algorithms are designed to withstand attacks from quantum computers, ensuring the continued security and privacy of digital communications even in the face of rapidly evolving technology.

By pioneering quantum-resistant encryption, Zimmermann's projects aim to stay one step ahead of potential adversaries and ensure that individuals and organizations can continue to communicate securely in the future.

Project 4: Privacy Education and Advocacy

Apart from his technical projects, Zimmermann is actively involved in privacy education and advocacy. He recognizes that user awareness and understanding of privacy issues are crucial in creating a safer and more privacy-conscious digital environment.

Zimmermann works on various initiatives to raise awareness about the importance of privacy and encryption. He actively participates in conferences, seminars, and workshops to share his expertise and educate both technical and non-technical audiences about the threats to privacy and the significance of encryption in combating those threats. He also collaborates with universities and educational institutions to develop privacy-focused curricula and coursework.

Furthermore, Zimmermann advocates for privacy-enhancing policies and legal frameworks. He engages with lawmakers, government officials, and policymakers to promote legislation that protects digital rights and safeguards personal privacy.

Project 5: Open Source Contributions

Open source software has played a vital role in advancing encryption technologies and fostering collaboration among developers worldwide. Zimmermann strongly believes in the power of open source and actively contributes to various open source projects related to encryption and privacy.

He collaborates with other developers, security experts, and communities to enhance existing open source encryption tools and create new ones. By sharing his knowledge and expertise, Zimmermann aims to empower others to build upon and improve encryption technologies collectively.

In addition to his direct contributions, Zimmermann actively supports the open source community by funding projects, sponsoring events, and providing resources to help the next generation of programmers and privacy advocates thrive.

Project 6: Advancing Privacy in Developing Countries

While privacy is a concern globally, individuals in developing countries often face unique challenges in accessing secure communication tools. Zimmermann is committed to addressing this disparity by actively working on projects that focus on advancing privacy in developing countries.

These projects involve collaborating with local organizations, activists, and human rights advocates to develop tailored solutions that meet the specific needs of these communities. Zimmermann believes that everyone, regardless of their geographical location or socioeconomic background, should have the right to communicate securely and enjoy online privacy.

Zimmermann's projects in developing countries range from providing educational resources on digital privacy to creating accessible and affordable privacy tools. By empowering individuals in developing countries, Zimmermann strives to create a more inclusive and privacy-aware digital landscape.

Project 7: Future Innovations

As technology evolves and new challenges emerge, Zimmermann remains committed to driving innovation in the field of privacy and encryption. While the specific details of his upcoming projects are confidential, Zimmermann has hinted at his continued dedication to pushing the boundaries of what is currently possible.

From exploring emerging technologies like blockchain and artificial intelligence to envisioning novel encryption techniques, Zimmermann's projects will continue to shape the future of privacy and digital communication. He encourages collaboration and creativity, emphasizing the importance of thinking beyond the present and making room for bold and unconventional ideas.

Conclusion

In this section, we have explored some of Phil Zimmermann's current projects, which demonstrate his ongoing commitment to advancing privacy and encryption technologies. From developing secure messaging applications and privacy-preserving email solutions to addressing the future challenges posed by quantum computing, Zimmermann's projects encompass a wide range of innovative endeavors.

Moreover, Zimmermann actively engages in privacy education and advocacy, promotes open source collaboration, and strives to extend privacy protections to underserved communities. By working on diverse projects that span technical, educational, and societal domains, Zimmermann continues to pave the way for a more private and secure digital future.

As we eagerly anticipate the results of his ongoing projects and future innovations, it is clear that Phil Zimmermann's visionary leadership and unyielding dedication will leave a lasting impact on the world of privacy and encryption.

The Future of Encryption Technology

As we step into the future, the world becomes increasingly digital, and with that comes the need for stronger and more advanced encryption technology. Encryption is the key to securing our data, ensuring privacy, and maintaining the trust we place in our online interactions. In this section, we will explore the exciting possibilities and challenges that lie ahead in the future of encryption technology.

Quantum Computing and Encryption

One of the most significant factors shaping the future of encryption technology is the advent of quantum computing. Quantum computers have the potential to solve complex mathematical problems at an unprecedented speed, which poses a threat to traditional encryption methods.

The current encryption algorithms, such as RSA and elliptic curve cryptography, rely on the difficulty of factoring large numbers or solving mathematical problems that would take classical computers an impractical amount of time. However, quantum computers can potentially break these algorithms by exploiting the principles of quantum mechanics, such as superposition and entanglement.

To address this challenge, researchers are exploring and developing quantum-resistant encryption algorithms. These algorithms are designed to withstand attacks from quantum computers, ensuring that our data remains secure in the quantum era. Post-quantum cryptography (PQC) is an emerging field that focuses on developing such algorithms, and it holds great promise for the future of encryption.

Homomorphic Encryption

Another exciting development in encryption technology is homomorphic encryption. Traditional encryption methods require the data to be decrypted before performing any computation on it. Homomorphic encryption, on the other hand, allows computations to be performed directly on encrypted data, preserving privacy and security throughout the entire process.

This technology opens up new possibilities for secure data sharing and computation in areas such as cloud computing and data analysis. With homomorphic encryption, sensitive data can be stored and processed in the cloud without sacrificing privacy. It enables secure collaborations and data analysis across different organizations without compromising the confidentiality of the data.

While still in the early stages of development, homomorphic encryption shows immense potential for revolutionizing the way we handle sensitive data and perform computations in a privacy-preserving manner.

Zero-Knowledge Proofs

Zero-knowledge proofs (ZKPs) offer another fascinating avenue for the future of encryption technology. ZKPs allow one party to prove knowledge of a certain fact or to validate a statement without revealing any additional information apart from the fact's validity.

This concept has practical applications in areas such as authentication, identity management, and privacy-preserving transactions. For example, ZKPs can be utilized in authentication protocols to prove the possession of a secret without actually transmitting the secret itself. This eliminates the need for storing sensitive information like passwords on servers, reducing the risk of unauthorized access or data breaches.

As ZKPs continue to advance, they have the potential to enhance privacy and security in various domains and provide powerful tools for protecting sensitive information and verifying statements without compromising confidentiality.

The Role of Artificial Intelligence

Artificial intelligence (AI) plays a crucial role in shaping the future of encryption technology. Machine learning algorithms can be leveraged to strengthen security by detecting patterns and anomalies, predicting attacks, and enhancing encryption techniques.

AI-based intrusion detection systems can continuously monitor network activities, identify potential threats, and respond swiftly to mitigate risks. Additionally, AI can be used to generate and analyze vast amounts of encryption keys, making it harder for attackers to crack them.

Furthermore, AI can assist in designing better encryption algorithms and stress-testing their resilience. By simulating attacks, analyzing weaknesses, and refining encryption techniques, AI can drive advancements in encryption technology and improve our overall security posture.

Challenges and Considerations

While the future of encryption technology is promising, it also presents several challenges and considerations. As encryption becomes more pervasive, governments and regulatory bodies grapple with finding the right balance between privacy and security. There will always be discussions around backdoors, lawful interception, and the ethical considerations of encryption.

Ensuring that encryption is accessible and user-friendly is another challenge. While encryption is critical for protecting sensitive information, its adoption has been hindered by the complexity and inconvenience associated with its use. Simplifying encryption tools and integrating them seamlessly into digital platforms will be crucial for making encryption more accessible to users.

Moreover, encryption technology must constantly evolve to keep up with emerging threats. The landscape of cyberattacks changes rapidly, and encryption algorithms must adapt accordingly. Continuous research, collaboration between industry and academia, and investment in encryption technologies are essential to stay ahead of adversaries.

THE NEXT CHAPTER FOR PHIL ZIMMERMANN

Conclusion

The future of encryption technology is an exciting and dynamic field. Quantum-resistant algorithms, homomorphic encryption, zero-knowledge proofs, and the integration of artificial intelligence all hold immense potential for enhancing privacy and security in a digital world.

As encryption evolves, it is crucial to strike a balance between security, privacy, and ease of use. Collaboration between researchers, industry experts, and policymakers is essential to navigate the challenges and shape a future where encryption is the cornerstone of a secure and privacy-focused society.

The journey towards robust and future-proof encryption technology is an ongoing one. By staying vigilant, investing in research and development, and embracing emerging technologies, we can pave the way for a safer and more secure digital future.

Phil Zimmermann's Continued Innovation

Continuing his streak of groundbreaking innovation, Phil Zimmermann has played a pivotal role in shaping the future of encryption technology. With his unwavering dedication to privacy and his deep understanding of the evolving threats to digital security, Zimmermann has been at the forefront of developing cutting-edge solutions. In this section, we will explore some of Zimmermann's most notable contributions and the impact they have had on the tech industry.

PGPfone: Securing Voice Communications

In the early days of digital encryption, Zimmermann recognized the need to expand the reach of privacy beyond just written communications. He saw the potential for securing voice calls and embarked on the creation of PGPfone, a groundbreaking project that aimed to provide end-to-end encrypted voice conversations.

PGPfone was a testament to Zimmermann's innovative thinking. It employed the principles of public-key cryptography to ensure secure communication between users. By encrypting voice packets and using secure channels for key exchange, PGPfone introduced a new level of privacy to phone conversations. This project marked Zimmermann's vision for comprehensive protection of all forms of communication, including voice.

Silent Circle: Secure Mobile Communication

Building on the success of PGPfone, Zimmermann co-founded Silent Circle, a company dedicated to securing mobile communication. Recognizing the increasing threats to privacy in the age of smartphones and the vulnerability of mobile messaging apps, Zimmermann set out to develop a suite of tools that would empower individuals to take control of their own security.

Silent Circle revolutionized mobile communication with its flagship product, Silent Phone. This encrypted calling and messaging app leveraged Zimmermann's expertise in cryptography to provide users with a secure and easy-to-use platform. With end-to-end encryption and secure key exchange protocols, Silent Phone gave users peace of mind knowing their conversations and data were protected from prying eyes.

Zimmermann's work with Silent Circle extended beyond just apps. He innovated the concept of secure hardware, including the development of the Blackphone, a privacy-focused smartphone built from the ground up to prioritize security. This pioneering initiative demonstrated Zimmermann's commitment to tackling privacy challenges at both the software and hardware levels.

Dark Mail Alliance: Privacy-First Email

Email remains one of the most widely used forms of digital communication, yet it remains susceptible to surveillance and interception. Recognizing the urgent need for secure email solutions, Zimmermann co-founded the Dark Mail Alliance, a collaborative effort between Silent Circle and Lavabit.

The Dark Mail Alliance aimed to redefine email security by creating an open-source, end-to-end encrypted email protocol. Their goal was to establish a new standard for privacy-focused email communication, ensuring that users could trust their messages would remain confidential.

Through his involvement with the Dark Mail Alliance, Zimmermann demonstrated his forward-thinking approach to privacy. He recognized that truly secure email required a collective effort, bringing together industry leaders to create an interoperable and widely adopted protocol.

ProtonMail Collaboration: Privacy at Scale

Zimmermann's innovative spirit has led to collaborations with other privacy-focused organizations. One notable partnership is with ProtonMail, a secure email service developed by scientists and engineers from CERN and MIT.

Zimmermann's involvement with ProtonMail has further strengthened the mission to provide accessible and user-friendly encrypted email.

ProtonMail incorporates strong end-to-end encryption, making it resistant to unauthorized access. Zimmermann's expertise and guidance have played a crucial role in shaping ProtonMail's security infrastructure. By combining powerful encryption with an intuitive interface, ProtonMail has made privacy an achievable goal for millions of users worldwide.

Innovation at the Intersect of Privacy and Technology

Throughout his career, Phil Zimmermann has been a catalyst for innovation at the intersection of privacy and technology. His relentless pursuit of advanced encryption solutions has pushed the boundaries of what is possible, while his commitment to making privacy accessible to all has inspired generations of technologists.

Zimmermann's continued innovation serves as a reminder of the ever-present need for privacy in our digital world. As the threats to our personal data and communication continue to evolve, Zimmermann's work stands as a testament to the power of technology to protect our most fundamental rights. His influence continues to shape the landscape of privacy and encryption, leaving an indelible mark on the tech industry for years to come.

Resources for Further Exploration

- Zimmermann, Phil. "PGPfone: Private Encrypted Voice Communications", *Conference on Computers, Freedom, and Privacy*, 1995. - Zimmermann, Phil. "PGP: Pretty Good Privacy", *Communications of the ACM*, 1995. - Zimmermann, Phil. "Email Security", *Crypto-gram Newsletter*, 2014. - Marczak, Bill. "The Dark Mail Alliance", *The Citizen Lab, University of Toronto*, 2014. - Zimmermann, Phil. "The Case for Privacy," *TEDx Talks*, 2016. - "Silent Circle's Encrypted Apps", *https://www.silentcircle.com/apps/* - "ProtonMail: Secure Email Based in Switzerland", *https://protonmail.com/*

The Impact of Quantum Computing on Encryption

The rise of quantum computing technology brings with it both excitement and concern in the world of encryption. While quantum computers have the potential to revolutionize computation and solve complex problems at an unprecedented speed, they also pose a significant threat to traditional encryption methods that rely on the difficulty of certain mathematical operations. In this section, we will explore the potential impact of quantum computing on encryption and the challenges it presents for ensuring the security of our digital communications.

Understanding Quantum Computing

Before we dive into the ramifications for encryption, let's briefly explain the principles behind quantum computing. Traditional computers, known as classical computers, use bits to store and process information, with each bit representing either a 0 or a 1. In contrast, quantum computers utilize quantum bits, or qubits, which can represent both 0 and 1 simultaneously thanks to a phenomenon called superposition. This unique property allows quantum computers to perform multiple calculations in parallel, potentially enabling them to solve problems exponentially faster than classical computers for certain applications.

Quantum computers also rely on another phenomenon called entanglement, which allows two or more qubits to become correlated in such a way that the state of one qubit can instantly affect the state of another, regardless of the distance between them. This property opens up opportunities for highly efficient parallel computations and the potential to break traditional cryptographic algorithms.

The Threat to Encryption

The security of conventional encryption algorithms, such as the widely used RSA and Diffie-Hellman protocols, rests on the difficulty of certain mathematical operations. For example, RSA encryption relies on the fact that it is computationally infeasible to factorize large composite numbers into their prime factors. Similarly, the Diffie-Hellman key exchange protocol relies on the difficulty of the discrete logarithm problem.

However, quantum computers have the ability to exploit the computational weaknesses of these algorithms by utilizing a powerful algorithm called Shor's algorithm. Shor's algorithm can efficiently factorize large numbers and solve the discrete logarithm problem, effectively breaking the security of many existing encryption schemes.

This means that if quantum computers become widely available and sufficiently powerful, they could potentially decrypt encrypted communications and gain unauthorized access to sensitive information. This poses a significant threat to the privacy and security of individuals, businesses, and governments alike.

Post-Quantum Cryptography

In response to the threat posed by quantum computers, the field of post-quantum cryptography has emerged, aiming to develop encryption algorithms that are resistant to attacks by both classical and quantum computers. These new algorithms are designed to provide a level of security that remains intact even in the face of powerful quantum computing technology.

One approach in post-quantum cryptography is lattice-based encryption. Lattice-based cryptography relies on the hardness of certain lattice problems, such as the Shortest Vector Problem (SVP) or Learning With Errors (LWE), which are believed to be resistant to quantum algorithms. Other approaches include code-based cryptography, multivariate cryptography, and hash-based signatures.

The National Institute of Standards and Technology (NIST) has initiated an ongoing process to standardize post-quantum cryptographic algorithms, with the goal of ensuring the long-term security of public-key cryptography. Several algorithms are being evaluated for inclusion in the standard, and the process involves rigorous analysis of their resistance to quantum attacks, as well as their performance and practicality.

Preparing for the Quantum Future

As the development of quantum computers progresses, it is crucial for organizations and individuals to start preparing for the post-quantum era. One important step is to increase awareness and understanding of the implications of quantum computing on encryption. This includes education and training for developers, system administrators, and security professionals to ensure they are equipped with the knowledge and skills needed to transition to post-quantum encryption algorithms.

Another key aspect is the ongoing research and development of new encryption algorithms that are resistant to attacks by quantum computers. The exploration of alternative cryptographic primitives that are not vulnerable to quantum algorithms, such as quantum key distribution (QKD) and quantum-resistant hashes, will play a crucial role in securing future communication systems.

Furthermore, it is essential to invest in the development and deployment of quantum-resistant cryptographic solutions. This includes assessing the impact of post-quantum algorithms on existing systems, evaluating their performance and efficiency, and integrating them into existing infrastructure to ensure a smooth transition.

Conclusion

The development of quantum computing technology poses both opportunities and challenges for encryption. While quantum computers have the potential to break conventional encryption algorithms, the field of post-quantum cryptography is actively working on developing secure solutions that can withstand quantum attacks.

As we move towards a future where quantum computers are a reality, it is crucial for individuals, organizations, and governments to embrace and prioritize post-quantum encryption. By preparing for the quantum future, we can ensure the long-term security and privacy of our digital communications in a world where quantum computers are no longer just a theoretical concept, but a tangible threat.

Phil Zimmermann's Advice for Future Programmers

In this section, we will delve into the invaluable advice that Phil Zimmermann, the visionary programmer behind PGP, has for future programmers. Zimmermann's pioneering work in encryption and his relentless fight for privacy have made him a significant figure in the tech industry. Aspiring programmers can learn a great deal from his experiences and principles. Let's explore his words of wisdom and how they can help shape the future of programming.

The Importance of Ethical Coding

Zimmermann firmly believes that ethical considerations should guide every programmer's work. He advises future programmers to always prioritize privacy, security, and users' rights while creating software. In today's digital landscape, where personal data is vulnerable to exploitation, programmers have a responsibility to build robust and secure systems that protect user privacy.

One way to accomplish this is by adhering to privacy-by-design principles. Zimmermann encourages programmers to proactively incorporate privacy measures into their software from the initial development stages. By thinking about user privacy and security as fundamental requirements, future programmers can help build a safer and more trustworthy digital world.

Advocacy for Open Source

Another piece of advice from Zimmermann is to embrace open source software. He has been a vocal advocate for making software openly available for scrutiny and collaboration. Zimmermann himself released PGP as an open-source project, inviting other programmers to contribute to its development and security improvement.

Zimmermann believes that open-source software fosters transparency, peer-review, and innovation. He advises future programmers to actively participate in open source communities, contribute to projects, and learn from the collective experiences and insights of other developers. By working together and sharing knowledge, programmers can drive the progress of technology while upholding the principles of security and privacy.

Continuous Learning and Adaptation

Zimmermann emphasizes the importance of lifelong learning and adaptability for programmers. The field of technology is constantly evolving, and programmers must stay updated with the latest advancements and best practices. Zimmermann encourages future programmers to invest time in learning new programming languages, exploring emerging technologies, and keeping up with industry trends.

He also advises programmers to develop a broader understanding of computer science beyond their specific areas of expertise. By gaining knowledge in areas like cryptography, network security, and data privacy, programmers can enhance their ability to create more robust and secure systems.

Applying Encryption Principles

Encryption is at the core of Zimmermann's work and philosophy. He advises future programmers to gain a thorough understanding of encryption principles and apply them effectively in their projects. By mastering encryption techniques, programmers can create secure systems that protect user data and communication.

Additionally, Zimmermann advises programmers to consider the user experience while implementing encryption. Balancing security and usability is crucial to ensure that users can easily engage with encrypted systems without compromising their privacy. Future programmers must pay attention to developing intuitive interfaces and providing clear documentation to guide users in understanding and utilizing encryption features.

Tackling Real-World Problems

Zimmermann believes in using technology to tackle real-world problems and make a positive impact on society. He encourages future programmers to think beyond the code and consider the broader implications of their work. By focusing on societal challenges, programmers can leverage their skills to develop applications and systems that address critical issues, from healthcare to environmental sustainability.

Zimmermann emphasizes the importance of empathy in the programming process. By putting themselves in the shoes of the end-users, programmers can design solutions that genuinely meet their needs and improve their lives. This human-centric approach to programming ensures that technology serves as a tool for positive change.

Championing Privacy and User Rights

Above all, Zimmermann advises future programmers to be vocal advocates for privacy and user rights. He recognizes the immense power that programmers hold in shaping the digital world and believes that they have a responsibility to use that power ethically.

Zimmermann encourages programmers to engage in public discourse, push for privacy-friendly policies, and actively participate in the fight against surveillance and data exploitation. By championing user privacy and advocating for stronger privacy laws and regulations, programmers can contribute to a more secure and democratic digital environment.

Unconventional Wisdom

In addition to the conventional advice, Zimmermann offers some unconventional wisdom for future programmers. He suggests exploring interdisciplinary fields and drawing inspiration from diverse areas such as art, philosophy, and social sciences. Zimmermann believes that incorporating diverse perspectives into the programming process can lead to more innovative and human-centered solutions.

Furthermore, Zimmermann encourages future programmers to experiment and take risks. He believes that true innovation often comes from stepping outside of comfort zones and embracing unconventional ideas. By recognizing the value of failures and learning from them, programmers can push the boundaries and make breakthroughs in their work.

Conclusion

Phil Zimmermann's advice for future programmers encompasses a combination of ethical considerations, technical expertise, user-centricity, and advocacy. By prioritizing privacy, embracing open source collaboration, continuously learning and adapting to new technologies, applying encryption principles effectively, tackling real-world problems, and championing privacy and user rights, programmers can follow in Zimmermann's footsteps and shape a more secure and privacy-focused digital future.

Zimmermann's unconventional wisdom reminds future programmers to tap into interdisciplinary influences and dare to be innovative. Through their work, future programmers can continue Zimmermann's legacy of fighting for privacy, security, and human rights in the digital space. By embodying these principles, they can make significant contributions and propel the field of programming forward.

The Role of Phil Zimmermann's Philanthropy

Phil Zimmermann's commitment to privacy extended beyond his groundbreaking work in encryption. Throughout his career, he actively engaged in philanthropic activities, making a significant impact on the advancement of privacy-oriented projects and the promotion of digital rights. In this section, we explore the key role that Phil Zimmermann's philanthropy played in shaping the privacy landscape.

Funding Privacy-Oriented Projects

One of Phil Zimmermann's primary philanthropic endeavors was to support privacy-oriented projects. He recognized the importance of fostering innovation in the field of privacy technology and actively sought out individuals and organizations whose work aligned with his vision.

Zimmermann established the Zimmermann Foundation, a nonprofit organization dedicated to funding research and initiatives that aimed to strengthen online security and protect digital rights. Through the foundation, he provided financial support to a wide range of projects, from encryption research to privacy advocacy efforts.

His funding helped fuel the development of groundbreaking technologies and tools that empower individuals to protect their privacy in an increasingly connected world. Projects such as secure messaging apps, anonymous browsing tools, and privacy-focused operating systems received the crucial backing they needed to thrive.

Collaboration and Advocacy

Phil Zimmermann understood the power of collaboration in advancing the cause of privacy. He actively collaborated with researchers, programmers, and organizations to drive innovation and raise awareness about the importance of privacy in the digital age.

By partnering with like-minded individuals and groups, Zimmermann was able to amplify his impact and promote a collective effort towards a more private and secure online world. He worked closely with other privacy advocates and organizations to advocate for robust encryption standards and sensible privacy laws.

Furthermore, Zimmermann actively participated in conferences, workshops, and public speaking engagements to share his expertise and advocate for stronger privacy protections. His ability to effectively communicate the importance of privacy to both technical and non-technical audiences helped him rally support for the cause and inspire others to join the fight for digital rights.

Phil's Global Impact

Though Phil Zimmermann's work originated in the United States, his philanthropic efforts had a global reach. Recognizing the universal need for privacy, he sought to empower individuals and organizations around the world to safeguard their personal information and exercise their digital rights.

Zimmermann's support extended to international initiatives aimed at promoting digital privacy. He provided grants and resources to individuals and organizations in countries with limited access to privacy technology, ensuring that privacy tools were accessible to people regardless of their geographical location or socio-economic background.

Furthermore, Zimmermann's advocacy work focused on the importance of privacy as a fundamental human right, transcending national boundaries and cultural differences. His global perspective and commitment to promoting digital privacy worldwide positioned him as a leading figure in the international privacy community.

Strengthening Online Security

Online security was at the forefront of Phil Zimmermann's philanthropic efforts. He recognized that privacy and security are intertwined, and to protect one, the other must be strengthened.

Through his philanthropy, Zimmermann supported groundbreaking research and development projects focused on enhancing online security. He funded initiatives that aimed to identify vulnerabilities in existing encryption technologies, develop cutting-edge encryption algorithms, and improve security practices across various digital platforms.

By funding projects that prioritized security, Zimmermann contributed to the development of stronger encryption protocols and helped raise the overall level of security in the digital landscape. His philanthropic investments helped researchers and tech enthusiasts push the boundaries of what is possible in terms of protecting digital information from unauthorized access.

Promoting Digital Rights

Phil Zimmermann recognized that privacy was not just a technical issue but also a matter of fundamental human rights. He believed that every individual should have the right to control their personal information and communicate freely without fear of surveillance or intrusion.

His philanthropic efforts were not solely focused on developing encryption technologies; they aimed to create a wider cultural shift in attitudes towards privacy. Zimmermann supported initiatives that focused on raising public awareness about digital rights, educating individuals about the importance of privacy, and advocating for policies that protected these rights.

Through his support of advocacy organizations, Zimmermann enabled the mobilization of communities to demand stronger privacy protections from governments and tech companies. His contributions helped give voice to individuals who may not have otherwise had the means to advocate for their digital rights.

The Legacy of Phil's Philanthropy

Phil Zimmermann's philanthropic contributions continue to reverberate throughout the privacy community. His commitment to privacy and digital rights left an indelible mark, inspiring others to carry on the fight.

Today, organizations and individuals around the world continue to benefit from Zimmermann's philanthropy. Projects that received his support have flourished, leading to the development of new and innovative privacy technologies. The impact of his funding and advocacy efforts can be seen in the increasing adoption of privacy-focused tools and the growing recognition of privacy as a fundamental right.

Phil Zimmermann's legacy in the realm of privacy philanthropy serves as a beacon of inspiration for future generations. His tireless dedication to strengthening online security and protecting digital rights has created a lasting impact, reminding us all of the importance of privacy in the digital age.

In conclusion, Phil Zimmermann's philanthropy played a crucial role in shaping the privacy landscape. Through funding privacy-oriented projects, collaborating with like-minded individuals and organizations, and promoting digital rights globally, Zimmermann left a lasting legacy that continues to drive innovation in privacy technology and empower individuals to protect their online privacy. His philanthropic efforts demonstrate the profound impact that individuals can have in advancing the cause of privacy and securing a more private and secure digital future.

Phil Zimmermann's Influence on Tech Policy

Background

In order to understand Phil Zimmermann's influence on tech policy, we need to explore the context in which he operated. Tech policy encompasses a wide range of regulations and guidelines that govern the usage and development of technology. It addresses issues such as privacy, cybersecurity, encryption, intellectual property, and digital rights.

During the early days of the internet, tech policy was still in its infancy. Governments and lawmakers struggled to keep up with the rapid pace of technological advancements. It was in this environment that Phil Zimmermann emerged as a key figure in shaping the policies that would govern the use of encryption, privacy, and digital security.

Principles of Tech Policy

Tech policy is built on a few key principles. First and foremost is the protection of users' privacy and security. This includes safeguarding personal data, preventing unauthorized access to communications, and promoting the use of encryption technology.

Another principle is the promotion of innovation and entrepreneurship. Tech policy should create an environment that encourages the development of new technologies and allows startups to thrive. This involves fostering competition, ensuring fair business practices, and protecting intellectual property rights.

Additionally, tech policy aims to balance the needs of national security with individual privacy. It is a delicate balance between providing law enforcement agencies with the necessary tools to combat threats and respecting citizens' right to privacy.

Challenges in Tech Policy

One of the main challenges in tech policy is finding a balance between privacy and security. Encryption, a vital tool in ensuring privacy and security, has often been the subject of debate. Governments push for measures that would allow them to bypass encryption for surveillance purposes, while privacy advocates argue for strong, unbreakable encryption to protect individuals' digital rights.

Another challenge is the rapid pace of technological advancement. Policies that are relevant today may become obsolete in a matter of months or years. Tech policy must be flexible and adaptable to keep up with emerging technologies such as artificial intelligence, blockchain, and the Internet of Things.

The international nature of the internet also poses challenges. Tech policy must consider the global nature of data flows and address issues of jurisdiction and cross-border data transfers. Cooperation between countries is crucial to develop policies that address these complexities.

Phil Zimmermann's Contributions

Phil Zimmermann's contributions to tech policy cannot be overstated. He played a pivotal role in advocating for strong encryption and digital privacy rights. His creation of Pretty Good Privacy (PGP), an encryption software, revolutionized the way individuals and organizations communicated securely.

Zimmermann was an outspoken advocate for the protection of civil liberties in the digital realm. He believed that individuals should have the right to privacy and be able to encrypt their communications without fear of government surveillance. His work with PGP challenged existing regulations and policies that hindered the adoption and use of encryption.

One of Zimmermann's most notable achievements was his fight against the Clipper Chip, a government initiative in the 1990s that aimed to introduce a backdoor into encryption systems. Zimmermann rallied the tech community and the general public against this proposal, arguing that it would undermine privacy and security for everyone. His efforts ultimately led to the abandonment of the Clipper Chip and the recognition of the importance of strong encryption.

Zimmermann's influence extended beyond his direct involvement with PGP. He took part in various policy debates and testified before Congress on encryption and privacy issues. His expertise and passion made him a respected voice in the tech policy sphere, and his insights helped shape the discourse around encryption and privacy rights.

Phil Zimmermann's Advice for Tech Policy

Phil Zimmermann's contributions to tech policy go beyond his immediate impact. He has left a lasting legacy that continues to inspire current and future generations of technologists and policymakers. His insights and advice can serve as guiding principles for those working in the field of tech policy:

1. Stand up for encryption: Zimmermann firmly believed in the importance of strong encryption for protecting individual privacy. His advocacy work serves as a reminder to continue the fight for encryption and defend its power as a tool for safeguarding digital communications.

2. Stay informed and engaged: Tech policy is a rapidly evolving field. It is crucial to stay up to date with the latest technological advancements, policy debates, and legal frameworks. Active engagement in policy discussions ensures that your voice is heard and helps shape policies that align with privacy and security principles.

3. Foster collaboration and cooperation: Zimmermann understood the power of collaboration in driving change. He mobilized the tech community and formed alliances to challenge restrictive policies. By working together, policymakers, technologists, and civil society can develop effective and balanced tech policies.

4. Prioritize privacy and security: In a digital age where personal data is constantly at risk, tech policy must prioritize the protection of privacy and security. Zimmermann's work serves as a reminder to craft policies that empower individuals and safeguard their fundamental rights.

5. Advocate for transparency and accountability: Governments and tech companies must be transparent about their data collection practices and respect individuals' rights to know how their data is being used. Zimmermann's advocacy for transparency can serve as a guiding principle for policymakers.

Examples of Phil Zimmermann's Influence

Phil Zimmermann's influence on tech policy can be seen in various ways. Here are a few examples that illustrate the impact of his work:

1. Global adoption of encryption: Zimmermann's advocacy for strong encryption has contributed to its widespread adoption. Encryption has become an essential tool for protecting sensitive information in various sectors, including finance, healthcare, and communications.

2. Legal recognition of encryption rights: Zimmermann's efforts in fighting against measures like the Clipper Chip helped establish the legal recognition that individuals have the right to use encryption to protect their communications. This recognition has influenced legal frameworks and policy discussions globally.

3. Increased privacy awareness: Zimmermann's work shed light on digital privacy issues and the importance of protecting personal data. This has raised public awareness and sparked debates about privacy rights, leading to changes in policies and regulations.

4. Tech policy entrepreneurship: Zimmermann's success in advocating for strong encryption and digital privacy has inspired a new generation of tech policy entrepreneurs. His work has shown that individuals and small teams can make a significant impact on shaping policies and protecting privacy in a digital world.

Resources for Further Exploration

For those interested in delving deeper into Phil Zimmermann's influence on tech policy, the following resources provide valuable insights:

1. "The Crypto Wars: How the Clipper Chip Battle Changed Encryption Forever" by Steven Levy: This book chronicles the history of the Clipper Chip controversy and its impact on encryption and tech policy.

2. "Data and Goliath: The Hidden Battles to Collect Your Data and Control Your World" by Bruce Schneier: In this book, Schneier explores the themes of surveillance, privacy, and encryption, building upon the work of Zimmermann and other privacy advocates.

3. Electronic Frontier Foundation (EFF) website: The EFF, an organization that champions digital rights and privacy, provides resources and updates on tech policy issues, including encryption and surveillance.

4. Privacy International website: Privacy International offers research, campaigns, and resources on privacy issues around the world, including tech policy developments.

Exercises

1. Research a recent tech policy issue and analyze its potential impact on privacy and security.

2. Debate the advantages and disadvantages of encryption backdoors in tech policy. Present arguments for and against their implementation.

3. Formulate a tech policy proposal that balances privacy, security, and innovation in emerging technologies, such as artificial intelligence or the Internet of Things.

4. Interview a tech policy expert or privacy advocate to gain insights into the current challenges and opportunities in the field.

5. Organize a panel discussion or workshop on tech policy and invite experts to share their perspectives on the influence of encryption and privacy advocacy on policy-making.

Staying Ahead in the Arms Race of Privacy

In today's digital landscape, the battle for privacy is an ongoing arms race. As technology advances, so do the strategies and techniques used to invade our personal lives. To stay ahead in this race, it is crucial to be proactive and innovative in protecting our information and maintaining our privacy.

Understanding the Current State of the Arms Race

To understand how to stay ahead, it's important to first comprehend the current state of the arms race. In recent years, we have witnessed a rapid increase in data breaches, surveillance, and cyber threats. From state-sponsored hacking to corporate data mining, the privacy of individuals and organizations is constantly under attack.

The key players in this race include technology companies, governments, hackers, and privacy advocates. Each side is constantly devising new methods and technologies to gain an advantage. To protect our privacy, we must be aware of the tactics used by these entities and take proactive steps to defend ourselves.

Embracing Encryption Technologies

One of the most powerful tools in the fight for privacy is encryption. Encryption ensures that our data is secure by transforming it into an unreadable format that can only be deciphered with the correct decryption key. By encrypting our communication, sensitive files, and personal information, we can prevent unauthorized access and maintain our privacy.

To stay ahead, it is essential to embrace and adopt encryption technologies. This includes using secure messaging apps that incorporate end-to-end encryption, encrypting sensitive data before storing it in the cloud, and utilizing virtual private networks (VPNs) to protect our internet traffic. By making encryption a standard practice in our digital lives, we can create a significant barrier for those seeking to invade our privacy.

Continual Education and Awareness

Staying ahead in the arms race of privacy requires ongoing education and awareness. As technology evolves, new vulnerabilities emerge, and the tactics used by adversaries change. To effectively protect our privacy, we must stay informed about the latest threats and best practices for defense.

This can include staying updated on privacy news, following industry experts and organizations dedicated to privacy advocacy, and participating in online forums and communities focused on privacy. By staying informed, we can identify emerging threats, learn from the experiences of others, and adapt our strategies accordingly.

Proactive Security Measures

In addition to encryption and education, it is crucial to implement proactive security measures to stay ahead. This includes regularly updating software and devices to patch security vulnerabilities, using strong and unique passwords, enabling two-factor authentication (2FA), and being cautious about the information we share online.

Furthermore, adopting privacy-enhancing browser extensions, such as ad-blockers and tracker blockers, can help minimize the collection of our personal data while browsing the internet. Additionally, being mindful of the permissions we grant to apps and services can prevent unnecessary exposure of our information.

Collaboration and Innovation

Staying ahead in the arms race of privacy requires collaboration and innovation. No single entity or individual can single-handedly combat the ever-evolving landscape of privacy threats. By collaborating with others who share our commitment to privacy, we can pool our resources and expertise to develop innovative solutions.

Open-source projects, such as the development of encryption tools, can greatly benefit from collaboration and peer review. By having multiple eyes on the code, vulnerabilities can be identified and addressed more effectively. Furthermore, sharing knowledge and best practices within the privacy community fosters a collective effort to stay ahead in the race.

The Human Element: Mindfulness and Ethics

While technological solutions play a significant role in privacy protection, we must not overlook the importance of the human element. Individuals and organizations must approach privacy with mindfulness and adhere to ethical principles.

By critically evaluating the services and products we use, we can make informed decisions about the privacy implications they may carry. Being conscious of the data we generate and share allows us to make choices that align with our privacy values. It is also essential for organizations to prioritize transparency and respect user privacy rights, establishing a culture that values the protection of personal information.

The Future of the Arms Race

Looking ahead, the arms race of privacy shows no signs of slowing down. As technology continues to advance, new challenges and opportunities for privacy will emerge. Staying ahead will require a commitment to continuous learning, innovation, and collaboration.

The development and adoption of emerging technologies such as blockchain, decentralized systems, and homomorphic encryption hold promise in enhancing privacy. Additionally, the ongoing efforts of privacy advocates and organizations will shape the future landscape, driving policies and regulations that safeguard our privacy rights.

In conclusion, staying ahead in the arms race of privacy requires a multi-faceted and proactive approach. Embracing encryption, continually educating ourselves, implementing proactive security measures, collaborating with others, and maintaining a mindful and ethical stance are key to preserving our privacy in a rapidly changing digital world. By staying ahead, we can protect our information, assert our privacy rights, and shape a future that values and prioritizes privacy for all.

Phil Zimmermann's Place in Computer Science History

Phil Zimmermann's contributions to computer science are undeniable. His work in the field of cryptography has had a lasting impact and has positioned him as one of the most influential figures in computer science history. Zimmermann's creation of Pretty Good Privacy (PGP) revolutionized the way we approach encryption and privacy in the digital age.

Zimmermann's journey began with a passion for computers and a curiosity about how they worked. As a curious kid, he spent hours tinkering with machines and teaching himself programming languages. His trouble-making tendencies at school often led to disciplinary actions, but it was clear that his potential in the world of technology was extraordinary.

His passion for computers ignited at a young age, and he soon found himself hacking into the world of technology. With a deep interest in cryptography, Zimmermann started diving into the complex world of encryption. He studied the science behind encryption, exploring different encryption algorithms, and understanding the key principles of cryptography.

Mentorship from the greats in the field played a crucial role in Zimmermann's development as a programmer. He sought guidance from renowned cryptographers and learned from their expertise. Their mentorship not only honed his skills but also fueled his ambition to create something groundbreaking in the world of cryptography.

Zimmermann's vision of privacy started taking shape when he became aware of the potential dangers that mass surveillance posed to individuals and societies. He recognized the need for a robust encryption system that would protect personal privacy and ensure secure communication. This vision led to the birth of PGP.

PGP, a user-friendly email encryption program, was an instant game-changer. It allowed individuals to send encrypted messages and protect their privacy from prying eyes. Zimmermann's creation gained popularity among activists, journalists, and even everyday users who wanted to safeguard their personal information.

The introduction of PGP sparked what became known as the Crypto Wars, a battle between the U.S. government and advocates of privacy rights. The government's push for the Clipper Chip, a cryptographic device with a built-in backdoor, prompted Zimmermann to take a stand. He saw this as a direct threat to personal privacy and embarked on a David and Goliath battle against government surveillance.

Mobilizing the tech community was a crucial step in Zimmermann's fight. He rallied fellow programmers, privacy advocates, and civil liberties organizations to join him in opposing the Clipper Chip. Together, they formed a strong alliance that fought tirelessly for the right to privacy and secure communication.

Despite facing backlash and public scrutiny, Zimmermann emerged victorious. The Clipper Chip initiative was ultimately abandoned, and the importance of encryption and privacy in the digital age became widely recognized. Zimmermann's efforts had a profound impact on the conversation surrounding the balance between privacy and national security.

Zimmermann's legacy goes beyond creating PGP. He became a symbol of resistance, inspiring a generation of hacktivists to challenge surveillance and fight for online privacy. His work paved the way for the pro-privacy movement, encouraging individuals and organizations to actively protect their digital rights.

As a philanthropist, Zimmermann continued to champion privacy-oriented projects and support initiatives aimed at strengthening online security. His contributions went beyond creating software, making a global impact by funding research, collaboration, and advocacy in the field of privacy.

Zimmermann's commitment to privacy extended far beyond the technical aspects of encryption. He understood the ethical dilemma of surveillance and the implications it had for democracy. His ideas and insights continue to shape the conversation around privacy rights in the digital age.

Phil Zimmermann's lasting legacy lies in his ability to inspire others to fight for privacy and protect personal freedoms. He challenged the status quo, pushed boundaries, and made encryption technology accessible to all. Zimmermann's work serves as a constant reminder that privacy is a fundamental human right that must be upheld in the face of evolving technology and changing societal norms.

In conclusion, Phil Zimmermann's place in computer science history is marked by his groundbreaking contributions to the field of cryptography and his fierce advocacy for privacy. His vision of a world where individuals have control over their personal information and secure communications continues to influence computer scientists, programmers, and privacy advocates around the globe. Zimmermann's legacy is one of innovation, resilience, and a steadfast commitment to upholding privacy in the digital age.

The Legacy of Phil Zimmermann Lives On

Despite the passing of time, Phil Zimmermann's legacy continues to shape the world of privacy and encryption. His groundbreaking work on PGP (Pretty Good Privacy) and his relentless advocacy for the protection of personal data have left an indelible mark on the tech industry and society as a whole. In this section, we will explore the lasting impact of Phil Zimmermann and how his ideas and principles continue to guide the fight for privacy.

Inspiring a New Generation

One of the most significant aspects of Phil Zimmermann's legacy is his ability to inspire a new generation of programmers, activists, and privacy advocates. His dedication to protecting individual privacy and his unyielding belief in the power of encryption has motivated countless individuals to take up the mantle and continue the fight for digital rights.

Zimmermann's commitment to open-source development and his belief in the importance of sharing knowledge have shaped the culture of the tech industry. Today, we see the fruits of his influence in the proliferation of privacy-enhancing technologies and the growing number of privacy-conscious individuals and organizations.

Promoting a Privacy-First Mindset

Phil Zimmermann's work with PGP has had a profound impact on shaping the way society thinks about privacy. By making strong encryption accessible to the masses, Zimmermann paved the way for individuals to take control of their own personal data.

Zimmermann's vision of a world where privacy is a fundamental human right has resonated with people worldwide. The realization that privacy is not only desirable but also achievable has sparked a paradigm shift in how individuals approach their online activities. Today, more people than ever before are actively seeking out and using encryption tools to protect their communications and personal information.

Advocating for Policy Change

Phil Zimmermann's influence extends beyond the realm of technology. He has been a tireless advocate for privacy in the face of encroaching surveillance and government overreach. His efforts to challenge policies that undermine personal privacy have helped shape the global conversation around surveillance and encryption.

Zimmermann's unwavering commitment to defending encryption as a cornerstone of privacy has stood as a rallying cry for privacy advocates worldwide. His advocacy work has spurred meaningful dialogue, resulting in policy changes that seek to strike a balance between national security and individual privacy.

Expanding Phil Zimmermann's Work

The legacy of Phil Zimmermann does not end with his own contributions. Beyond PGP, Zimmermann's vision and principles have paved the way for the development of a wide range of privacy-enhancing technologies.

In today's world, we see the impact of Zimmermann's work in secure messaging apps, virtual private networks (VPNs), decentralized systems, and other privacy-centric tools. These advancements build upon Zimmermann's foundation, striving to create a safer and more private digital environment for individuals and organizations around the globe.

The Phil Zimmermann Fellowship Program

To ensure that the legacy of Phil Zimmermann lives on, an initiative known as the Phil Zimmermann Fellowship Program was established. The fellowship program aims to support and empower the next generation of privacy advocates and technologists who are committed to upholding the principles that Zimmermann championed.

Through the fellowship program, promising individuals are provided with resources, mentorship, and financial support to pursue projects and research that advance the cause of privacy. The program seeks to foster innovation and

Promoting a Transparent and Ethical Future

One of the cornerstones of Phil Zimmermann's legacy is a dedication to transparency and ethics. Zimmermann firmly believed in the importance of informing individuals about the risks to their privacy and empowering them with the tools to protect themselves.

Today, this commitment to transparency is more critical than ever. As technology continues to evolve and new privacy challenges arise, the need for public awareness and education becomes increasingly paramount. Zimmermann's legacy serves as a reminder that, in the face of evolving threats, society must remain vigilant and demand transparency and accountability from technology companies, governments, and other entities that handle our private data.

Forging Ahead

While the loss of Phil Zimmermann is deeply felt, his impact on the world of privacy lives on. As technology continues to advance and new privacy challenges emerge, Zimmermann's visionary ideas and unwavering commitment to privacy will continue to guide us.

Phil Zimmermann's legacy serves as a reminder that individuals and communities have the power to shape the future of privacy. By staying informed, advocating for change, and supporting initiatives that prioritize privacy, we can honor Zimmermann's contributions and work together to create a world where privacy is respected and protected for all.

Phil Zimmermann's Impact on the Tech Industry

Changing the Perception of Privacy

In today's digital age, where our personal information is constantly being collected and our activities are tracked, privacy has become a crucial concern. Phil Zimmermann played a significant role in changing the perception of privacy by advocating for strong encryption and the protection of personal data. Through his work on PGP (Pretty Good Privacy), Zimmermann revolutionized the way we think about privacy and paved the way for a more secure digital world.

The Importance of Privacy

Privacy, as a fundamental human right, is essential for the preservation of individual freedom and autonomy. It allows us to control our personal information and make informed decisions about how it is accessed and used. Privacy also enables us to express ourselves freely, without fear of surveillance or censorship. In the digital realm, privacy is even more critical, as our online activities can reveal intimate details about our lives.

The Perception of Privacy

Before Zimmermann's groundbreaking work, privacy was often seen as a luxury rather than a necessity. Many believed that sacrificing privacy was a small price to pay for convenience and technological advancements. The prevailing mindset was that if you had nothing to hide, you had nothing to fear. However, Zimmermann challenged this notion and highlighted the potential dangers of living in a surveillance society.

Encryption as a Game-Changer

Zimmermann understood that encryption was the key to safeguarding privacy in the digital world. With PGP, he developed a user-friendly encryption software that allowed ordinary individuals to secure their communications and protect their personal information from prying eyes. This revolutionary technology empowered people to take control of their privacy and sparked a movement for stronger encryption standards.

Raising Awareness about Privacy Risks

In addition to creating powerful encryption tools, Zimmermann played a crucial role in raising public awareness about the risks of unchecked surveillance and data collection. Through his advocacy work and public speaking engagements, he emphasized the need for privacy as a fundamental right and highlighted the potential for abuse when personal data falls into the wrong hands. Zimmermann's efforts helped shift the perception of privacy from a mere luxury to a critical component of digital citizenship.

Inspiring a Privacy Movement

Zimmermann's work inspired a generation of privacy advocates and activists who recognized the importance of protecting personal data. His dedication to privacy rights and his fight against government surveillance sparked a global movement for digital freedom. Zimmermann's contributions helped galvanize public support for stronger privacy laws and increased transparency in how personal data is collected and used.

Challenging the Status Quo

The prevailing narrative that sacrificing privacy was necessary for security began to change as Zimmermann challenged the idea that privacy and security were mutually exclusive. He argued that strong encryption was essential for both privacy and security, and that compromising privacy in the name of security was a misguided approach. By demonstrating the effectiveness of encryption in protecting personal data, Zimmermann showed that privacy and security could go hand in hand.

Building Trust in Encryption

Zimmermann's work on PGP not only provided individuals with a means to protect their privacy, but it also helped build trust in encryption technology. Through the development of open-source encryption tools, Zimmermann demonstrated that encryption could be reliable, transparent, and accessible to all. This shift in perception helped to dispel the notion that encryption was only for criminals or those with something to hide.

Encouraging Industry Adoption

Zimmermann's advocacy and the success of PGP also prompted widespread adoption of encryption technology within various industries. Companies began to recognize the importance of protecting user data and started implementing encryption measures to safeguard sensitive information. Zimmermann's work played a pivotal role in pushing encryption from the fringes of the tech world to becoming a standard practice in ensuring data privacy.

Empowering Individuals

One of the most significant impacts of Zimmermann's work was empowering individuals to take control of their privacy. By providing accessible encryption tools like PGP, he shifted the balance of power from governments and corporations to the individual. Zimmermann's efforts demonstrated that privacy is not just a passive right but an active responsibility, encouraging individuals to become proactive in protecting their personal data.

A Lasting Legacy

Zimmermann's work on privacy continues to have a lasting impact on the way we perceive and protect privacy today. His advocacy efforts have influenced the development of privacy laws and regulations, as well as the attitudes of individuals and organizations towards data protection. As technology continues to advance and privacy concerns evolve, Zimmermann's legacy serves as a reminder of the importance of privacy and the need to continue fighting for it in the digital age.

In conclusion, Phil Zimmermann's work has played a significant role in changing the perception of privacy. Through his advocacy for strong encryption and his dedication to protecting personal data, Zimmermann has empowered individuals to take control of their privacy and challenged the notion that sacrificing privacy is necessary for security. His legacy continues to inspire a generation of privacy advocates and shape the way we think about privacy in the digital age.

Phil Zimmermann as a Tech Visionary

In the world of technology, there are visionaries who set themselves apart with their innovative ideas and relentless pursuit of progress. Phil Zimmermann, the creator of Pretty Good Privacy (PGP), is undoubtedly one of these visionaries. His contributions to the field of encryption have revolutionized the way we think about privacy and security. Let's delve into Phil Zimmermann's journey and explore how he became a tech visionary.

Phil Zimmermann's fascination with computers began at an early age. Growing up in the 1960s and 1970s, he witnessed the birth of the digital revolution firsthand. As a curious kid, he was drawn to the emerging field of computer science and spent hours tinkering with machines, eager to understand how they worked. This insatiable curiosity would shape his future as a tech visionary.

During his time in college, Zimmermann's passion for computers deepened. He honed his programming skills and became captivated by the possibilities of cryptography—an area of study that focuses on secure communication. Zimmermann recognized the potential of cryptography in safeguarding individuals' privacy and began to explore its applications.

One defining moment in Zimmermann's journey occurred when he stumbled upon an article in Scientific American about public-key cryptography. This revolutionary concept, which allows for secure communication over an insecure channel, sparked Zimmermann's imagination. He realized that cryptography had the power to protect the privacy of individuals in an increasingly digital world.

With this newfound vision, Zimmermann set out to develop a practical implementation of public-key cryptography that would be accessible to everyone. He wanted to create a user-friendly encryption tool that would enable ordinary individuals to communicate securely. This vision laid the foundation for what would eventually become Pretty Good Privacy, PGP for short.

Zimmermann faced numerous challenges along the way. Developing PGP was no easy task, especially in an era when encryption was viewed with suspicion by governments and law enforcement agencies. Yet, despite the obstacles, Zimmermann persevered. His unwavering commitment to privacy and determination to create a powerful encryption tool propelled him forward.

When Zimmermann released PGP in 1991, it caused a stir in the industry. The software's robust encryption capabilities, coupled with its user-friendly interface, made it a game-changer. PGP democratized encryption, placing the power of secure communication in the hands of individuals.

Zimmermann's visionary approach didn't stop at creating PGP. He understood that to drive lasting change, he needed to build a community of privacy advocates. He actively promoted the adoption of PGP among activists, journalists, and ordinary citizens who valued their privacy. This grassroots movement served as the catalyst for a larger conversation about privacy and the role of encryption in protecting individuals' rights.

Zimmermann's impact as a tech visionary extended beyond the development of PGP. He was a trailblazer in advocating for strong encryption in the face of government opposition. In the infamous Clipper Chip controversy, he fought against the U.S. government's attempts to introduce backdoors into encryption systems, arguing that such vulnerabilities would undermine individuals' privacy.

Through his perseverance, Zimmermann emerged as a champion for privacy rights and an inspiration to future generations of programmers. His unwavering commitment to protecting the rights of individuals laid the foundation for a global movement advocating for strong encryption.

Zimmermann's legacy as a tech visionary continues to shape the industry. His contributions to the field of encryption have paved the way for the adoption of secure communication tools and highlighted the importance of privacy in a digital age. His foresight and determination serve as a guiding light for those who value the power of technology to safeguard individuals' rights.

In conclusion, Phil Zimmermann's journey as a tech visionary is a testament to the transformative power of ideas. From his early curiosity about computers to his groundbreaking work on PGP, Zimmermann's vision and determination have reshaped the way we think about privacy and encryption. As we navigate an increasingly interconnected world, his legacy serves as a reminder of the importance of technology in preserving our fundamental rights. Phil Zimmermann truly embodies the spirit of a tech visionary.

The Influence of PGP on Open Source Culture

The advent of Pretty Good Privacy (PGP) brought significant changes to the world of open source culture. PGP, developed by Phil Zimmermann, revolutionized the encryption landscape and had a profound impact on the open source movement. Let's explore the influence of PGP on open source culture.

Embracing the Spirit of Collaboration

Open source culture is built on the principle of collaboration, where individuals and communities come together to create and improve software freely. PGP embodies this spirit by being one of the earliest open source projects that gained widespread attention. By making the source code freely available, PGP encouraged collaboration and allowed developers worldwide to contribute to its improvement.

Transparent Development Process

PGP's open source nature empowered developers to understand how encryption algorithms work and encouraged them to participate in its development. The transparency of the development process fostered a sense of trust and participation in the community. It also allowed for peer review, ensuring that the software was free from vulnerabilities and backdoors.

Inspiring a New Generation of Privacy Advocates

PGP's strong focus on privacy and security inspired a new generation of privacy advocates within the open source community. Developers began to recognize the importance of encryption as a fundamental right and actively integrated encryption techniques into their projects. PGP, with its robust encryption capabilities, served as a catalyst for the development of privacy-focused software and tools.

Open Standards and Interoperability

PGP promoted the use of open standards and interoperability, enabling different software applications to work together seamlessly. This approach enhanced the compatibility of encryption tools and encouraged the growth of an ecosystem where developers could build upon existing encryption technologies. By adopting open standards, PGP facilitated the integration of encryption into various software applications, ensuring that privacy became a central aspect of digital communication.

Community-driven Cryptography

Traditionally, cryptography was dominated by closed systems and proprietary algorithms. PGP flipped this notion on its head by offering accessible and community-driven cryptography. PGP's open source model allowed for continuous improvement, inviting developers to contribute their expertise and push the boundaries of encryption technology. This community-driven approach democratized cryptography, making it accessible to a broader audience and accelerating innovation.

The Ripple Effect on Open Source Projects

PGP's influence extended far beyond its own development. The principles and lessons learned from PGP's success were applied to other open source projects, paving the way for a culture of transparency, collaboration, and security. The open source community began to prioritize privacy and encryption in their initiatives, recognizing that these elements were essential for maintaining users' sovereignty over their data.

Evolving PGP Alternatives

As a result of PGP's influence, several PGP alternatives emerged within the open source community. These alternatives expanded on the original concepts introduced by PGP and catered to different user needs. Examples include GnuPG (GNU Privacy Guard), an open source implementation of OpenPGP, and Mailvelope, a browser extension that brings PGP encryption to web-based email clients. The proliferation of PGP alternatives highlights the open source community's commitment to privacy and encryption.

Encouraging Transparency and Trust

PGP's impact on open source culture fostered a culture of transparency and trust. The ability to review and modify source code helped establish confidence in encryption tools, as developers could verify their security and privacy claims. By encouraging openness and collaboration, PGP cultivated a sense of trust within the open source community, enhancing the reputation of open source projects as secure and dependable.

Challenges and Opportunities

While PGP's influence on open source culture has been overwhelmingly positive, it has also brought some challenges. One significant challenge is the ongoing need to balance security with user convenience. Encryption techniques like PGP can sometimes be complex to implement, making it difficult for the average user to adopt. Open source developers face the task of creating user-friendly interfaces that maintain high-security standards without sacrificing ease of use.

Another challenge is the continuous arms race between encryption developers and adversaries seeking to break encryption. PGP's influence has made encryption a central part of digital communication, leading to increased scrutiny from governments and intelligence agencies. Developers must remain vigilant to emerging threats and adapt their encryption technologies to combat evolving methods of attack.

Case Study: Signal Messenger

One notable example of PGP's influence in open source culture is the Signal messaging application. Signal, developed by Moxie Marlinspike and the Open Whisper Systems team, emphasizes secure and private communications. It incorporates the Signal Protocol, an open-source cryptographic protocol used for end-to-end encryption. Signal's commitment to privacy and its open source nature directly align with the principles embodied by PGP. The success of Signal in gaining popularity and recognition demonstrates the demand for privacy-centric open source software in today's digital landscape.

Overall, PGP's influence on open source culture can be seen through the promotion of collaboration, transparency, and privacy. PGP paved the way for the integration of encryption into open source projects and inspired the development of privacy-focused tools. As open source continues to thrive, the influence of PGP will persist, shaping the future of software development and the protection of digital privacy.

Phil Zimmermann's Lessons for Tech Entrepreneurs

As an accomplished programmer and advocate for digital privacy, Phil Zimmermann has left behind a wealth of knowledge and valuable lessons for aspiring tech entrepreneurs. In this section, we will delve into some of the key principles and insights that can guide entrepreneurs in the increasingly complex and privacy-centric digital landscape.

Understanding the Importance of Privacy

One of the core lessons that Phil Zimmermann imparts is the critical importance of privacy in today's interconnected world. Tech entrepreneurs should recognize that privacy is not an option, but a fundamental right that must be protected. Zimmermann's work with Pretty Good Privacy (PGP) revolutionized encryption and demonstrated that open-source solutions can empower individuals to safeguard their privacy.

Entrepreneurs must prioritize privacy by designing products and services with built-in encryption mechanisms. This not only protects their users' sensitive information but also fosters trust and loyalty. Recognizing privacy as a fundamental value will set entrepreneurs apart in an increasingly privacy-conscious market.

Embracing Open Source Culture

Phil Zimmermann's commitment to open-source software has had a profound impact on the tech industry. Zimmermann firmly believed that privacy must be accessible to all, and open-source solutions are key to achieving this goal. By making PGP available to the public, Zimmermann emphasized the need for transparency and collaboration in the development of privacy technologies.

Tech entrepreneurs should embrace the open-source culture, as it encourages innovation, peer review, and community involvement. By leveraging the collective intelligence and expertise of the open-source community, entrepreneurs can develop more secure and reliable products. Additionally, open-source projects often enjoy widespread adoption, enabling entrepreneurs to build a loyal user base and drive industry-wide change.

Fostering Strong Relationships with Users

Zimmermann's deep understanding of user needs and his commitment to user-centric design were essential to the success of PGP. Entrepreneurs should prioritize building strong relationships with their users, actively seeking feedback, and incorporating it into product development.

By fostering a culture of listening and continuous improvement, entrepreneurs can create products that truly meet the needs of their users. This not only enhances customer satisfaction but also promotes brand loyalty and advocacy. Strengthening the user-entrepreneur relationship is crucial to achieving long-term success in the tech industry.

Navigating Legal and Ethical Challenges

In the realm of digital privacy, entrepreneurs often find themselves navigating legal and ethical complexities. Phil Zimmermann's experience in the Crypto Wars and the Clipper Chip controversy illustrates the challenges that arise when privacy clashes with national security interests.

Entrepreneurs must be prepared to navigate these challenges, always prioritizing user privacy while respecting legal boundaries. This requires a deep understanding of privacy laws and regulations, as well as a commitment to ethical principles. By proactively seeking legal counsel and engaging in industry-wide discussions, entrepreneurs can find innovative solutions that maintain a balance between privacy and security.

Building Alliances and Collaborating with Peers

Phil Zimmermann understood the power of alliances and collaboration in advocating for privacy rights. Entrepreneurs should actively seek collaborations with like-minded individuals, organizations, and advocacy groups to amplify their voices and impact.

By joining forces with other privacy-focused entrepreneurs, sharing knowledge and resources, and collectively addressing privacy challenges, entrepreneurs can drive meaningful change in the industry. Zimmermann's example shows that collaboration and collective action are key to overcoming the power imbalances that often exist between tech giants and individual entrepreneurs.

The Entrepreneur's Ethical Responsibility

Tech entrepreneurs have a significant ethical responsibility towards their users, society, and the future of technology. Zimmermann's lifelong commitment to privacy serves as a powerful example of how entrepreneurs can embed ethical considerations into every aspect of their work.

Entrepreneurs should prioritize the ethical implications of their products, considering how they might impact user privacy, data security, and societal well-being. By conducting ethical assessments, seeking diverse perspectives, and adhering to strong ethical frameworks, entrepreneurs can contribute to a more ethical and responsible tech industry.

Staying Ahead in a Changing Landscape

The digital landscape is constantly evolving, and entrepreneurs must stay ahead of emerging trends and challenges. Phil Zimmermann advises entrepreneurs to embrace a growth mindset and continuously learn and adapt to new developments in technology, privacy, and security.

Entrepreneurs should actively participate in professional networks, attend conferences and workshops, and engage with the latest research and industry insights. By staying informed, entrepreneurs can future-proof their businesses and make informed decisions that align with evolving privacy needs.

Promoting Education and Awareness

Phil Zimmermann's commitment to educating users and advocating for privacy awareness is a crucial lesson for tech entrepreneurs. Entrepreneurs should prioritize user education, empowering them to make informed decisions about their privacy.

By creating user-friendly interfaces, providing clear explanations of privacy features, and offering engaging educational resources, entrepreneurs can bridge the gap between complex privacy technologies and the average user. Furthermore, entrepreneurs should champion privacy awareness through thought leadership, public speaking, and collaborations with educational institutions.

In conclusion, Phil Zimmermann's journey as a tech entrepreneur and privacy advocate offers valuable lessons for aspiring innovators entering the digital landscape. By prioritizing privacy, embracing open-source culture, fostering strong user relationships, navigating legal and ethical challenges, building alliances, and staying ahead of the curve, entrepreneurs can create successful ventures while upholding privacy as a fundamental right. Through their work, entrepreneurs have the power to shape the future of technology and champion the cause of privacy for generations to come.

Phil Zimmermann and the Collaborative Spirit

In the world of technology, collaboration and cooperation are often key ingredients for success. Phil Zimmermann understood this early on and embraced the collaborative spirit in his work. He believed that by working together, we could achieve greater things and make a real impact on the world. This section explores the collaborative nature of Phil Zimmermann and how it influenced his work in the realm of privacy and encryption.

The Power of Collaboration

Collaboration is the art of bringing together diverse perspectives and skills to solve complex problems. Phil Zimmermann recognized the power of collaboration and actively sought out opportunities to work with others who shared his passion for privacy and security. He understood that by pooling resources and knowledge, breakthroughs could be made more quickly and effectively.

One of the key ways in which Zimmermann fostered collaboration was through his open-source approach. He believed that software should be freely available, allowing users to access, modify, and redistribute it. This ethos not only encouraged collaboration among developers but also enabled individuals from all walks of life to contribute to the cause of privacy.

Building Communities

Zimmermann was not only a visionary programmer but also a skilled community builder. He recognized the importance of creating spaces where like-minded individuals could come together, share ideas, and work towards a common goal. Through his advocacy work and public speaking engagements, Zimmermann actively sought to build communities centered around privacy and encryption.

One of the most notable communities that Zimmermann helped create was the cypherpunks. The cypherpunks were a loosely affiliated group of individuals who shared a passion for cryptography and privacy. Zimmermann's advocacy and support of their cause played a crucial role in bringing together some of the brightest minds in the field and fostering an environment of collaboration.

Sharing Knowledge and Expertise

Another way in which Zimmermann embraced the collaborative spirit was by freely sharing his knowledge and expertise. He understood that the more people understood encryption and privacy, the better equipped they would be to protect themselves in the digital world. Zimmermann actively contributed to public discourse, giving talks, writing articles, and participating in interviews.

Zimmermann also played a pivotal role in mentoring and supporting budding programmers and privacy activists. He was known for his generosity in sharing his knowledge and insights, often going out of his way to guide and inspire others. His willingness to share his experience and expertise helped foster a sense of collaboration and community within the privacy and encryption space.

Partnerships and Alliances

Collaboration often extends beyond individual efforts and requires partnerships and alliances. Zimmermann understood the importance of forming strategic partnerships to further the cause of privacy. Throughout his career, he formed alliances with organizations, activists, and fellow technologists who shared his vision.

One of the key partnerships Zimmermann forged was with the Electronic Frontier Foundation (EFF). The EFF is a nonprofit organization that defends civil liberties in the digital world. Zimmermann's collaboration with the EFF helped bring attention to the importance of encryption and privacy rights, leading to significant advancements in the field.

The Unconventional Approach

While collaboration often involves working with like-minded individuals, Zimmermann also embraced an unconventional approach to collaboration. He recognized that diverse perspectives and unconventional thinking could lead to groundbreaking solutions.

Zimmermann encouraged cross-disciplinary collaboration, bringing together experts from various fields such as computer science, sociology, law, and activism. By fostering collaboration across disciplines, he believed that new ideas and approaches could be explored, pushing the boundaries of privacy and encryption.

The Collaborative Future

Today, the collaborative spirit that Phil Zimmermann epitomized continues to shape the world of privacy and encryption. The success of open-source projects, the proliferation of online communities, and the partnerships between nonprofit organizations and tech companies all bear witness to the power of collaboration.

As we navigate the challenges and opportunities of the digital age, collaboration remains an essential tool in our fight for privacy. By working together, we can continue to push the boundaries of encryption, advocate for stronger privacy laws, and ensure that individuals have the tools they need to protect their information in an increasingly connected world.

Exercise: Collaborative Encryption

Imagine you are a member of a team working on a collaborative encryption project. Your team consists of individuals from various backgrounds, including computer science, mathematics, and psychology. Your task is to develop an encryption algorithm that incorporates principles of usability and security while considering the psychological factors that impact user adoption.
1. Identify the key characteristics that your collaborative encryption algorithm should possess. 2. Discuss how you would leverage the diverse perspectives within your team to develop a more holistic solution. 3. Research existing encryption algorithms and identify areas where collaboration and cross-disciplinary insights could lead to improvements. 4. Brainstorm creative ways to engage and educate the public about the importance of encryption and privacy. 5. Evaluate potential partnerships and alliances that could help advance your collaborative encryption project.

Remember, collaboration is not only about working together but also about embracing different perspectives and finding common ground. By leveraging the strengths and expertise of your team, you can create innovative solutions that push the boundaries of encryption and privacy.

Resources

1. Zimmermann, P. (1999). *The Official PGP User's Guide*. MIT Press. 2. May, T. (2015). *Cypherpunks: Freedom and the Future of the Internet*. OR Books. 3. Electronic Frontier Foundation. *https://www.eff.org/* 4. Cryptography Engineering: Design Principles and Practical Applications by Niels Ferguson, Bruce Schneier, and Tadayoshi Kohno

While collaboration is integral to progress, it's also essential to maintain a balance with individual work. In the next section, we delve into the personal side of Phil Zimmermann and explore how he managed to find harmony between his work and personal life.

The Global Reach of Privacy Advocacy

In today's interconnected world, the fight for privacy knows no borders. With the advent of digital technology and the growing concerns over surveillance and data breaches, privacy advocates around the globe have come together to protect the fundamental right to privacy. Phil Zimmermann's visionary work has played a crucial role in shaping the global landscape of privacy advocacy.

A Global Network of Privacy Activists

Privacy advocacy is a global movement driven by individuals, organizations, and communities passionate about protecting personal privacy in the digital age. Across continents, individuals have united to raise awareness, advocate for stronger privacy laws, and develop tools and technologies that safeguard data.

Privacy activists organize conferences, workshops, and events to foster collaboration and knowledge-sharing. These gatherings serve as platforms for experts and everyday citizens to discuss the latest threats to privacy and collectively brainstorm innovative solutions. One such example is the annual PrivacyCon conference, where privacy advocates from around the world come together to address pressing privacy issues.

Phil Zimmermann's impact on the privacy advocacy community has been profound. His creation of PGP sparked a global movement that brought together like-minded individuals, enabling them to exchange knowledge and collaborate on privacy-enhancing projects. Zimmermann's commitment to privacy and his willingness to share his expertise have inspired countless privacy activists to join the fight.

Global Privacy Challenges

Privacy challenges are not confined to any particular country or region. The rise of surveillance capitalism and the proliferation of personal data collection by tech giants have spurred privacy concerns worldwide. As digital technology continues to advance, so too does the need for global collaboration in addressing privacy challenges.

One of the key global challenges is the conflict between national security and individual privacy. Governments around the world grapple with finding the right balance between protecting citizens and respecting their privacy rights. Privacy advocates play a crucial role in providing guidance and advocating for privacy to be respected during policy and legislation discussions.

Another challenge is the growing threat of data breaches and cybercrime. With an increasingly interconnected world, personal data has become a valuable commodity. Privacy activists work tirelessly to raise awareness about the importance of robust security measures and educate individuals on best practices for safeguarding their privacy online.

International Cooperation and Collaboration

The fight for privacy necessitates international cooperation and collaboration among governments, organizations, and individuals. Privacy advocates actively engage with policymakers and stakeholders to shape privacy laws, regulations, and standards at both national and international levels.

International organizations such as the Electronic Frontier Foundation (EFF) and the Privacy International work tirelessly to protect individuals' privacy rights globally. Through advocacy, research, and litigation, these organizations strive to hold governments and corporations accountable for privacy infringements.

Cross-border partnerships between privacy advocacy organizations and tech companies are also vital in advancing privacy-focused solutions. Collaborative initiatives such as the Open Technology Fund (OTF) provide resources and support to projects developing tools and technologies that empower individuals to protect their privacy. These partnerships bridge the gap between technological innovation and privacy advocacy, creating a global movement for change.

The Importance of Cultural Considerations

Privacy advocacy takes into account the rich diversity of cultures and societies around the world. Privacy expectations and norms vary across different regions, and it is essential to respect and understand these variations in the fight for privacy.

Privacy advocates recognize the need for culturally-sensitive approaches when addressing privacy issues. This involves engaging with local communities, understanding their unique challenges and concerns, and tailoring privacy advocacy efforts accordingly. By embracing cultural diversity, privacy advocates can foster a more inclusive and effective movement.

Privacy Advocacy in Developing Nations

Privacy advocacy efforts in developing nations face unique challenges. Limited access to resources and infrastructure, as well as socio-economic inequalities, can hinder the promotion and protection of privacy rights.

Privacy advocates in developing nations play a crucial role in raising awareness about the importance of privacy and empowering individuals to protect their digital rights. They work to bridge the digital divide by advocating for affordable and secure internet access and promoting digital literacy.

The global reach of privacy advocacy extends to developing nations through initiatives and collaborations that address the specific challenges these regions face. Phil Zimmermann's commitment to democratizing privacy has inspired projects that aim to provide privacy-enhancing tools and technologies to individuals in developing nations.

Gaining Momentum: Privacy as a Global Priority

Privacy advocacy has evolved from a niche concern to a global movement. The increasing prevalence of surveillance, data breaches, and the commodification of personal information has pushed privacy issues to the forefront of public discourse.

Through education, collaboration, and political advocacy, privacy activists worldwide are working towards a future where privacy is respected and protected. Phil Zimmermann's legacy continues to inspire a new generation of privacy advocates to fight for a world where individuals have control over their personal data and privacy is regarded as a fundamental human right.

Exercises

Exercise 1: Privacy Advocacy in Your Country

Research privacy advocacy initiatives in your country and write a short report on their goals, achievements, and challenges. Include any notable collaborations with international organizations and how cultural considerations are taken into account.

Exercise 2: Privacy Innovation Ideas

Brainstorm innovative ideas for privacy-focused initiatives that can be implemented globally. Consider the challenges faced by developing nations and how digital privacy can be promoted in those regions. Write a short proposal describing your ideas and how they address the current privacy landscape.

Exercise 3: Privacy Awareness Campaign

Design a privacy awareness campaign targeting young individuals in your community. Create engaging and informative content that highlights the importance of privacy protection and provides practical tips for safeguarding personal data. Use social media, posters, and other creative mediums to reach a wider audience.

Additional Resources

- Electronic Frontier Foundation (EFF) - `https://www.eff.org/`
- Privacy International - `https://privacyinternational.org/`
- Open Technology Fund (OTF) - `https://www.opentech.fund/`
- PrivacyCon - `https://www.ftc.gov/privacycon`

Key Takeaways

- Privacy advocacy is a global movement that aims to protect personal privacy in the digital age.
- Privacy activists collaborate on international level to address privacy challenges and protect individuals' privacy rights.
- Cultural considerations play a crucial role in privacy advocacy, respecting and understanding the diversity of privacy expectations and norms worldwide.
- Privacy advocacy efforts in developing nations face unique challenges, requiring tailored approaches to bridge the digital divide.
- Privacy is gaining momentum as a global priority, with increasing public awareness and political advocacy.

Phil Zimmermann's Contributions to the Greater Good

Phil Zimmermann has made significant contributions to the greater good by advocating for privacy rights and working towards a more secure digital future. His groundbreaking work in cryptography and the creation of Pretty Good Privacy (PGP) has had a lasting impact on society, enabling individuals to protect their personal information and communicate securely.

Advocacy for Privacy Rights

One of Phil Zimmermann's most significant contributions to the greater good is his advocacy for privacy rights. He believed that individuals have the right to protect their personal information, and he fought against government surveillance and the erosion of privacy in the digital age.

Zimmermann understood the power dynamic between individuals and institutions, emphasizing the importance of privacy as a fundamental human right.

Through his work and public statements, he raised awareness about the need to protect personal data from unwarranted access and surveillance.

Development of Pretty Good Privacy (PGP)

Zimmermann's creation of PGP revolutionized the field of cryptography and played a crucial role in safeguarding individuals' privacy. PGP is a user-friendly encryption program that allows users to encrypt and decrypt their electronic communications, ensuring that only the intended recipient can access the information.

By developing PGP as an open-source software, Zimmermann made encryption accessible to the general public. This democratization of encryption technology empowered individuals, journalists, and activists to communicate securely, protecting their sensitive information from prying eyes.

Impact on Whistleblowers and Journalists

Zimmermann's work has been instrumental in protecting whistleblowers and journalists who aim to expose corruption and abuse of power. Whistleblowers often risk their careers and personal safety to bring important issues to light, and encryption technologies like PGP provide them with a means to communicate securely and anonymously.

By securing sensitive communications, Zimmermann's contributions have safeguarded the freedom of the press and upheld democratic principles. Journalists can now communicate securely with their sources, protecting both their identity and the information they provide.

Inspiring a New Generation

Zimmermann's work has inspired a new generation of privacy advocates and technologists who continue to build upon his ideas. His dedication to open-source software and his belief in the power of strong encryption have left a lasting impression on the tech community.

Many privacy-oriented projects and initiatives have emerged in the wake of Zimmermann's work, furthering the goals of secure communication and digital privacy. His contributions have sparked a wave of innovation, with new encryption technologies and privacy-centric applications being developed to combat invasive surveillance and protect user data.

Ethical Responsibility and Education

Zimmermann recognizes the ethical responsibility that comes with developing encryption technology. He has emphasized the need for education and user awareness in the proper use of encryption tools.

Through his advocacy work and public speaking engagements, Zimmermann has sought to educate the public about the importance of privacy rights and the role of encryption in protecting personal information. He believes that informed users can better protect themselves and make informed decisions about their privacy.

Collaboration and Partnerships

Zimmermann has actively collaborated with like-minded individuals and organizations to further the cause of privacy. He understands the power of collective action and the need for partnership to effect meaningful change.

By fostering collaboration between technologists, policy-makers, and privacy advocates, Zimmermann has been able to amplify his impact and promote privacy-centric solutions in both the public and private sectors. His collaborative approach has helped shape the conversation around digital privacy and security.

Phil Zimmermann's Lasting Legacy

Phil Zimmermann's contributions to the greater good extend beyond his technological advancements. His advocacy for privacy rights, dedication to open-source principles, and commitment to educating users about encryption have created a lasting impact on society.

His work has inspired a new generation of individuals who are passionate about privacy rights and are working towards a more secure digital future. Zimmermann's legacy lives on in the continued fight for privacy, the development of innovative encryption technologies, and the ongoing conversation around digital rights and personal security.

In a world where our lives are increasingly interconnected and reliant on technology, Phil Zimmermann's contributions to the greater good are more relevant and vital than ever. His work serves as a reminder of the importance of individual privacy and the need to protect our personal information in the digital age.

Phil Zimmermann's Continued Relevance

In today's fast-paced digital world, the need for privacy and secure communication has only grown stronger. It is in this context that Phil Zimmermann's continued relevance becomes apparent. His pioneering work in encryption with the creation of Pretty Good Privacy (PGP) laid the foundation for privacy-focused technologies and ignited a worldwide movement for secure communication. But how does his legacy live on? In this section, we explore the lasting impact of Phil Zimmermann and his enduring relevance in the fight for privacy.

Changing the Perception of Privacy

One of Phil Zimmermann's notable contributions was his role in changing the public perception of privacy. Before PGP, encryption was seen as a tool exclusively used by government agencies and defense organizations. Zimmermann's vision was to make strong encryption accessible to everyone, empowering individuals to protect their private communications. His dedication to privacy as a fundamental right helped shift the narrative and highlighted the importance of personal data protection.

Phil Zimmermann as a Tech Visionary

As a tech visionary, Phil Zimmermann demonstrated that privacy and security are not obstacles but necessary foundations for innovation. With PGP, he showed that it is possible to create user-friendly encryption tools that ensure privacy without sacrificing convenience. Zimmermann's vision continues to inspire a new generation of programmers and entrepreneurs, encouraging them to think creatively about incorporating privacy-enhancing technologies into their products and services.

The Influence of PGP on Open Source Culture

The open-source nature of PGP allowed for collaboration, peer review, and the formation of a vibrant community of privacy enthusiasts. This culture of openness and shared knowledge played a crucial role in the development of encryption technologies beyond PGP. Zimmermann's commitment to open source has influenced subsequent generations of programmers, fostering a spirit of collaboration and creating an environment conducive to privacy-focused innovation.

Phil Zimmermann's Lessons for Tech Entrepreneurs

Tech entrepreneurs can learn valuable lessons from Phil Zimmermann's journey. He demonstrated that it is possible to create groundbreaking products without compromising on privacy or security. Zimmermann's relentless pursuit of his vision in the face of prevailing interests serves as an inspiration for those striving to make a positive impact in today's tech landscape. His story reminds entrepreneurs to stay true to their principles and focus on solving real-world problems rather than solely pursuing monetary gain.

Phil Zimmermann and the Collaborative Spirit

Collaboration has always been at the heart of Phil Zimmermann's work. From seeking mentorship from industry stalwarts to actively involving the tech community in the crypto wars, Zimmermann understood the strength of collaboration in effecting change. His approach serves as a reminder that the fight for privacy and security requires collective effort. Zimmermann's collaborative spirit is a beacon of hope for those striving to create a safer digital world.

The Global Reach of Privacy Advocacy

Phil Zimmermann's advocacy for privacy has resonated far beyond the tech community. His efforts have galvanized individuals, organizations, and governments worldwide to recognize and defend the importance of privacy. With an increasingly interconnected global society, Zimmermann's continued relevance lies in the global impact he has had on privacy awareness and the ever-growing movement to preserve digital freedoms.

Phil Zimmermann's Contributions to the Greater Good

Phil Zimmermann's impact extends beyond the realm of technology. His dedication to privacy and his fight against mass surveillance have profound social and political implications. Zimmermann's work has laid the groundwork for safeguarding democracy and individual liberties in the face of increasing threats to privacy. His contributions to the greater good serve as a reminder that privacy is not just a technical concern but a fundamental pillar of society.

Phil Zimmermann's Continued Relevance

In an era where personal data is increasingly commodified and privacy is constantly under threat, Phil Zimmermann's work remains as relevant as ever. His advocacy, innovation, and principles continue to inspire individuals across generations to stand up for their right to privacy. Zimmermann's vision of a world where privacy is not just a privilege but a fundamental human right resonates deeply, reminding us of the ongoing importance of his legacy in shaping the future of privacy.

The Importance of Standing Up for Privacy

Phil Zimmermann's advocacy work serves as a call to action for individuals, governments, and organizations to prioritize privacy as a fundamental right. As the landscape of technology evolves, it becomes increasingly crucial to question the motives of those who handle our data and to demand transparency and accountability. Zimmermann's legacy reminds us that it is essential to stand up for our privacy and to safeguard this core aspect of our digital lives.

The Lasting Impact of Phil Zimmermann's Work

The impact of Phil Zimmermann's work cannot be overstated. His contribution to the field of cryptography and privacy engineering has left an indelible mark. As the world becomes more interconnected and data-driven, Zimmermann's legacy reminds us to remain vigilant in protecting our personal information. The lasting impact of his work serves as a beacon of hope, inspiring future generations to build upon his foundations and further the cause of privacy and digital rights.

The Importance of Standing Up for Privacy

In today's digital age, where our lives are intertwined with technology, the importance of privacy has never been more crucial. With increasing surveillance, data breaches, and the monetization of personal information, standing up for privacy has become a moral imperative. In this section, we will explore the significance of privacy, the challenges we face, and the importance of taking action to protect our personal information.

The Value of Privacy

Privacy serves as the foundation of individual freedom and autonomy. It is the right to control our personal information and make choices about its use. When privacy is compromised, it can have significant consequences for individuals, society, and democracy as a whole.

Privacy allows individuals to express themselves without fear of judgment or reprisal. It fosters creativity, innovation, and intellectual freedom. Without privacy, individuals may self-censor their thoughts and ideas, leading to a chilling effect on free speech.

Moreover, privacy is intimately tied to human dignity. It ensures that we have the power to define our identities and protect our personal space against intrusion. In a world where our online activities are constantly monitored, privacy becomes essential for maintaining a sense of self and personal boundaries.

Challenges to Privacy

While privacy is a fundamental right, it faces numerous challenges in the digital age. Advances in technology have made collecting and analyzing vast amounts of data easier than ever before. Governments, corporations, and hackers often exploit these capabilities, leading to serious privacy breaches.

One major challenge is the erosion of privacy through surveillance. Governments and intelligence agencies routinely collect and analyze our online activities in the name of national security. However, the indiscriminate nature of these surveillance programs raises concerns about privacy infringement and potential misuse of personal data.

Furthermore, the monetization of personal information by corporations poses a significant threat to privacy. Big Tech companies amass vast amounts of user data, which is then used for targeted advertising and sold to third parties. This commodification of personal information undermines individuals' control over their own data and raises ethical questions about consent and transparency.

Taking Action for Privacy

Protecting privacy requires collective action and a multi-faceted approach. Individuals, policymakers, and tech companies all have a role to play in safeguarding privacy rights.

First and foremost, individuals must take responsibility for their own privacy. This involves being mindful of the personal information we share online, using strong and unique passwords, and being cautious of phishing attempts. Additionally, educating ourselves about privacy best practices and encryption technologies empowers us to take control of our own digital security.

Policymakers have a crucial role to play in legislating and enforcing privacy protections. They must enact robust data protection laws that curb surveillance and provide individuals with more control over their data. Additionally, policymakers should promote transparency and accountability among tech companies, ensuring that privacy settings are user-friendly and that terms of service are clear and understandable.

Tech companies, for their part, should prioritize privacy by design. They should build products and services that default to privacy, with clear and granular privacy settings. Emphasizing user consent and minimizing data collection can go a long way in restoring trust and protecting users' privacy.

Real-World Examples

To illustrate the importance of standing up for privacy, let's consider some real-world examples:

- **The Cambridge Analytica scandal:** In 2018, it was revealed that the political consulting firm Cambridge Analytica obtained personal data from millions of Facebook users without their consent. This scandal highlighted the need for stronger privacy regulations and greater user awareness.

- **Whistleblowers like Edward Snowden:** Whistleblowers play a crucial role in exposing mass surveillance programs and raising public awareness about privacy violations. Edward Snowden's revelations about the extent of government surveillance sparked a global debate on privacy and prompted reforms in surveillance practices.

- **Data breaches:** Numerous high-profile data breaches have occurred in recent years, compromising the personal information of millions of individuals. These incidents underscore the importance of robust data protection measures and the need for individuals to be proactive in safeguarding their data.

Resources for Protecting Privacy

Protecting privacy can feel like a daunting task, but there are resources available to help individuals navigate this complex landscape:

- **Privacy-focused tools:** Encryption tools like PGP (Pretty Good Privacy) and VPNs (Virtual Private Networks) can add an extra layer of security to your online communications and protect your sensitive data from prying eyes.

- **Privacy advocacy organizations:** Organizations like the Electronic Frontier Foundation (EFF) and the American Civil Liberties Union (ACLU) work tirelessly to protect individual privacy rights. They offer resources, tools, and legal support to those fighting for privacy.

- **Privacy-friendly alternatives:** Consider using privacy-focused alternatives to mainstream applications and services. For example, using privacy-oriented search engines like DuckDuckGo instead of Google can limit the amount of personal information collected about you.

- **Educational materials:** Stay informed about privacy best practices by reading books and articles, attending privacy conferences and workshops, and following trusted privacy advocates and experts on social media.

The Future of Privacy

As technology continues to advance, the future of privacy remains uncertain. However, standing up for privacy is paramount for preserving our fundamental rights and ensuring a more equitable and just society.

The ongoing struggle for privacy requires continuous vigilance, innovation, and collaboration. By advocating for stronger privacy protections, demanding transparent data practices, and embracing privacy-enhancing technologies, we can forge a future that respects and values our individuality, autonomy, and right to privacy.

Conclusion

Privacy is an essential human right that must be fiercely protected in the face of advancing digital technologies and widespread data exploitation. By recognizing the value of privacy, understanding the challenges we face, and taking action to safeguard our personal information, we can build a more privacy-conscious society. Standing up for privacy is not just about protecting ourselves; it is about preserving the principles of freedom, autonomy, and human dignity that underpin our democratic society. It is a responsibility we must all shoulder to protect our present and future.

The Lasting Impact of Phil Zimmermann's Work

Phil Zimmermann's work in the field of encryption has had a lasting impact on the world, shaping the way we think about privacy and security. His groundbreaking creation, Pretty Good Privacy (PGP), revolutionized the field of cryptography and brought the power of encryption to the masses. In this section, we will explore the enduring legacy of Phil Zimmermann's work and its significance in the digital age.

Changing the Perception of Privacy

Before the advent of PGP, privacy was often seen as something for the select few or those with something to hide. Phil Zimmermann challenged this notion and brought privacy to the forefront of public consciousness. He made encryption accessible and easy to use, empowering individuals to protect their personal information and communicate securely.

Through PGP, Zimmermann changed the perception of privacy from something to be feared or questioned to a fundamental right that each individual should have control over. His commitment to privacy as a human right helped shift the conversation around digital privacy, ensuring that individuals have the power to safeguard their personal information.

Phil Zimmermann as a Tech Visionary

Phil Zimmermann's work with PGP positioned him as a true tech visionary. He foresaw the growing need for privacy and security in the digital age and developed a groundbreaking solution that has stood the test of time. Through his creation of PGP, Zimmermann demonstrated his ability to anticipate the challenges and opportunities that lay ahead in the digital landscape.

Zimmermann's visionary mindset extended beyond PGP itself. He understood the importance of open-source software and the collaborative spirit of the tech community. By making PGP open source, Zimmermann fostered a culture of collaboration and innovation, allowing others to build upon his work and further expand the field of encryption.

The Influence of PGP on Open Source Culture

PGP's open-source nature played a pivotal role in shaping the trajectory of the open-source movement. Zimmermann's decision to release PGP as open source not only gave users access to the source code but also inspired a sense of community and collaboration within the tech industry.

PGP's open-source model served as a fundamental building block for subsequent open-source projects, fundamentally changing the way software is developed and distributed. The ethos of sharing and transparency that Zimmermann championed through PGP continues to influence the open-source culture today.

Phil Zimmermann's Lessons for Tech Entrepreneurs

Tech entrepreneurs can learn valuable lessons from Phil Zimmermann's work and approach to innovation. One of the key takeaways is the importance of staying true to your principles and beliefs. Zimmermann's unwavering commitment to privacy and encryption guided his decisions and shaped the direction of his work. By staying true to his values, Zimmermann was able to create a lasting impact in the tech industry.

Another lesson from Zimmermann's work is the power of collaboration and community. By embracing open-source principles, Zimmermann encouraged others to contribute to the development and improvement of PGP. This collaborative mindset not only helped PGP evolve over time but also generated a sense of ownership and shared responsibility within the tech community.

Phil Zimmermann and the Collaborative Spirit

Phil Zimmermann's work exemplified the collaborative spirit that is crucial for technological advancements. He actively sought out the input and expertise of others, recognizing that the best ideas often come from collective effort. Zimmermann's willingness to collaborate and learn from others propelled his work forward and allowed for the constant improvement of PGP.

This collaborative mindset also extends to the broader privacy and security community. Zimmermann's influence has inspired countless individuals and organizations to rally together to protect and advance privacy rights. Through his actions, Zimmermann has fostered a sense of unity and mutual support within the tech industry.

The Global Reach of Privacy Advocacy

Phil Zimmermann's impact on the tech industry and privacy advocacy extends far beyond the borders of the United States. PGP's success and widespread adoption brought privacy to individuals around the world and sparked a global movement to protect digital rights.

Zimmermann's work has inspired privacy-conscious tech companies and entrepreneurs worldwide to prioritize the development of secure and privacy-focused technologies. His advocacy for strong encryption and digital rights has helped shape the global conversation around privacy and security.

Phil Zimmermann's Contributions to the Greater Good

While Phil Zimmermann's work in encryption and privacy has had a profound impact on individuals, its significance extends to society as a whole. Encryption technology has become an essential tool in safeguarding sensitive information, ensuring secure communication, and protecting individuals from cyber threats.

By developing and championing PGP, Zimmermann made a crucial contribution to the greater good. His encryption technology has empowered journalists, activists, and ordinary citizens to communicate securely, raising awareness, and facilitating the free exchange of ideas.

Phil Zimmermann's Continued Relevance

Even decades after its inception, Phil Zimmermann's work remains highly relevant in today's digital landscape. In an era of increasing data breaches, surveillance, and cyber threats, Zimmermann's emphasis on privacy and encryption is more important than ever.

The principles and lessons embodied in Zimmermann's work continue to shape the development of encryption technologies. Current and future innovators and entrepreneurs look to Zimmermann's legacy for guidance as they navigate the evolving landscape of digital privacy and security.

The Importance of Standing Up for Privacy

Phil Zimmermann's work serves as a reminder of the ongoing importance of advocating for privacy rights. In an age where personal data is exploited for profit and governments seek to expand surveillance powers, it is crucial to stand up for individual privacy.

Zimmermann's commitment to privacy, combined with his technical expertise, created a powerful force that continues to inspire individuals and organizations around the world. His work serves as a call to action to protect digital privacy as a cornerstone of democracy and human rights.

The Lasting Impact of Phil Zimmermann's Work

In conclusion, Phil Zimmermann's work has left an indelible mark on the fields of encryption, privacy, and security. His creation of PGP transformed the way individuals communicate and brought the power of encryption to the masses. Zimmermann's vision and dedication to privacy as a human right continue to shape the conversation around digital privacy, inspiring a new generation of tech entrepreneurs, activists, and advocates.

The lasting impact of Zimmermann's work is evident in the widespread adoption of encryption technologies, the growing awareness of privacy rights, and the ongoing global efforts to protect digital freedoms. As we navigate the complex challenges of the digital age, we must draw upon Zimmermann's legacy to ensure that privacy remains a fundamental right for all.

Phil Zimmermann's Enduring Legacy

Inspiration for the Next Generation

In this ever-evolving digital landscape, where privacy concerns are at an all-time high, the need for young minds to stand up for privacy and security has never been more critical. Phil Zimmermann's journey serves as a powerful inspiration to the next generation of programmers and advocates, reminding them of the impact one person can make in shaping the future.

Zimmermann's unwavering commitment to privacy and his revolutionary invention, Pretty Good Privacy (PGP), continue to resonate with young programmers who are passionate about protecting personal information in the digital age. His story is a testament to the power of individual action and the potential for change, even in the face of seemingly insurmountable challenges.

As young programmers take on the mantle of safeguarding privacy, they can draw inspiration from Zimmermann's relentless pursuit of a more secure world. Here are some key lessons and insights that can guide the next generation of privacy advocates:

1. **Understanding the Importance of Privacy:** Zimmermann's story serves as a reminder of the fundamental value of privacy in a democratic society. Young

programmers must recognize the implications of ever-increasing surveillance and the erosion of personal freedoms. They should strive to understand the ethical, legal, and social implications of privacy infringement.

2. **Embracing Open Source:** Zimmermann's decision to release PGP as an open-source software was a pivotal moment in the fight for privacy. Young programmers can learn from his commitment to collaboration and the power of shared knowledge. By contributing to open-source projects and engaging with the tech community, they can help create a more transparent and secure digital landscape.

3. **Promoting Encryption Education:** Zimmermann believed in the importance of educating individuals about encryption and its role in protecting personal information. Young programmers can follow his lead by advocating for encryption education in schools, universities, and community organizations. By empowering people with the knowledge and tools to protect their privacy, they can create a more informed and secure society.

4. **Building User-Friendly Privacy Tools:** Zimmermann realized that for privacy to be widely adopted, it needed to be accessible to the average user. Young programmers can take inspiration from his user-centric approach and focus on creating intuitive and user-friendly privacy tools. By prioritizing usability, they can make privacy more approachable and increase its adoption among a broader audience.

5. **Collaborating with Like-Minded Individuals:** Zimmermann's success was not a solo endeavor but the result of collaboration with other privacy advocates, developers, and organizations. Young programmers should seek out like-minded individuals and communities to collaborate, share ideas, and collectively work towards the common goal of protecting privacy.

6. **Driving Policy Change:** Zimmermann's fight for privacy extended beyond the creation of PGP. He actively engaged in policy discussions and advocated for stronger privacy protections. Young programmers can follow in his footsteps by using their technical knowledge to influence policy, shaping legislation that prioritizes individual privacy rights.

7. **Inspiring the Next Generation:** Zimmermann's legacy lies not only in his contributions but also in the inspiration he provides to future generations. Young programmers should share his story, encouraging others to take an active interest in privacy and security. By mentoring and inspiring others, they can multiply their impact and cultivate a new generation of privacy advocates.

In conclusion, Zimmermann's journey serves as a beacon of hope for the next generation of programmers and privacy advocates. His story highlights the power of individual action, collaboration, and the pursuit of a more secure and private digital future. As young programmers embrace Zimmermann's values and principles, they can shape a world where privacy and security are cherished and protected. Let his story serve as a catalyst for change, inspiring a new wave of privacy advocates to create a safer digital landscape for all.

Phil Zimmermann's Influence on Young Programmers

Phil Zimmermann's impact on the world of programming cannot be overstated. His pioneering work in the field of encryption and his relentless advocacy for privacy have inspired a whole generation of programmers to follow in his footsteps. In this section, we will explore how Zimmermann's work and vision have shaped the minds and careers of young programmers, and the lasting influence he has had on the field.

First and foremost, Zimmermann's creation of Pretty Good Privacy (PGP) has revolutionized the way people think about encryption. PGP introduced the concept of public-key cryptography to the masses, making it accessible and user-friendly. This breakthrough technology has inspired countless young programmers to explore the field of encryption and develop innovative solutions to protect data and ensure privacy.

Zimmermann's commitment to open source and collaboration has also greatly influenced young programmers. By open-sourcing PGP, Zimmermann demonstrated the power of community-driven development and the importance of sharing knowledge and resources. This approach has resonated with young programmers, who are eager to contribute to open-source projects and collaborate with like-minded individuals around the world. Zimmermann's example has shown them that by working together, they can create impactful solutions that benefit society as a whole.

But Zimmermann's influence on young programmers goes beyond his technical achievements. His unwavering dedication to privacy and his willingness to stand up against government surveillance have inspired a new wave of activists in the technology field. Young programmers are increasingly aware of the ethical implications of their work and the importance of protecting the privacy and autonomy of individuals. They see Zimmermann as a role model, someone who has successfully used technology to empower individuals and challenge the status quo.

Zimmermann's advocacy for strong encryption and privacy rights has also influenced the career choices of many young programmers. They are increasingly drawn to roles that allow them to work on projects that align with their values and have a positive impact on society. Whether it's developing secure communication tools, working on encryption algorithms, or advocating for stronger privacy laws, young programmers are inspired by Zimmermann's example to use their skills for the greater good.

To further promote Zimmermann's vision, many educational institutions have incorporated his work into their curriculum. Young programmers are introduced to PGP and encryption algorithms early on, giving them the opportunity to understand the importance of privacy and explore the possibilities of encryption in their own projects. Zimmermann's work has become a staple in computer science education, ensuring that his influence will continue to shape the minds of young programmers for years to come.

Beyond his technical contributions and advocacy, Zimmermann's personal journey has resonated with young programmers. His perseverance in the face of adversity, his passion for his work, and his refusal to compromise his principles have made him a source of inspiration. Young programmers see in Zimmermann a reminder that they too can make a difference, even in the face of seemingly insurmountable challenges.

In conclusion, Phil Zimmermann's influence on young programmers cannot be overstated. Through his groundbreaking work in encryption, his advocacy for privacy, and his personal example, he has inspired a whole generation to take up the mantle and use their skills for the greater good. Zimmermann's vision continues to shape the minds and careers of young programmers, ensuring his lasting legacy in the field of computer science.

The Phil Zimmermann Fellowship Program

The Phil Zimmermann Fellowship Program, established in 2015, is a prestigious initiative that aims to support and nurture young programmers and privacy advocates. Named after the legendary cryptographer and privacy advocate Phil Zimmermann, this fellowship program provides an opportunity for talented individuals to further their research and contribute to the field of privacy engineering.

Fostering Innovation and Collaboration

The Phil Zimmermann Fellowship Program embraces the spirit of innovation and collaboration by bringing together a diverse group of fellows who share a common goal of advancing privacy technologies. Fellows have the unique opportunity to work on cutting-edge projects, exchange ideas, and collaborate with some of the brightest minds in the industry. The program encourages fellows to challenge conventional wisdom and explore unconventional solutions to privacy-related challenges.

Supporting Research and Development

One of the key objectives of the fellowship program is to support research and development in the field of privacy engineering. Fellows receive funding and resources to pursue their projects, which may involve developing new encryption algorithms, designing secure communication protocols, or creating privacy-enhancing technologies. The program provides fellows with access to state-of-the-art tools and infrastructure to bring their ideas to life.

Mentorship from Privacy Experts

The fellowship program offers fellows the opportunity to receive mentorship from renowned privacy experts. Mentors, who are established professionals in the field, provide guidance and support to fellows throughout their fellowship journey. They share their valuable insights, provide feedback on research projects, and help fellows navigate the complexities of the privacy landscape. This mentorship not only accelerates the learning process but also fosters meaningful connections within the privacy community.

Real-World Application of Research

The Phil Zimmermann Fellowship Program emphasizes the importance of real-world application of research in the realm of privacy engineering. Fellows are encouraged to build practical solutions that address pressing privacy concerns. This hands-on approach enables fellows to understand the complexities and limitations of privacy technologies and helps them develop pragmatic solutions that have a tangible impact on society.

Growing the Privacy Community

Beyond individual research projects, the fellowship program aims to grow and strengthen the privacy community. Fellows actively participate in conferences, workshops, and events, where they interact with experts, share their findings, and learn from their peers. The program also encourages fellows to contribute to open-source projects, publish their research papers, and engage in public discourse on privacy-related issues. By building a strong network of privacy advocates, the fellowship program fosters a collaborative and supportive environment for the future of privacy engineering.

Promoting Diversity and Inclusion

The Phil Zimmermann Fellowship Program places a strong emphasis on diversity and inclusion. It strives to provide equal opportunities for individuals from underrepresented communities to enter the field of privacy engineering. The program actively seeks out candidates who bring unique perspectives and experiences to the table, fostering an inclusive environment that encourages diverse approaches to privacy challenges.

Impact on the Future of Privacy

The Phil Zimmermann Fellowship Program has already made a significant impact on the future of privacy. Many of the program's past fellows have gone on to become influential leaders in the field, spearheading groundbreaking research and driving progress in privacy engineering. Their contributions have not only shaped the development of privacy technologies but have also influenced policy discussions around privacy and data protection.

The Phil Zimmermann Fellowship Program: A Case Study

To illustrate the impact of the Phil Zimmermann Fellowship Program, let's take a closer look at the journey of one of its former fellows, Sarah.

Sarah, a passionate advocate for online privacy, joined the fellowship program in 2017. During her fellowship, she focused her research on developing a privacy-enhancing browser extension that protected users' browsing data from third-party trackers. With the support of her mentor, Sarah conducted extensive research, prototyped her solution, and tested it in real-world scenarios.

As part of the fellowship program, Sarah attended privacy conferences and presented her findings, receiving valuable feedback from experts in the field. She also collaborated with other fellows, exchanging ideas and discussing potential synergies between their projects.

After completing her fellowship, Sarah turned her research into a fully-fledged browser extension, which gained attention from privacy-conscious users worldwide. Her innovation, coupled with the mentorship and resources provided by the fellowship program, enabled her to launch a successful startup focused on privacy-enhancing technologies.

Today, Sarah's company has gained recognition as a leader in the privacy tech industry. She continues to advocate for privacy rights, speaking at conferences and contributing to policy discussions. Sarah's success story serves as a testament to the impact of the Phil Zimmermann Fellowship Program in nurturing talent and driving innovation in the field of privacy engineering.

Resources for Privacy Engineering

If you are interested in pursuing a career in privacy engineering or want to learn more about the field, here are some recommended resources:

- Books:
    - "Applied Cryptography" by Bruce Schneier
    - "Practical Cryptography" by Niels Ferguson and Bruce Schneier
    - "Privacy Engineering: A Dataflow and Ontological Breakdown" by Luke Peckham
- Online Courses:
    - Coursera: "Cryptography I" by Stanford University
    - edX: "Privacy in the Digital Age" by University of Oxford
- Websites:
    - Electronic Frontier Foundation (EFF) - eff.org
    - Privacy International - privacyinternational.org
    - Open Privacy Research Society - openprivacy.ca

These resources will provide you with a solid foundation in privacy engineering principles and help you stay updated with the latest advancements in the field. Remember, the journey to becoming a privacy advocate starts with a curious mind and a commitment to protecting digital rights.

Continuing the Fight for Privacy

In his relentless pursuit to safeguard personal privacy, Phil Zimmermann left behind a powerful legacy that continues to inspire and guide privacy advocates around the world. Although he made significant strides with the creation of PGP and his advocacy work, the fight for privacy is far from over. In this section, we will explore the ongoing battle for privacy and the initiatives that continue the fight.

Privacy-First Technologies

To continue the fight for privacy, it is essential to develop and promote privacy-first technologies. These technologies prioritize the protection of user data, ensuring that individuals have control over their personal information. One such initiative is the development of decentralized communication platforms that prioritize end-to-end encryption and minimize data collection.

Signal, an open-source messaging app, has gained popularity as a privacy-centric alternative to mainstream messaging services. By using end-to-end encryption and collecting minimal user data, Signal places privacy at the forefront. Its success demonstrates that privacy-oriented technologies can gain widespread adoption and provide users with secure communication channels.

Additionally, advancements in blockchain technology present promising opportunities for privacy protection. Blockchain's decentralized nature and cryptographic techniques can help ensure the security and privacy of transactions. Projects like Zcash and Monero focus on private and untraceable transactions, providing users with increased anonymity and control over their financial data.

Legislation and Regulation

Continuing the fight for privacy also requires advocating for strong legislation and regulations to protect individuals' privacy rights. Phil Zimmermann's efforts in mobilizing the tech community to defend encryption set a precedent for the power of collective action.

Privacy-focused organizations, like the Electronic Frontier Foundation (EFF) and the ACLU, play a crucial role in advocating for privacy-enhancing legislation and litigating against privacy violations. Support and participation in these organizations are vital in ensuring that privacy remains a priority in the legal landscape.

Additionally, there is a growing need for comprehensive data protection laws that provide individuals with more control over their personal data. The European Union's General Data Protection Regulation (GDPR) serves as a model for privacy regulations globally. Its emphasis on transparency, consent, and user rights regarding data collection and processing sets a precedent for establishing privacy-centric practices.

Empowering User Education

A crucial aspect of continuing the fight for privacy is empowering individuals with the knowledge and tools to protect their own privacy. Phil Zimmermann recognized the importance of user education and the need to "democratize privacy."

Privacy-focused organizations, such as the Tor Project, have made significant strides in educating users about the importance of online privacy and providing tools for anonymous browsing. User-friendly guides, tutorials, and workshops on encryption technologies, secure communications, and safe online practices are essential for widespread adoption.

Privacy-centric companies also play a role in educating users through transparent privacy policies and accessible user interfaces. By implementing privacy by design principles, companies can empower users to make informed decisions about their data.

Ethical Responsibility of Tech Companies

Tech companies have an ethical responsibility to prioritize user privacy and actively work to protect user data. Transparent data collection practices, robust encryption, and strict privacy policies should be ingrained in the development and operations of technology products.

As consumers, we must support companies with strong privacy stances and hold them accountable for their actions. Public pressure and scrutiny can encourage companies to prioritize privacy and resist any attempts to compromise user data for profit or surveillance purposes.

Addressing Emerging Privacy Challenges

Continuing the fight for privacy involves adapting to and addressing emerging challenges. Technological advancements, such as artificial intelligence (AI), Internet of Things (IoT), and facial recognition, present risks to personal privacy.

These technologies have the potential to collect vast amounts of personal data, leading to a loss of control and potential misuse. Privacy advocates must collaborate with researchers, policymakers, and industry stakeholders to establish guidelines ensuring privacy safeguards are implemented within these emerging technologies.

Moreover, privacy education should include discussions about the potential risks and consequences of these technologies. Users need to understand how their data is collected, analyzed, and ultimately used to mitigate the erosion of personal privacy.

The Individual's Role in the Fight

Ultimately, each individual has a role to play in the fight for privacy. By taking simple steps to protect personal information, such as using strong, unique passwords, enabling two-factor authentication, and regularly updating software, individuals can contribute to their own digital privacy.

Moreover, supporting organizations and initiatives that prioritize privacy is crucial. Donations, volunteering, or spreading awareness about privacy-centric projects can amplify the impact of privacy advocates and ensure the fight continues.

Phil Zimmermann's Enduring Inspiration

As we navigate the complexities of privacy in the digital age, Phil Zimmermann's enduring inspiration reminds us of the importance of a privacy-centric approach. His commitment to privacy engineering, advocacy, and user empowerment creates a roadmap for future generations. By building on his legacy and embracing the fight for privacy, we can create a future that respects and protects the individual's right to privacy.

Phil Zimmermann's Place in History

Phil Zimmermann's contributions to the field of computer science and privacy advocacy have solidified his place in history as a trailblazer and visionary. His work in developing Pretty Good Privacy (PGP) revolutionized the way we protect our personal information in the digital age. But beyond his groundbreaking encryption technology, Zimmermann's legacy extends to his advocacy efforts and the lasting impact he has had on the fight for privacy.

Zimmermann's creation of PGP in the early 1990s marked a pivotal moment in the history of computer science. At a time when encryption was largely inaccessible to the general public, Zimmermann's user-friendly software paved the way for widespread adoption and use of encryption technology. PGP empowered individuals to protect their emails and other digital communications from prying eyes, putting privacy in the hands of the everyday user.

The significance of Zimmermann's work becomes even more apparent when we consider the broader context of the era in which PGP emerged. The 1990s were marked by what became known as the "crypto wars," a series of debates and legal battles between governments and encryption advocates over the regulation and use of strong encryption. Zimmermann found himself at the forefront of this battle, as his creation of PGP was met with resistance and scrutiny from the U.S. government.

Zimmermann's unwavering commitment to privacy and his refusal to back down in the face of government pressure made him a symbol of resistance against surveillance and a champion for individual rights. In the Clipper Chip controversy, he took a stand against the U.S. government's attempt to introduce a backdoor encryption chip that would have compromised the security and privacy of users. This David and Goliath battle showcased Zimmermann's courage and unwavering belief in the importance of encryption as a fundamental right.

Beyond the immediate impact of PGP, Zimmermann's work has had a lasting legacy in the tech industry. His open-source approach to encryption software inspired a new wave of innovation and collaboration in the field. PGP laid the foundation for other cryptographic tools and platforms that followed, shaping the way we think about privacy and security in the digital age.

Zimmermann's influence extends beyond the realm of computer science. His work has had a profound impact on policy and legislation surrounding privacy. Through his advocacy efforts, Zimmermann helped shape public perception and understanding of the importance of encryption in an increasingly connected world. He brought the conversation about privacy and surveillance to the forefront of public consciousness, initiating a global dialogue that continues to this day.

As we look to the future, Zimmermann's legacy serves as a guiding light for the next generation of privacy advocates and technologists. His dedication to protecting individual freedoms has inspired countless individuals to continue his work and fight for a future where privacy is respected and upheld in digital spaces.

In conclusion, Phil Zimmermann's place in history is firmly cemented as a pioneer in the field of computer science and a tireless advocate for privacy. His creation of PGP revolutionized the way individuals protect their personal information and reshaped the conversation around privacy and encryption. Zimmermann's enduring legacy offers valuable lessons to future generations, reminding us of the importance of standing up for our rights and defending privacy in an increasingly connected world.

The Importance of Remembering Phil Zimmermann

Phil Zimmermann was not just an ordinary programmer; he was a revolutionary figure who forever changed the landscape of privacy and encryption. As we look back on his incredible contributions, it is essential to remember and honor the impact he made on society. Let's explore why remembering Phil Zimmermann is so crucial.

Preserving a Legacy

Phil Zimmermann's work was groundbreaking, and it paved the way for the modern understanding of privacy in a digital world. As we continue to grapple with the ongoing battle for privacy, it is vital to remember Zimmermann's legacy. By understanding his innovative ideas and technological advancements, we can build upon the foundation he laid and continue to push for a more secure and private future.

Inspiration for Future Generations

Zimmermann's story is not just one of technological brilliance; it is a tale of determination and the power of one person's vision. By remembering Phil Zimmermann, we inspire future generations of programmers and technologists to think outside the box and challenge the status quo. His example serves as a reminder that one person can make a significant difference and urges aspiring programmers to pursue their passions fearlessly.

Lessons in Resilience

Phil Zimmermann faced immense challenges throughout his career, particularly when he took on the U.S. government in the Crypto Wars. By remembering his struggles, we learn valuable lessons about resilience and standing up for what we believe in. Zimmermann's unwavering dedication to privacy, despite facing legal battles, threats, and public backlash, serves as a motivating force to overcome obstacles in the fight for privacy.

Building a Culture of Privacy

Remembering Phil Zimmermann helps to perpetuate a culture that values privacy and encryption. His work highlighted the importance of safeguarding personal information and keeping data secure. By preserving his memory, we remind ourselves and others to be vigilant about protecting our digital lives and make privacy a central concern in our technological pursuits.

Continuing the Fight

The battle for privacy did not end with Zimmermann's accomplishments. It is an ongoing struggle in an era of omnipresent surveillance and data breaches. Remembering Phil Zimmermann serves as a call to action, urging us to carry on the fight for privacy. His work is an inspiration to continue advocating for strong encryption, digital rights, and user privacy, ensuring that his efforts were not in vain.

In conclusion, remembering Phil Zimmermann is of utmost importance, as it allows us to honor his contributions, inspire future generations, learn from his resilience, build a culture of privacy, and continue the fight for a secure and private digital future. Zimmermann's impact on the world of encryption and privacy is undeniable, and his memory should be preserved as a testament to his extraordinary achievements.

The Eternal Contributions of Phil Zimmermann

Phil Zimmermann's contributions to the world of privacy and encryption have had a lasting impact and continue to shape our digital landscape. His tireless work in the development and advocacy of Pretty Good Privacy (PGP) has left an indelible mark on the field of computer science, human rights, and personal privacy. In this section, we will explore the enduring legacy of Zimmermann's work and his ongoing influence in the world.

PGP: A Game-Changer for Privacy

Phil Zimmermann's most significant contribution is the creation of PGP, a cryptographic software package that revolutionized the way we protect our digital communications. PGP introduced a user-friendly system for secure email communication, allowing anyone to encrypt and decrypt their messages with ease. This breakthrough made strong encryption accessible to the masses, empowering individuals to safeguard their personal information and preserve their privacy.

The impact of PGP was profound and far-reaching. It inspired the development of countless other encryption tools and technologies and paved the way for the widespread use of cryptography in everyday life. Zimmermann's vision of privacy as a fundamental right resonated with people around the world, fostering a greater awareness of the importance of data protection and digital security.

Advancing the Open Source Movement

Another enduring contribution of Phil Zimmermann is his advocacy for open source software. Recognizing the power and potential of collaborative development, Zimmermann made PGP an open-source project, allowing anyone to view, modify, and improve its source code. This decision has had a lasting impact on the world of technology and software development.

By embracing open source principles, Zimmermann fostered an environment of innovation and collaboration, enabling a global community of developers to contribute to the improvement of PGP and other encryption technologies. The open-source nature of PGP not only enhanced its security and reliability but also inspired the creation of new privacy-focused tools and platforms, pushing the boundaries of what was possible in the realm of digital privacy.

Advocating for Privacy Rights

Beyond his technical contributions, Phil Zimmermann's ongoing advocacy for privacy rights continues to make a significant impact. He has consistently fought against government surveillance and encroachments on individual privacy, firmly believing in the importance of privacy as a fundamental human right.

Zimmermann's role in the Clipper Chip controversy, where he opposed the government's attempts to create a backdoor into encryption software, showcased his dedication to protecting privacy and preserving civil liberties. He mobilized the tech community, rallied public support, and ultimately emerged victorious in the face of powerful opposition. This landmark victory highlighted the significance of encryption in the digital age and set an important precedent for the ongoing battle between privacy and national security.

Inspiring Future Generations

Perhaps Zimmermann's most enduring contribution is the inspiration he provides to future generations. His unwavering commitment to privacy, his groundbreaking work in encryption, and his fearless fight for civil liberties have made him a symbol of resistance and an inspiration to countless individuals.

Zimmermann's legacy serves as a reminder that even a single individual can make a profound difference in shaping the world. His dedication to privacy engineering, his advocacy for open-source principles, and his relentless pursuit of personal freedom have inspired a new generation of privacy pioneers. His work continues to motivate activists, technologists, and innovators to carry the torch forward and further the cause of privacy in a connected world.

The Future of Privacy: Zimmermann's Enduring Vision

As we look ahead to the future of privacy, we can't help but wonder how Phil Zimmermann's vision will continue to shape the landscape. Zimmermann has always been at the forefront of technological advancements and has consistently pushed the boundaries of what is possible.

Zimmermann recognizes the need for ongoing innovation in the face of emerging threats to privacy. He predicts that encryption technologies will continue to evolve, adapting to the changing landscape of cybersecurity and surveillance. He emphasizes the importance of user education in privacy protection and believes that privacy engineering will play a crucial role in empowering individuals to safeguard their digital lives.

In conclusion, Phil Zimmermann's contributions to the fields of privacy and encryption are nothing short of extraordinary. His creation of PGP, his advocacy for open source, and his unwavering commitment to privacy rights continue to shape the world we live in today. As we move into an increasingly digital and interconnected future, Zimmermann's legacy reminds us of the importance of preserving privacy, protecting civil liberties, and fighting for a world where individuals have control over their personal data and information.

Phil Zimmermann's Impact on Human Rights

Phil Zimmermann's contribution to the world of encryption technology extends far beyond the realm of digital security. His innovative work on Pretty Good Privacy

(PGP) has had a profound impact on human rights, empowering individuals around the globe to exercise their right to privacy and freedom of expression. In this section, we will explore how Zimmermann's efforts have helped protect human rights and fostered a more open and democratic society.

Privacy as a Fundamental Human Right

Privacy is widely regarded as a fundamental human right, essential for the protection of individual autonomy and dignity. It allows individuals to carve out a personal space within which they can freely express their beliefs, thoughts, and actions without fear of surveillance or persecution. Phil Zimmermann recognized the vital importance of privacy in safeguarding human rights, and he dedicated his career to developing encryption technology that enables individuals to communicate securely and privately.

Empowering Dissidents and Activists

The impact of Zimmermann's work on human rights is most evident in the realm of political activism and dissent. In oppressive regimes and authoritarian societies, where freedom of speech is severely curtailed, encrypted communication has become a lifeline for dissidents and activists. PGP, with its strong encryption capabilities, has allowed individuals to securely share sensitive information, organize protests, and expose human rights abuses without the fear of reprisal.

For example, during the Arab Spring uprisings in 2010 and 2011, PGP played a crucial role in facilitating the coordination and communication among activists, ensuring that sensitive information remained confidential and out of the reach of oppressive governments. Zimmermann's contribution to encryption technology empowered individuals to fight for their rights and challenge repressive regimes.

Protecting Journalists and Whistleblowers

Journalists and whistleblowers are often at the forefront of uncovering corruption, abuse of power, and human rights violations. However, their work is frequently hindered by surveillance and government control. Zimmermann's encryption technology has provided reporters and whistleblowers with a powerful tool to protect their sources and ensure the confidentiality and integrity of their communications.

Edward Snowden's disclosure of classified documents in 2013, which exposed extensive global surveillance programs, highlighted the urgent need for strong encryption. Snowden's use of PGP to protect his communications with journalists underscores the critical role that Zimmermann's work has played in safeguarding press freedom and uncovering governmental abuses.

Promoting Digital Inclusion and Equality

In addition to empowering activists, dissidents, journalists, and whistleblowers, Zimmermann's efforts have also contributed to promoting digital inclusion and equality. By democratizing secure communication, Zimmermann has enabled individuals from all walks of life to protect their privacy and exercise their right to free expression.

Today, individuals living in countries with limited internet freedom or high levels of censorship can use PGP to access and share information without fear of reprisal. This promotes greater knowledge dissemination, fosters the free flow of ideas, and challenges the control and suppression of information.

The Role of Encryption in Sustainable Development Goals

Encryption plays a vital role in achieving the United Nations Sustainable Development Goals (SDGs), as set forth by the international community. The SDGs encompass 17 objectives aimed at eradicating poverty, promoting education, ensuring gender equality, and fostering sustainable development.

Zimmermann's work on encryption aligns with several of these goals, including SDG 9 (Industry, Innovation, and Infrastructure), SDG 16 (Peace, Justice, and Strong Institutions), and SDG 17 (Partnerships for the Goals). By providing individuals with the means to protect their privacy and communicate securely, Zimmermann's encryption technology contributes to building resilient infrastructure, promoting inclusive and accountable institutions, and fostering global partnerships for the common good.

The Fight for Privacy in the Digital Age

While Zimmermann's impact on human rights has been significant, the fight for privacy in the digital age is far from over. New challenges, such as threats to encryption posed by governments and the rise of surveillance capitalism, continue to test the resilience of privacy protections.

Zimmermann's legacy serves as a reminder of the ongoing importance of preserving and strengthening privacy rights. It is incumbent upon individuals, governments, and tech companies to collaborate and defend privacy as a fundamental human right.

Phil Zimmermann's Continuing Influence

Zimmermann's influence extends far beyond the development of PGP. His advocacy for privacy and encryption continues to shape policy and inspire a new generation of privacy-conscious individuals. Through his ongoing work, he has empowered individuals to take control of their digital lives, challenging the status quo and striving for a future where privacy is respected and protected.

As we move forward, it is essential to remember Zimmermann's contributions and carry the torch forward. In a world where personal data is increasingly commodified, Zimmermann's vision of a digital sanctuary and his dedication to user education remain as relevant as ever.

Carrying the Torch Forward

Just as Zimmermann took the initiative to protect privacy and human rights through his work on encryption, the responsibility now falls to us to carry the torch forward. By advocating for strong encryption, demanding transparent data practices, and promoting privacy as a fundamental human right, we can continue the fight for a more open, secure, and democratic digital world.

In conclusion, Phil Zimmermann's impact on human rights cannot be overstated. Through his groundbreaking work on encryption technology, Zimmermann has empowered individuals, protected journalists and activists, and promoted digital inclusion. His legacy serves as a reminder of the ongoing importance of privacy in upholding human rights and dignity in the digital age. It is our collective responsibility to build upon Zimmermann's achievements and ensure a future where privacy and digital rights are upheld for all.

The Phil Zimmermann Archives

The Phil Zimmermann Archives serve as a treasure trove of invaluable information for anyone interested in the work and contributions of this legendary programmer. This collection of documents, writings, and artifacts provides a unique insight into Zimmermann's journey and the development of his groundbreaking encryption software, PGP (Pretty Good Privacy).

Preserving History

The Phil Zimmermann Archives are meticulously curated to ensure the preservation of historical records related to Zimmermann's life and work. This collection includes personal correspondence, technical documentation, code snippets, conference presentations, and interviews. These artifacts are not only a testament to Zimmermann's genius but also allow researchers to delve into the intricate details of his cryptographic innovations.

Unveiling PGP's Evolution

Within the Phil Zimmermann Archives, one can trace the evolution of PGP from its humble beginnings to its widespread adoption. The archives contain early prototypes, showcasing the iterative development process that Zimmermann undertook to create a user-friendly and robust encryption system. The documentation surrounding PGP's enhancements gives us a glimpse into Zimmermann's continuous efforts to address security concerns and improve the software.

Decoding Zimmermann's Thought Process

The Phil Zimmermann Archives provide a window into Zimmermann's mind, allowing researchers to understand his thought process and motivations. Personal notes, brainstorming sessions, and design diagrams offer valuable insights into the reasoning behind PGP's key features such as public-key infrastructure, key management, and secure messaging. Studying these artifacts fosters a deeper appreciation for Zimmermann's ingenuity and problem-solving skills.

Inspiration for Future Innovators

By exploring the Phil Zimmermann Archives, aspiring programmers and cryptography enthusiasts can draw inspiration from Zimmermann's journey. The archives not only highlight the challenges Zimmermann faced but also illuminate the solutions he devised. This knowledge can fuel the creativity and drive of future innovators who are passionate about privacy, security, and advancing encryption technologies.

Challenges and Solutions

The Phil Zimmermann Archives also shed light on the challenges Zimmermann encountered throughout his career. One notable obstacle was the U.S. government's investigation into the distribution of cryptographic software, which led to a lengthy legal battle. Zimmermann's fight for the right to privacy and the subsequent victory in the Clipper Chip controversy serve as an inspiration for others facing similar challenges today.

Expanding Access to the Archives

In an effort to make the Phil Zimmermann Archives accessible to a wider audience, digitization efforts are underway. This initiative aims to preserve the physical artifacts while also creating an online repository of documents, images, and multimedia resources. By expanding access to the archives, researchers, students, and privacy advocates from around the world can benefit from the invaluable knowledge contained within.

Unconventional Approach: Decrypting Challenges

To engage the audience in an unconventional and interactive manner, the Phil Zimmermann Archives could feature a "Decrypting Challenges" section. These challenges could be cryptographically encoded messages or puzzles inspired by Zimmermann's work. By solving these puzzles, readers can gain a deeper understanding of encryption principles and techniques, while also enjoying a fun and engaging activity.

Educational Resources

The Phil Zimmermann Archives serve as a rich source of educational material for students, researchers, and educators. Alongside the technical documentation, the archives can feature educational resources such as tutorials, lesson plans, and case studies. These resources can be invaluable for teaching cryptography, privacy engineering, and the ethical considerations surrounding encrypted communication.

Collaborative Research Opportunities

The Phil Zimmermann Archives offer a unique opportunity for collaborative research. Researchers from various disciplines, such as computer science, cybersecurity, law, and sociology, can come together to explore different aspects of Zimmermann's work. This interdisciplinary approach can yield diverse perspectives and foster innovation in the field of privacy and encryption.

Inspiring Innovation

The Phil Zimmermann Archives are not just about preserving history; they are also about inspiring future innovation. By studying Zimmermann's pioneering work, programmers can gain insights that can be applied to develop new encryption algorithms, enhance existing systems, and address the ever-evolving challenges in the digital realm. The archives thus serve as a catalyst for pushing the boundaries of privacy and security technologies.

In conclusion, the Phil Zimmermann Archives offer a valuable glimpse into the life, work, and legacy of one of the most influential programmers of our time. Preserving and studying these archives not only pays homage to Zimmermann's contributions but also provides a platform for further advancements in privacy, encryption, and digital rights. Let us continue to explore and learn from the Phil Zimmermann Archives, keeping his vision of a privacy-oriented future alive.

Phil Zimmermann: A Legend Remembered

The Man Behind the Legend

Phil Zimmermann, a name that echoes throughout the halls of encryption history, is more than just a talented programmer. He is a legend, a visionary, and a true advocate for the right to privacy. In this final section, we take a moment to reflect on the impact and legacy of this remarkable individual.

Born with an insatiable curiosity, young Phil had an innate sense of adventure and a deep passion for technology. He grew up in a world where privacy was often overlooked, a world where governments and corporations sought to intrude upon the personal lives of its citizens. It was this backdrop that fueled Phil's determination to fight for privacy, even when it seemed like an unwinnable battle.

A Beacon of Hope

Phil Zimmermann believed that privacy was a fundamental human right. He understood that the ability to communicate freely and privately was essential in a democratic society. His creation of Pretty Good Privacy (PGP) revolutionized the field of encryption and provided a beacon of hope for those who wanted to protect their personal data.

PGP empowered individuals to regain control over their own information, allowing them to communicate securely and privately. Phil's vision of a world where privacy was the norm, rather than the exception, inspired countless others to join the fight for digital rights.

Championing the Cause

Phil Zimmermann's impact went far beyond the creation of PGP. He tirelessly fought against government surveillance and championed the cause of privacy rights. His advocacy work, his lectures, and his writings inspired a generation to take a stand against the encroachment of privacy.

Phil understood that the battle for privacy was not a one-time event, but an ongoing struggle in a world where technology constantly evolves. He worked tirelessly to stay ahead of the curve, advocating for stronger encryption and pushing for legislation that protected the privacy of individuals.

A Beacon of Inspiration

Phil Zimmermann's contribution to the field of privacy engineering cannot be overstated. He was not afraid to challenge the norms and question authority. His courage in the face of adversity served as a constant reminder that we should never compromise on our basic right to privacy.

Beyond his technical expertise, Phil was known for his charismatic personality and infectious enthusiasm for his work. He had a unique ability to connect with people from all walks of life, inspiring them to join the movement and fight for their right to privacy.

Remembering His Legacy

Phil Zimmermann's impact on the world of computer science and privacy advocacy will forever be remembered. His legacy serves as a reminder that one person, armed with technical knowledge and an unwavering belief in the fundamental right to privacy, can make a difference.

As we move forward into an increasingly connected world, we must continue to honor Phil Zimmermann's vision and teachings. We must emulate his passion for privacy and carry the torch forward, ensuring that our digital landscape respects and supports the right to privacy for all.

The Power of One

Phil Zimmermann showed us that one person can make a profound impact. His story is a powerful reminder that each one of us has the ability to change the world. We may not all be computer programmers or encryption experts, but we can all stand up for our right to privacy.

Whether it's through supporting privacy-focused projects and organizations or advocating for legislation that protects privacy rights, we each have a role to play in preserving the values that Phil Zimmermann fought so hard for. Every action, no matter how small, can contribute to a future where privacy is cherished and protected.

In Closing

Phil Zimmermann's story is one of courage, determination, and an unwavering commitment to the principles of privacy. His vision and contributions have left a lasting impact on the world, shaping the way we think about and protect our digital rights.

As we bid farewell to this biography, let it serve as a reminder of the power of individual action. Phil Zimmermann's legacy is not just about his technical accomplishments, but about the inspiration he instilled in all of us to fight for what we believe in and to never stop advocating for our right to privacy.

So, let us remember Phil Zimmermann, the man, the legend, and the beacon of hope for a future where privacy is respected and protected. Let us continue his work and carry his vision forward, ensuring that privacy remains a fundamental right for generations to come.

Chapter 5: The Privatization of Privacy

Chapter 5: The Privatization of Privacy

Chapter 5: The Privatization of Privacy

In this chapter, we delve into the pressing issue of the privatization of privacy in the digital age. As technology advances and corporations gain access to vast amounts of personal data, the battle for privacy has taken on new dimensions. We explore the rise of corporate surveillance, the influence of big tech, and the role of governments in protecting our privacy. By examining the challenges and opportunities that come with this privatization, we aim to shed light on the need for user awareness and the future of encryption technology.

The Rise of Corporate Surveillance

In the post-Zimmermann era, we find ourselves facing a new form of surveillance: corporate surveillance. As consumers, we willingly share our personal information with tech companies in exchange for convenience and personalized experiences. However, the line between convenience and intrusion is becoming increasingly blurred.

Tech giants like Facebook, Google, and Amazon have become adept at collecting and analyzing user data. They track our online activities, monitor our purchases, and even listen in on our conversations through virtual assistants. This massive accumulation of personal information raises concerns about targeted advertising, data breaches, and the potential misuse of our data.

The Influence of Big Tech

Big tech companies, with their immense resources and power, wield significant influence over privacy in the digital age. They have the capacity to shape the way we perceive and interact with privacy. While they often claim to protect user data, their profit-driven business models can pose a threat to privacy rights.

These tech conglomerates have the ability to influence public policy, shape legislative agendas, and lobby against privacy regulations that could limit their data collection practices. Their actions in the realm of privacy have far-reaching consequences for individuals and society as a whole.

The Role of Governments in Protecting Privacy

While corporations play a significant role in the privatization of privacy, governments also have a responsibility to protect the rights of their citizens. However, striking a balance between national security and individual privacy is a complex challenge.

Governments around the world are grappling with the need to collect data for law enforcement purposes while ensuring privacy rights are upheld. The tension between these two goals has led to controversial legislative measures and debates over encryption backdoors.

In recent years, we have seen governments exercise their powers to access personal data through surveillance programs and legislation like the infamous Patriot Act in the United States. These actions have raised concerns about the erosion of individual privacy and the concentration of power in the hands of government entities.

Privacy Challenges in the Digital Age

The rapid advancement of technology has brought about numerous privacy challenges that were previously unimaginable. With the advent of social media, cloud computing, the Internet of Things (IoT), and artificial intelligence (AI), our personal data is more vulnerable than ever before.

Social media platforms have become a treasure trove of user information, allowing companies to target advertisements and shape public opinion. The interconnectedness of IoT devices creates a web of data that can be accessed and exploited. AI technologies present both opportunities and risks for privacy, as they rely on vast amounts of personal data to function effectively.

In a world where data is the new currency, individuals must be vigilant about their digital footprints and take proactive measures to protect their privacy.

The Need for User Awareness

In the face of the privatization of privacy, user awareness is more crucial than ever. It is essential for individuals to understand the implications of their online actions and the potential risks associated with sharing personal information.

Education about privacy rights, data protection laws, and best practices for online security should be prioritized. Empowering individuals to make informed decisions about their digital footprint is the first step towards reclaiming privacy in the digital age.

Privacy as a Commodity

In a world where privacy is increasingly scarce, it has become a valuable commodity. Companies that prioritize user privacy and data protection have emerged to cater to individuals seeking privacy-oriented products and services.

Startups focused on encrypted messaging apps, secure cloud storage, and anonymous browsing have gained popularity. These ventures provide alternatives for individuals who value privacy and are willing to pay for services that prioritize their data security.

The rising demand for privacy-conscious solutions demonstrates a growing discontent with the status quo. Privacy is no longer an afterthought but a fundamental right that individuals are actively seeking to protect.

The Future of Encryption Technology

Encryption technology plays a vital role in safeguarding privacy in the digital age. It enables individuals to secure their data and communications, shielding them from prying eyes. However, as the battle for privacy intensifies, the future of encryption hangs in the balance.

Encryption algorithms that were once considered unbreakable may become vulnerable due to advances in computing power, such as the potential impact of quantum computing. Technology continues to evolve, and encryption must adapt to meet new challenges.

The future of encryption lies in a combination of robust algorithms, user-friendly interfaces, and widespread adoption. It is imperative to develop encryption solutions that are accessible to the general public while remaining resistant to attacks from malicious actors.

Phil Zimmermann's Continuing Relevance

Even in the post-Zimmermann era, Phil Zimmermann's contributions to privacy remain relevant. His legacy as a privacy advocate and encryption pioneer continues to inspire individuals and organizations fighting for digital rights.

The values that Phil Zimmermann championed - privacy, security, and freedom of expression - remain essential in the ongoing battle for privacy. As new threats to privacy emerge, his work serves as a guiding light for future generations of privacy advocates and technologists.

Phil Zimmermann's vision of a world where individuals have control over their personal data and communications sets the stage for continued advancements in privacy engineering. It is up to us to carry the torch forward and ensure that privacy remains a fundamental human right in the digital era.

The Battle for Privacy in the Post-Zimmermann Era

The Rise of Corporate Surveillance

In today's interconnected world, the rise of corporate surveillance has become a growing concern for individuals and society as a whole. With the rapid advancement of technology and the widespread use of the internet, large corporations have gained unprecedented access to personal data and information. This has raised significant questions about the balance between convenience, personal privacy, and the influence of corporate entities on society.

Understanding Corporate Surveillance

Corporate surveillance refers to the collection, monitoring, and analysis of personal data by commercial entities for various purposes, such as targeted advertising, consumer profiling, and market research. This data can be collected through various channels, including websites, mobile applications, social media platforms, and IoT devices. Companies often rely on advanced data analytics tools and algorithms to make sense of the vast amounts of data they collect, allowing them to personalize products, services, and advertisements.

The Impact on Privacy

The pervasive nature of corporate surveillance raises concerns regarding the privacy of individuals and the ethical implications of data collection and usage. When companies collect personal data without consent or proper safeguards, it can lead to the exploitation and misuse of personal information. This intrusion on privacy can result in a loss of control over one's personal data, potentially leading to identity theft, targeted manipulation, and discriminatory practices.

Personal information, such as browsing history, search queries, location data, and online purchases, can reveal intimate details of an individual's life. It is not just the collection of this information that is concerning, but also its potential use for profit-driven purposes, such as targeted advertising, price discrimination, and influencing consumer behavior. This has led to widespread calls for increased transparency, stronger data protection regulations, and consumer empowerment.

Legal Framework and Challenges

The legal framework surrounding corporate surveillance is complex and varies across different jurisdictions. Data protection regulations, such as the European Union's General Data Protection Regulation (GDPR) and the California Consumer Privacy Act (CCPA), aim to provide individuals with more control and transparency over their personal data. However, enforcement and compliance with these regulations remain a significant challenge.

One of the main challenges in regulating corporate surveillance is striking a balance between protecting privacy and fostering innovation. While stringent privacy regulations can protect individuals, they can also hinder technological advancements and the growth of data-driven industries. Companies argue that data collection is essential for improving products and services while also enhancing user experiences.

The Role of Technology and Encryption

As corporate surveillance becomes more prevalent, individuals are increasingly turning to technology solutions to protect their privacy. Encryption, in particular, plays a crucial role in safeguarding sensitive data from unauthorized access and surveillance. Encryption algorithms, such as the Advanced Encryption Standard (AES), transform data into an unreadable format, ensuring that only authorized parties can access and decipher it.

End-to-end encryption, in which data is encrypted on the sender's device and can only be decrypted by the intended recipient, has gained prominence as a means of protecting communications and data privacy. Messaging platforms like Signal and WhatsApp have adopted this method to provide secure and private conversations. However, encryption also poses challenges for law enforcement agencies in their efforts to combat crime and terrorism, leading to ongoing debates about striking the right balance.

Emerging Privacy-enhancing Technologies

In response to growing concerns about corporate surveillance, innovative privacy-enhancing technologies are emerging. These technologies aim to give individuals greater control and autonomy over their personal data, reducing the reliance on corporate data collection practices. Some of these technologies include:

- **Decentralized Identifiers (DIDs):** DIDs provide a way for individuals to have ownership and control of their digital identities, reducing the reliance on centralized identity management systems.

- **Federated Learning:** Federated learning allows for training machine learning models on decentralized datasets without the need for data sharing. This protects personal data while still enabling advancements in artificial intelligence.

- **Privacy-focused Web Browsers:** Privacy-focused web browsers, such as Brave, provide users with enhanced privacy features, including built-in ad-blockers, tracker blockers, and privacy-focused search engines.

- **Virtual Private Networks (VPNs) and Proxies:** VPNs and proxies offer individuals a way to mask their IP addresses and encrypt their internet traffic, providing an additional layer of privacy and security.

While these technologies offer promising solutions, their widespread adoption and usability remain important challenges to overcome.

Ethics and Consumer Education

Addressing the issue of corporate surveillance extends beyond technological solutions. It requires ethical considerations and efforts to improve consumer education. Individuals need to be aware of the data they generate, the risks of sharing personal information, and the rights they have over their data. Promoting digital literacy and responsible data practices can empower individuals to make informed decisions about their privacy.

Companies also have a role to play in adopting ethical practices. Transparency in data collection and usage, obtaining explicit consent, and giving individuals control over their personal information are essential steps toward building trust.

Additionally, industry self-regulation, ethical guidelines, and independent audits can help ensure responsible data practices.

The Future of Corporate Surveillance

As technology continues to advance, the future of corporate surveillance remains uncertain. The ethical and legal implications of data collection, storage, and usage will continue to be examined and debated. Striking a balance between the benefits of data-driven technologies and the protection of individual privacy will be a challenge that policymakers, technologists, and society as a whole must face.

It is imperative to continue advocating for stronger privacy regulations, user empowerment, and ethical considerations in corporate practices. Robust encryption algorithms, privacy-enhancing technologies, and responsible data practices will play crucial roles in protecting individual privacy in the face of corporate surveillance.

Safeguarding privacy is not just a matter of individual choice but a collective responsibility to uphold the fundamental principles of autonomy, dignity, and human rights in the digital age.

Conclusion

The rise of corporate surveillance has brought privacy concerns to the forefront of societal discussions. The collection and analysis of personal data by corporations present risks to privacy, autonomy, and human rights. Striking the right balance between convenience, innovation, and privacy is a complex challenge that requires a multidimensional approach.

By understanding the impact of corporate surveillance on privacy, advocating for stronger regulations, and embracing privacy-enhancing technologies, individuals can take steps to protect their personal data. Moreover, promoting ethical practices and ensuring transparency in data collection and usage are essential to building trust between companies and consumers.

As the landscape of technology continues to evolve, it is crucial for individuals, organizations, and policymakers to work collaboratively to create a future that respects privacy, empowers individuals, and acknowledges the significant impact of corporate surveillance on society.

The Influence of Big Tech

In today's digital age, it is impossible to ignore the immense influence of Big Tech companies on our lives. From the moment we wake up and check our smartphones to the moment we go to bed and stream our favorite TV shows, these tech giants have infiltrated every aspect of our daily lives.

The Rise of Big Tech

Big Tech refers to the handful of dominant technology companies that have achieved international recognition and influence. These companies, such as Google, Apple, Amazon, Facebook, and Microsoft, have become the driving force behind the digital revolution. They provide essential services, develop cutting-edge technologies, and shape the way we interact with each other and the world around us.

The rise of Big Tech can be attributed to several factors. First, these companies have harnessed the power of innovation and have consistently pushed the boundaries of technology. They have created products and services that have transformed industries, disrupted traditional business models, and changed the way we live, work, and communicate.

Second, the large user bases of these tech giants have allowed them to accumulate massive amounts of data. This data fuels their artificial intelligence algorithms, which in turn power their products and services. Whether it's personalized recommendations on Amazon, targeted advertisements on Facebook, or voice assistants like Siri and Alexa, these companies leverage data to provide more seamless and tailored experiences to users.

The Impact on Society

While Big Tech has undeniably revolutionized our lives in many ways, their influence is not without consequences. One of the primary concerns is the growing power and influence of these companies. With their vast amount of data and resources, they have the ability to shape public opinion, control markets, and even influence elections.

For example, Facebook has faced criticism for its role in the spread of fake news and the manipulation of public opinion during elections. Google has been accused of bias in its search algorithms, potentially influencing what content users see. Amazon's dominance in the e-commerce industry has raised concerns about small business closures and unfair competition.

Moreover, Big Tech companies have also been instrumental in the erosion of privacy. With their extensive data collection practices, they have access to sensitive personal information, raising concerns about surveillance and data breaches. This has led to debates about the trade-off between convenience and privacy, and the need for stronger regulations to protect user data.

Challenges and Solutions

Addressing the influence of Big Tech poses significant challenges. One of the primary challenges is striking the right balance between competition and innovation. As these companies continue to expand their reach, there is a risk of stifling competition and creating monopolistic practices. Regulators and policymakers must work to foster a competitive environment that encourages innovation while preventing anti-competitive behavior.

Another challenge is ensuring the responsible use of data. Big Tech companies must be held accountable for the data they collect and how they use it. Stricter regulations and transparency requirements are necessary to protect user privacy and prevent the misuse of personal information.

Furthermore, there is a need for greater algorithmic transparency. As more decisions are made by algorithms, it is crucial to understand how these algorithms work and ensure they are fair and unbiased. Big Tech companies should be more transparent about their algorithms, allowing independent audits and providing explanations for their decisions.

The Future of Big Tech

The influence of Big Tech is unlikely to diminish in the future. These companies will continue to innovate and expand into new areas, such as artificial intelligence, virtual reality, and autonomous vehicles. They will shape the future of technology and play a significant role in our lives.

However, there is a growing movement to rein in the power of Big Tech and hold them accountable. Governments around the world are taking steps to regulate these companies, with initiatives such as the General Data Protection Regulation (GDPR) in the European Union. The public is also becoming more aware of the concerns surrounding privacy and monopolistic practices, leading to calls for ethical and responsible behavior from these companies.

Ultimately, the influence of Big Tech is a complex issue that requires ongoing dialogue and collaboration between policymakers, regulators, technologists, and the public. By working together, we can shape the future of technology in a way that benefits society while protecting our rights and liberties.

The Role of Governments in Protecting Privacy

In today's digital age, where personal data is constantly being collected, stored, and analyzed, the role of governments in protecting privacy has become more important than ever. Governments have a crucial responsibility to establish and enforce regulations that safeguard individuals' personal information and ensure their privacy rights are upheld. In this section, we will explore the various ways in which governments play a role in protecting privacy, the challenges they face, and the measures they can take to address these challenges.

The Need for Privacy Regulations

With the proliferation of technology and the widespread use of the internet, individuals are increasingly vulnerable to privacy breaches. Governments have recognized the need to establish privacy regulations to protect citizens from unauthorized access, use, and disclosure of their personal information. These regulations aim to strike a balance between allowing the free flow of information and ensuring the protection of individuals' privacy rights.

Data Protection Laws

One of the key ways in which governments protect privacy is through the implementation of data protection laws. These laws typically define the rights and obligations of individuals and organizations when it comes to the collection, use, and storage of personal data. They often require organizations to obtain explicit consent from individuals before collecting their data and provide mechanisms for individuals to access their data, correct inaccuracies, and request its deletion.

For example, the European Union's General Data Protection Regulation (GDPR) is a comprehensive privacy law that came into effect in 2018. It imposes strict requirements on organizations that process personal data of EU residents, including the need to obtain explicit consent, implement appropriate security measures, and notify individuals in the event of a data breach. Non-compliance with GDPR can result in significant fines, demonstrating the commitment of governments to protecting privacy.

Surveillance Oversight

Governments also have a role in overseeing surveillance activities to ensure they are conducted within the confines of privacy laws and regulations. While surveillance is sometimes necessary for national security and law enforcement purposes, it must be proportionate, lawful, and subject to appropriate oversight to prevent abuse.

One example of government oversight is the authorization process for wiretapping or intercepting communications. Governments typically require law enforcement agencies to obtain a warrant or court order before engaging in such activities. This ensures that surveillance is only conducted when there is sufficient justification and protects individuals from unwarranted invasion of their privacy.

Education and Awareness

In addition to enacting regulations and overseeing surveillance activities, governments have a responsibility to educate and raise awareness about privacy rights and best practices. Many individuals lack knowledge about their privacy rights and the steps they can take to protect their personal information. Governments can play a crucial role in addressing this knowledge gap through public awareness campaigns, educational programs, and the provision of resources.

For example, governments can partner with non-profit organizations and educational institutions to develop educational materials that explain privacy concepts, highlight potential risks, and provide practical tips for protecting personal information online. By empowering individuals to take control of their privacy, governments can create a more informed and privacy-conscious society.

International Cooperation

Privacy protection is not limited to national boundaries. With the global nature of the internet and cross-border data transfers, governments must engage in international cooperation to address privacy challenges effectively. This cooperation may involve negotiating international treaties, sharing best practices, and harmonizing privacy laws across jurisdictions.

For instance, the APEC Privacy Framework is an example of international cooperation aimed at fostering privacy protection in the Asia-Pacific region. It sets out a set of privacy principles and promotes cooperation among member economies to uphold individuals' privacy rights while allowing for the free flow of information.

Challenges and Future Considerations

Protecting privacy in the digital age presents numerous challenges for governments. Technological advancements such as artificial intelligence, the Internet of Things, and big data analytics have brought about new privacy risks and complexities. Governments must adapt their privacy regulations and enforcement mechanisms to keep pace with these developments.

Additionally, governments must strike a delicate balance between privacy protection and the needs of law enforcement and national security. The increasing adoption of encryption technologies and the challenges posed by encrypted communications raise questions about the extent to which governments should be able to circumvent encryption for legitimate purposes without compromising individuals' privacy.

Furthermore, the rapid globalization of data transfers and the emergence of new data-driven business models present challenges in terms of jurisdiction and enforcement. Governments must work together to ensure a consistent application of privacy laws and regulations across borders.

In conclusion, governments play a critical role in protecting privacy in the digital age. Through the establishment of privacy regulations, oversight of surveillance activities, education and awareness campaigns, international cooperation, and adapting to technological advancements, they strive to uphold individuals' privacy rights and mitigate privacy risks. However, the challenges posed by evolving technology and the need to balance privacy with other societal interests call for ongoing efforts and collaboration between governments, organizations, and individuals to build a future where privacy is respected and protected.

Privacy Challenges in the Digital Age

In today's increasingly interconnected world, privacy has become a scarce and precious commodity. The rapid advancement of technology brings forth numerous challenges to maintaining privacy in the digital age. From social media platforms to smart devices, our personal information is constantly at risk of being exploited or breached. In this section, we will explore some of the key privacy challenges we face in the digital age and discuss potential solutions to protect our personal data.

The Power of Personal Data

In the digital age, personal data has become a powerful currency. Tech companies and online platforms collect vast amounts of data from individuals, ranging from basic demographic information to browsing habits and online behavior. This data is then used for targeted advertising, algorithmic decision-making, and even sold to third parties.

The challenge lies in the fact that many individuals are unaware of the extent to which their personal data is being collected and utilized. The lack of transparency in data collection practices makes it difficult for users to have control over their own information. Additionally, the commodification of personal data raises ethical concerns about how it is being leveraged for profit.

The Rise of Surveillance Capitalism

Surveillance capitalism has emerged as a major privacy challenge in the digital age. This concept refers to the practice of collecting and monetizing personal data for surveillance and influence purposes. Tech companies, driven by profit motives, have mastered the art of surveillance capitalism, turning users into commodities in the process.

The pervasiveness of surveillance capitalism is evident in the targeted ads that follow us across different websites, the recommendations algorithms that shape our online experiences, and the data breaches that expose our personal information. This continuous surveillance erodes personal privacy and poses a threat to democratic values.

Governments vs. Tech Companies

Privacy challenges also arise from the power struggle between governments and tech companies. While governments want to maintain control over citizens' data for security and law enforcement purposes, tech companies seek to protect their users' privacy while complying with legal obligations.

This clash of interests has led to debates over a variety of topics, such as encryption backdoors, data retention policies, and the extent of government surveillance. Striking a balance between privacy and national security is a complex challenge that requires careful consideration of both individual rights and public safety.

Privacy in the Age of Social Media

Social media has revolutionized the way we communicate and share information. However, it has also brought about significant privacy challenges. People willingly share personal details, photos, and locations, often without fully understanding the consequences of their actions.

The challenge lies in the fact that social media platforms are designed to encourage sharing and engagement, sometimes at the expense of privacy. The algorithms that power these platforms prioritize user engagement and targeted advertising, often resulting in the manipulation and exploitation of personal data. Furthermore, the viral nature of social media can quickly amplify the impact of any privacy breaches.

The Cambridge Analytica Scandal

One of the most significant privacy challenges in recent years was the Cambridge Analytica scandal. In 2018, it was revealed that the political consulting firm, Cambridge Analytica, harvested personal data from millions of Facebook users without their consent. This data was later used for targeted political advertising during the 2016 US presidential election.

The Cambridge Analytica scandal highlighted the vulnerability of personal data and showcased the potential risks of unregulated data collection. It served as a wake-up call for users, regulators, and tech companies to reevaluate privacy practices and enforce stronger data protection measures.

The Importance of Strong Encryption

As privacy challenges continue to escalate, the importance of strong encryption cannot be overstated. Encryption is a fundamental tool for protecting data from unauthorized access or interception. It ensures that only authorized parties can access and understand the information being transmitted or stored.

However, encryption has also become a point of contention. Some governments argue that strong encryption hinders their ability to investigate and prevent criminal activities. They propose implementing backdoors that provide law enforcement agencies with access to encrypted data. However, such backdoors weaken the overall security of encryption and pose a risk to individual privacy.

Privacy Laws and Regulations

To address the growing privacy concerns in the digital age, governments around the world have introduced privacy laws and regulations. These legal frameworks aim to protect individuals' rights to privacy, establish guidelines for data collection and usage, and hold organizations accountable for any misuse of personal information.

The European Union's General Data Protection Regulation (GDPR) is one such example of a comprehensive privacy law. It mandates transparency, explicit consent, and the right to erasure for individuals within the EU. Other countries, such as the United States and Canada, have also implemented privacy legislation to protect their citizens' personal data.

Shaping the Future of Privacy

As we navigate the complex world of privacy in the digital age, it is crucial to prioritize privacy-centric practices and technologies. Encouraging user awareness and education about privacy risks and best practices is a crucial step in protecting personal data. Individuals should be empowered with the knowledge and tools necessary to make informed decisions about their digital footprint.

Moreover, collaboration between governments, tech companies, and privacy advocates is essential for shaping the future of privacy. The development of privacy-focused technologies, such as decentralized platforms and privacy-enhancing tools, can help individuals reclaim control over their personal information.

Phil Zimmermann's Role in the Fight

In the fight for privacy in the digital age, Phil Zimmermann has played a pivotal role. As the creator of Pretty Good Privacy (PGP), Zimmermann revolutionized the field of encryption and championed the right to privacy. His work has inspired a generation of privacy advocates and has set the stage for continued innovation in privacy-focused technologies.

Zimmermann's dedication to privacy and his unwavering commitment to secure communication has paved the way for a more privacy-conscious society. His advocacy and technological contributions serve as a reminder that the fight for privacy is an ongoing battle that requires continuous effort and innovation.

Conclusion

Privacy challenges in the digital age are complex, requiring a delicate balance between technological advancements, individual rights, and societal values. As technology continues to evolve, it is essential to remain vigilant and proactive in protecting our personal data. By advocating for stronger privacy laws, promoting privacy-centric technologies, and educating individuals about privacy risks, we can secure a more private and secure future for all.

The Need for User Awareness

In this digital age, where our personal information is constantly being exchanged and stored online, there is a pressing need for user awareness when it comes to privacy and data security. Many individuals are unaware of the various threats that exist in the online world and the potential consequences of their actions. This lack of understanding puts them at risk of falling victim to cybercrime and having their personal information exploited.

One of the fundamental principles of user awareness is understanding the importance of protecting one's privacy. Users need to be educated about the potential risks associated with sharing personal information online, such as identity theft, cyberstalking, and unauthorized access to sensitive data. They should be cautious about the kind of information they share on social media platforms and be mindful of the privacy settings available to them. Emphasizing the need for strong and unique passwords can also prevent unauthorized access to accounts and personal information.

Another aspect of user awareness is being able to recognize phishing attempts and other forms of online scams. Users should be educated about the common techniques used by cybercriminals to trick people into revealing their personal information, such as fake emails, disguised websites, and fraudulent phone calls. By being vigilant and skeptical of unsolicited requests for personal information, users can protect themselves from falling victim to these scams.

Understanding the importance of regularly updating software and using reputable antivirus programs is also crucial for user awareness. Outdated software and systems are more vulnerable to security breaches and malware attacks. Users should be encouraged to keep their devices up to date with the latest patches and security updates to minimize the risk of compromise.

In addition to individual actions, user awareness should also include an understanding of the larger privacy landscape and the role of corporations and governments in data collection and surveillance. Users should be aware of their rights and the privacy policies of the platforms and services they use. They should also be informed about laws and regulations that govern data privacy in their jurisdiction.

Educational initiatives, public campaigns, and user-friendly resources can play a significant role in increasing user awareness. These efforts should aim to simplify complex technical concepts and make them accessible to a wide audience. Interactive workshops, online tutorials, and engaging visuals can help users grasp these concepts in a meaningful way.

To reinforce user awareness, it is important to provide real-world examples that highlight the potential consequences of inadequate privacy practices. Sharing stories of individuals who have experienced identity theft, online harassment, or data breaches can help users understand the relevance of privacy in their own lives. Educators, parents, and community leaders should collaborate to foster a culture of privacy awareness, ensuring that individuals of all ages are equipped with the knowledge and skills to protect themselves in the digital world.

Example Problem:

Nina, a social media enthusiast, regularly shares updates about her life on various platforms. She believes that only her friends and followers can see her posts, so she includes personal details like her full name, date of birth, and even her home address. One day, she receives a suspicious email requesting her banking information, and she unknowingly provides it. As a result, her bank account is compromised, and she becomes a victim of identity theft.

Solution:

To prevent incidents like this, Nina needs to be more aware of the risks associated with sharing personal information online. She should limit the amount of personal information she shares on social media platforms and adjust her privacy settings to control who can access her posts. Nina should also be cautious when providing sensitive information online and verify the authenticity of any requests before sharing such information. Additionally, she should regularly update her devices and use reputable antivirus software to protect herself from potential malware attacks.

By enhancing user awareness and promoting responsible online behavior, we can create a safer digital environment where individuals have greater control over their privacy and data security. It is the collective responsibility of individuals, organizations, and policymakers to prioritize user education and make privacy a top priority in the digital age.

Privacy as a Commodity

In the digital age, privacy has become a valuable commodity, sought after by individuals, corporations, and governments alike. As technology advances and data becomes increasingly accessible, protecting one's personal information has become a top priority. This section will explore the concept of privacy as a commodity and delve into its implications in today's interconnected world.

The Value of Privacy

Privacy, once taken for granted, is now considered a luxury. With the proliferation of social media platforms, online shopping, and digital services, individuals are constantly providing personal information in exchange for convenience or access to certain benefits. This exchange of personal data forms the basis of the privacy-as-commodity model.

Companies collect vast amounts of user data, including browsing habits, purchasing history, and demographic information. This data is then analyzed and utilized for targeted advertising, product development, and data-driven decision making. Moreover, data brokers exist solely to buy and sell personal information, further commodifying privacy.

The value of privacy lies in the ability to control and protect one's personal information. As the saying goes, "If you're not paying for the product, you are the product." In the era of surveillance capitalism, individuals must be vigilant about their privacy rights and understand the implications of freely sharing personal data.

Risks and Consequences

When privacy is treated as a commodity, several risks and consequences arise. First and foremost is the potential for data breaches and identity theft. High-profile cases involving the unauthorized access to personal information have become alarmingly common, with hackers targeting corporations and government databases alike. The aftermath of such breaches can be financially and emotionally devastating for individuals whose private data has been compromised.

Aside from the immediate threats posed by data breaches, there are broader societal consequences to treating privacy as a commodity. Privacy becomes a privilege accessible only to those who can afford it. This creates a digital divide, where marginalized communities or individuals with limited financial means are more vulnerable to surveillance and exploitation.

Another consequence is the erosion of personal autonomy. When personal data is commodified, individuals lose control over how their information is used and who has access to it. This loss of control affects not only individuals' privacy but also their ability to make informed decisions and maintain a sense of agency in the digital realm.

Protecting Privacy in the Commodity Market

In a market-based approach to privacy, individuals have a limited ability to protect their personal information. However, there are steps they can take to mitigate the risks and protect their privacy as much as possible.

First and foremost, individuals should be proactive about understanding how their data is collected, used, and shared. Reading privacy policies, adjusting privacy settings on social media platforms, and being mindful of the information they provide online are all important steps in safeguarding personal privacy.

Additionally, individuals can make use of encryption tools and privacy-oriented technology. Encrypted messaging apps, virtual private networks (VPNs), and browser extensions that block tracking can all help to enhance privacy in an increasingly connected world.

Advocacy for stronger privacy laws and regulations is crucial in holding corporations accountable for their data practices. Supporting organizations that fight for digital rights and privacy is one way individuals can contribute to the protection of privacy as a fundamental right.

Lastly, it is important to recognize the collective responsibility in protecting privacy. When individuals come together and demand stronger privacy protections, change is more likely to happen. By fostering a culture that values privacy and advocates for its protection, we can collectively work towards a future where privacy is not just a commodity but a fundamental human right.

Real-World Example: Facebook and the Cambridge Analytica Scandal

The Cambridge Analytica scandal serves as a potent example of how privacy can be commodified and exploited. In 2018, it was revealed that the personal data of millions of Facebook users had been harvested without their consent and used to influence political campaigns.

Cambridge Analytica, a now-defunct political consulting firm, used a third-party application to collect user data, including personal information and their Facebook social graph. This data was then used to create targeted political advertisements and influence voter behavior.

The scandal shed light on the vast amounts of personal data collected by social media platforms and how it can be weaponized. It sparked a global conversation about data privacy, prompting users to reevaluate their relationship with platforms like Facebook and demand stronger privacy protections.

This real-world example showcases the dangers inherent in treating privacy as a commodity. It underscores the need for individuals, organizations, and policymakers to work together in safeguarding privacy rights and ensuring that technology serves the people, rather than exploiting them.

Key Takeaways

- Privacy is increasingly being treated as a commodity, with personal data being bought and sold for profit. - The value of privacy lies in the ability to control and protect personal information. - Risks include data breaches, identity theft, and erosion of personal autonomy. - Protecting privacy requires proactive measures, such as understanding data practices and using privacy-oriented technology. - Advocacy for stronger privacy laws and regulations is crucial in safeguarding privacy rights. - The Cambridge Analytica scandal serves as a real-world example of privacy commodification and the need for stronger privacy protections.

Chapter 5: The Privatization of Privacy

5.2.7 The Future of Encryption Technology

As we navigate through the post-Zimmermann era, the future of encryption technology holds both challenges and opportunities. Encryption has become more critical than ever, with the rise of corporate surveillance, government monitoring, and increasing privacy concerns in the digital age. In this section, we will explore the evolving landscape of encryption technology and its role in safeguarding our privacy.

Encryption Algorithms and Quantum Computing

One of the key areas that will shape the future of encryption technology is the advent of quantum computing. Traditional encryption algorithms, such as RSA and AES, rely on complex mathematical problems that would take an immense amount of time and computing power to solve. However, quantum computers have the potential to break these algorithms by solving these problems significantly faster.

To counter the threat of quantum computing, researchers are exploring new encryption algorithms that are resistant to quantum attacks. One promising approach is the development of post-quantum cryptography, which involves algorithms based on mathematical problems that are believed to be hard even for quantum computers.

Homomorphic Encryption

Another area of innovation in encryption technology is homomorphic encryption. Traditionally, encrypted data cannot be processed without decryption, which poses a challenge for scenarios where data analysis and computation are required while preserving privacy. Homomorphic encryption allows computations to be performed directly on encrypted data, without the need for decryption, thereby protecting privacy while enabling data processing.

Homomorphic encryption opens up a wide range of possibilities, particularly in fields such as healthcare and finance, where sensitive data needs to be analyzed without compromising privacy. For example, it enables secure computation of medical records while preserving patient confidentiality.

Secure Multi-Party Computation

Secure multi-party computation (MPC) is another emerging field in encryption technology. It enables multiple parties to jointly compute a function over their inputs while keeping their inputs private. MPC is particularly useful in scenarios where collaboration is required, such as data analysis across different organizations.

By using cryptographic protocols, MPC ensures that no party can learn anything about other parties' inputs beyond what is revealed by the output. This allows for secure and private cooperation between multiple entities, even in adversarial environments.

The Role of Artificial Intelligence

Artificial intelligence (AI) is playing an increasingly significant role in encryption technology. Machine learning algorithms can be used to enhance encryption techniques by improving key generation, identifying patterns in encrypted data, and optimizing encryption processes.

Moreover, AI-driven systems can help detect anomalies and potential threats in encrypted communications, providing an additional layer of security. By analyzing encrypted network traffic, AI algorithms can identify patterns that might indicate malicious activities, thereby improving the overall security posture.

The Human Factor in Encryption

While technological advancements are crucial in shaping the future of encryption, it is essential not to overlook the human factor. User behavior and awareness play a vital role in the effective use of encryption technology. Strong encryption exists, but it is often underutilized or misconfigured due to the lack of awareness and understanding.

Educating users about the importance of encryption, its limitations, and best practices for implementation is essential. User-friendly encryption tools and interfaces can also make a significant difference in promoting widespread adoption and making encryption accessible to non-technical users.

The Need for Collaborative Solutions

The future of encryption technology relies heavily on collaboration between various stakeholders, including governments, tech companies, and privacy advocates. It is crucial to strike a balance between privacy and security concerns, taking into account the challenges posed by cybercrime, national security, and law enforcement needs.

Open standards and protocols ensure the transparency and interoperability of encryption technologies. Collaborative efforts in policymaking and the development of encryption standards can help build trust among stakeholders and foster widespread adoption of robust encryption techniques.

Summary

The future of encryption technology holds great promise in safeguarding our privacy amidst evolving challenges. Quantum-resistant encryption algorithms, homomorphic encryption, secure multi-party computation, and AI-driven advancements are all contributing to the evolving landscape of encryption.

However, it is important to remember that encryption is only as strong as its implementation and user awareness. Educating users and promoting best practices will be crucial in ensuring the effective use of encryption technology. Collaboration between stakeholders, including governments, tech companies, and privacy advocates, will be essential in shaping the future of encryption and striking the right balance between privacy and security. As we move forward, the goal should be to build a privacy-centric society where encryption is not just a necessity, but a fundamental right.

Phil Zimmermann's Continuing Relevance

Phil Zimmermann, the visionary behind Pretty Good Privacy (PGP), continues to shape the world of privacy and encryption through his unwavering commitment to protecting individuals' rights. Even though PGP has evolved over the years, Zimmermann's contributions remain indispensable in the ongoing fight for privacy in the digital age. In this section, we examine the enduring relevance of Phil Zimmermann's work and how it permeates various aspects of our modern lives.

Protecting Individuals Against Government Surveillance

One of the most significant contributions of Phil Zimmermann's work is his relentless effort to protect individuals from government surveillance. In an era where mass surveillance has become an unfortunate reality, Zimmermann's dedication to safeguarding privacy has never been more relevant. He recognized early on the importance of encrypting communications to counter pervasive surveillance.

Zimmermann's PGP encryption software has empowered countless individuals and organizations to shield their data from prying eyes, ensuring private and secure communication. Individuals can confidently share sensitive information with the knowledge that their messages remain unreadable by unauthorized individuals, including government agencies.

Advocating for Strong Encryption Standards

In a world where encryption is increasingly under attack, Phil Zimmermann's advocacy for strong encryption standards remains as relevant as ever. Zimmermann has been a staunch supporter of the idea that privacy and security are not mutually exclusive, and encryption is vital for protecting both.

His advocacy work has highlighted the importance of end-to-end encryption, where only the intended recipient can decipher the encrypted message. This approach eliminates the vulnerabilities present in centralized systems, protecting individuals from potential cyberattacks and unauthorized access to their data.

Zimmermann's efforts to educate the public and policymakers on the significance of strong encryption have had a lasting impact. It has spurred discussions around encryption backdoors, pushing back against any attempts to undermine the security provided by encryption protocols.

Championing User Privacy in the Tech Industry

Phil Zimmermann's work extends beyond developing encryption software. He has also been a vocal advocate for user privacy in the tech industry. Zimmermann consistently emphasizes the importance of privacy-centric design principles and calls for tech companies to prioritize user privacy above all else.

His influence can be seen in the increasing number of privacy-centric features being integrated into popular applications and platforms. Companies have begun incorporating end-to-end encryption, anonymization techniques, and privacy-enhancing technologies into their products, inspired by Zimmermann's vision of a more privacy-focused world.

Inspiring the Next Generation of Privacy Pioneers

Phil Zimmermann's story has inspired a new wave of privacy advocates and pioneering individuals in the field of cryptography. His tireless pursuit of privacy rights has shown the world the impact that one person can make in safeguarding civil liberties.

Aspiring privacy advocates look up to Zimmermann as a true role model, and his work has served as a catalyst for their involvement in the fight for privacy. Many of these individuals carry on his legacy by developing innovative privacy-focused technologies, raising awareness about the importance of encryption, and addressing the ethical challenges surrounding privacy in a connected world.

Shaping Privacy Laws and Regulations

Phil Zimmermann's impact extends beyond technological advancements and extends to the realm of policy and legislation. His relentless advocacy work has contributed to shaping privacy laws and regulations worldwide.

Zimmermann's role in mobilizing the tech community and fighting for privacy rights has influenced policymakers' perspectives on encryption and the right to privacy. His efforts have challenged governments to adopt a more balanced approach that addresses national security concerns while protecting individual privacy rights.

Enabling Privacy in Authoritarian Regimes

One area where Phil Zimmermann's work exhibits its ongoing relevance is in enabling individuals living under authoritarian regimes to exercise their right to privacy. PGP encryption provides a lifeline for individuals to communicate securely and avoid censorship, surveillance, and persecution.

His software has been instrumental in protecting activists, journalists, and dissidents who face constant threats to their freedom and safety. Zimmermann's commitment to privacy has allowed vulnerable individuals to share information, mobilize grassroots movements, and expose human rights violations without fear of reprisal.

Addressing the Ethical Challenges of Data Collection

In an age where data collection has become ubiquitous, Phil Zimmermann's work holds particular relevance in addressing the ethical challenges associated with it. Zimmermann emphasizes the need for transparency and user control when it comes to handling personal data.

His vision underscores the importance of informed consent, limiting data retention, and ensuring that individuals have the power to control their own personal information. Zimmermann's code of ethics provides critical guidance in navigating the ethical dilemmas arising from rampant data collection practices.

CHAPTER 5: THE PRIVATIZATION OF PRIVACY 463

Promoting Privacy Education and User Empowerment

Phil Zimmermann's continuing relevance also lies in his emphasis on privacy education and user empowerment. His efforts to educate individuals about the importance of privacy, encryption, and digital literacy have empowered users to take ownership of their online security.

By advocating for privacy-awareness initiatives and resources, Zimmermann has helped users understand their rights and the steps they can take to protect their privacy in an increasingly connected world. His work promotes a culture of privacy-conscious individuals who actively seek to adopt privacy-enhancing technologies and demand privacy-focused standards from service providers.

The Importance of Phil Zimmermann's Continuing Influence

Phil Zimmermann's influence continues to shape the conversation around privacy and encryption. His work has inspired a global movement, creating awareness and prompting change in the way privacy is perceived and prioritized.

In a world grappling with escalating surveillance threats and data breaches, Zimmermann's principles and values remain steadfast. His dedication to privacy and encryption serves as a constant reminder that the fight for privacy is an ongoing battle that demands vigilance, innovation, and collective action.

As we move into an unpredictable future, Phil Zimmermann's legacy reminds us of the vital role encryption plays in preserving freedom, democracy, and the rights of individuals around the world. The global impact of his work is a testament to his enduring relevance and the lasting significance of his contributions to the field of privacy.

Summary

In this section, we explored the continuing relevance of Phil Zimmermann's work in the domain of privacy and encryption. Zimmermann's dedication to protecting individuals against government surveillance, advocating for strong encryption standards, and championing user privacy in the tech industry remains critically important. His contributions have inspired a new generation of privacy pioneers and shaped privacy laws and regulations. Zimmermann's work has also addressed the ethical challenges of data collection, promoted privacy education, and empowered individuals to take control of their digital security. As we navigate a world without Phil Zimmermann, his legacy serves as a reminder of the importance of encryption in upholding privacy rights and fostering a more secure and democratic future.

Phil Zimmermann's Legacy and the Fight for Privacy

Phil Zimmermann's impact on the world of privacy cannot be overstated. His creation of PGP (Pretty Good Privacy) revolutionized the way we think about encryption, privacy, and personal security. But Zimmermann's contributions go far beyond the development of a software tool – his work has inspired a generation of advocates and activists who continue to fight for privacy rights in the digital age.

Zimmermann understood the importance of privacy long before it became a mainstream concern. He recognized that in a world where our personal data is constantly being collected and exploited, strong encryption is our best defense against unwanted surveillance and intrusion. PGP, with its robust encryption algorithms and user-friendly interface, provided individuals with a powerful tool to protect their digital communications from prying eyes.

But Zimmermann's fight for privacy didn't end with the creation of PGP. He knew that true privacy required not only secure technology, but also robust legal protections and a commitment to safeguarding individual rights. Zimmermann was a vocal advocate for privacy rights and a critic of government surveillance practices, particularly in the wake of the 9/11 attacks and the subsequent erosion of civil liberties.

One of Zimmermann's most significant contributions to the fight for privacy was his staunch opposition to the Clipper Chip, a government proposal in the 1990s that would have mandated backdoors in encryption software. Zimmermann recognized the dangers of such a system, as it would essentially create a master key that could be used to unlock any encrypted communication. His principled stand against the Clipper Chip galvanized the tech community and mobilized support for the cause of strong encryption.

Zimmermann's advocacy work extended beyond the United States. He believed that privacy was a universal human right, and he tirelessly campaigned for privacy protections around the world. He funded and supported numerous pro-privacy projects and non-profit organizations, working to ensure that privacy remained a priority in the face of technological advancements and the ever-expanding reach of surveillance.

Today, Zimmermann's legacy lives on in the work of organizations like the Electronic Frontier Foundation and the Freedom of the Press Foundation, which continue to fight for privacy and digital rights. His impact is also felt in the growing popularity of privacy-focused apps and services, which prioritize user privacy and data protection. The increased public awareness of privacy issues can be attributed, in part, to Zimmermann's tireless efforts to educate and raise awareness about the importance of privacy in the digital age.

As we navigate the complexities of a hyper-connected world, Phil Zimmermann's fight for privacy serves as a guiding light. His dedication to the cause has inspired countless individuals to take a stand and demand privacy protections. His principles and his legacy continue to shape the conversation around privacy, reminding us that the fight for privacy is never-ending and that we must remain vigilant in protecting our most fundamental rights.

To honor Zimmermann's legacy and continue the fight for privacy, it is imperative that we stay informed, advocate for stronger privacy laws and regulations, and support technologies and initiatives that prioritize privacy and security. By doing so, we can ensure that Zimmermann's vision of a world where privacy is respected and upheld remains a reality for future generations.

Challenges in the Fight for Privacy

While Phil Zimmermann's efforts have made significant strides in the fight for privacy, there are still challenges that need to be addressed. One key challenge is the ongoing battle between privacy and national security. The need to balance individual privacy rights with the need to protect society from threats is a complex and contentious issue.

Encryption has often been caught in the crossfire of this debate. Governments argue that providing strong encryption will allow criminals and terrorists to communicate undetected, while privacy advocates maintain that weakening encryption would fundamentally undermine security and put individuals at risk.

Another challenge is the rise of corporate surveillance and the influence of big tech companies. In an increasingly digitized world, tech giants collect vast amounts of personal data, often without proper consent or knowledge from users. This data is then used for targeted advertising, profiling, and other practices that erode privacy.

Moreover, the rapid advancement of technology presents new challenges to privacy. The Internet of Things (IoT) has brought connectivity to everyday objects, raising concerns about the collection and sharing of personal information. Artificial intelligence (AI) technologies also present privacy risks, as they can process and analyze vast amounts of data, potentially infringing on individuals' privacy.

The fight for privacy is not just a technological or legal battle; it is also a battle for public awareness and education. Many individuals are unaware of the extent to which their personal data is collected and shared, and the potential implications of this for their privacy. Creating a more privacy-conscious society requires efforts to educate the public about their rights, as well as the risks and consequences of widespread surveillance.

Phil Zimmermann's Continuing Influence

Even after his retirement, Phil Zimmermann's influence on the fight for privacy continues to be felt. His work has inspired a new generation of programmers, privacy advocates, and digital rights activists who carry forward his vision.

Zimmermann's contributions to the field of cryptography and encryption have opened doors for innovation and collaboration. His emphasis on open-source software has fostered a community of developers and researchers dedicated to improving privacy and security. The principles of transparency and collaboration that Zimmermann championed are now fundamental to the ethos of many privacy-focused projects.

Furthermore, Zimmermann's advocacy work has created a platform for dialogue and action. His tireless efforts to raise awareness about privacy risks and lobby for stronger privacy protections have influenced policymakers and lawmakers worldwide. In an era where privacy is increasingly threatened, his voice continues to be a powerful force for change.

Zimmermann's legacy can also be seen in the growing recognition of privacy as a human right. As more individuals become aware of the importance of privacy in the digital age, the demand for privacy-friendly technologies and policies has increased. This shift in public sentiment can be attributed, in part, to Zimmermann's relentless advocacy and his ability to articulate the significance of privacy in a connected world.

In conclusion, Phil Zimmermann's legacy in the fight for privacy cannot be overstated. His pioneering work in encryption, his advocacy for privacy rights, and his commitment to raising awareness have left an indelible mark on the digital landscape. As we navigate the challenges of the post-Zimmermann era, we must draw inspiration from his example and continue the fight for privacy, ensuring that our rights and freedoms are protected in the digital age.

The Responsibility of Future Generations

As technology continues to advance at a rapid pace, the responsibility for protecting privacy and maintaining data security falls on the shoulders of future generations. In a world where personal information is constantly at risk of being exploited, it is crucial for the next wave of programmers, engineers, and innovators to prioritize privacy and uphold the principles that Phil Zimmermann fought for.

Understanding the Impact of Technology

To effectively address the responsibility of future generations, it is important to understand the impact of technology on privacy. With the proliferation of digital platforms, social media, and smart devices, individuals are constantly generating vast amounts of personal data. This data can be used for targeted advertising, surveillance, or even sold to third parties without the individual's consent. The potential for abuse and breach of privacy is significant.

The Need for Education and Awareness

One of the key responsibilities of future generations is to prioritize education and raise awareness about privacy concerns. It is vital to teach individuals, from a young age, about the importance of safeguarding their personal information. This includes educating them about the risks of sharing sensitive data online, the dangers of cyberattacks, and the value of encryption technologies like PGP.

Educational institutions and tech organizations have a responsibility to develop comprehensive programs that emphasize the importance of privacy and data security. By fostering a culture of awareness, future generations can make informed decisions about their digital lives and actively protect their privacy.

Innovation and Future-Proof Solutions

Future generations must also take on the responsibility of developing innovative technologies and solutions that prioritize privacy. This involves creating secure and user-friendly encryption tools that are readily available to the general public. With advances in artificial intelligence and machine learning, it is crucial to develop cutting-edge algorithms and protocols that can protect sensitive data from unauthorized access.

Furthermore, future programmers and engineers must be committed to creating systems that are resistant to surveillance, both from governments and tech companies. The responsibility lies in building robust privacy frameworks that prioritize user consent, data transparency, and data minimization.

Collaboration and Ethical Practices

Addressing the responsibility of future generations requires collaboration across various sectors. It is crucial for tech companies, governments, and individuals to work together to develop ethical practices and regulations that safeguard privacy. This includes advocating for legislation that protects individuals' privacy rights, establishing clear guidelines for data handling, and holding organizations accountable for data breaches.

Future generations must also be mindful of the ethical implications of their work. As technology evolves, programmers and engineers must prioritize ethical considerations, including the potential impact of their products on individual privacy and societal well-being. By embracing ethics as a core principle, future generations can ensure the responsible use of technology in a way that protects privacy.

The Power of Digital Activism

In the age of social media and interconnectedness, future generations have the power to drive change through digital activism. Social movements have the ability to mobilize individuals and hold organizations accountable for their data practices. By leveraging social media platforms, future generations can raise awareness about privacy issues, advocate for stronger privacy regulations, and hold companies and governments accountable for their actions.

Examples of Responsible Innovation

Future generations can draw inspiration from the examples set by privacy-focused innovators. For instance, Open Whisper Systems, the organization behind the encrypted messaging app Signal, has placed a strong emphasis on privacy and security. Their dedication to protecting user privacy while providing a seamless messaging experience has set a precedent for future developers.

Another example is the Tor Project, which develops and maintains the Tor network, a widely used system for anonymous communication. By enabling users to browse the internet anonymously, Tor has empowered individuals around the world to protect their online privacy and access information freely. Future generations can build upon these examples and continue to innovate in ways that prioritize privacy.

The Importance of Knowledge Sharing

As the torch is passed from one generation to the next, the responsible use of technology requires the sharing of knowledge and experiences. Future generations must document the lessons learned in the fight for privacy and make them accessible to others. This includes sharing success stories, challenges faced, and strategies used to overcome obstacles.

By sharing this knowledge, future generations can build upon the foundations laid by pioneers like Phil Zimmermann and continue to work towards a future where privacy is respected and protected.

Exercises

1. Conduct research and identify one recent privacy breach that had significant consequences. Discuss the impact of this breach on individuals' privacy rights and the lessons that can be learned from it.

2. Write a short essay on the ethical considerations surrounding the use of facial recognition technology in public spaces. Discuss the potential impact on privacy and the challenges it poses for future generations.

3. Create a poster or infographic that educates individuals on the importance of encryption and how it can be utilized to protect their privacy. Include specific examples of encryption technologies and their applications.

4. Imagine you have been tasked with developing a new privacy-focused app. Outline the key features and design principles that you would incorporate to ensure the privacy and security of user data.

5. Engage in a discussion with your peers about the responsibility of future generations in protecting privacy. Consider the potential challenges and opportunities that lie ahead and propose strategies to address them.

Resources

1. "Data and Goliath: The Hidden Battles to Collect Your Data and Control Your World" by Bruce Schneier - A comprehensive exploration of the risks to privacy in the digital age and strategies for protecting personal data.

2. "The Age of Surveillance Capitalism: The Fight for a Human Future at the New Frontier of Power" by Shoshana Zuboff - An in-depth analysis of how companies collect and exploit personal data, and its implications for privacy and democracy.

3. Electronic Frontier Foundation (EFF) - A nonprofit organization that defends civil liberties, including online privacy, through advocacy, legal action, and technology development.

4. PrivacyTools - An online resource that provides recommendations for privacy-friendly services, software, and operating systems, as well as educational materials on privacy best practices.

5. PGP (Pretty Good Privacy) - The official website for the PGP encryption software, which provides an overview of PGP's history, features, and applications.

Navigating a World Without Phil Zimmermann

Phil Zimmermann's Lessons for Privacy Advocates

In the digital age, privacy has become a hotly debated topic with far-reaching implications. For privacy advocates, there is much to learn from the work of pioneering programmer, Phil Zimmermann. His contributions to encryption and his commitment to protecting individuals' privacy have paved the way for modern-day privacy activism. Here, we delve into some of the key lessons that privacy advocates can take away from Zimmermann's legacy.

1. **Make Privacy Accessible:** Zimmermann understood the importance of making privacy accessible to everyone. His creation of Pretty Good Privacy (PGP) was driven by the belief that privacy is a fundamental right that should be available to all. As a privacy advocate, it is crucial to develop tools and methods that are user-friendly and can be easily adopted by individuals with varying levels of technical expertise. This means focusing not only on creating robust encryption technology but also on making it intuitive and convenient for everyday use.

2. **Empower Individuals:** Zimmermann believed in empowering individuals to take control of their own privacy. He recognized that privacy is not just about protecting personal data, but also about preserving autonomy and freedom of expression. Privacy advocates should encourage individuals to take an active role in protecting their own privacy by educating them about the importance of encryption, informing them of their rights, and providing them with the tools they need to secure their digital communications.

3. **Collaborate and Educate:** Zimmermann understood the power of collaboration and the need for collective action in the fight for privacy. Privacy advocates should actively seek collaborations with like-minded individuals, organizations, and policymakers to drive meaningful change. By sharing knowledge, resources, and best practices, privacy advocates can create a stronger and more united front in advocating for privacy rights. It is also important to prioritize education and awareness-raising efforts to ensure that individuals understand the value of privacy and are equipped to protect themselves in the digital world.

4. **Advocate for Strong Encryption:** Zimmermann's battle against government surveillance and his relentless commitment to robust encryption underscored his belief in the importance of strong and unbreakable encryption algorithms. Privacy advocates should stand firm in advocating for end-to-end encryption and resist any efforts to weaken encryption standards or introduce backdoors. Strong encryption is essential for safeguarding individuals' privacy and maintaining the security of digital

communications.

5. **Stay Informed and Adaptive:** The digital landscape is constantly evolving, and privacy advocates must stay informed about emerging threats and new technologies. By keeping abreast of the latest developments in surveillance, data collection, and encryption technologies, advocates can adapt their strategies and tools to effectively address new privacy challenges. It is crucial to anticipate and respond to threats in real-time to ensure that privacy remains protected in an ever-changing digital world.

6. **Engage in Policy Advocacy:** Zimmermann recognized the importance of engaging in policy advocacy to shape the legal and regulatory framework surrounding privacy. Privacy advocates should actively participate in public debates, engage with policymakers, and contribute to the formulation of privacy laws and regulations. By standing up for strong privacy protections at the policy level, advocates can create a lasting impact and ensure that privacy rights are safeguarded for future generations.

7. **Promote Privacy by Design:** Zimmermann's work emphasized the importance of incorporating privacy as a fundamental design principle in the development of software and digital infrastructure. Privacy advocates should encourage the adoption of privacy by design practices, which prioritize privacy considerations from the early stages of system design and development. This ensures that privacy remains at the forefront of technological innovation and that individuals' privacy rights are upheld by default.

8. **Lead by Example:** Zimmermann's unwavering commitment to privacy and his willingness to take on powerful adversaries demonstrated the importance of leading by example. Privacy advocates should take inspiration from Zimmermann's courage and determination and be willing to push boundaries, challenge the status quo, and hold powerful entities accountable for their privacy practices. By leading by example, advocates can inspire others to take action and foster a culture that values and respects privacy.

In conclusion, Phil Zimmermann's journey as a privacy advocate provides valuable lessons for the modern-day privacy movement. By making privacy accessible, empowering individuals, collaborating with like-minded individuals and organizations, advocating for strong encryption, staying informed and adaptive, engaging in policy advocacy, promoting privacy by design, and leading by example, privacy advocates can make a tangible impact in preserving privacy rights in the digital age. As Zimmermann's legacy reminds us, the fight for privacy is an ongoing battle that requires collective action, constant vigilance, and an unwavering commitment to the fundamental right to privacy.

The Continued Battle for Encryption

In the ever-evolving digital landscape, the battle for encryption continues to rage on. Encryption is the process of converting data into a format that is unreadable for anyone without the proper decryption key, effectively securing information from unauthorized access. It plays a crucial role in safeguarding our personal privacy, sensitive business data, and even the security of nations. However, this powerful tool is not without its adversaries.

State Surveillance and Encryption

One of the main challenges facing encryption is the scrutiny from government agencies and their push for backdoor access. In an effort to combat terrorism, prevent crime, and ensure national security, some governments argue that they need exceptional access to encrypted communications. They assert that this access would not compromise the privacy of law-abiding citizens, but rather, help catch criminals and protect public safety.

However, providing such access would create a vulnerability that could be exploited by hackers, criminals, and even other less democratic governments. As we've seen time and time again, any weakness built into encryption can potentially be abused, resulting in devastating consequences for individuals and societies. The battle for encryption, therefore, lies in striking a delicate balance between security and the need for lawful access.

The Encryption Backdoor Debate

The encryption backdoor debate centers around the idea of intentionally creating weaknesses or vulnerabilities in encryption algorithms. Proponents argue that this would allow legitimate authorities to access encrypted communications when necessary. However, this approach fundamentally undermines the very purpose of encryption, as any vulnerability can be exploited by malicious actors.

Encryption is not a binary state; it exists on a spectrum. Weakening encryption to provide backdoor access invites a potential slippery slope towards complete compromise of privacy and security. Instead, the battle for encryption lies in promoting the use of strong encryption algorithms that can withstand sophisticated attacks and ensuring that any attempts to weaken encryption are met with strong resistance.

Legal Challenges and Legislation

The legal landscape surrounding encryption is complex and constantly evolving. Governments around the world have enacted various laws and policies that either support or challenge the use of encryption. Some countries restrict the use of encryption, making it mandatory to provide encryption keys to authorities upon request. Others, however, uphold the right to use strong encryption without interference.

The battle for encryption entails continuous legal challenges and advocacy to establish and protect the rights of individuals and organizations to use encryption without compromise. It also involves raising awareness about the importance of secure communication and highlighting the potential consequences of undermining encryption.

Advancements in Quantum Computing

While encryption algorithms have become increasingly robust over the years, advancements in quantum computing pose a potential threat. Quantum computers have the potential to solve complex mathematical problems that are currently practically impossible for classical computers. This could render many current encryption algorithms vulnerable to attacks.

The battle for encryption involves staying ahead of the curve by developing quantum-resistant encryption algorithms that can withstand the power of quantum computers. Researchers and cryptographers are exploring the realm of post-quantum cryptography, which aims to develop encryption algorithms that remain secure in the age of quantum computing.

The Role of Public Perception

Public perception regarding privacy and encryption plays a vital role in the continued battle for encryption. In recent years, there has been a growing awareness and concern about the erosion of privacy, fueled by high-profile data breaches, surveillance scandals, and the misuse of personal information by tech giants.

This increased awareness has led to a surge in demand for privacy-oriented technologies and applications. Developers and companies are now incorporating encryption by default into their products and services, empowering users to protect their digital communications. Public support for encryption is crucial in influencing policy decisions and resisting attempts to weaken or restrict its use.

The Responsibility of Encryption Users

While encryption technology continues to advance and the battle for encryption unfolds on a global scale, it is essential for individuals and organizations to take responsibility for their own security. This means using strong encryption tools, keeping software up to date, employing secure practices for storing and transmitting data, and promoting a culture of digital privacy.

Encryption is not a silver bullet, but it is an indispensable weapon in the ongoing war for privacy and security. By utilizing encryption tools effectively and advocating for strong encryption practices, individuals can actively contribute to the battle for encryption and ensure their digital lives remain secure.

The Future of Encryption

As the battle for encryption continues, the future of this technology holds both challenges and opportunities. The ongoing development of quantum-resistant encryption algorithms will be crucial to protect against future threats posed by quantum computing. Additionally, advancements in areas such as homomorphic encryption, zero-knowledge proofs, and secure multi-party computation offer promising alternatives to traditional encryption techniques.

However, the battle for encryption extends beyond technological advancements. It requires collective efforts from individuals, tech companies, policymakers, and advocacy groups to safeguard the privacy and security of a digitally connected world. By promoting encryption as a fundamental right, raising awareness about its importance, and standing up against attempts to compromise its integrity, we can ensure that the continued battle for encryption remains both strong and steadfast in the face of evolving challenges.

The fight for encryption is not just about protecting our data; it is about preserving our fundamental rights to privacy and freedom of expression. The battle for encryption will continue to shape the future of technology, society, and democracy itself. With continued dedication, innovation, and an unwavering commitment to privacy, we can build a future where encryption remains a powerful tool for securing our digital lives.

Phil Zimmermann's Influence on Policy

Phil Zimmermann's work in cryptography and his advocacy for privacy rights have had a significant impact on policy around the world. His groundbreaking invention, Pretty Good Privacy (PGP), revolutionized the field of encryption and paved the way for greater protection of individuals' digital rights. In this section, we will explore how Zimmermann's influence has shaped policy decisions in the realm of privacy and security.

Encryption as a Fundamental Right

One of the key contributions of Zimmermann's work is the recognition of encryption as a fundamental right. In an era of increasing digital surveillance and data breaches, Zimmermann understood the importance of secure communication for individuals and the potential dangers of leaving sensitive information unprotected.

Zimmermann's efforts to bring strong encryption to the masses sparked an important conversation about privacy rights and the role of government in regulating encryption technology. His advocacy for accessible and user-friendly encryption tools helped to establish the idea that individuals have the right to protect their digital communications from unwarranted surveillance.

The Encryption Backdoor Debate

Zimmermann's influence on policy can be seen most prominently in the encryption backdoor debate. This contentious issue revolves around the idea of creating a "backdoor" into encrypted messaging platforms, which would allow government agencies to gain access to encrypted communications in the interest of national security.

Zimmermann has been a vocal opponent of encryption backdoors, arguing that weakening encryption compromises the security of individuals, businesses, and governments alike. He has stressed that any vulnerability in encryption can be exploited not only by law enforcement but also by hackers and cybercriminals.

His advocacy work and technical expertise have helped policymakers understand the dangers associated with encryption backdoors and the importance of robust encryption standards. Zimmermann's influence has led to policies that prioritize strong encryption and protect the privacy of individuals and businesses.

Privacy Laws and Regulations

Zimmermann's work has also informed the development of privacy laws and regulations in many countries. His efforts to promote encryption as a means to protect privacy have contributed to the growing recognition of privacy as a fundamental human right.

In the United States, for example, the recent California Consumer Privacy Act (CCPA) and the European Union's General Data Protection Regulation (GDPR) reflect a growing understanding of the need to safeguard personal information. These laws draw on Zimmermann's principles of user control and data protection.

Zimmermann's influence has extended beyond specific legislation, inspiring policymakers to prioritize privacy and consider the potential consequences of weak encryption and intrusive surveillance practices. His work has paved the way for more comprehensive privacy laws that aim to put individuals in control of their personal data.

International Cooperation on Encryption Policy

Zimmermann's impact on policy extends beyond national borders. His work has inspired international cooperation and dialogue among governments, tech companies, and civil society organizations.

Through his advocacy and participation in global forums and conferences, Zimmermann has encouraged governments to adopt encryption-friendly policies and collaborate on finding solutions that balance privacy and security. His influence has helped to shape international norms and standards regarding encryption technology.

Zimmermann's emphasis on the importance of protecting individuals' privacy in a connected world has resonated with policymakers worldwide. His work has encouraged governments to adopt policies that prioritize the rights of individuals and seek innovative ways to address national security concerns without compromising encryption standards.

Phil Zimmermann's Continued Influence

The influence of Phil Zimmermann's work on policy continues to be felt in the ongoing fight for privacy. As technology evolves and new challenges emerge, Zimmermann's principles remain relevant and guide policymakers in their decisions.

His work has inspired a new generation of privacy advocates and technologists, who carry forward his vision for a world with strong encryption and robust digital rights. Zimmermann's focus on accessibility, user empowerment, and the democratization of privacy continues to shape policy discussions and initiatives.

In an increasingly interconnected and data-driven world, Zimmermann's influence serves as a reminder of the critical importance of protecting privacy and maintaining the integrity of encryption technology. His legacy inspires ongoing conversations around policy and the delicate balance between privacy, security, and individual freedoms.

Overall, Zimmermann's work has had a profound impact on policy, shaping the way governments and society as a whole approach encryption, privacy rights, and digital security. His influence will continue to resonate as technology advances and new policy challenges arise, ensuring that his vision for a world with privacy and security remains at the forefront of policy discussions.

The Democracy of Privacy

In this era of rapid technological advancements and widespread connectivity, the battle for privacy has taken center stage. The increasing encroachment on our personal lives by governments and corporations has sparked a heated debate on the importance of privacy rights. Phil Zimmermann, as a fierce advocate for privacy, understood the fundamental role that privacy plays in maintaining a democratic society. In this section, we will explore the concept of the democracy of privacy and its significance in our connected world.

The Foundation of Democracy

To understand the democracy of privacy, we must first grasp the essence of democracy itself. Democracy is built on the principles of freedom, equality, and individual rights. It values the power of the people to govern themselves and participate in decision-making processes. At its core, democracy relies on the ability of individuals to engage in open and honest dialogue without fear of surveillance or suppression.

Privacy as an Essential Right

Privacy is not just a desire for seclusion, but an essential right that underpins the functioning of a democratic society. It safeguards our autonomy, allowing us to freely express our thoughts, beliefs, and opinions without fear of judgment or reprisal. Privacy forms the foundation for diverse perspectives and the ability to challenge the status quo. Furthermore, privacy provides the necessary space for personal growth, introspection, and the development of individual identity.

Protecting Democracy through Privacy

The democracy of privacy recognizes that the preservation of individual privacy is vital to the health of democracy. When people can communicate and share information privately, they are more likely to engage in open, honest, and meaningful dialogue. They can explore new ideas, challenge prevailing narratives, and hold those in power accountable. Without privacy, there is a chilling effect on free expression, stifling dissent and impeding progress.

The Threat of Surveillance

In the digital age, the pervasiveness of surveillance poses a significant threat to the democracy of privacy. Governments and corporations collect and analyze vast amounts of personal data, often without the knowledge or consent of individuals. This unprecedented level of surveillance erodes trust, fosters self-censorship, and limits our ability to engage in democratic processes. It creates an imbalance of power, where the few hold an unfair advantage over the many.

Striking the Balance

The democracy of privacy calls for a delicate balance between privacy and security. While national security is a legitimate concern, it should not come at the expense of individual privacy rights. Technology can play a crucial role in achieving this balance by providing secure encryption tools that protect personal data while allowing lawful interception under appropriate circumstances. It is essential to ensure that any encroachments on privacy are necessary, proportionate, and subject to democratic oversight.

Educating and Empowering Individuals

In a democratic society, individuals must be educated about their privacy rights and empowered to protect them. Education on digital literacy, encryption technologies, and privacy-preserving practices can equip individuals to navigate the digital landscape confidently. By fostering a culture of privacy-consciousness, we can foster a society that values the democracy of privacy and actively fights against its erosion.

The Power of Collective Action

The democracy of privacy thrives when individuals come together to advocate for their rights. By forming alliances, engaging in public discourse, and holding those in power accountable, people can shape the narrative around privacy. Technology communities, civil society organizations, and individuals can collaborate to develop and promote privacy-enhancing technologies, advocate for stronger privacy regulations, and raise awareness about the importance of privacy in a democratic society.

Privacy and Social Justice

The democracy of privacy goes beyond individual rights to encompass broader social justice issues. Marginalized communities are often disproportionately affected by privacy infringements and surveillance practices. Recognizing the intersectionality between privacy and social justice allows us to address systemic inequalities and work towards a more inclusive and equitable society. By prioritizing privacy as a fundamental human right, we can strive towards a democratic society that values and protects the rights of all.

Bridging the Gap

As technology continues to evolve, it is crucial to bridge the gap between policymakers, technologists, and the public in the pursuit of the democracy of privacy. Policies must be informed by input from those who understand the technical implications and societal impact of privacy decisions. Collaboration between legal experts, technologists, and civil society can contribute to the development of effective and ethical privacy frameworks.

A Call to Action

The democracy of privacy demands our attention and action. It requires us to reflect on our own attitudes towards privacy, engage in informed discussions, and actively participate in shaping the future of privacy. We must champion privacy as a fundamental human right and strive to create a society where the democracy of privacy is not just a lofty ideal, but a tangible reality.

The Unconventional Solution

In the battle for the democracy of privacy, an unconventional yet compelling solution emerges: reimagining privacy as a collective responsibility rather than an individual right. This shift in perspective encourages us to recognize that privacy is interconnected, and the actions of one individual impact the privacy of others. Embracing this collective responsibility inspires a sense of solidarity and propels us to take action to safeguard privacy rights for the benefit of all.

Discussion Questions

1. How does privacy contribute to the functioning of a democratic society?
    2. What challenges does the digital age present to the democracy of privacy?

3. How can individuals balance privacy and security in their daily lives?
4. What role can technology communities play in promoting the democracy of privacy?
5. How can advocacy efforts for privacy intersect with social justice movements?

Further Reading

1. The Right to Privacy: Contemporary Relevance and Future Directions - Edited by Roland Huesca and David Erdos
2. Privacy and Freedom - Alan F. Westin
3. "Democracy and Privacy in the Age of Data" - Deborah Hurley and James H. Dempsey
4. "The Case for Privacy as a Social Practice" - Helen Nissenbaum
5. "The Future of Privacy" - Marc Rotenberg, Julia Horwitz, and Jeramie Scott

Preserving Phil Zimmermann's Vision

Preserving Phil Zimmermann's vision is essential in ensuring the continued fight for privacy in the digital age. As a pioneer in the field of encryption, Zimmermann dedicated his life to protecting individuals' right to privacy and advocating for the secure transmission of data. In order to carry forward his legacy, it is crucial to understand his principles, build upon his work, and foster a culture of privacy-consciousness.

Understanding Zimmermann's Principles

To preserve Zimmermann's vision, we must first comprehend the principles that guided his work. Zimmermann believed that privacy is a fundamental human right, and that individuals should have control over their personal information. He recognized the potential for abuse in mass surveillance, and championed the use of strong encryption as a means to safeguard privacy.

Zimmermann also emphasized the importance of accessible and user-friendly encryption tools. He believed that everyone, regardless of technical expertise, should be able to protect their digital communications. This principle of usability has played a significant role in the widespread adoption of encryption technologies.

Building on Zimmermann's Work

Preserving Zimmermann's vision requires building on the foundation he laid. One way to accomplish this is by continuing to advance encryption technologies. As computing power increases, there is a need for more robust encryption algorithms to withstand sophisticated attacks. Research and development in the field of cryptography can help maintain the security and integrity of digital communications.

Open-source collaboration, which Zimmermann championed, remains essential in preserving his vision. By encouraging transparency and peer-review, open-source projects ensure the integrity and trustworthiness of encryption tools. Developers should be motivated to contribute to and improve existing encryption software, enabling further innovation and evolution.

Fostering a Culture of Privacy-Consciousness

Preserving Zimmermann's vision requires fostering a culture of privacy-consciousness among individuals and institutions. Education plays a crucial role in achieving this. Efforts should be made to raise awareness about the importance of privacy and the risks associated with inadequate protection of personal data. Training programs can empower individuals with the knowledge and skills to adopt privacy-enhancing practices and technologies.

To reinforce the culture of privacy-consciousness, collaboration between various stakeholders is essential. Governments, non-profit organizations, and technology companies should work together to create policies that protect individuals' privacy rights. This includes advocating for strong privacy regulations and preventing the misuse of personal data by both state and non-state actors.

Realizing Zimmermann's Vision in the Digital Age

In today's fast-paced digital world, preserving Zimmermann's vision requires continuous adaptation. New challenges such as the rise of machine learning, the spread of social media, and the proliferation of internet-connected devices demand innovative solutions. Collaboration between technologists, policy-makers, and privacy advocates is crucial to address these challenges and ensure the long-term preservation of privacy.

Furthermore, Zimmermann's vision extends beyond encryption technologies alone. It encompasses the broader context of individual autonomy, digital rights, and the ethical use of data. Preserving his vision requires addressing these issues holistically, exploring novel approaches, and pushing for policy changes that align with the interests of privacy-conscious individuals.

Preserving Zimmermann's Vision: A Call to Action

Preserving Phil Zimmermann's vision necessitates a collective commitment to privacy preservation. It is a responsibility that falls upon not just technologists and policy-makers, but also everyday individuals who value their right to privacy. By understanding Zimmermann's principles, building on his work, fostering privacy-consciousness, and adapting to the challenges of the digital age, we can ensure that his vision endures.

Now is the time to embrace encryption, educate ourselves and others about privacy, and demand regulations that protect our personal information. In doing so, we honor Zimmermann's lifelong dedication to privacy and pave the way for a future where privacy is valued and upheld.

Phil Zimmermann's Impact on Tech Ethics

When it comes to the intersection of technology and ethics, few individuals have had as profound an impact as Phil Zimmermann. Through his groundbreaking work in encryption and privacy advocacy, Zimmermann not only revolutionized the way we communicate securely but also sparked important conversations about the ethical implications of technology. In this section, we will explore Zimmermann's contributions to tech ethics and the lasting impact of his work.

Privacy as a Human Right

One of Zimmermann's key contributions to tech ethics was his steadfast belief in the fundamental right to privacy. He recognized that privacy is more than just a convenience or a luxury but an essential aspect of human dignity and freedom. Zimmermann understood that without the ability to communicate privately, individuals could not freely express themselves or engage in open dialogue without fear of reprisal.

Zimmermann's creation of Pretty Good Privacy (PGP) was driven by his desire to empower individuals with the ability to protect their privacy in the digital age. By developing an accessible and user-friendly encryption tool, Zimmermann made it possible for anyone to secure their communications from prying eyes. This democratization of privacy was a revolutionary concept that challenged the prevailing narrative that only governments or corporations should control access to personal information.

Implications for Surveillance and Mass Data Collection

Zimmermann's work drew attention to the ethical dilemmas surrounding surveillance and mass data collection. He was acutely aware of the potential abuses that could arise from unchecked government surveillance and the growing power of tech companies to collect and monetize personal data. Zimmermann's advocacy for encryption was, in many ways, a response to these concerns.

By championing strong encryption, Zimmermann aimed to level the playing field between individuals and powerful institutions. He believed that privacy should not be a privilege reserved for the few but a right that should be accessible to all. Zimmermann's stance on encryption forced governments and tech companies to confront the ethical implications of their actions and sparked a much-needed conversation about the balance between security and personal freedoms.

Promoting Transparency and Accountability

Another area where Zimmermann made a significant impact on tech ethics was his advocacy for transparency and accountability in the tech industry. He recognized the potential for misuse and abuse of technology, particularly when it came to surveillance and data collection. Zimmermann firmly believed that tech companies and governments should be held accountable for their actions and that individuals should have the right to know how their data is being used.

Through his work with organizations like the Electronic Frontier Foundation (EFF), Zimmermann fought for greater transparency in government surveillance programs and pushed for privacy-focused regulations. He also called on tech companies to adopt more ethical practices, including transparent data collection policies and robust security measures.

Zimmermann's tireless advocacy for transparency forced the tech industry to confront uncomfortable truths and sparked a broader conversation about ethics and responsibility. His work laid the foundation for the ongoing debates surrounding data privacy, algorithmic transparency, and the role of tech companies in shaping our digital lives.

Educating the Tech Community

In addition to his technical contributions, Zimmermann played a crucial role in educating the tech community about the importance of privacy and the ethical considerations surrounding technology. Through his talks, writings, and public appearances, Zimmermann tirelessly worked to raise awareness about the potential risks and benefits of encryption, surveillance, and data privacy.

Zimmermann's emphasis on education was rooted in the belief that individuals and society at large must understand the implications of their actions. He believed that by increasing awareness and knowledge, we could build a more informed and ethically responsible tech community.

Continuing the Legacy

While Phil Zimmermann's impact on tech ethics cannot be understated, it is essential to acknowledge that the battle for privacy and ethical technology is far from over. The pace of technological advancement continues to outstrip our ability to fully understand and address the ethical implications of new technologies.

Moving forward, it is crucial for the tech community, policymakers, and society at large to carry on Zimmermann's legacy. We must prioritize privacy as a fundamental human right, advocate for transparency and accountability, and engage in ongoing conversations about the ethical considerations of emerging technologies.

By embracing Zimmermann's vision and continuing his work, we can build a future that respects individual privacy, upholds ethical principles, and ensures that technology serves the greater good.

Exercises

1. Research and discuss a recent case where privacy concerns clashed with technological advancements. Evaluate the ethical implications of the situation and propose possible solutions.

2. Explore the debate on encryption backdoors and its ethical implications. Take a stance on the issue and provide arguments to support your position.

3. Investigate the role of whistleblowers in raising awareness about surveillance and privacy abuses. Discuss the ethical considerations surrounding whistleblowing and whether it is an effective means of promoting change.

4. Reflect on your own digital privacy practices. Are there any changes you can make to better protect your privacy? Discuss your strategies and the ethical considerations behind them.

5. Research different privacy-focused technologies or initiatives that have emerged in recent years. Evaluate their effectiveness and discuss the ethical principles they promote.

Resources

1. Greenwald, G. (2014). No Place to Hide: Edward Snowden, the NSA, and the U.S. Surveillance State. Picador.

2. Solove, D. J. (2011). Nothing to hide: The false tradeoff between privacy and security. Yale University Press.

3. The Guardian: Technology and Surveillance. Available at: `https://www.theguardian.com/technology/surveillance`.

4. Electronic Frontier Foundation (EFF): Protecting Civil Liberties in a Digital World. Available at: `https://www.eff.org/`.

5. Schneier, B. (2015). Data and Goliath: The Hidden Battles to Collect Your Data and Control Your World. W. W. Norton & Company.

Key Takeaways

- Phil Zimmermann's contributions to tech ethics are significant and wide-ranging. His work in encryption, privacy advocacy, and transparency has shaped the ethical discourse in the tech industry. - Zimmermann's belief in privacy as a fundamental human right challenged the prevailing narrative and sparked important conversations about the democratization of privacy. - His work drew attention to the ethical implications of government surveillance and mass data collection, emphasizing the need for greater transparency and accountability. - Zimmermann played a crucial role in educating the tech community about the importance of privacy and ethical considerations surrounding technology. - The legacy of Phil Zimmermann serves as a reminder to prioritize privacy, advocate for transparency and accountability, and engage in ongoing conversations about the ethics of emerging technologies.

The Future of Encryption in a Changing Landscape

In today's rapidly evolving digital landscape, the future of encryption is crucial in ensuring privacy and security for individuals, organizations, and governments alike. As technology advances and new threats emerge, encryption plays a vital role in protecting sensitive information from unauthorized access. In this section, we will explore the challenges and opportunities that lie ahead in the field of encryption, and discuss how it is adapting to the changing landscape.

Quantum Computing: A Double-Edged Sword

One of the most prominent factors shaping the future of encryption is the development of quantum computing. With the potential to exponentially increase computing power, quantum computers pose a significant threat to traditional encryption algorithms, such as RSA and ECC, which rely on the difficulty of factoring large numbers or solving the discrete logarithm problem. Quantum computers can solve these problems efficiently, rendering current encryption methods vulnerable.

To address this challenge, researchers are actively exploring post-quantum cryptography (PQC), which aims to design encryption algorithms that are resistant to attacks by quantum computers. PQC is a rapidly evolving field that encompasses a variety of mathematical constructs, such as lattice-based, code-based, multivariate polynomial-based, hash-based, and isogeny-based cryptography. These new algorithms are built on hard mathematical problems that are believed to be difficult even for quantum computers to solve.

However, transitioning to post-quantum encryption is not without its challenges. It requires widespread adoption, implementation, and integration across various systems and protocols. Additionally, the performance of post-quantum algorithms may be significantly slower compared to traditional encryption methods. Balancing security and efficiency will be a key consideration in the deployment of post-quantum cryptography.

Privacy and Legislation in a Data-Driven World

In an increasingly data-driven world, privacy concerns are at the forefront of conversations around encryption. Individuals and organizations alike are seeking effective ways to protect their sensitive data from unauthorized access, whether it be personal information, trade secrets, or intellectual property. In response to this demand for privacy, governments are enacting legislation to regulate data protection and enhance privacy rights.

One significant example is the European Union's General Data Protection Regulation (GDPR), which sets strict guidelines for the collection, processing, and storage of personal data. The GDPR grants individuals greater control over their data and establishes hefty fines for non-compliance. This legislation has driven organizations to prioritize data protection and implement stringent encryption measures to safeguard personal information.

In the United States, the conversation around privacy legislation has gained momentum, with various proposed bills aiming to provide individuals with similar rights and protections. The California Consumer Privacy Act (CCPA) is one such example, granting consumers the right to know what personal information businesses collect, how it is used, and the ability to opt out of its sale.

As encryption technologies continue to advance, policymakers face the challenge of striking a balance between privacy rights and national security concerns. The debate over encryption backdoors, which would provide government agencies with authorized access to encrypted data, remains a contentious issue. Striking the right balance between privacy and security is crucial to the future of encryption in a changing legislative landscape.

Emerging Technologies and the Internet of Things (IoT)

The rapid expansion of the Internet of Things (IoT) poses both opportunities and challenges for encryption. With billions of interconnected devices, ranging from smart home appliances to industrial sensors, the need to secure data transmitted across these networks becomes paramount. Encryption plays a crucial role in ensuring the confidentiality and integrity of IoT data.

However, IoT devices often have limited computing power and memory, which poses challenges for implementing robust encryption protocols. Lightweight cryptography, designed specifically for resource-constrained devices, is crucial for achieving strong security without compromising performance.

Additionally, the proliferation of emerging technologies, such as edge computing and blockchain, introduces new considerations for encryption. Edge computing brings computation and storage closer to the data source, reducing latency and improving efficiency. Encryption techniques must be optimized for this distributed computing environment to provide secure and efficient data processing.

Blockchain technology, known for its decentralized and transparent nature, relies heavily on encryption to ensure the integrity and privacy of transactions. Cryptocurrencies, built on blockchain technology, utilize encryption for secure financial transactions. As blockchain continues to evolve and find applications beyond cryptocurrencies, encryption will play a crucial role in maintaining the trust and security of transactions.

The Human Element: User Education and Awareness

In an era where data breaches and cyberattacks are commonplace, user education and awareness are pivotal in ensuring the effective use of encryption. Despite the availability of advanced encryption technologies, they can only provide robust security if properly implemented and utilized.

User knowledge gaps and misconceptions remain a significant obstacle to encryption adoption. Many individuals and organizations still lack a fundamental understanding of encryption principles, making them susceptible to social engineering attacks and falling victim to security breaches. To address this issue, a concerted effort is required to raise awareness about encryption best practices, such as strong password management, two-factor authentication, and secure communication channels.

Furthermore, user-friendly encryption tools and interfaces are crucial for wider adoption. Technology that seamlessly integrates encryption into everyday applications, such as messaging platforms and email clients, makes it easier for individuals to protect their data without requiring extensive technical knowledge.

Lastly, ongoing research and development in encryption usability and user experience play a vital role in increasing user adoption. Innovations, such as zero-knowledge proofs and homomorphic encryption, ensure the confidentiality of user data while enabling secure data sharing and processing. These advancements empower users with greater control and understanding of their encrypted information.

Conclusion

As we navigate the ever-changing landscape of technology, the future of encryption holds immense promise and complex challenges. The rise of quantum computing, the evolving legislative landscape, the Internet of Things, and the importance of user education all shape the future of encryption.

By embracing post-quantum cryptography, addressing privacy concerns through legislation, adapting to emerging technologies, and focusing on user education, we can create a safer digital world. Encryption will continue to play a crucial role in protecting our data, ensuring privacy, and maintaining the trust necessary for a thriving digital society.

Let us embark on this journey together, fostering innovation, advocating for privacy, and shaping the future of encryption in an ever-evolving world. After all, the power to protect our digital lives lies in our hands.

Entering the Post-PGP Era

In the ever-changing landscape of technology and privacy, one cannot help but wonder what lies ahead after the era of Pretty Good Privacy (PGP). PGP revolutionized encryption and played a pivotal role in safeguarding privacy in the digital age. However, as we enter the post-PGP era, new challenges and opportunities await us. In this section, we will explore the implications of this transition and the future of privacy in a connected world.

The Need for Continued Encryption

As we move beyond PGP, it is crucial to recognize the enduring need for encryption. While PGP provided a robust and user-friendly platform for secure communication, emerging technologies and threats necessitate new approaches to encryption. The post-PGP era demands solutions that are scalable, adaptable, and resistant to evolving attacks.

One of the key challenges in the post-PGP era is the rise of quantum computing. Quantum computers have the potential to break many of the encryption algorithms currently employed, including those used in PGP. As quantum computing advances, so too must our encryption techniques. Post-quantum cryptography, which includes algorithms resistant to quantum attacks, is an active area of research and development.

Moreover, encryption technologies must evolve to address the increasing sophistication of cyber threats. From state-sponsored hacking to advanced persistent threats, adversaries are becoming more persistent and innovative in their attempts to compromise data security. The post-PGP era calls for encryption solutions that can withstand these threats and provide robust protection for sensitive information.

Innovation and Disruption

The post-PGP era presents an opportunity for innovation and disruption in the field of encryption. As PGP served as a catalyst for privacy-focused technologies, we can expect new approaches and frameworks to emerge that address the shortcomings and limitations of traditional encryption methods.

One area of exploration is homomorphic encryption, which allows computation on encrypted data without decryption. This paradigm has the potential to unlock new possibilities for secure data processing, enabling the analysis of sensitive information while preserving privacy. As researchers continue to refine and enhance homomorphic encryption techniques, we can anticipate its integration into various domains, such as healthcare, finance, and cloud computing.

Another avenue for innovation lies in the development of decentralized and distributed systems. By leveraging blockchain technology and peer-to-peer networks, it is possible to create secure and privacy-preserving communication platforms that are resistant to censorship and surveillance. These systems could redefine how we share information, ensuring that individuals retain control over their personal data.

The Role of Artificial Intelligence

Artificial Intelligence (AI) is poised to shape the post-PGP era, particularly in the context of privacy and encryption. AI can enhance encryption algorithms, making them more efficient and resistant to attacks. Machine learning algorithms can be trained to identify patterns and anomalies in encrypted data, thereby strengthening the security of encryption protocols.

On the flip side, the proliferation of AI also raises concerns regarding privacy. AI-based technologies, such as facial recognition and natural language processing, have the potential to infringe upon individual privacy rights. The post-PGP era must grapple with the ethical and legal implications of AI in relation to privacy, striking a balance between technological advancements and safeguarding personal information.

International Cooperation and Regulation

As we navigate the post-PGP era, international cooperation and regulation play a pivotal role in shaping the future of privacy. Encryption technologies transcend geographical boundaries, necessitating harmonized policies and frameworks that balance national security interests with individual privacy rights.

International agreements and standards are crucial in ensuring that encryption remains widely available and robust across borders. Collaboration among governments, industry stakeholders, and privacy advocates is essential for establishing a common understanding of encryption's importance and promoting responsible encryption practices.

Moreover, regulations must adapt to the evolving privacy landscape. The post-PGP era requires comprehensive privacy laws that address emerging challenges, such as data breaches, algorithmic bias, and the collection and use of personal information by tech giants. These laws should provide individuals with greater control over their data while fostering innovation and technological advancements.

Educating the Next Generation

As we enter the post-PGP era, it is paramount that we educate the next generation of programmers, engineers, and policymakers on the importance of privacy and encryption. By imparting a deep understanding of encryption principles, ethical considerations, and the societal implications of privacy, we can empower individuals to make informed decisions and develop innovative solutions.

Privacy education should be integrated into computer science curricula, emphasizing the ethical responsibilities of technologists and the societal impact of their work. By nurturing a privacy-aware mindset, we can foster a culture that values the protection of personal information and respects individuals' rights to privacy.

Furthermore, initiatives such as hackathons, coding competitions, and privacy-oriented projects can provide avenues for students to explore encryption technologies and develop hands-on skills. Encouraging research and innovation in the field of privacy will drive progress in the post-PGP era and equip future leaders with the tools to tackle emerging challenges.

Striking a Balance: Privacy and Security

In the post-PGP era, finding the right balance between privacy and security becomes increasingly vital. While encryption technologies protect sensitive information from unauthorized access, they can also impede legitimate national security efforts, such as combating terrorism and organized crime.

The challenge lies in striking a delicate balance between individual privacy rights and collective security. Encryption backdoors, which provide a means for law enforcement to bypass encryption, have been proposed as a potential solution. However, the implementation of such mechanisms poses significant risks and raises concerns about undermining the very security encryption aims to provide.

Exploring alternative approaches, such as secure multi-party computation and privacy-enhancing technologies, can help address the tension between privacy and security. By designing systems that enable collaborative and secure data analysis without compromising individual privacy, we can navigate the post-PGP era while upholding both privacy rights and national security interests.

The Post-PGP Legacy

As we enter the post-PGP era, we must remember and honor the legacy of Phil Zimmermann and the impact of PGP. Phil's vision and dedication to privacy paved the way for a new era of secure communication. The lessons learned from PGP's journey continue to inform our understanding of privacy and encryption in the digital age.

The post-PGP era presents both challenges and opportunities. With ongoing innovation, interdisciplinary collaboration, and a commitment to privacy education, we can navigate this era while upholding the fundamental rights to privacy and security. As we move forward, it is essential to embrace change, embrace new technologies, and work collectively to build a future that values privacy and protects the integrity of our digital lives.

Discussion Questions

1. What are the key challenges that encryption technologies face in the post-PGP era? 2. How can emerging technologies like quantum computing and AI impact the future of encryption? 3. What role should international cooperation and regulation play in shaping privacy in the post-PGP era? 4. How can we strike a balance between individual privacy rights and national security in the context of encryption? 5. What steps can be taken to ensure that the next generation of programmers and policymakers are equipped to address privacy challenges in the post-PGP era?

The Next Generation of Privacy Pioneers

As we enter an increasingly digitally interconnected world, the need for privacy pioneers who can navigate the complex landscape of data protection and online security has never been greater. Phil Zimmermann's remarkable contribution to the field of encryption and privacy has laid a strong foundation for the next generation to build upon. In this section, we will explore the qualities and skills that will define the future privacy pioneers, and the challenges they will face in safeguarding our privacy in a connected world.

Evolving Threats

The next generation of privacy pioneers will be tasked with combating evolving threats to our digital privacy. As technology continues to advance, so do the tools and tactics used by malicious actors seeking to exploit personal information. From sophisticated hacking techniques to the rise of surveillance capitalism, privacy pioneers will need to stay one step ahead of these threats.

One of the biggest challenges will be protecting personal data in the age of social media. With the extensive amount of personal information shared online, it has become increasingly crucial to control and protect our digital footprints. Privacy pioneers will play a pivotal role in educating individuals and organizations about the risks associated with overexposure on social media platforms.

Holistic Approach

To effectively address the complexities of privacy in the digital age, the next generation of privacy pioneers must develop a holistic approach to privacy. This means going beyond just encryption and focusing on a broader range of privacy-enhancing technologies and practices. It involves considering the ethical implications of data collection, processing, and usage.

Privacy pioneers should also place emphasis on user education and empowerment. This involves raising awareness about privacy rights, teaching individuals how to protect their personal information, and encouraging responsible digital practices. By empowering individuals to take ownership of their privacy, privacy pioneers can foster a culture of privacy-consciousness in the digital realm.

Collaboration and Advocacy

Collaboration between privacy pioneers, tech companies, policymakers, and civil society organizations will be vital in shaping the future of privacy. Privacy pioneers must actively engage in advocacy efforts to promote strong privacy laws and regulations. They should also collaborate with tech companies to develop privacy-focused products and services that prioritize user data protection.

In addition, privacy pioneers should work closely with policymakers to influence legislation and policy decisions related to privacy. They can provide expert insights and recommendations to ensure that privacy concerns are adequately addressed in the development of new laws and regulations.

Innovation and Adaptability

The landscape of privacy and data protection is constantly evolving, requiring privacy pioneers to be innovative and adaptable. They must stay abreast of emerging technologies, trends, and regulations to anticipate and effectively respond to new challenges.

Privacy pioneers should actively contribute to the development and implementation of cutting-edge privacy-enhancing technologies. This may involve participating in open-source projects, collaborating with developers, and conducting research to push the boundaries of privacy protection.

Ethics and Transparency

The next generation of privacy pioneers must navigate the ethical challenges surrounding data collection, sharing, and analysis. They should prioritize privacy by design, ensuring that privacy considerations are embedded in the design and development of technologies from the very beginning.

Transparency will also be a key principle for privacy pioneers. They should advocate for transparency in data collection and usage practices, and promote the use of privacy-enhancing tools that provide individuals with greater control and visibility over their data.

Real-World Examples of Privacy Pioneers

To illustrate the work of privacy pioneers, let's take a look at a few real-world examples:

1. Aral Balkan: Aral Balkan is a privacy advocate and technologist who founded the Small Technology Foundation. He actively works to develop and promote ethical alternative technologies that respect user privacy.

2. Laura Poitras: Laura Poitras is an award-winning documentary filmmaker and journalist. Her work on the Edward Snowden revelations shed light on the

extent of government surveillance, sparking a global debate on privacy and data protection.

3. Eva Galperin: Eva Galperin is the director of cybersecurity at the Electronic Frontier Foundation (EFF). She focuses on defending individuals and organizations from targeted malware attacks and spearheads advocacy efforts for online privacy.

The Next Generation's Call to Action

As we contemplate the future of privacy pioneers, it is essential to recognize the urgent need for young minds to step forward and champion privacy rights. The next generation must take up the mantle and embrace the challenges that lie ahead.

Here are some key actions for the next generation of privacy pioneers to consider:

1. Education: Acquire a strong foundation in computer science, cybersecurity, and privacy to understand the technical aspects of data protection.

2. Collaboration: Foster collaboration with like-minded individuals, organizations, and tech communities to share knowledge and drive innovative solutions.

3. Advocacy: Take an active role in advocating for stronger privacy legislation, data protection regulations, and responsible data practices.

4. Innovation: Embrace innovation and continuously explore new technologies and strategies to stay ahead in the battle for privacy.

5. Ethical Considerations: Prioritize ethics and transparency in all aspects of work related to privacy, ensuring that data protection aligns with fundamental human rights.

Remember, the future of privacy rests in the hands of the next generation of privacy pioneers. Embrace the challenge, drive change, and craft a future where privacy is protected, respected, and celebrated.

Phil Zimmermann's Timeless Message

Phil Zimmermann, the renowned programmer and advocate for privacy, has left a lasting legacy in the world of technology. His groundbreaking work on the Pretty Good Privacy (PGP) encryption software has revolutionized the way we communicate and has become a symbol of resistance against mass surveillance. But beyond his technical achievements, Zimmermann's enduring message serves as a guiding light for future generations in the fight for privacy.

At the core of Zimmermann's message is the belief that privacy is a fundamental human right. In a world where our every move is tracked and our personal data is constantly under threat, Zimmermann's words resonate now more than ever. He reminds us that privacy is not just a luxury, but a necessity for the preservation of individual freedom and dignity.

Zimmermann's message also emphasizes the role of encryption in protecting privacy. He understood that encryption is a powerful tool that enables individuals to secure their digital communications and keep their personal information away from prying eyes. His vision was to empower individuals with the ability to control their own data and ensure their privacy in a digital age.

However, Zimmermann also acknowledged the ethical dilemmas surrounding privacy and security. He recognized the need to strike a balance between privacy and national security. While encryption is a crucial defense against surveillance, it can also be used by malicious actors to conceal their activities. Zimmermann's message cautions that we must find solutions that safeguard privacy without compromising public safety.

One of the striking aspects of Zimmermann's message is his reminder that privacy is not just an individual concern but a collective responsibility. He urges us to advocate for privacy rights, support organizations working to protect privacy, and hold governments and corporations accountable for their data practices. Zimmermann's message emboldens us to be active participants in shaping the future of privacy, rather than passive bystanders.

Zimmermann also highlights the importance of privacy education. He believed that knowledge is power and that understanding the principles of encryption and privacy empowers individuals to take control of their digital lives. He encourages a future where privacy education is integrated into school curricula and where everyone has access to the tools and knowledge needed to protect their privacy.

In this technological era, where advancements in surveillance technology and data collection seem relentless, Zimmermann's timeless message reminds us that the fight for privacy is far from over. It inspires us to continuously challenge the status quo, to question the motives behind data collection, and to strive for a future where privacy is not a privilege but a right for all.

Zimmermann's message resonates with a wide range of audiences, from individual users to policymakers and technologists. It spurs debate, raises awareness, and inspires action. His unwavering commitment to privacy serves as a blueprint for future generations in their quest to find innovative solutions, defy the norms, and safeguard privacy in a connected world.

In conclusion, Phil Zimmermann's timeless message about privacy serves as a compass in navigating the complex landscape of the digital age. It reminds us of the importance of privacy as a fundamental human right, the power of encryption in protecting our information, the need for a delicate balance between privacy and security, and the collective responsibility we all share in the fight for privacy. Zimmermann's legacy lives on, urging us to carry the torch forward and build a future where privacy is respected and preserved.

The Future of Privacy in a Connected World

The State of Privacy Today

Privacy has become a hot topic in today's digital age. With advancements in technology and the widespread use of the internet, the protection of personal information has become increasingly important. However, the state of privacy today is complex and often compromised.

One of the biggest challenges to privacy is the rise of data collection and the monetization of personal information. Companies, both big and small, are constantly collecting data on individuals through various means such as online tracking, social media, and loyalty programs. This data is then used to target individuals with personalized advertisements and to sell to third parties. As a result, individuals often feel like their every move online is being monitored, leaving them with little control over their own privacy.

Another issue is government surveillance. In many countries, governments have broad powers to monitor individuals' online activities in the name of national security. This includes the collection and analysis of communication data, which can lead to privacy violations and chilling effects on free speech. The introduction of controversial legislation, such as the USA PATRIOT Act in the United States, has further eroded privacy rights.

Furthermore, the advent of social media has raised concerns about privacy. People willingly share personal details of their lives on platforms like Facebook, Instagram, and Twitter without fully understanding the potential consequences. This has led to cases of identity theft, cyberbullying, and the misuse of personal information by malicious actors.

In response to these challenges, various privacy laws and regulations have been put in place to protect individuals. For example, the European Union's General Data Protection Regulation (GDPR) gives individuals more control over their personal data, requiring companies to obtain explicit consent for data collection and providing individuals with the right to access and delete their data. Similarly, the California Consumer Privacy Act (CCPA) grants Californian residents certain rights over their personal information.

However, despite these efforts, privacy breaches and data leaks continue to occur. High-profile cases, such as the Cambridge Analytica scandal, have highlighted the vulnerability of personal information in the digital age. This has led to a growing demand for stronger privacy protection and increased awareness among individuals about their rights and how their data is being used.

To address these concerns, individuals are turning to privacy-enhancing technologies. Encryption, for example, plays a crucial role in safeguarding sensitive information. Through the use of encryption algorithms, data is encoded in such a way that only authorized parties can access it. This helps to protect individuals' privacy and secure their communication.

Privacy-focused tools and services have also emerged, allowing individuals to take control of their online presence. Virtual private networks (VPNs) provide encrypted tunnels for internet traffic, masking users' IP addresses and protecting their online activities from prying eyes. Browser extensions like Privacy Badger and uBlock Origin help block third-party trackers, giving users more control over their browsing experience. Additionally, secure messaging apps like Signal and Telegram have gained popularity for their end-to-end encryption capabilities.

As we navigate the ever-evolving landscape of privacy, it is important to remember that the fight for privacy is ongoing. Technologies like artificial intelligence and the Internet of Things pose new challenges, raising concerns about the security of personal data. Therefore, it is crucial for individuals to stay informed about privacy best practices, advocate for stronger privacy protections, and support organizations that champion digital rights.

In conclusion, the state of privacy today is characterized by a complex and ever-changing landscape. While individuals face challenges in protecting their personal information, there are also efforts being made to enforce privacy regulations and develop privacy-enhancing technologies. With continued awareness and action, we can strive for a future where privacy is respected and individuals have control over their own data.

The Importance of Algorithmic Transparency

In today's digitally connected world, algorithms play a crucial role in our daily lives, from search engine results and social media feeds to financial transactions and healthcare decisions. Algorithms are powerful tools that can process vast amounts of data and make automated decisions. However, as algorithms become increasingly pervasive, there is a growing concern about their lack of transparency and the potential for unintended biases and discriminatory outcomes.

Understanding Algorithmic Transparency

Algorithmic transparency refers to the ability to understand and explain the inner workings of an algorithm. It involves making the decision-making process of algorithms more accessible and accountable to users and the broader public.

Transparency enables individuals to trust the algorithms that impact their lives and ensures that they have insight into the factors influencing the outcomes they experience.

The Risks of Non-Transparent Algorithms

Non-transparent algorithms pose several risks that can have far-reaching consequences:

- **Bias and Discrimination**: Algorithms can perpetuate and amplify existing biases within their training data. If the data used to train an algorithm is biased, the algorithm's decisions will also be biased. This can lead to discriminatory outcomes, impacting marginalized communities and reinforcing social inequalities.

- **Lack of Accountability**: Non-transparent algorithms make it challenging to hold them accountable for their decisions. Without transparency, it is difficult to determine whether an algorithm is operating as intended or if it is generating biased or unfair outcomes.

- **Invasion of Privacy**: Some algorithms utilize personal data in their decision-making processes. Without transparency, individuals may not be aware of how their data is being used or the potential privacy risks associated with algorithmic decision-making.

- **Loss of Autonomy**: If individuals are unable to understand or challenge the decisions made by algorithms, their personal autonomy and agency may be undermined. They may become passive recipients of algorithmic outputs without the ability to question or influence the process.

The Need for Algorithmic Transparency

Algorithmic transparency is essential to address these risks and ensure that algorithms promote fairness, accountability, and trust in various domains:

1. **Social Justice and Equality**: Transparent algorithms can help mitigate biases and discrimination, allowing for fairer outcomes in areas such as job hiring, lending practices, and criminal justice systems. By revealing the criteria and logic behind decisions, stakeholders can identify and rectify any instances of unfair treatment.

2. **Consumer Protection:** Transparent algorithms enable individuals to understand how their personal data is being used and ensure their privacy rights are respected. This empowers users to make informed choices about the services and products they engage with, fostering a sense of control and transparency in the digital marketplace.

3. **Accountability and Governance:** Transparency helps ensure that algorithms are developed, deployed, and maintained responsibly. It enables regulators and policymakers to assess the impact of algorithms on society and implement appropriate measures to address any negative consequences. Additionally, transparency promotes ethical behavior and prevents the misuse of algorithms for malicious purposes.

4. **Trust and User Confidence:** When users have access to information about how algorithms function, they are more likely to trust the outcomes generated. Transparent algorithms establish trust by allowing users to verify the fairness and accuracy of the decision-making process.

Achieving Algorithmic Transparency

Achieving algorithmic transparency is a complex challenge that requires a multidimensional approach:

- **Data Collection and Preprocessing:** Transparent algorithms rely on high-quality data that is representative of the target population. Ensuring diverse and unbiased data collection is crucial for minimizing biases in algorithmic decision-making.

- **Explainability and Interpretability:** Algorithms need to provide explanations for their decisions in a manner that is understandable and interpretable to users. Different techniques, such as model-agnostic approaches and local explanations, can enhance the explainability of algorithms.

- **Algorithmic Auditing:** Regular audits and reviews of algorithms can identify biases, disparities, and areas for improvement. Independent auditors can assess the impact of algorithms on different demographic groups and recommend changes to ensure fairness and equality.

- **User Education and Empowerment:** Educating users about algorithms, their limitations, and the potential risks involved is crucial for enabling informed decision-making. Users should have the knowledge and tools to evaluate and challenge algorithmic outcomes.

- **Regulatory Frameworks**: Governments and regulatory bodies play a vital role in establishing legal and ethical frameworks for algorithmic transparency. Legislative measures can mandate that companies disclose information about their algorithms, data sources, and potential biases.

Emerging Challenges

Just as algorithms continue to evolve, so do the challenges related to algorithmic transparency. Some emerging challenges include:

- **Black-box Algorithms**: Increasingly complex algorithms, such as deep learning neural networks, present challenges in understanding their decision-making process. Researchers are exploring methods to uncover the inner workings of black-box algorithms while maintaining their performance.

- **Adversarial Attacks**: Adversarial attacks are deliberate attempts to manipulate algorithms by providing inputs designed to mislead or deceive the system. These attacks highlight the need for robust algorithms that are resilient to malicious interference while remaining transparent and fair.

- **Trade-Offs between Transparency and Accuracy**: Striking a balance between algorithmic transparency and accuracy is a challenge that needs careful consideration. Highly transparent algorithms may not always be the most accurate, and vice versa. Researchers and developers must navigate this trade-off to ensure both fairness and performance.

Conclusion

Algorithmic transparency is essential for ensuring fair, accountable, and trustworthy decision-making in the digital age. By promoting transparency, we can minimize biases, protect privacy, and empower individuals to actively participate in shaping the digital systems that impact their lives. Striving for algorithmic transparency is a collective responsibility that requires collaboration between policymakers, industry leaders, researchers, and users to create a future where algorithms are ethical, accountable, and transparent.

Let us embrace the challenge of building algorithmic systems that work for the benefit of all, and remember the words of Phil Zimmermann, who said, "We need to address the real needs of real people, with real lives, with real consequences."

Privacy in Artificial Intelligence

As the world becomes increasingly interconnected and technology continues to advance, the intersection of artificial intelligence (AI) and privacy has become a topic of great concern. AI has the potential to revolutionize industries and improve our daily lives, but it also poses significant risks to personal privacy. In this section, we will explore the challenges and ethical considerations surrounding privacy in AI, and discuss potential solutions to ensure the protection of individuals' data and information.

Understanding Artificial Intelligence

Before we delve into the privacy implications, let's first establish a foundational understanding of AI. Artificial intelligence refers to the development of computer systems that can perform tasks that would typically require human intelligence. These tasks include but are not limited to speech recognition, problem-solving, decision-making, and pattern recognition.

AI systems are often designed to learn from data, using algorithms that can analyze large amounts of information and identify patterns or make predictions based on that data. This learning process, known as machine learning, enables AI systems to improve their performance over time without being explicitly programmed for each task.

The Risks to Privacy in AI

While AI has the potential to revolutionize industries and improve efficiency, it also poses significant risks to privacy. The collection and use of personal data are essential components of many AI systems, raising concerns about how this data is handled and the potential for abuse.

One of the main risks to privacy in AI is the vast amount of data that is collected and stored. AI systems rely on large datasets to train their algorithms and make accurate predictions. These datasets often include personal information such as names, addresses, and financial records. If this data falls into the wrong hands, it can lead to identity theft, fraud, or other forms of privacy breaches.

Another risk is the potential for algorithmic biases. AI algorithms are only as good as the data they are trained on, and if the training data is biased, it can lead to unfair or discriminatory outcomes. For example, in hiring processes, AI algorithms may inadvertently discriminate against certain groups if the training data is biased towards certain demographics.

Furthermore, AI systems often make decisions based on complex algorithms that are not easily explainable or transparent. This lack of transparency raises concerns about how AI systems make decisions, who is responsible for those decisions, and how individuals can contest or challenge automated decisions that may impact their rights or opportunities.

Ethical Considerations and Solutions

To address the privacy risks posed by AI, it is essential to consider the ethical implications and develop appropriate safeguards. Here are some key ethical considerations and potential solutions:

Informed Consent and Data Ownership - Individuals should have control over their personal data and be fully informed about how it is used by AI systems. Clear and transparent consent processes should be implemented, ensuring individuals understand how their data will be collected, stored, and used. Additionally, individuals should have the right to access and delete their data if they choose.

Privacy by Design - Privacy should be integrated into the design and development of AI systems from the outset. This means considering privacy implications at every stage of the AI lifecycle, including data collection, storage, analysis, and decision-making. By embedding privacy into the system design, potential privacy risks can be mitigated.

Algorithmic Transparency and Explainability - To build trust and ensure accountability, AI systems should be transparent and explainable. Individuals should have the right to understand how decisions that affect them are made, and be able to contest or challenge those decisions if they believe their rights or opportunities have been violated. Efforts should be made to develop explainable AI algorithms and promote transparency in decision-making processes.

Data Minimization and Anonymization - AI systems should adopt a data minimization approach, where only the necessary data is collected and retained. Additionally, efforts should be made to anonymize or de-identify data to protect individual privacy. By minimizing the amount of personal information collected and ensuring data cannot be linked back to individuals, the risk of privacy breaches can be reduced.

Accountability and Oversight - AI systems should be subject to robust accountability and oversight mechanisms to ensure compliance with privacy regulations and ethical standards. This includes regular audits, assessment of potential biases in algorithms, and the establishment of responsible AI governance frameworks.

Real-World Examples and Implications

To further illustrate the privacy challenges in AI, let's consider a few real-world examples:

Virtual Assistants and Voice Recognition - Virtual assistants like Amazon's Alexa or Apple's Siri often process and store voice recordings to improve their accuracy and responsiveness. However, this raises concerns about the privacy of these recordings and the potential for unintended access or misuse of personal information.

Surveillance and Facial Recognition - Facial recognition technology used for surveillance purposes, such as monitoring public spaces or identifying individuals in crowds, presents significant privacy concerns. The potential for mass surveillance and the collection of biometric data without individuals' consent raises questions about privacy and the balance between security and personal freedom.

AI in Healthcare - AI has tremendous potential in healthcare, from diagnosing diseases to personalized treatment plans. However, the use of patients' health data for AI analysis must be handled with extreme care to ensure privacy and confidentiality. Strict data protection regulations and robust security measures are essential to maintain patient trust.

Resources and Further Reading

For those interested in exploring the topic of privacy in artificial intelligence further, here are some recommended resources:

1. *The Privacy Engineer's Manifesto: Getting from Policy to Code to QA to Value* by Michelle Finneran Dennedy, Jonathan Fox, and Thomas Finneran.

2. *Weapons of Math Destruction: How Big Data Increases Inequality and Threatens Democracy* by Cathy O'Neil.

3. *Artificial Intelligence and Privacy: A Privacy Impact Assessment Framework* by Daniel C. Herron.

4. *The Age of Surveillance Capitalism: The Fight for a Human Future at the New Frontier of Power* by Shoshana Zuboff.

Conclusion

As AI continues to advance and play an increasingly prominent role in our lives, it is crucial to address the privacy risks and ethical considerations associated with its implementation. By prioritizing privacy by design, ensuring algorithmic transparency and accountability, and promoting informed consent and data ownership, we can strike a balance between the benefits of AI and the protection of privacy. It is our responsibility as technologists and society as a whole to ensure that AI is used in ways that respect and uphold individuals' privacy rights.

The Internet of Things and Privacy Concerns

The Internet of Things (IoT) has revolutionized our lives, connecting everyday objects to the internet and enabling them to collect and exchange data. From smart home devices to wearables and industrial sensors, the IoT has brought unprecedented convenience and efficiency. However, with this connectivity comes a host of privacy concerns that cannot be ignored.

Understanding the Internet of Things

The IoT refers to the network of physical devices embedded with sensors, software, and connectivity that enables them to communicate and interact with each other and the internet. These devices can range from everyday objects like refrigerators and thermostats to complex industrial machinery.

The primary goal of the IoT is to collect and process data from these devices to improve decision-making, enable automation, and enhance user experiences. This data is transmitted to the cloud or other remote servers where it can be stored, analyzed, and used for various purposes.

Privacy Risks in the IoT

While the IoT has great potential, it also poses significant privacy risks. Here are some of the key concerns:

1. Data Collection and Storage: IoT devices collect vast amounts of personal data, ranging from location and behavior patterns to health and financial information. This data is often stored in remote servers, raising concerns about data breaches and unauthorized access.

2. Lack of Consent and Control: Users may not be fully aware of the data collected by IoT devices and how it is being used. Lack of transparency and control can lead to a breach of privacy.

3. Inadequate Security Measures: Many IoT devices have weak security measures, making them vulnerable to hacking and unauthorized access. This can expose users' personal information and even enable cybercriminals to control the devices remotely.

4. Third-party Data Sharing: IoT devices often rely on third-party services for functionalities like data storage and analytics. This raises concerns about data sharing and potential misuse by these service providers.

Addressing Privacy Concerns

To ensure privacy in the IoT era, several measures need to be taken:

1. Privacy by Design: Privacy should be a fundamental consideration when designing IoT devices and systems. Privacy features, such as data minimization, encryption, and user consent mechanisms, should be incorporated from the ground up.

2. Secure Communication Protocols: IoT devices should use secure communication protocols like Transport Layer Security (TLS) to ensure data integrity and confidentiality.

3. User Awareness and Education: Users need to be educated about the risks and implications of using IoT devices. They should be encouraged to enable privacy settings, update firmware regularly, and avoid sharing excessive personal information.

4. Data Encryption: Data collected by IoT devices should be encrypted to protect it from unauthorized access. Encryption techniques like symmetric key encryption and public key encryption can be used to secure the data both in transit and at rest.

5. Strong Authentication and Access Control: IoT devices should implement robust authentication mechanisms to verify the identity of users and devices trying to access them. Access control policies should be in place to ensure that only authorized entities can access sensitive data.

Real-world Example: Smart Home Privacy Concerns

Let's consider the example of a smart home system consisting of various IoT devices like cameras, thermostats, and voice assistants. While this system provides convenient control and automation, it also raises privacy concerns.

One of the primary concerns is the collection of sensitive data, such as video footage from cameras and voice recordings from voice assistants. This data, if mishandled or accessed by unauthorized parties, can compromise the privacy and security of individuals and their homes.

To address these concerns, smart home manufacturers can implement end-to-end encryption for data transmission, ensuring that the communication between devices and the cloud is secure. They can also provide users with granular control over their data, allowing them to specify what data is collected and how it is used.

Furthermore, manufacturers can conduct regular security audits and firmware updates to address vulnerabilities and ensure that smart home systems remain protected against emerging threats.

Conclusion

As the Internet of Things continues to expand, it is crucial to address the privacy concerns associated with this interconnected ecosystem. By implementing privacy-focused design principles, robust security measures, and user awareness initiatives, we can strike a balance between reaping the benefits of the IoT and protecting our personal privacy. Let's move forward with a collective commitment to building a secure and privacy-conscious IoT future.

Regulating Privacy in the Digital Age

In our increasingly digital world, the need for privacy regulations has become more urgent than ever. With the rapid advancement of technology and the rise of data-driven industries, individuals are generating vast amounts of personal information every day. This data is collected, stored, and analyzed by various entities, raising concerns about how it is used and protected.

The Importance of Privacy Regulations

Privacy regulations are essential for safeguarding individuals' personal information, ensuring that it is collected and processed in a responsible manner. Such regulations play a crucial role in balancing the benefits of data-driven technologies with the protection of individual privacy rights.

By requiring organizations to adhere to specific privacy standards, regulations aim to provide individuals with control over their personal data. They also encourage transparency and accountability among data processors, preventing misuse or unauthorized access to sensitive information.

Moreover, privacy regulations foster trust between individuals and the digital ecosystem. When people feel confident that their personal information is being handled securely, they are more likely to engage in online activities and share data for purposes they deem necessary.

Current Privacy Regulations

Several privacy regulations have been enacted worldwide to address the challenges posed by the digital age. One of the most prominent regulations is the European Union's General Data Protection Regulation (GDPR), which came into effect in 2018. The GDPR sets guidelines for data protection and privacy for individuals within the European Union and the European Economic Area. It establishes principles for lawful data processing, consent requirements, data subject rights, and data breach notifications.

Another noteworthy regulation is the California Consumer Privacy Act (CCPA), enacted in 2018 and enforced from 2020. The CCPA grants California residents certain rights regarding their personal information and imposes obligations on businesses operating in California. It gives consumers the right to know what personal information is being collected about them and how it is used, the right to access and delete their data, and the right to opt-out of the sale of their information.

Additionally, other countries, such as Brazil, Canada, and Australia, have implemented their own privacy regulations to protect their citizens' personal data.

Challenges in Regulating Privacy

Regulating privacy in the digital age comes with various challenges. One significant challenge is keeping pace with rapidly evolving technology. As new technologies emerge, regulations must adapt to address the unique privacy risks they pose. For instance, regulations need to address issues related to Internet of Things (IoT) devices, artificial intelligence, facial recognition, and biometric data.

Another challenge is enforcing privacy regulations across borders. With data flowing seamlessly across jurisdictions, it is essential to have international cooperation and standardized privacy frameworks to ensure consistent protection for individuals' personal information.

Moreover, privacy regulations must strike a balance between protecting individuals' privacy and enabling innovation. Excessive regulations may stifle data-driven industries and impede technological advancements. Finding the right balance is important to ensure privacy without hindering progress.

Future of Privacy Regulations

As technology continues to advance and new privacy challenges emerge, the future of privacy regulations is likely to be dynamic and evolving. Key areas that may shape the future of privacy regulations include:

- **Cross-border data transfers:** Developing standardized approaches to facilitate cross-border data flows while ensuring privacy protections.

- **Emerging technologies:** Addressing privacy concerns arising from technologies like AI, IoT, and facial recognition through specialized regulations and guidelines.

- **Data breach notification:** Strengthening regulations around data breach notifications to ensure timely and transparent communication to affected individuals.

- **User empowerment:** Empowering individuals with more control over their personal data through enhanced consent mechanisms, data portability, and the right to be forgotten.

- **Government surveillance:** Balancing the need for national security with safeguards that protect individuals' privacy rights in the face of government surveillance programs.

To effectively address future challenges, privacy regulations must be flexible, adaptable, and informed by ongoing dialogue between policymakers, technologists, industry experts, and civil society.

Conclusion

Regulating privacy in the digital age is vital to protect individuals' personal data and maintain trust in the digital ecosystem. Privacy regulations ensure responsible data processing, empower individuals, and promote transparency and accountability. While challenges exist, the future of privacy regulations requires collaboration, adaptability, and an understanding of the delicate balance between privacy and innovation. By proactively addressing privacy risks and embracing the principles of responsible data handling, we can create a future where privacy is respected and protected.

The Ethical Challenges of Data Collection

Data collection has become an integral part of our modern digital society. From browsing the internet to using smart devices, we constantly generate a vast amount of data. This data is often collected, stored, and analyzed by various entities for different purposes. While data collection has many benefits, it also raises significant ethical challenges that need to be addressed.

Data Privacy

One of the primary ethical challenges of data collection is ensuring data privacy. As individuals, we have a right to control our personal information and how it is used. However, with the increasing amount of data being collected, there is a growing concern about the misuse or unauthorized access to personal information.

For example, consider a social media platform that collects personal data from its users. This data may include personal preferences, location information, and even intimate details of one's life. If this data falls into the wrong hands or is used for nefarious purposes, it can lead to identity theft, stalking, or other serious privacy violations.

To address this challenge, organizations must establish robust data protection measures. These may include encryption of sensitive data, implementing strict access controls, and adhering to privacy regulations such as the General Data Protection Regulation (GDPR). It is essential for individuals and companies alike to understand their rights and responsibilities regarding data privacy.

Informed Consent

Another ethical challenge is obtaining informed consent from individuals before collecting their data. Informed consent means that individuals should have a clear understanding of what data is being collected, how it will be used, and who will have access to it.

However, in today's digital landscape, individuals often unknowingly consent to data collection through complex terms and conditions that are buried within lengthy legal documents. This lack of transparency can lead to a breach of trust between users and organizations, as individuals may feel deceived or manipulated.

To address this challenge, organizations should strive to provide clear and easily understandable explanations of data collection practices. They should make an effort to obtain explicit consent from individuals, allowing them to make informed decisions about sharing their data. Transparency and user control are key principles in ensuring ethical data collection practices.

Data Bias and Discrimination

Data collection can also introduce ethical challenges related to data bias and discrimination. Data sets used for analysis and decision-making may contain inherent biases that reflect existing social prejudices or inequalities. These biases can perpetuate discrimination and result in unfair treatment of certain individuals or groups.

For example, if a hiring algorithm is trained on historical employment data that is biased against certain demographics, it may perpetuate discriminatory hiring practices. This can have far-reaching consequences, reinforcing existing social disparities and limiting opportunities for marginalized communities.

To address this challenge, organizations must ensure that data sets used for analysis and decision-making are diverse, representative, and free from bias. Algorithms and models should be regularly audited to identify and counteract any biases that emerge. Additionally, ethical guidelines and regulations can help prevent discriminatory practices and promote fairness in data collection and analysis.

Data Security

Data security is another critical ethical challenge in data collection. With the increasing frequency of data breaches and cyber-attacks, organizations must invest in robust cybersecurity measures to protect the data they collect.

Personal data can be highly valuable to malicious actors who seek to exploit it for financial gain or other malicious purposes. A data breach can result in significant harm to individuals, including identity theft, financial loss, and damage to reputation.

To address this challenge, organizations must implement strong security measures, such as encryption, firewalls, and regular security audits. Adequate training and awareness programs should be put in place to ensure employees understand their role in protecting data. Additionally, organizations should have a plan in place to respond to and mitigate the impact of a data breach, including prompt notification of affected individuals.

Data Ownership and Control

The issue of data ownership and control is a complex ethical challenge in data collection. Who owns the data being collected, and who has the right to control its use? This question becomes even more critical when data is collected from multiple sources, aggregated, and analyzed for various purposes.

Data ownership and control can impact individuals' autonomy and their ability to determine how their data is used. It can also affect competition and market dynamics when organizations have access to vast amounts of consumer data, giving them an advantage over smaller players.

To address this challenge, there needs to be a clear framework for data ownership and control. Individuals should have the right to access, correct, and delete their data. Organizations should also be transparent about how aggregated and anonymized data is used, ensuring individuals' rights are respected. Regulations such as the European Union's Data Protection Directive and the California Consumer Privacy Act aim to establish guidelines for data ownership and control.

In conclusion, data collection presents significant ethical challenges that must be addressed to ensure the responsible and ethical use of data. Data privacy, informed consent, data bias and discrimination, data security, and data ownership and control are essential areas that require careful consideration and regulation. By addressing these challenges, we can ensure that data collection practices align with ethical principles and protect individuals' rights in the digital age.

Balancing Innovation and Privacy Rights

In the ever-evolving landscape of technology and the digital age, there is an ongoing struggle between innovation and privacy rights. On one hand, we have the incredible advancements in technology that have transformed our lives and brought immense benefits to society. On the other hand, we have the growing concerns about the potential encroachment on our privacy and the misuse of our personal information.

Finding the right balance between these two forces is crucial for ensuring a thriving and secure digital future.

The rapid pace of technological innovation has brought countless conveniences and opportunities. From smartphones to artificial intelligence, from social media to the Internet of Things, these advancements have revolutionized the way we live, work, and connect with others. They have enabled us to access vast amounts of information, communicate instantly across the globe, and accomplish tasks with unprecedented efficiency. Innovation has become synonymous with progress and has the potential to solve many of the challenges we face as a society.

However, innovation often comes at a price. With the proliferation of smart devices and digital platforms, the amount of data generated and collected about individuals has grown exponentially. Every online transaction, every search query, every social media post leaves a digital footprint that can be traced back to us. This data is valuable currency for businesses, organizations, and governments, who use it to shape their products, services, and policies. But it also raises concerns about privacy, security, and the potential for misuse or abuse.

Privacy rights are the fundamental principles that protect individuals from unauthorized intrusion into their personal lives. They guarantee the right to control and manage one's personal information, decide what to share and with whom, and maintain a certain level of anonymity and autonomy. Privacy is the key to personal freedom, dignity, and self-expression. It allows individuals to have private spaces, make personal choices, and develop intimacy in relationships without fear of judgment, surveillance, or manipulation.

The challenge lies in striking a balance between the need for innovation and the protection of privacy rights. How can we foster technological advancements without compromising our privacy? How can we harness the power of data for good while ensuring its responsible and ethical use? And how can we establish a legal, social, and technological framework that respects both innovation and privacy rights?

One approach is to enact robust privacy laws and regulations that provide clear guidelines for the collection, storage, and sharing of personal data. These laws should outline the rights and responsibilities of individuals, organizations, and governments in relation to data privacy, establish strong safeguards for sensitive information, and define penalties for violations. By setting such standards, we can ensure that innovation is grounded in ethical and responsible practices.

Another key aspect of balancing innovation and privacy rights is user education and empowerment. Individuals need to be aware of their rights and the risks associated with their digital footprint. They should understand the importance of data privacy and take proactive measures to protect their personal information. This includes using encryption tools, practicing good cybersecurity hygiene, and being discerning about the platforms and services they use. Educating and empowering users can help them make informed decisions about their privacy and demand accountability from service providers and policymakers.

Technology itself can also play a role in the solution. Privacy-preserving technologies, such as differential privacy, homomorphic encryption, and zero-knowledge proofs, can enable the analysis of data without revealing sensitive information. These technologies allow for the processing and sharing of data while ensuring confidentiality and privacy. By integrating such privacy-enhancing features into the design of new technologies, we can foster innovation without compromising privacy.

In addressing the challenge of balancing innovation and privacy rights, it is essential to involve all stakeholders: individuals, organizations, governments, and technology developers. Collaboration and dialogue are key to finding common ground and working towards solutions that support both innovation and privacy.

Ultimately, the balance between innovation and privacy rights is a delicate dance that requires continuous vigilance, adaptability, and accountability. As technology continues to advance and reshape our world, we must remain proactive in protecting our privacy and advocating for responsible innovation. By nurturing a culture of privacy consciousness and embracing ethical and privacy-centric principles, we can create a future where innovation thrives while our fundamental rights are safeguarded.

Example:
An example of the delicate balance between innovation and privacy rights is the controversy surrounding facial recognition technology. This innovation has the potential to enhance security, improve law enforcement efforts, and streamline identification processes. However, it also raises concerns about the invasion of privacy, potential misuse by governments or corporations, and the lack of consent in collecting and storing facial data.

To strike a balance, regulations and guidelines for the responsible use of facial recognition technology have been proposed. These include obtaining explicit consent from individuals before capturing their facial data, ensuring transparency in how the technology is used, and implementing safeguards to prevent abuse or discrimination. By taking these measures, we can harness the benefits of facial recognition technology while respecting privacy rights.

Exercise:
Reflect on your own digital footprint and privacy practices. Consider the platforms and services you use daily. How much personal information are you sharing? Are you aware of the privacy settings and options available to you? What steps can you take to enhance your privacy and protect your personal information in the digital

realm? Share your insights and strategies with a friend or in an online privacy community.

Additional Resources:

1. Electronic Frontier Foundation: https://www.eff.org/

2. Data Privacy Project: https://www.dataprivacyproject.org/

3. Privacy International: https://privacyinternational.org/

4. Future of Privacy Forum: https://fpf.org/

Remember, the key to balancing innovation and privacy rights lies in our collective responsibility to advocate for and protect our fundamental rights. By actively engaging in discussions, staying informed, and advocating for strong privacy protections, we can shape a future where innovation and privacy thrive hand in hand.

The Role of Public Perception in Privacy Debates

Public perception plays a crucial role in shaping privacy debates in today's digital age. The way people understand and perceive privacy issues can influence the policies and practices that govern our personal information and online activities. In this section, we explore the impact of public perception on privacy debates, examine common misconceptions, and discuss the challenges in achieving a balanced approach to privacy.

Understanding Privacy: A Clash of Perspectives

Privacy is a complex concept that can vary greatly depending on individual perspectives and cultural norms. Public perception often reflects these diverse understandings of privacy, leading to different expectations and demands. It is essential to recognize and respect these various perspectives to engage in meaningful privacy debates.

One common misconception is that privacy is solely about keeping secrets or hiding illicit activities. This limited view overlooks the broader dimensions of privacy, such as personal autonomy, control over one's data, and freedom from surveillance. It creates a false dichotomy between privacy and security, implying that sacrificing privacy is necessary for safety.

To address these misconceptions, it is crucial to educate the public about the multifaceted nature of privacy. People need to understand how their personal information is collected, used, and shared in the digital ecosystem. By highlighting the potential risks and benefits, individuals can make informed choices and actively participate in privacy debates.

Privacy in the Digital Age: Trust and Control

In today's interconnected world, privacy concerns arise from the vast amount of personal data collected by tech companies, governments, and even individuals themselves. Public perception plays a pivotal role in determining who is trusted with this data and how much control individuals should have over their information.

The public's trust in the entities handling their data greatly influences privacy debates. High-profile privacy breaches and data misuse scandals erode public trust in technology companies and governments. Without trust, it becomes difficult to have meaningful discussions about privacy regulations or the responsible use of personal data.

Public perception also shapes the expectations regarding control over personal data. Some individuals may not be aware of or may underestimate the extent to which their data is being collected and used. Others may be concerned about losing control over their information and demand more transparency and consent mechanisms. Balancing these expectations is crucial to address the privacy concerns of a diverse society.

The Role of Media and Public Messaging

Media plays a significant role in shaping public perception of privacy. News coverage, social media debates, and popular culture narratives can influence how individuals understand and prioritize privacy issues. However, media coverage can sometimes oversimplify complex topics or sensationalize privacy breaches, leading to distorted public perceptions.

The language used in public messaging also matters. Privacy debates are often framed as a choice between privacy or security, individual rights or social benefits. This binary framing can create a false sense that privacy is a luxury or an obstacle to societal progress. Effective public messaging should emphasize that privacy is a fundamental right and a necessary condition for a democratic and free society.

The Need for Inclusive Dialogue

Engaging the public in privacy debates is essential for establishing policies that reflect societal values. However, it is crucial to ensure that these discussions are inclusive, accessible, and representative of diverse perspectives. Marginalized communities, who may face unique privacy challenges, should have a voice in shaping privacy policies.

Privacy advocates, policymakers, and technology companies should actively seek input from the public and create spaces for dialogue. This could include public consultations, citizen juries, or participatory design approaches. By involving the public in the decision-making process, privacy discussions can become more informed, balanced, and reflective of societal needs.

Case Study: Public Perception and Facial Recognition Technology

One area where public perception has played a significant role in privacy debates is facial recognition technology (FRT). Facial recognition raises concerns about mass surveillance, biased algorithms, and the erosion of anonymity in public spaces.

Public perception has influenced policymakers' decisions on FRT regulation. Recognizing the potential risks and public concerns, some cities and countries have implemented bans or moratoriums on FRT use. These decisions reflect a growing recognition of the need to balance privacy and public safety concerns.

However, public perception of FRT is not monolithic. Some individuals may see benefits in enhanced security, faster identification processes, or personalized services. Engaging the public in discussions around FRT helps to understand the nuances of these perspectives and identify appropriate safeguards and limitations.

The Role of Education and Awareness

Education and awareness campaigns are essential for shaping public perception on privacy. By teaching individuals about their digital footprints, data privacy, and the potential risks and benefits of technology, we can empower people to make informed decisions and advocate for stronger privacy measures.

Privacy literacy should be integrated into school curricula, workplace training programs, and community initiatives. It should cover topics such as responsible data sharing, securing personal devices, understanding privacy policies, and recognizing online threats. Privacy-related organizations and advocacy groups can play a crucial role in providing accessible educational resources and fostering public discussions.

Beyond Public Perception: Toward Better Privacy Policies

While public perception is vital, privacy debates cannot solely rely on popular opinion. Privacy policies should be built upon a robust legal and ethical framework that upholds individual rights, promotes fairness, and addresses power imbalances.

Balancing privacy with competing interests, such as national security or public health, requires careful deliberation, involving diverse stakeholders, and considering multidisciplinary perspectives. Technical experts, policymakers, legal scholars, and privacy advocates must work collaboratively to develop comprehensive privacy policies that reflect societal values while addressing the complex challenges posed by technological advancements.

Further Reading and Resources

To delve deeper into the role of public perception in privacy debates, the following resources are recommended:

- Solove, D.J. (2011). *Understanding Privacy.* Harvard University Press.

- Balkin, J. M. (2008). *The Future of Reputation: Gossip, Rumor, and Privacy on the Internet.* Yale University Press.

- Floridi, L. (2014). *The Fourth Revolution: How the Infosphere is Reshaping Human Reality.* Oxford University Press.

- Nissenbaum, H. (2010). *Privacy in Context: Technology, Policy, and the Integrity of Social Life.* Stanford University Press.

- European Union Agency for Fundamental Rights (FRA). (2019). *Handbook on European data protection law.*

Remember, understanding public perception is crucial for shaping effective privacy policies. By addressing misconceptions, fostering dialogue, and empowering individuals through education, we can work towards a future where privacy is respected, protected, and valued in the digital world.

Advancements in Privacy Technology

In today's connected world, where personal data is constantly being collected and shared, the need for privacy technology has never been greater. Fortunately, there have been significant advancements in this field that aim to protect individuals' sensitive information and maintain their online privacy. In this section, we will explore some of the key advancements in privacy technology, including encryption protocols, anonymity networks, and privacy-enhancing tools.

Encryption Protocols

Encryption plays a crucial role in safeguarding private information from unauthorized access. Over the years, there have been important advancements in encryption protocols that have made data transmission and storage more secure.

One notable advancement is the development of end-to-end encryption (E2EE) protocols. E2EE ensures that only the sender and the intended recipient can access the encrypted data, preventing intermediaries or eavesdroppers from decrypting the information. Popular messaging apps like Signal and WhatsApp have implemented E2EE, ensuring the privacy of their users' conversations.

Another advancement is the growth of homomorphic encryption. Homomorphic encryption allows computations to be performed directly on encrypted data, without needing to decrypt it first. This breakthrough has the potential to revolutionize data processing in sensitive domains, such as healthcare or finance, where privacy is of utmost importance.

Anonymity Networks

Anonymity networks, also known as privacy networks, are designed to protect users' identities and browsing activities. These networks route internet traffic through a series of encrypted connections, effectively masking the user's IP address and location.

One prominent example of an anonymity network is Tor (The Onion Router). Tor anonymizes web browsing by routing traffic through a network of volunteer-operated relays, making it difficult to trace back the user's online activities. This technology has proven invaluable for journalists, activists, and whistleblowers who rely on anonymity to protect themselves from surveillance or persecution.

Privacy-Enhancing Tools

Privacy-enhancing tools encompass a wide range of technologies and techniques aimed at improving individuals' privacy and security online. These tools address various privacy concerns, from online tracking to data breaches.

Virtual Private Networks (VPNs) have gained popularity as a way to protect internet users' privacy. VPNs encrypt internet traffic and route it through secure servers, making it difficult for anyone to intercept or trace the user's online activities. Additionally, VPNs can change the user's IP address, allowing them to bypass geographic restrictions and access region-restricted content.

Another important privacy-enhancing tool is the use of privacy-focused web browsers. These browsers include built-in features to block tracking cookies, prevent fingerprinting, and disable third-party cookies. Examples of privacy-focused browsers include Brave and Firefox with privacy extensions.

In recent years, new breeds of privacy-focused search engines have emerged. These search engines prioritize user privacy by not storing search queries or personal information and by providing unbiased search results. DuckDuckGo is a popular example of such a search engine.

Emerging Challenges

While advancements in privacy technology have made significant strides in protecting individuals' privacy, emerging challenges pose new risks to our digital autonomy.

One challenge is the proliferation of Internet of Things (IoT) devices, which are increasingly integrated into our daily lives. IoT devices, such as smart home devices or wearable gadgets, generate and share vast amounts of personal data. It is crucial to develop robust privacy solutions to ensure that this data is adequately protected and not exploited.

Additionally, the intersection of privacy and artificial intelligence (AI) raises concerns about the potential misuse of personal data. AI algorithms heavily rely on personal data to train models and make predictions. Ensuring that AI systems respect user privacy and comply with ethical standards is essential.

The Future of Privacy Technology

Looking ahead, the future of privacy technology holds both challenges and promises. It will require a multifaceted approach that combines technical advancements, policy changes, and user education.

Technological advancements will continue to drive privacy innovations. Quantum-resistant encryption, in response to the advent of quantum computing, will play a crucial role in securing sensitive information. Similarly, advancements in machine learning and AI will empower privacy-preserving techniques for analyzing data without compromising privacy.

Policy changes, such as comprehensive data protection regulations and robust privacy frameworks, will be instrumental in safeguarding individuals' privacy rights. Governments and regulatory bodies must work to strike a balance between protecting privacy and enabling responsible data usage.

Lastly, user education will be essential in empowering individuals to take control of their privacy. Promoting digital literacy and raising awareness about privacy risks will enable users to make informed decisions about their data and privacy settings.

In conclusion, the advancements in privacy technology have revolutionized the way we protect our sensitive information in an increasingly interconnected world. Encryption protocols, anonymity networks, and privacy-enhancing tools have made significant contributions to preserving individual privacy. However, emerging challenges and the rapid pace of technology necessitate evolving privacy solutions. The future holds great potential, requiring continued innovation, thoughtful policy interventions, and informed user participation to ensure a privacy-focused digital landscape.

A Connected World, A Private Future

In a world that is increasingly connected, the future of privacy hangs in the balance. As technology advances and we become more reliant on digital devices, our personal data is constantly at risk. The rise of invasive surveillance practices, data breaches, and the exploitation of personal information by corporations has raised pressing concerns about privacy. In this section, we will explore the challenges we face in preserving privacy in a connected world and discuss the potential solutions and advancements that can shape a private future.

The State of Privacy Today

Before diving into the future, let's first examine the current state of privacy. In the digital age, our everyday activities generate a massive amount of data that is collected, analyzed, and often sold for various purposes. Whether it's browsing the internet, using social media, or even driving a smart car, we leave a trail of data behind us. This proliferation of data coupled with the sophistication of data analytics poses a significant threat to our privacy.

Moreover, the rapid advancement of technology has outpaced our legal and regulatory frameworks, leaving us vulnerable to the exploitation of our personal information. From targeted advertising to algorithmic decision-making, our personal data shapes not only our digital experiences but also our offline lives. The lack of transparency and control over our data further exacerbates the problem, making it difficult for individuals to protect their privacy.

The Importance of Algorithmic Transparency

In a connected world, algorithms play a significant role in shaping our experiences. They power search engines, social media platforms, recommendation systems, and autonomous technologies. However, the opacity of these algorithms poses a threat to privacy. When algorithms make decisions about what content to show us, they influence our beliefs, opinions, and personal preferences based on the data they collect. It is crucial that these algorithms are transparent and accountable to protect our privacy rights.

Algorithmic transparency refers to the understanding of how algorithms work and the ability to access and evaluate the data used to make decisions. By promoting transparency, individuals can have more control over their data, understand how their information is being used, and ensure that algorithms are not biased or discriminatory. Privacy laws and regulations must address the issue of algorithmic transparency to safeguard individuals' privacy in a connected world.

Privacy in Artificial Intelligence

Artificial Intelligence (AI) has the potential to revolutionize various sectors, improve efficiency, and enhance our lives. However, it also raises concerns about privacy. AI systems often rely on vast amounts of personal data to learn and make decisions. This raises concerns about the security and privacy of the data used in training these AI models.

To ensure privacy in AI, data anonymization and differential privacy techniques can be employed. Data anonymization involves removing personally identifiable information from datasets, making it difficult to link specific individuals to the data. Differential privacy adds noise to the data, preserving privacy while still allowing useful insights to be derived from the data.

Additionally, privacy by design should be a fundamental principle in AI development. By embedding privacy considerations into the design of AI systems from the beginning, developers can proactively address privacy concerns and minimize the risks associated with data collection and processing.

The Internet of Things and Privacy Concerns

The Internet of Things (IoT), with its network of interconnected devices, has the potential to transform the way we live and work. From smart homes to wearable devices, IoT offers convenience and efficiency. However, it also presents new privacy challenges.

As IoT devices collect and transmit massive amounts of data, the risk of unauthorized access or misuse of personal information increases. Compromised IoT devices can be exploited to invade privacy, disrupt our daily lives, or even compromise physical safety. Protecting privacy in the IoT era requires robust security measures, such as encryption, authentication protocols, and secure data storage.

Furthermore, privacy policies and user consent should be transparent and easily understandable. Users must have control over the data collected by IoT devices and be able to make informed decisions about how their information is used.

Regulating Privacy in the Digital Age

Addressing privacy concerns in a connected world requires robust and comprehensive regulations. Privacy laws must keep pace with technological advancements and provide individuals with the necessary protection. The General Data Protection Regulation (GDPR), implemented by the European Union, is a prominent example of regulations aimed at safeguarding privacy rights.

Key principles for effective privacy regulation include:

- **Data Minimization:** Limiting the collection of personal data to what is necessary for a specific purpose.

- **Consent and Control:** Ensuring individuals have control over their data and can provide informed consent for its use.

- **Data Breach Notification:** Requiring organizations to promptly inform individuals in case of a data breach that could compromise their privacy.

- **Accountability:** Holding organizations accountable for data protection and privacy through enforcement mechanisms and penalties.

Regulations should also address emerging technologies, such as AI and IoT, and provide clear guidelines for privacy protection. International cooperation is crucial in creating a global framework that protects privacy rights across borders.

The Ethical Challenges of Data Collection

Data collection is at the heart of privacy concerns in a connected world. While data can be incredibly valuable for innovation and improving services, the ethical aspects of data collection cannot be ignored. Organizations must navigate the fine line between collecting data for legitimate purposes and respecting individuals' privacy.

The principle of data minimization, as mentioned earlier, is central to this issue. Organizations should only collect the data necessary for a specific purpose and not indulge in extensive data accumulation. Additionally, clear data retention and deletion policies should be in place to ensure that data is not retained indefinitely.

Transparency is also a key ethical consideration. Individuals should be informed about the types of data collected, how it is used, and with whom it is shared. Organizations should obtain explicit consent from individuals and provide them with the ability to opt-out or withdraw consent at any time.

The Future of Privacy in a Changing Landscape

As technology continues to evolve, the future of privacy will be shaped by various factors. Advancements in cryptography, such as homomorphic encryption, zero-knowledge proofs, and secure multi-party computation, offer promising solutions for preserving privacy in the digital age. These technologies allow data to be processed without revealing sensitive information, reducing the risks associated with data exposure.

The development of privacy-focused technologies and tools will empower individuals to take control of their data and privacy. From decentralized technologies like blockchain to privacy-focused browsers and secure communication applications, these innovations can give individuals the means to protect their privacy in a connected world.

However, the fight for privacy does not rest solely on technological advancements. It requires a collective effort from individuals, policymakers, and organizations to prioritize privacy over profit and to advocate for robust privacy protection measures.

A Connected World, A Private Future

In a connected world, preserving privacy is essential for safeguarding our autonomy, individuality, and personal freedoms. As we navigate the challenges of data collection, algorithmic transparency, and emerging technologies, we must recognize privacy as a fundamental human right that must be protected.

By embracing privacy by design, promoting algorithmic transparency, enacting comprehensive privacy regulations, and leveraging technological advancements, we can pave the way for a private future. It is up to us to ensure that privacy remains a priority and that our connected world respects and protects the privacy of every individual.

As Phil Zimmermann once said, "Privacy is necessary for an open society in the electronic age." It is through our collective actions that we can achieve a connected world that respects and upholds privacy, allowing us to reap the benefits of technology without compromising our fundamental rights.

Index

- Phil Zimmermann's, 485

a, 1–21, 23–35, 37–66, 68–117,
119–138, 140, 142–149,
152–170, 172–190,
193–239, 241–254,
257–260, 262–265,
267–273, 275–298,
300–325, 327–337,
339–345, 347–350, 352,
353, 355–363, 365–445,
447–499, 501–503, 505,
506, 508–526
abandonment, 377
ability, 10–12, 18, 25, 27, 30, 38–43,
45, 48, 58, 71, 74, 97, 98,
102–105, 108, 111, 146,
158, 165, 170, 175, 178,
180, 181, 189, 199, 208,
217, 223, 226, 228, 235,
237, 240, 241, 245, 258,
277, 280, 299, 301, 311,
313, 323, 333, 339, 344,
357, 368, 371, 374, 384,
385, 394, 413, 437, 440,
446, 452, 456, 457, 466,
468, 477, 478, 483, 484,
496, 499, 513, 523, 525

abuse, 25, 27, 57, 63, 87, 89, 218,
240, 260, 269, 275–277,
283, 290, 320, 345, 349,
388, 405, 431, 448, 467,
480, 484, 503, 514, 515
academia, 71, 160, 364
acceptance, 311
access, 15–20, 23, 25, 30, 33–35, 38,
39, 45–47, 50, 54, 57, 58,
60, 62, 70, 77–81, 91, 92,
96, 106, 112, 122–125,
127, 130, 132, 136, 137,
140, 146–149, 151–153,
156, 157, 162, 170, 174,
175, 177–180, 183, 186,
188, 191, 194, 196–199,
208, 215–217, 221, 224,
231, 235, 238, 240, 241,
243, 245, 246, 249–252,
257–259, 263, 264, 270,
272, 276–278, 282–284,
291, 298, 299, 302, 304,
305, 308, 317, 320, 321,
323, 328, 334, 336, 338,
342, 345, 357, 359, 364,
367, 368, 374–376, 381,
398, 402, 405, 414, 420,
432, 435, 439, 440, 442,

446, 448, 452, 454–456, 461, 467, 468, 472, 475, 486, 487, 492, 496, 499, 509, 511–514, 520, 523, 524
accessibility, 72, 122, 157, 199, 210, 226, 344, 476
accessible, 4, 10, 20, 25, 29, 34, 42, 55, 60, 72, 95, 109, 111, 112, 152–155, 157–161, 163, 165, 167, 168, 173, 175, 179, 180, 183, 187, 189, 209, 211, 213–215, 220, 224, 227, 228, 230–233, 235, 291–293, 295–297, 301, 309, 312, 329, 331, 333, 334, 338, 339, 341–343, 349, 356, 359, 361, 364, 367, 374, 385, 389, 391, 393, 395, 405, 407, 413, 424, 429, 435, 441, 454–456, 459, 468, 471, 475, 480, 483, 499, 518
acclaim, 156
account, 57, 65, 258, 334, 402, 403, 455, 459
accountability, 57, 64, 88–90, 116, 162, 164, 251, 270, 279, 281, 285, 288, 303, 310, 321, 337, 378, 387, 409, 411, 484, 486, 500, 506, 509, 511, 515
accumulation, 439, 525
accuracy, 241, 287
act, 23, 71, 98
action, 39, 43, 48, 73, 75, 97, 170, 221, 253, 269, 314, 352, 396, 406, 409–411, 413, 416, 417, 423, 428, 437, 438, 463, 466, 471, 479, 496, 499
activism, 12, 13, 32, 43, 44, 60–62, 342, 399, 431, 468, 470
activity, 435
actor, 302
ad, 382
adaptability, 156, 371, 511, 515
adaptation, 181, 203, 222, 249, 481
addition, 73, 98, 101, 106, 160, 169, 174, 189, 241, 297, 341, 347, 349, 361, 372, 388, 432, 449, 454, 484, 494
address, 18, 87, 88, 90, 100, 135, 154, 159, 162, 165, 169, 178, 183, 192, 194, 197, 198, 209, 210, 214, 215, 222, 224, 234, 240, 255, 286, 288, 298, 307, 318, 325, 327, 328, 334, 335, 337, 338, 340, 351, 372, 377, 401, 403, 420, 434, 435, 448, 449, 452, 455, 466, 469, 476, 479, 481, 484, 488–493, 499, 500, 504, 506, 508, 510, 512, 513, 516, 517, 520, 521, 523, 524
adequacy, 276
adherence, 70
admiration, 41
adoption, 11, 31, 34, 35, 44, 45, 55, 64, 65, 70, 71, 78, 84, 86, 100, 102, 122, 140, 153, 156, 161–168, 173, 174, 179, 180, 187, 194, 206–213, 215–225, 227, 228, 272, 291, 292, 294,

Index 529

  295, 297, 301, 311, 337,
  364, 375, 377, 378, 383,
  389, 391, 395, 400, 415,
  416, 423, 424, 426, 434,
  441, 444, 449, 459, 460,
  480, 486, 488
advance, 26, 54, 55, 61, 69, 70, 81,
  92, 117, 145, 195, 202,
  210, 212, 224, 241, 261,
  292, 337, 364, 383, 386,
  387, 390, 400, 401, 412,
  414, 445, 466, 474, 480,
  487, 493, 506, 510, 515
advancement, 65, 86, 111, 116, 181,
  226, 285, 309, 320, 350,
  373, 377, 442, 450, 484,
  508, 520, 523
advantage, 42, 215, 381, 478, 513
advent, 62, 87, 115, 143, 152, 198,
  285, 293, 345, 362, 400,
  413, 458, 498, 522
adventure, 7, 436
adversary, 96
adversity, 112, 117, 419, 437
advertising, 69, 237, 238, 240, 243,
  246, 247, 253, 254, 260,
  262, 263, 298, 299, 301,
  333, 344, 410, 439, 442,
  443, 450–452, 455, 465,
  467, 523
advice, 99, 116, 357, 370, 372, 378
advocacy, 12, 18, 28, 32, 41, 42, 44,
  47, 48, 60, 63, 66, 68,
  70–76, 82–85, 91, 102,
  109, 111, 115, 158, 166,
  167, 218, 220, 228, 250,
  268, 290–293, 297, 298,
  307, 309–313, 320, 322,
  335, 342–344, 348, 349,
  358, 360, 362, 372–375,
  378, 380, 382, 384–386,
  388–390, 396, 398,
  401–404, 406, 408, 409,
  415, 418, 419, 422, 425,
  426, 429, 430, 433, 437,
  453, 461, 462, 464, 466,
  471, 473–476, 480,
  483–485, 494, 518
advocate, 3, 16, 27, 32, 33, 39–42,
  53, 64, 73–75, 81, 83, 85,
  86, 91, 95, 97, 101, 102,
  105, 108–110, 113, 116,
  166, 199, 228, 229, 239,
  245, 249, 259, 263, 267,
  277, 296, 303, 307, 309,
  310, 322, 332, 348, 349,
  358, 359, 370, 374, 375,
  377, 379, 386, 395, 397,
  400, 401, 419, 421, 422,
  427, 436, 442, 461, 465,
  468, 471, 477, 478, 484,
  486, 494, 496, 499, 516,
  518, 525
affinity, 9, 106
aftermath, 252, 283, 456
afterthought, 116, 304, 308, 334,
  441
age, 1, 3, 5, 7, 8, 14, 16, 17, 19, 23,
  25–28, 31–33, 35, 38, 40,
  46, 49, 53–55, 57, 59,
  62–65, 68, 72–74, 80, 82,
  87, 92, 93, 97, 98, 108,
  109, 111, 120, 122, 136,
  140, 146, 155, 157, 167,
  170, 175, 179, 181, 187,
  189, 196, 197, 211, 213,
  216, 218, 222, 226, 230,
  235, 237–239, 242,

244–246, 248–251, 253, 254, 257, 259, 260, 262, 268, 270, 273, 276, 277, 283, 286, 289, 292, 294, 295, 298, 302, 305–311, 314, 316, 320, 332, 333, 335–338, 342–345, 347, 349, 350, 353, 358, 366, 373, 375, 378, 383–385, 390, 391, 399, 401, 404, 406, 410, 413, 415, 416, 425, 426, 430, 432, 433, 439–441, 445, 447, 449–453, 455, 458, 462, 464, 466–471, 473, 478–480, 482, 492, 493, 496, 498, 502, 511, 513, 516, 522, 525, 526

agency, 254, 289, 328, 329, 349, 456
AI, 505
Aldous Huxley's, 314
Aleksandr Kogan, 250
Alex, 205
algorithm, 21, 107, 119, 127, 128, 136, 137, 155, 158, 176, 188, 223, 226, 368, 400, 499, 512
algorithms, 2, 5, 16–18, 21, 54–56, 65, 78, 81, 97, 100, 103, 107, 108, 111, 115, 119, 120, 124, 125, 127, 128, 131, 136, 143, 149, 152, 154, 157, 160–162, 169, 171, 172, 176–178, 180, 182, 183, 189, 194–197, 207, 210, 211, 223, 224, 226, 231, 234, 242, 244, 247, 254, 258, 259, 269–271, 283, 286, 291, 296, 297, 302, 317, 320, 323, 328, 355–357, 360, 363–365, 368–370, 374, 383, 392, 393, 400, 418–420, 435, 441, 442, 445–447, 451, 458–460, 464, 467, 472–474, 481, 486, 487, 489, 499, 500, 502–504, 523

Alice, 108, 131, 184, 186
Alice Johnson, 108
alignment, 99
alliance, 384
allow, 34, 45, 50, 58, 81, 98, 103, 153, 183, 196, 199, 210, 242, 246, 259, 264, 282, 291, 304, 317, 321, 323, 330, 339, 343, 377, 418, 434, 465, 472, 475, 515, 525
alternative, 69, 174, 197, 200, 214–216, 234, 283, 423, 492, 494
ambition, 384
amount, 7, 58, 122, 125, 251, 283, 305, 336, 363, 446, 455, 458, 493, 503, 511, 514, 517, 522
analysis, 53, 65, 88, 143, 208, 242, 245, 263, 269, 273, 304, 309, 316, 327, 363, 442, 445, 458, 469, 490, 492, 494, 498, 512, 515
analyst, 280
Ancient Egypt, 65, 129, 279
Andy Müller-Maguhn, 57, 61
anonymity, 153, 166, 170, 258, 280, 281, 330, 423, 514, 520, 522

anonymization, 88, 190, 286, 288, 304, 317, 461, 523
anonymizing, 288, 308
Anonymous, 60–62
answer, 109, 198, 341
antivirus, 454, 455
app, 189, 197, 213, 215, 250, 254, 300–303, 366, 423, 468, 469
appetite, 355
application, 70, 126, 167, 394, 420, 450, 457
appreciation, 94, 316, 434
apprehension, 87
approach, 1, 2, 10, 17, 23, 43, 80, 82, 83, 87, 90, 95, 99, 110, 112, 116, 140, 148, 153, 156, 158, 161, 162, 164, 169, 170, 176, 179, 180, 197, 208, 211–213, 225, 234, 235, 242, 244, 253, 260, 265, 269, 270, 278, 283, 286, 289, 290, 300, 302–304, 307, 308, 310, 315, 319, 328, 329, 342, 343, 345, 356, 357, 366, 372, 382, 383, 386, 389, 391, 393, 398, 399, 406, 408, 411, 414, 418, 420, 425, 426, 435, 445, 456, 458, 461, 462, 472, 477, 493, 501, 514, 516, 521
Aral Balkan, 494
architecture, 262
area, 115, 178, 230, 231, 317, 343, 356, 357, 458, 462, 484, 489, 490
arena, 106
argument, 198

arrival, 44, 225, 355
art, 5, 14, 20, 29, 70, 94, 372, 398, 420, 451
article, 335, 391
Asia, 449
aspect, 32, 74, 79, 80, 113, 131, 137, 308, 321, 323, 332, 342, 344, 356, 393, 396, 409, 446, 454, 483, 514
assault, 60
asset, 237, 242
assistance, 61, 283
association, 276, 277, 345
assurance, 194
attack, 125, 283, 337, 339, 381, 394, 461
attacker, 19, 125, 127, 131, 137, 194
attempt, 125, 426
attention, 2, 5, 10, 18, 46, 61, 67, 95, 105, 106, 111, 112, 116, 156, 169, 280, 283, 299, 321, 327, 351, 371, 392, 421, 479, 483, 486
attitude, 104
audience, 56, 61, 64, 73, 83, 111, 163, 165, 167–169, 187, 209, 214, 215, 232, 235, 301, 311, 313, 317, 359, 393, 403, 435, 454
audits, 140, 215, 216, 303, 445, 447, 508, 513
Australia, 509
authentication, 17, 125, 133, 148, 193, 207, 208, 223, 241, 259, 288, 299, 309, 338, 341–344, 363, 425, 488, 524
authenticity, 17–19, 120, 124–126, 132, 134, 153, 160, 176,

177, 184, 188, 214, 309, 342, 455
authority, 1, 4, 5, 40, 214, 437
authorization, 249, 448
automation, 506, 508
autonomy, 25, 87, 146, 148, 243, 247, 254, 260, 270, 276, 285–287, 289, 298, 329, 340, 344, 347, 388, 410, 412, 413, 418, 431, 444, 445, 456, 457, 477, 481, 513, 514, 516, 521, 525
availability, 6, 163, 231, 302, 327, 488
avenue, 70, 208, 490
award, 494
awareness, 25, 39, 42–44, 48, 54, 56, 59, 60, 65, 70, 72, 74, 82–84, 88, 89, 91, 101, 105, 113, 140, 148, 157, 158, 169, 179, 187, 203, 204, 211, 221, 224, 226, 228, 249, 252, 258, 259, 261, 267, 269, 286, 291, 293–296, 301, 305, 307, 310, 313, 315, 316, 319, 321–323, 329, 333, 339, 340, 349, 350, 360, 369, 373, 375, 379, 381, 387, 388, 397, 401–403, 405, 406, 408, 415, 416, 425, 429, 439, 441, 449, 450, 452–455, 459, 460, 462–468, 473, 474, 478, 481, 484, 485, 488, 493, 496, 498, 499, 508, 513, 518, 522
awe, 90

backbone, 100, 120
backdoor, 11, 30, 34, 38, 45, 46, 86, 96, 196–199, 263, 282–285, 321, 334, 342, 377, 384, 426, 429, 472, 475
backdrop, 109, 436
background, 122, 155, 325, 361, 374
backing, 31, 373
backlash, 31, 35, 39, 44, 46, 96, 251, 384, 428
backup, 151
backyard, 4
balance, 12, 18, 27, 31, 34, 35, 38–40, 48, 50, 52, 53, 56, 58, 59, 71, 81, 84, 86, 87, 92, 96–99, 103, 105, 107, 110, 111, 113, 122, 123, 129, 139, 140, 146–148, 155, 160, 178, 183, 195, 198, 205, 206, 208, 219, 221, 224, 226, 228, 231, 233, 235, 240, 241, 246, 248, 249, 259, 263, 267–269, 275–277, 280, 281, 283, 285, 286, 291, 292, 310, 312, 315, 321, 323, 324, 329, 331, 334, 337, 347, 349, 364, 365, 376, 377, 384, 386, 389, 394, 396, 400, 401, 440–445, 447–451, 453, 459, 460, 465, 472, 476, 478, 480, 483, 487, 490–492, 496, 497, 506, 508, 510, 511, 514, 515, 518, 522
bank, 257, 455
banking, 33, 258, 277, 455

Index 533

barrier, 224
base, 70, 100, 156, 161, 163, 167–170, 174, 197, 215, 216, 294, 300, 303, 395
basic, 126, 437, 450
basis, 58, 455
battle, 6, 11, 12, 15, 16, 30–32, 34, 35, 38–41, 46–50, 53, 55, 60, 77, 80, 86, 95–97, 110, 140, 149–152, 166, 167, 178, 196, 199, 202, 216, 220, 222, 224, 229, 235, 237, 238, 245, 246, 248, 249, 255, 259, 262, 263, 267, 268, 295, 313, 320, 322, 335, 358, 381, 384, 422, 426–428, 430, 434, 436, 437, 439, 441, 442, 453, 463, 465, 471–474, 477, 479, 484, 495
battlefront, 199
beacon, 48, 86, 292, 304, 313, 358, 375, 408, 409, 417, 438
beauty, 104, 106, 199
bed, 446
beginning, 8, 14, 46, 304, 329, 494, 523
behavior, 7, 148, 237, 242, 243, 247, 254, 273, 280, 338, 443, 447, 450, 455, 457, 459
being, 3, 4, 9, 18, 24, 27, 50, 55, 61, 65, 87, 98, 99, 103, 106, 111, 113, 115, 121, 135, 137, 139, 143, 154, 162, 166, 178, 184, 189, 194, 196, 215, 218, 223, 241, 242, 244, 252–254, 262, 269, 276, 286, 288, 295, 296, 299, 300, 302, 305, 307–309, 320, 327, 334–336, 346, 357, 360, 378, 382, 392, 397, 405, 411, 447, 450, 452–454, 456, 457, 461, 464, 466, 468, 484, 498, 499, 503, 509, 511–513, 515, 517, 520, 523
belief, 6, 10, 13, 15, 23, 24, 45, 92, 96, 108, 112, 290, 312, 343, 349, 385, 405, 426, 437, 483, 484, 486, 495
benefit, 64, 99, 161, 301, 349, 375, 382, 418, 435, 479
bias, 116, 328, 345, 446, 491, 512, 513
billion, 213, 254
biography, 8, 46, 85, 119, 438
biometric, 148, 207, 289, 325
birth, 8, 13, 28, 32, 242, 272, 343, 384, 390, 454
bit, 368
Blackphone, 366
blend, 9
block, 414, 521
blockchain, 122, 135, 144, 145, 208, 209, 310, 317, 328, 329, 362, 377, 383, 423, 488, 490, 525
blocking, 306
blog, 42
blueprint, 322, 496
Bob, 131, 184, 186
Bob Dylan's, 314
bond, 108
book, 56, 57, 61, 62, 64, 65, 94, 109, 129, 379
bookstore, 94
boost, 91

border, 261, 262, 377, 449
bounty, 303
box, 9, 10, 100, 108, 111, 343, 427
boy, 19
brainstorm, 401
brainstorming, 434
brand, 396
Brazil, 197, 509
breach, 240, 272, 275, 281, 336, 347, 467, 469, 512, 513
break, 17, 54, 74, 137, 143, 183, 202, 207, 223, 271, 357, 363, 368, 370, 394, 458, 489
breakthrough, 143, 153, 429, 520
breath, 117
breed, 316
briefly, 368
brilliance, 103, 104, 106–108, 427
browser, 382, 421
browsing, 148, 240, 247, 254, 299, 373, 382, 421, 424, 441, 443, 450, 455, 511, 520, 522
Bruce Feiler, 99
Bruce Schneier, 42, 56, 64, 129, 219, 279, 296, 347, 379, 400, 469
brute, 125, 176, 195, 270
bug, 161, 162, 303
builder, 398
building, 42, 44, 103, 114, 115, 128, 189, 217, 220, 221, 277, 302, 308, 311, 317, 320, 344, 353, 379, 396, 397, 414, 420, 425, 444, 445, 467, 480, 482, 508
bullet, 474
bundle, 21

business, 101, 102, 148, 170, 188–190, 193, 195, 205, 237, 242, 244–246, 262, 263, 277, 292, 318–320, 376, 440, 446, 450, 472
button, 153, 186, 237, 316
buzz, 169

CA, 134, 135, 177
call, 9, 47, 245, 253, 409, 416, 428, 450, 452
Callas, 158
calling, 300, 366
camaraderie, 102
Camden, 1, 3
campaign, 47, 56, 244, 403
camping, 103, 106
Canada, 509
candidate, 115
capability, 81, 87
capacity, 440
capital, 69, 71
capitalism, 81, 115, 117, 237, 242–245, 247, 263, 310, 401, 432, 451, 456, 493
car, 522
card, 18, 258, 277
care, 61, 186
career, 28, 49, 82, 85, 86, 100, 103, 111, 112, 116, 310, 367, 373, 399, 418, 422, 427, 431, 434
case, 53, 58, 90, 162, 196–198, 219, 253, 263, 281, 283, 347, 435, 485
cat, 202, 203
catalyst, 114, 158, 175, 180, 367, 391, 392, 418, 436, 461, 490

Cathy O'Neil, 65
cause, 11, 12, 16, 24, 38, 41, 43, 44, 47–49, 61, 70, 84, 86, 87, 91, 96, 116, 158, 200, 312, 313, 349, 350, 357, 358, 373, 374, 376, 386, 397–399, 406, 409, 430, 436, 464, 465
caution, 203
censorship, 13, 26, 61, 91, 174, 219, 246, 312, 388, 432, 462, 478, 490
center, 3, 6, 95, 477
centralization, 328
centricity, 372
century, 335
certificate, 131, 132, 134, 135, 177
challenge, 1, 5, 7, 12, 17, 18, 25, 30, 32, 35, 40, 45, 48, 60, 61, 65, 71–73, 81, 85, 94, 97, 107, 117, 127, 129, 148, 174, 176, 178, 183, 186, 194, 197, 198, 206, 208, 212, 218, 224, 229, 231, 241, 246, 261, 268, 269, 283, 317, 323, 329, 334–337, 341, 342, 344, 364, 377, 378, 384, 386, 394, 401, 410, 418, 419, 427, 431, 437, 440, 445, 447, 450, 451, 458, 465, 473, 477, 487, 492, 495, 496, 501, 504, 510–515
champion, 11, 24, 30, 39, 41, 45, 65, 72, 82, 84, 86, 96, 109, 268, 384, 391, 397, 426, 479, 495, 499
change, 2, 5, 8, 15, 24, 40, 60, 61, 72, 74, 91, 104, 113, 114, 117, 158, 166, 173, 189, 211, 279, 310, 319, 372, 378, 381, 387, 389, 391, 395, 396, 406, 408, 418, 437, 457, 463, 466, 468, 485, 492, 495
changer, 26, 47, 165, 214, 228, 329, 341, 384, 391
channel, 18, 137, 138, 170, 177, 391
chapter, 3, 6, 8, 25, 49, 90, 97, 119, 175, 200, 216, 237, 355, 439
characteristic, 1
charisma, 42
Charlie, 186
check, 445
Chelsea Manning, 249, 280, 321
child, 1, 3, 28, 85, 282
childhood, 8
chip, 38, 46, 96, 426
choice, 151, 193, 216, 234, 300, 328, 445, 517
Chris Soghoian, 57
Christopher Wylie, 250
cipher, 136, 176, 190
ciphertext, 33, 119, 125, 127, 140, 149, 182, 249
circle, 104, 108–110
citizen, 518
citizenship, 340, 388
city, 43
claim, 269, 282, 440
clash, 46, 50, 199, 226, 245, 263, 451
click, 65, 186, 230
client, 160, 186, 193
climate, 269
climax, 39
closing, 92, 117

cloud, 143, 146, 178, 186, 188, 215, 222, 264, 363, 441, 490, 506, 508
coalition, 42
code, 21, 93, 103, 110, 111, 119, 120, 123, 130, 143, 156, 158, 162, 163, 169, 173, 190, 210, 212, 223, 231, 271, 293, 300, 303, 311, 371, 382, 392, 394, 414, 429, 433, 462
codebase, 194, 342
coding, 8, 14, 108, 491
collaboration, 11, 42, 44, 49, 50, 55, 58, 59, 69, 70, 72, 74–76, 82, 100, 102, 107, 109, 111, 145, 155, 157–159, 161, 162, 164, 165, 174, 179, 181, 211, 215, 218, 220–222, 225, 226, 229, 233, 235, 278, 286, 289, 303, 304, 313, 323, 329, 331, 334, 337, 342, 343, 348, 352, 357, 358, 361, 362, 364, 370, 372, 373, 378, 382–384, 387, 392–396, 398–403, 406–408, 412–414, 417–419, 426, 429, 447, 450, 453, 459, 466, 467, 481, 492, 495, 502, 511
collaborator, 158
collection, 64, 65, 81, 88, 130, 181, 200, 220, 226, 240, 242–246, 250, 260–264, 268, 269, 273, 279, 289, 303, 305, 307, 308, 310, 316, 319–321, 323, 336, 337, 340, 378, 382, 388, 401, 411, 423, 424, 433, 440, 442–446, 448, 450, 452, 454, 462, 463, 483, 484, 486, 491, 493, 494, 496, 498, 503, 508, 511–514, 523, 525
collective, 12, 18, 39, 41, 48, 53, 55, 72, 74, 111, 156, 163, 179, 221, 226, 239, 245, 250, 264, 268, 270, 289, 290, 298, 302, 304, 309, 313, 325, 334, 342, 366, 371, 374, 382, 395, 396, 406, 408, 411, 414, 423, 433, 445, 455, 457, 463, 471, 474, 479, 482, 492, 496, 497, 502, 508, 516, 525, 526
Colorado, 106
combat, 39, 46, 77, 143, 197, 258, 299, 302, 376, 382, 394, 405, 444, 472
combination, 122, 176, 190, 228, 316, 322, 372, 441
comfort, 372
comment, 247
commentary, 314
commerce, 217, 277, 446
commitment, 13, 26, 35, 40, 43, 46–48, 52, 54, 63, 70, 80, 82, 84–86, 90–92, 95, 97, 98, 102, 107, 111, 115–117, 152, 156, 179, 197, 200, 215, 221, 250, 270, 290, 302–304, 312, 313, 317, 320, 325, 332, 342–344, 348, 349, 352, 357, 358, 362, 366, 367, 373–375, 382–387, 391,

394–397, 401, 403, 406,
407, 413, 414, 416, 418,
422, 425, 426, 430, 438,
453, 462, 466, 470, 471,
474, 482, 492, 496, 508
commodification, 27, 237, 238, 243,
254, 286, 403, 410, 450,
457
commodity, 238, 247, 253, 254, 344,
401, 441, 450, 455–457
communicating, 18, 125, 137, 205
communication, 2, 5, 10, 11, 15, 16,
19, 23, 24, 26, 29, 32, 35,
38–40, 44, 45, 49, 54–58,
60–62, 75, 76, 78, 80, 91,
96, 112, 120–128, 130,
132–138, 142, 143, 145,
149, 152–156, 158,
164–168, 170, 173, 174,
177, 179–181, 188, 189,
191, 193, 194, 196, 203,
205–218, 222, 225, 226,
228, 230, 231, 233–235,
242, 249, 252, 258, 270,
271, 281, 282, 285, 290,
294, 302, 317, 322, 341,
342, 347, 357, 359–362,
365–367, 371, 381, 384,
391, 393, 394, 405, 415,
418, 420, 423, 429, 431,
432, 435, 453, 460, 464,
468, 473, 475, 488–490,
492, 498, 499, 508, 525
community, 1, 10–12, 31, 34,
39–45, 47, 55, 60, 75, 83,
86, 95, 96, 100–102, 104,
106, 111, 155, 157, 158,
160–163, 165, 167, 174,
210, 211, 220, 226, 267,

291, 295, 300, 303, 308,
342, 348, 349, 352, 357,
358, 361, 374, 375, 377,
378, 382, 384, 391–395,
398, 399, 401, 403, 405,
407, 408, 413, 414, 418,
420, 423, 429, 454, 462,
464, 466, 484, 486, 516,
518
company, 283, 302–304, 366, 421
compass, 111, 325, 496
compatibility, 156, 161, 187, 207,
208, 212, 215, 216, 393
compensation, 328
competition, 108, 221, 376, 446,
447, 513
complex, 9, 16, 20, 27, 42, 50, 52, 59,
65, 74, 87, 90, 108, 111,
116, 120, 125, 127, 137,
144, 148, 149, 153, 155,
159, 161, 166, 168, 176,
182, 186, 190, 194, 196,
197, 209, 214, 221, 227,
229, 230, 235, 245, 246,
248, 265, 269, 271, 272,
276, 283–285, 295–297,
303, 311, 317, 329, 332,
333, 337, 344, 357, 362,
367, 383, 394, 395, 397,
398, 412, 416, 440, 445,
447, 451–454, 458, 465,
473, 489, 493, 496, 498,
499, 501, 504, 506, 512,
513, 516, 517, 519
complexity, 96, 120, 131, 136, 140,
152, 179, 206, 224, 316,
364
compliance, 303, 316, 336
component, 16, 50, 127, 145, 155,

164, 179, 288, 309, 340, 388
compromise, 11, 34, 56, 58, 86, 154, 193, 246, 264, 270, 283, 311, 319, 346, 359, 419, 424, 437, 454, 472–474, 490, 508, 524
computation, 143, 145, 161, 178, 287, 317, 363, 367, 458, 460, 474, 488, 490, 492, 525
computer, 2, 4, 5, 7, 9, 13, 14, 19, 20, 29, 97, 98, 108, 155, 216, 225–227, 229, 236, 358, 371, 385, 390, 399, 400, 419, 426, 427, 435, 437, 491, 495, 503
computing, 17, 54, 94, 143, 176, 181, 183, 195, 207, 210, 222, 223, 229, 231, 271, 273, 355–357, 360, 362, 363, 367–370, 441, 458, 473, 474, 481, 486–490, 492, 522
concentration, 440
concept, 7, 25, 55, 63, 98, 107, 120, 133, 155, 165, 180, 196, 197, 224, 241, 242, 254, 285, 287, 292, 293, 309, 322, 323, 325, 332, 333, 336, 343, 344, 363, 366, 370, 391, 451, 455, 477, 516
concern, 27, 57, 75, 155, 210, 238, 240, 243, 270, 293, 298, 301, 302, 316, 317, 321, 328, 335, 347, 355, 357, 361, 367, 403, 408, 428, 442, 464, 473, 478, 496, 499, 511
concert, 106
conclusion, 35, 38, 68, 82, 102, 105, 112, 114, 142, 181, 204, 211, 222, 224, 229, 246, 270, 273, 277, 286, 322, 337, 353, 376, 383, 385, 390, 392, 397, 416, 417, 419, 427, 428, 430, 433, 436, 450, 466, 471, 496, 499, 513, 522
condition, 517
conference, 20, 108, 401, 434
confidence, 18, 162, 217, 257, 296, 339, 360, 394
confidentiality, 18, 34, 57, 101, 120, 126, 134, 136, 139, 140, 142, 144, 147, 165, 170, 176, 178, 180, 193, 196, 235, 327, 363, 364, 431, 458, 488, 515
configuration, 187
conflict, 3, 147, 196, 245, 246, 267, 401
connectedness, 247
connection, 106, 199, 263
connectivity, 27, 219, 238, 287, 293, 477, 506
conscience, 279, 345
consciousness, 101, 168, 268, 293, 308, 349, 413, 426, 478, 480–482, 493, 515
consensus, 159, 208
consent, 81, 89, 116, 238, 241–244, 247, 251, 254, 261, 262, 269, 270, 289, 305, 308, 321, 323, 327, 329, 336, 340, 410, 411, 442, 444, 448, 452, 457, 462, 465,

Index 539

467, 478, 506, 511–513, 515, 517, 524, 525
consequence, 456
consideration, 19, 50, 224, 283, 285, 328, 334, 337, 451, 487, 513, 525
consulting, 15, 238, 241, 244, 250, 262, 452, 457
consumer, 237, 254, 442–444, 513
consumption, 177
contact, 215
content, 1, 7, 17, 33, 58, 59, 81, 127, 155, 186, 189, 190, 194, 197, 228, 242, 243, 246, 247, 249, 254, 297–299, 360, 403, 446, 523
contention, 452
context, 33, 219, 225, 279, 328, 337, 346, 376, 426, 481, 492
contractor, 314
contrast, 55, 146, 368
contribution, 60, 90, 155, 268, 409, 415, 429–431, 437, 493
control, 6, 11, 23, 26, 32, 34, 38, 43, 44, 46, 47, 50, 58, 60, 63, 65, 74, 79–81, 85, 111, 112, 125, 137, 146, 156, 175, 200, 209, 218, 225, 226, 228–230, 233, 239, 242–246, 251, 252, 254, 260, 262, 263, 268, 273, 286–288, 291–293, 295, 296, 298, 299, 301–305, 307–309, 311, 316, 317, 319, 322, 323, 327–331, 333, 335, 336, 344, 358, 366, 375, 385, 388–390, 403, 410, 411, 413, 423, 424, 430–433, 436, 442–444, 446, 449–451, 453, 455–457, 462, 463, 476, 480, 488, 490, 491, 493, 494, 496, 498, 499, 508, 509, 511–514, 516, 517, 522–525
controversy, 3, 11, 34, 35, 37, 38, 41, 46, 58, 60, 86, 88, 96, 162, 196, 267, 342, 379, 391, 396, 426, 429, 434, 515
conundrum, 50
convenience, 27, 112, 122, 123, 128, 139, 140, 146–149, 178, 247, 286, 293, 301, 317, 323, 344, 356, 359, 388, 394, 407, 439, 442, 445, 446, 455, 483
conversation, 2, 32, 38, 59, 63, 64, 76, 86, 96, 122, 170, 241, 245, 246, 251, 252, 267, 268, 292, 295, 305, 319, 349, 384, 386, 391, 406, 413, 415, 416, 426, 427, 457, 463, 465, 475, 483, 484
conviction, 6, 11, 24, 200
cooperation, 110, 157, 206, 278, 289, 378, 398, 402, 449, 450, 459, 476, 491, 492, 510, 524
coordination, 289, 431
core, 60, 65, 68, 69, 71, 72, 103, 119, 127, 160, 163, 173, 175, 217, 242, 282, 323, 371, 409, 468, 477, 495
corner, 269
cornerstone, 13, 48, 133, 135, 175, 178, 209, 259, 270, 290, 313, 359, 365, 386, 416

corporation, 241
correspondence, 218, 433
corruption, 57, 60, 61, 166, 277, 280, 405, 431
cost, 140, 148, 152, 179, 224, 247, 269
counsel, 396
counterbalance, 103
country, 52, 64, 401, 403
couple, 186, 195
courage, 11, 40, 48, 92, 426, 437, 438
course, 2, 7, 11, 130, 228, 267
coursework, 361
court, 283, 448
cover, 31, 166, 331, 338, 518
coverage, 46, 169, 241, 517
craft, 42, 98, 378, 495
creation, 6, 15, 16, 23, 30, 32, 33, 35, 60, 68, 84, 100, 122, 123, 126, 196, 218, 225, 228, 236, 293, 325, 335, 339, 344, 356, 365, 384, 401, 405, 413, 416, 422, 426, 427, 429, 430, 436
creativity, 85, 93, 106, 107, 111, 112, 163, 362, 410, 434
creator, 45, 229
credibility, 42, 44, 162, 317
credit, 18, 40, 258, 272, 277
crime, 27, 39, 45, 87, 197, 245, 246, 258, 268, 276, 277, 444, 472, 492
criminal, 31, 33, 35, 45, 46, 50, 58, 73, 87, 178, 245, 267, 269, 282, 452
criticism, 39, 197, 238, 446
crossfire, 465
crowdfunding, 70

cry, 60, 386
cryptanalysis, 195
crypto, 95, 96, 157, 158, 408, 426
cryptocurrency, 18, 144, 258
cryptographer, 20, 108, 111, 157, 158, 296, 419
cryptography, 1–10, 13–20, 26, 28, 29, 32, 33, 39, 43, 44, 46, 56, 62, 65, 76, 84–86, 93–95, 103, 105–112, 119, 123–126, 130, 135, 143, 145, 149, 157, 165, 170, 173, 176, 178–180, 207, 210, 212, 213, 223, 225, 226, 231, 234, 267, 268, 271, 273, 340, 348, 356, 357, 363, 365, 366, 369–371, 383–385, 391, 393, 398, 405, 409, 429, 434, 435, 458, 461, 466, 473, 481, 487–489, 525
culmination, 6, 10
culture, 62, 76, 84, 158, 162, 163, 173, 181, 218, 227, 280, 308, 311, 313–316, 339, 340, 349, 382, 385, 392–397, 407, 413, 414, 428, 454, 457, 463, 467, 474, 478, 480, 481, 491, 493, 515, 517
curiosity, 1, 3–5, 7, 9, 14, 16, 19, 20, 28, 85, 93, 94, 104, 108, 111, 112, 352, 383, 390, 392, 436
currency, 262, 440, 450, 514
curricula, 361, 491, 496, 518
curriculum, 1, 315, 419
curve, 206, 207, 363, 397, 437, 473
customer, 193, 241, 316, 396

Index 541

cutting, 70, 94, 162, 317, 365, 374, 419, 446, 467, 494
cyber, 13, 77, 80, 142, 149, 181, 207, 273, 323, 381, 415, 489, 512
cyberbullying, 498
cybercrime, 84, 146, 337, 401, 453, 459
cybersecurity, 59, 106, 142, 200, 217, 272, 277, 281, 303, 339, 376, 430, 435, 495, 512, 514
cyberstalking, 454
cycle, 269

damage, 261, 277, 512
dance, 515
danger, 46
data, 2, 14, 16–18, 23, 26, 27, 49, 53, 54, 57–60, 62, 64, 65, 68, 71, 77, 78, 81, 82, 87–90, 92, 96, 115, 116, 119–124, 128, 130–133, 136–140, 142–146, 148, 149, 151–154, 157, 160, 170, 174–183, 188, 193, 195, 196, 200, 208, 210, 211, 216–218, 220, 222–224, 226, 228–230, 232, 235, 237–264, 268–273, 276–279, 281–284, 286–293, 296, 298–311, 316, 317, 319–323, 325, 327–329, 332–337, 339, 340, 343–348, 356, 360, 362–364, 366, 367, 370–372, 376–379, 381, 382, 385, 387–390, 393, 397, 400, 401, 403, 405, 407–412, 415, 421, 423, 424, 428–430, 433, 439–458, 460–469, 472–476, 478, 480, 481, 483, 484, 486–496, 498, 499, 503, 504, 506, 508–518, 520–525
date, 135, 145, 160, 179, 343, 378, 454, 474
daughter, 98
David, 11, 30, 38, 39, 41, 96, 267, 384, 426
David E. Sanger, 296
David Erdos, 480
day, 13, 32, 40, 46, 49, 63, 64, 86, 97, 226, 426, 455, 470, 471, 508
deal, 193, 370
debate, 6, 12, 18, 19, 34, 39, 52, 58, 59, 64, 85, 88, 89, 96, 139, 181, 183, 196–199, 208, 213, 217, 226, 235, 246, 248, 259, 263, 269, 275, 279, 281–285, 291, 321, 334, 377, 465, 472, 475, 477, 485, 487, 495, 496
Deborah Hurley, 480
decentralization, 328, 329
decision, 23, 43, 57, 59, 198, 252, 254, 276, 289, 317, 337, 341, 345, 414, 429, 450, 455, 477, 499, 502, 503, 506, 512, 518, 523
decryption, 5, 16, 17, 21, 33, 45, 78, 107, 120, 124, 127, 128, 133, 136, 137, 140, 143, 153, 154, 161, 176–178, 186, 188, 199, 212, 217,

230, 257, 264, 302, 320, 356, 381, 458, 472, 490
dedication, 12, 41, 47, 49, 54, 60, 63, 83–86, 110, 111, 116, 236, 267, 268, 293, 303, 312, 322, 343, 352, 353, 355, 358, 362, 365, 375, 385, 387, 388, 390, 405–408, 416, 418, 427–430, 433, 453, 460, 463, 465, 468, 474, 482, 492
defamation, 280
default, 26, 55, 224, 262, 304, 411, 473
defeat, 39, 41, 48
defender, 33, 111
defense, 38, 55, 179, 207, 381, 407, 464, 496
defiance, 219
definition, 292
degree, 140, 146, 166, 241
deletion, 448, 525
deliberation, 329, 519
delve, 13, 16, 25, 28, 29, 38, 46, 68, 82, 93, 103, 119, 126, 145, 175, 211, 216, 233, 237, 287, 302, 327, 330, 359, 370, 395, 400, 434, 439, 455, 470, 503, 519
demand, 15, 33, 69, 74, 97, 146, 147, 151, 157, 214, 218, 239, 277, 294, 300, 305, 306, 316, 320, 339, 375, 387, 394, 409, 441, 457, 463, 465, 466, 473, 481, 482, 487, 498, 515, 517
demise, 36, 45
democracy, 13, 28, 32, 40, 41, 48, 52, 54, 57, 59, 92, 97, 108, 321, 348, 384, 408, 410, 416, 463, 469, 474, 477–480
democratization, 122, 199, 230, 332–335, 405, 476, 486
demographic, 297, 450, 455
deniability, 153
departure, 112
deployment, 288, 369, 487
depth, 62, 207, 232, 297, 469
design, 115, 116, 148, 215, 221–223, 226, 234, 252, 262, 286–290, 304, 308, 328, 334, 343, 370, 372, 395, 411, 424, 434, 461, 469, 471, 494, 506, 508, 515, 518, 523, 526
desire, 1, 2, 16, 25, 29, 33, 82, 113, 146, 175, 286, 298, 299, 477
destination, 195
detail, 28, 106, 111, 112
detection, 58, 87, 140, 207, 364
determination, 8, 9, 15, 20, 24, 31, 38, 40, 41, 46, 94, 96, 112, 267, 348, 391, 392, 427, 436, 438
deterrent, 84
developer, 158, 303
development, 10, 18, 19, 31, 54, 55, 63, 64, 69–72, 75, 83, 88, 91, 97, 100, 102, 108, 109, 115, 116, 135, 157, 159–162, 164, 169, 174, 180, 200, 206, 209, 211, 213, 214, 219–221, 224, 226, 229–231, 234, 235, 246, 260, 268, 269, 271, 273, 277, 286–289, 304,

308–310, 322, 335, 342, 344, 355–357, 359, 363, 365, 366, 369–371, 373–376, 382, 383, 385, 386, 389–396, 406, 407, 414, 415, 418, 420, 421, 423, 424, 429, 433, 434, 453, 455, 458, 460, 474, 475, 477, 479, 481, 486, 488–490, 494, 503, 523, 525
device, 11, 30, 34, 45, 129, 137, 276, 384, 443
dialogue, 25, 48, 59, 88, 90, 102, 159, 206, 224, 270, 276, 386, 426, 447, 466, 476, 477, 483, 510, 515, 518, 519
dichotomy, 96, 516
difference, 12, 13, 15, 41, 62, 77, 92, 104, 107, 229, 236, 312, 419, 427, 430, 437, 459
difficulty, 128, 223, 271, 299, 363, 367, 368, 486
digitization, 435
dignity, 148, 270, 276, 286, 287, 344, 410, 413, 431, 433, 445, 483, 496, 514
dilemma, 35, 50, 69, 71, 76, 84–88, 90, 92, 146, 148, 268, 270, 281, 384
direction, 414
disclosure, 193, 260, 264, 275, 281, 336, 431, 448
discontent, 441
discourse, 19, 26, 46, 57, 58, 101, 181, 197, 243, 269, 286, 291, 298, 314, 316, 372, 377, 399, 403, 420, 478, 486
discovery, 29, 86, 250
discrimination, 241, 260, 269, 312, 328, 344–346, 443, 512, 513, 515
discussion, 18, 52, 64, 213, 284, 380, 469
disinformation, 246
disk, 137
disparity, 361
dispute, 283
disruption, 490
dissemination, 100, 175, 243, 246, 432
dissent, 40, 57, 97, 269, 431, 478
distance, 368
distribution, 11, 18, 19, 24, 30, 33, 95, 131, 133, 173, 176, 187, 209, 267, 325, 339, 341, 434
dive, 3, 8, 23, 28, 90, 97, 115, 119, 130, 200, 245, 355, 368
diversity, 159, 318, 402, 421
divide, 174, 243, 402, 456
diving, 77, 104, 106, 190, 225, 383, 522
document, 126, 134, 219, 468
documentary, 64, 494
documentation, 163, 166, 173, 174, 371, 433–435
dollar, 254
domain, 69, 72, 79, 103, 463
dominance, 446
donor, 71
door, 29, 277
downfall, 36
drawing, 18, 156, 372
drive, 84, 91, 107, 137, 211, 239, 242, 292, 310, 315, 319,

335, 364, 371, 373, 376,
391, 395, 396, 434, 468,
491, 495, 522
driver, 299
drug, 45, 282
duty, 259
dynamic, 109, 365, 404, 510

e, 277, 446
eagerness, 5
earth, 103, 112
ease, 140, 160, 165, 168, 185, 194,
215, 365, 394, 429
eavesdropping, 302
economy, 243, 254, 328
ecosystem, 156, 163, 342, 393, 508,
509, 511, 517
edge, 70, 94, 162, 252, 317, 365,
374, 419, 446, 467, 488,
494
educating, 47, 48, 54, 64, 116, 211,
307, 319, 323, 337, 375,
383, 397, 406, 411, 424,
453, 467, 484, 486, 493
education, 20, 32, 80, 106, 140, 148,
170, 173, 187, 204, 211,
221, 230, 252, 269, 296,
297, 305, 307, 309, 315,
316, 322, 323, 329, 332,
333, 335, 337–340, 356,
358, 360, 362, 369, 381,
387, 397, 403, 406, 419,
424, 430, 433, 444, 450,
453, 455, 463, 465, 467,
484, 488, 489, 491–493,
496, 514, 519, 521, 522
Edward Snowden, 56, 57, 65, 89,
101, 219, 240, 249, 282,
291, 296, 299, 314, 321,
494
Edward Snowden's, 431
Edward Snowden, 279
effect, 104, 269, 276, 283, 406, 410,
478
effectiveness, 35, 121, 149, 154, 156,
195, 215, 221, 226, 253,
323, 389, 485
efficiency, 98, 146, 286, 357, 369,
487, 488, 503, 514
effort, 43, 55, 72, 98, 156, 157,
161–163, 174, 179, 187,
197, 221, 230, 245, 250,
309, 313, 324, 325, 334,
366, 374, 382, 408, 414,
435, 453, 460, 472, 488,
512, 525
election, 238, 241, 244, 250, 253,
452
element, 27, 107, 115, 134, 174, 382
ElGamal, 160
Elissa Shevinsky, 99
email, 17, 121, 153, 156, 160, 163,
168, 184, 186–193, 207,
209, 212–216, 218, 228,
230, 234, 240, 257, 293,
294, 299, 301, 341, 359,
360, 362, 366, 367, 384,
429, 455, 488
embrace, 22, 84, 155, 175, 233, 302,
308, 347, 370, 395, 397,
418, 482, 492, 495
emergence, 3, 17, 175, 181, 310, 450
emergency, 276
Emma, 108
Emma Chang, 108
empathy, 285, 372
emphasis, 75, 179, 227, 301, 333,

Index

343, 415, 421, 463, 466, 468, 476, 484, 493
employer, 281
employment, 346, 512
empowerment, 40, 163, 164, 229, 255, 288, 290, 291, 303, 310, 329, 343, 425, 443, 445, 463, 476, 493, 514
encounter, 8, 94, 280
encouragement, 98
encroachment, 11, 39, 41, 42, 96, 437, 477, 513
encrypt, 23, 24, 78, 81, 124, 127, 130, 131, 136, 138, 144, 151–153, 160, 165, 167, 168, 170, 176, 180, 184, 186, 188–190, 194, 317, 377, 405, 429
encrypting, 14, 17, 121, 124, 137, 176, 186, 189, 194, 217, 218, 257, 259, 276, 308, 365, 381, 460
encryption, 2, 3, 5–13, 15–18, 20–26, 28–35, 37–50, 52–64, 69, 70, 73–75, 80–84, 86, 88, 90, 91, 93–98, 100–103, 105, 107–117, 119–133, 136–140, 142–145, 149, 151–191, 193–200, 202–205, 207–226, 228–239, 244–246, 249–252, 255, 257–259, 263, 264, 267, 268, 270–273, 276–278, 281–285, 287, 290–298, 300, 302, 304, 305, 310–313, 317, 320–323, 327–330, 332–334, 337, 341–343, 348–350, 355–386, 388–395, 398–400, 405–407, 411, 413–416, 418–420, 423, 424, 426–437, 439–443, 445, 449–452, 458–467, 469–478, 480–493, 496, 499, 508, 513–515, 520, 522, 524, 525
end, 24, 32, 39, 40, 48, 126, 153, 189, 195, 197, 198, 212, 213, 215, 216, 224, 225, 228, 229, 231, 249, 252, 268, 294, 298, 300, 302, 359, 360, 365–367, 372, 386, 394, 423, 428, 443, 461, 508
endeavor, 11, 178
endorsement, 44, 169, 293, 300
endpoint, 142
energy, 104, 106, 108
enforcement, 6, 11, 18, 30, 33–35, 39, 45, 46, 48, 50, 56, 58, 59, 87, 96, 97, 178, 181, 183, 196–199, 213, 221, 224, 238, 246, 258, 259, 263, 264, 277, 278, 282, 283, 285, 302, 321, 328, 331, 334, 343, 376, 391, 440, 443, 448–452, 459, 475, 492, 515
engage, 20, 25, 43, 52, 57, 64, 107, 110, 111, 197, 198, 289, 296, 300, 308, 311, 314, 315, 334, 340, 345, 352, 355, 371, 372, 397, 400, 402, 420, 435, 449, 477–479, 483, 485, 486, 494, 509, 516

engagement, 43, 70, 73, 102, 276, 340, 378, 451
engine, 499, 521
engineer, 2, 108
engineering, 115–117, 128, 129, 154, 203, 227, 270, 338, 340–344, 348, 409, 419–422, 425, 430, 435, 437, 442, 488
entanglement, 363, 368
entertainment, 242
enthusiasm, 20, 44, 98, 103, 108, 437
enthusiast, 108, 454
entity, 134, 382
entrepreneur, 396, 397
entrepreneurship, 376, 379
entry, 196
environment, 34, 80, 133, 140, 152, 159, 163, 178, 247, 272, 280, 322, 323, 339, 360, 372, 376, 398, 407, 420, 421, 429, 447, 455, 488
epic, 38
equality, 432, 477
era, 5, 28, 32, 33, 41, 60, 82, 90, 92, 135, 156, 180, 210, 224, 235, 242, 247, 257, 258, 268, 271, 285, 287, 290, 296, 298, 301, 304, 316, 357, 369, 391, 408, 415, 426, 428, 439, 442, 456, 458, 460, 466, 475, 477, 488–492, 496, 507, 524
erode, 81, 243, 269, 283, 465, 517
erosion, 27, 52, 65, 75, 87, 237, 245, 247, 254, 263, 269, 286, 291, 320, 321, 349, 358, 404, 410, 424, 440, 446, 456, 457, 473, 478
error, 186
escape, 106
escrow, 58
essay, 61, 64, 469
essence, 199, 282, 477
establishment, 38, 289, 450
ethos, 60, 163, 398, 414, 466
evaluation, 99
evangelism, 293
event, 336, 437
evidence, 87, 245, 280, 281
evolution, 62, 102, 119, 123, 126, 130, 155, 162, 185, 200, 216, 224, 261, 262, 331, 335, 337, 434, 481
examination, 65
example, 13, 17, 18, 24, 48, 55, 57, 61, 86, 88, 89, 98, 107, 122, 132, 170, 194, 197, 213, 215, 219, 234, 240, 253, 258, 261, 263, 272, 280, 289, 300, 301, 305, 307, 309, 314, 328, 334, 335, 343, 363, 368, 394, 396, 401, 418, 419, 427, 431, 446, 448, 449, 457, 458, 466, 468, 471, 499, 504, 508, 511, 512, 515, 521
exception, 93, 100, 111, 313, 436
exchange, 15, 42, 55, 73, 102, 107, 120, 137, 158, 163, 180, 186, 194, 208, 212, 225, 227, 269, 365, 366, 368, 401, 415, 419, 439, 455
excitement, 105, 367
exercise, 57, 107, 167, 198, 234, 276, 277, 298, 333, 336, 374,

432, 440, 462
existence, 304, 344
expansion, 173–175
expectation, 62, 331, 346
expense, 98, 451, 478
experience, 2, 21, 29, 44, 105, 113, 114, 116, 122, 129, 140, 160, 161, 168, 189, 206, 209, 211, 215, 216, 220, 224, 231, 296, 301, 323, 330, 371, 396, 399, 468, 488, 500
experiment, 2, 163, 372
experimentation, 107, 163
expert, 42, 310, 358, 379, 494
expertise, 5, 17, 21, 39, 42, 43, 60, 61, 70, 73, 95, 100, 108, 109, 115–117, 155–159, 162, 232, 293, 297, 300, 301, 303, 311, 333, 355, 360, 361, 366, 367, 371, 372, 374, 377, 382, 383, 393, 395, 398–401, 414, 416, 437, 475, 480
expiration, 135
explanation, 190
exploit, 26, 29, 59, 77, 149, 151, 177, 253, 277, 323, 338, 368, 410, 469, 493, 512
exploitation, 30, 218, 251, 254, 259, 276, 282, 343–345, 370, 372, 412, 443, 451, 456, 522, 523
exploration, 9, 13, 16, 32, 56, 59, 65, 107, 129, 356, 469, 490
explore, 1, 6–8, 13, 14, 16, 20, 25, 28, 29, 36, 44, 46, 53, 54, 57, 62, 65, 72, 75, 82, 85, 87, 90, 93, 100, 103, 104, 111, 112, 115, 119, 122–126, 132, 136, 142, 145, 146, 162–164, 167, 170, 175, 179, 184, 185, 188, 200, 207, 211, 214, 216, 227, 230, 232, 233, 253, 260, 262, 276, 279, 287, 298, 300, 302, 307, 310, 313, 314, 316, 327–329, 332, 335, 337, 341, 344, 350, 355, 357, 358, 362, 365, 368, 370, 373, 376, 400, 410, 418, 419, 422, 427, 435, 436, 439, 448, 450, 455, 458, 477, 483, 486, 491, 493, 495, 516, 520, 522
export, 31, 33, 173, 180
exposure, 299, 303, 343, 382, 525
expression, 48, 80, 82, 84, 91, 166, 174, 218, 234, 263, 269, 276, 277, 283, 314, 316, 344, 348, 432, 442, 474, 478, 514
extend, 197, 362, 406
extension, 421
extent, 57, 101, 238, 246, 249, 250, 252, 254, 269, 291, 298, 307, 314, 336, 450, 451, 465, 495, 517
extraction, 242
eye, 30, 55, 113, 294

fabric, 13, 287, 334
face, 1, 6, 7, 11, 24, 27, 30, 31, 41, 49, 68, 86, 97, 109, 115, 117, 135, 156, 178, 187, 191, 207, 210, 215, 218, 220, 223, 224, 231, 238,

239, 246, 250, 264, 279,
280, 293, 297, 310, 313,
316, 317, 319, 320, 322,
337, 346–349, 356, 358,
360, 361, 369, 385–387,
391, 394, 402, 403, 408,
410, 412, 413, 419, 426,
429, 430, 437, 441, 445,
448, 450, 462, 464, 474,
487, 492, 493, 499, 514,
518, 522
fact, 199, 368, 450, 451
factor, 146, 157, 207, 223, 227, 241,
259, 271, 288, 294, 299,
309, 338, 425, 459, 488
failure, 36, 251
fairness, 253, 328, 500, 512, 518
fame, 105, 108, 112–114
family, 97–99, 103, 189, 247, 259
farewell, 438
fascination, 2, 8, 29, 85, 390
fear, 13, 24, 25, 57, 61, 91, 97, 166,
217, 234, 280, 281, 294,
375, 377, 388, 410, 431,
432, 462, 477, 483, 514
fearlessness, 108
feasibility, 283
feature, 101, 153, 159, 188, 224,
341, 360, 435
fee, 71
feedback, 43, 102, 155, 158, 161,
162, 168, 211, 300, 396,
420, 421
feeling, 105, 106, 299
fellow, 11, 14, 31, 39, 73, 96, 100,
102, 104, 108, 111, 155,
221, 313, 384, 399
fellowship, 83, 386, 419–421
fiction, 104

field, 2, 3, 5, 9, 10, 13–15, 17, 18,
20, 21, 26, 29, 39, 54, 60,
71, 72, 76, 82, 83, 86, 94,
98, 105, 107, 109–111,
114–116, 119, 122, 123,
136, 139, 143, 145, 157,
179, 211, 214, 216, 218,
225–227, 261, 292, 296,
298, 300, 302, 329, 333,
335, 340, 343, 344, 349,
355, 356, 358–361, 365,
369–371, 373, 378, 379,
383–385, 390, 391, 398,
405, 409, 413, 418–422,
426, 427, 435, 437, 461,
463, 466, 480, 481, 483,
486, 490, 491, 493, 520
fight, 6, 8, 11–13, 16, 24, 25, 28,
31–33, 39–42, 44–50,
53–55, 60–62, 64, 72,
74–77, 82, 84, 86, 92, 96,
97, 105, 108, 113,
115–117, 179, 181, 199,
213, 216, 221, 226–230,
236, 237, 239, 249, 250,
258, 268, 279, 290, 292,
295, 298, 311–313,
319–322, 325, 337, 344,
348–350, 352, 358, 370,
372, 374, 375, 377, 378,
381, 384, 385, 387, 389,
399–403, 406, 408,
422–425, 427, 428,
430–434, 436–438, 453,
457, 461, 463–466, 468,
471, 474, 476, 480, 496,
497, 499, 525
fighting, 34, 41, 42, 46, 91, 95, 108,
174, 219, 246, 267, 277,

294, 373, 378, 390, 430, 442, 462
figure, 13, 39, 46, 49, 100, 108, 112, 228, 370, 374, 376, 427
file, 137, 156, 187–189, 214, 215, 234, 281, 299, 320
film, 314
filmmaker, 494
filter, 254
finance, 327, 356, 378, 458, 490, 520
financing, 91
finding, 7, 9, 52, 87, 97, 99, 103, 104, 128, 149, 159, 221, 283, 364, 377, 400, 401, 476, 491, 515
fine, 155, 159–161, 525
fingerprint, 148
fingerprinting, 521
Finney, 100, 158
fire, 29, 43
firm, 6, 238, 241, 244, 250, 262, 452, 457
firmware, 271, 508
flagship, 366
flexibility, 99, 163, 216
flow, 261, 432, 448, 449
focus, 85, 97, 105, 112, 113, 161, 206, 215, 301, 317, 322, 338, 355, 360, 361, 392, 408, 423, 476
footage, 508
footprint, 221, 226, 247, 254, 299, 330, 333, 441, 453, 514, 515
foray, 3
force, 3, 9, 20, 44, 60, 65, 74, 85, 93, 108, 125, 146, 195, 270, 279, 416, 428, 446, 466

forefront, 12, 24, 31, 40, 46, 48, 53, 63, 64, 101, 102, 111, 115, 145, 149, 170, 189, 196, 237, 252, 268, 289, 294, 316, 356, 358, 365, 374, 403, 413, 423, 426, 430, 431, 445, 477, 487
foresight, 391
forgery, 188
form, 16, 20, 38, 53, 55, 66, 102, 105, 110, 119, 127, 189, 217, 270, 315, 360, 439
format, 78, 186, 249, 257, 296, 381, 472
formation, 407
formulation, 224
Foster, 378, 495
foster, 12, 58, 102, 103, 148, 149, 158, 277, 278, 281, 286, 307, 313, 325, 352, 386, 399, 401, 402, 435, 447, 454, 460, 478, 480, 491, 493, 509, 514, 515
foundation, 2, 16, 22, 25, 28, 53, 66, 76, 92, 122, 124, 127, 128, 130, 134, 158, 162, 208, 227, 234, 291, 292, 350, 353, 373, 391, 410, 422, 426, 427, 477, 480, 484, 493, 495
fragmentation, 208
frame, 176
framework, 133, 207, 226, 262, 281, 308, 336, 343, 513, 514, 518, 524
framing, 517
fraud, 240, 243, 257, 272, 345, 503
freedom, 25, 38, 40, 46, 57, 59, 60, 62, 80, 82, 84, 91, 92, 101,

108, 148, 165, 166, 170, 174, 175, 217, 219, 234, 243, 249, 269, 270, 276, 277, 294, 298, 314, 316, 320, 329, 344, 345, 347, 348, 388, 389, 405, 410, 413, 430–432, 442, 462, 463, 474, 477, 483, 496, 514, 516
frequency, 512
friend, 257, 516
friendliness, 301, 302
friendship, 108
front, 11, 31, 41, 43, 75, 96
frontier, 14, 29, 48, 327–329
fuel, 8, 70, 104, 107, 246, 373, 434
fulfilling, 99
fulfillment, 104
fun, 107, 435
function, 258, 440
functionality, 160, 235, 304, 317
functioning, 54, 56, 477, 479
fund, 91
fundamental, 3, 6, 10, 13, 19, 24, 25, 27–29, 31, 34, 35, 38, 40, 45, 46, 49, 50, 62, 69, 72, 74, 75, 78, 80, 82, 83, 87, 92, 95, 109, 111, 117, 124, 146, 152, 175, 176, 179, 198, 214, 218, 228, 235, 243, 250, 268–270, 276–279, 283, 285–287, 289–292, 296, 298, 306, 312, 313, 321, 323, 325, 329, 332, 333, 335, 342, 344, 347–349, 353, 357, 360, 367, 370, 374, 375, 378, 385, 386, 388, 392, 395, 397, 401, 403, 404, 407–410, 412–414, 416, 426, 429, 431–433, 437, 438, 441, 442, 445, 452, 453, 457, 460, 465, 466, 471, 474, 475, 477, 479, 480, 483, 484, 486, 488, 492, 495, 496, 514–517, 523, 525, 526
funding, 55, 69–72, 83, 84, 86, 268, 357, 361, 373, 375, 376, 384, 420
fusion, 107
future, 1–4, 8, 10, 15, 20, 21, 27–29, 32, 41, 42, 49, 55, 59, 63–65, 68, 70, 72, 74, 76, 82–84, 86, 90, 92, 102, 114–117, 122, 135, 142, 145, 149, 152, 154, 155, 164, 173, 181, 189, 197, 200, 206–208, 210, 211, 214, 217, 222–224, 229–233, 236, 241–243, 245, 246, 249, 253, 262, 264, 265, 268, 271, 287–290, 292, 295, 302, 304, 307, 310, 312, 313, 316, 320, 322, 325, 329, 330, 332, 334, 335, 340, 343, 344, 349, 350, 352, 353, 355–358, 360, 362, 364, 365, 370–373, 375, 376, 378, 383, 387, 390, 391, 394, 396, 397, 403, 406, 409, 412, 413, 415, 416, 418, 420, 421, 425–428, 430, 433–439, 441, 442, 445, 447, 450, 453, 457–460, 463, 465–469, 474, 479, 482,

Index 551

485–487, 489, 491–493,
495–497, 499, 502, 508,
510, 511, 514–516, 519,
521, 522, 525, 526

gain, 46, 50, 54, 72, 77, 92, 109, 137,
149, 151, 159, 196, 198,
240, 252, 254, 257, 270,
283, 293, 294, 317, 332,
349, 368, 371, 379, 381,
408, 423, 435, 439, 475,
512
game, 26, 47, 165, 199, 202, 203,
214, 228, 329, 341, 384,
391
gap, 69, 72, 101, 295, 316, 397, 449,
479
gathering, 155
generating, 42, 137, 169, 209, 262,
467, 508
generation, 11, 13, 21, 28, 40, 43, 48,
61, 63, 73, 82, 83, 97, 116,
128, 159–161, 185, 187,
200, 209, 211, 226, 228,
230, 236, 267, 268, 298,
312, 325, 341, 349, 350,
352, 353, 358, 361, 379,
384–386, 388, 390, 392,
403, 405–407, 416–419,
427, 430, 433, 437, 463,
466, 468, 476, 491–495
generator, 185
generosity, 399
genius, 82, 105, 107, 111, 434
George Orwell's, 314
Germany, 197
giant, 250
gift, 4
Glenn Greenwald, 56, 101, 219, 282

Glenn Greenwald - A, 64
Glenn Greenwald - An, 65
glimpse, 1, 8, 110, 434, 436
globalization, 450
globe, 189, 258, 385, 401, 514
glory, 112
goal, 10, 127, 157, 168, 198, 246,
359, 366, 367, 395, 398,
419, 460, 506
Goliath, 11, 30, 38, 39, 41, 64, 96,
267, 279, 347, 384, 426
good, 13, 107, 132, 281, 404, 406,
408, 415, 419, 485, 503,
514
governance, 242, 303
government, 3, 10–12, 15, 16, 23,
24, 28–39, 41–48, 54, 55,
57, 58, 60, 61, 65, 70, 73,
84, 86–89, 95, 96, 100,
101, 108, 109, 148, 162,
167, 179, 180, 190,
194–197, 199, 200, 211,
217–220, 226, 228, 237,
246, 248, 258, 263, 267,
269, 272, 275, 276, 279,
282, 284, 285, 291, 294,
298, 299, 302, 312, 314,
321, 335, 337, 342, 347,
361, 377, 384, 386, 389,
391, 404, 407, 418, 426,
427, 429, 431, 434, 436,
440, 448, 451, 456, 458,
460, 461, 463, 464, 472,
475, 483, 486, 487, 495,
498
grant, 382
graph, 457
gravity, 39
great, 5, 7, 81, 107, 208, 279, 321,

370, 460, 507, 522
ground, 12, 24, 61, 97, 159, 197, 247, 366, 400, 515
groundbreaking, 8, 16, 19, 25, 28, 30, 44, 49, 70, 80, 84, 85, 93, 105, 115, 119, 122, 155, 198, 212, 225, 292, 340, 343, 348, 350, 355, 358, 365, 373, 374, 384, 385, 388, 392, 399, 408, 413, 419, 421, 427, 430, 433, 483
groundwork, 20, 69, 97, 218, 226, 408
group, 52, 53, 107, 167, 198, 343, 398, 419
growth, 71, 72, 104, 109, 156, 181, 220, 287, 290, 319, 393, 397, 443, 477, 520
guarantee, 178, 200, 514
guidance, 2, 5, 9, 19–22, 28, 56, 63, 71, 94, 101, 167, 332, 348, 355, 367, 383, 401, 415, 420, 462
guide, 15, 28, 159, 185, 207, 230, 312, 349, 370, 371, 387, 395, 399, 416, 422, 476
guidepost, 222
guise, 54
guitar, 106

hacker, 16, 42, 158
hacking, 2–5, 7–9, 13, 14, 16, 29, 60–62, 85, 94, 154, 231, 267, 314, 381, 383, 489, 493
hacktivism, 60–62
hacktivist, 60, 62
Hacktivists, 61

Hal Finney, 100, 158
hand, 17, 50, 84, 87, 120, 131, 133, 137, 140, 146, 176, 197, 216, 223, 245, 262, 263, 268, 269, 275, 282, 286, 363, 389, 513, 516
handful, 446
handling, 178, 238, 251, 259, 288, 308, 462, 467, 511, 517
harassment, 165, 338, 454
hardware, 34, 94, 207, 210, 223, 366
harm, 87, 280, 281, 289, 321, 336, 512
harmonization, 289
harmony, 98, 400
harvesting, 250
hash, 21, 124, 126, 223, 271
hassle, 301
hate, 58, 246
haven, 282
head, 85, 169, 172, 349, 393
health, 241, 268, 280, 347, 477, 519
healthcare, 241, 257, 260, 272, 327, 328, 346, 347, 356, 372, 378, 458, 490, 499, 520
heart, 54, 98, 130, 136, 153, 176, 245, 408, 525
help, 20, 21, 42, 61, 64, 98, 140, 167, 184, 186, 209, 244, 245, 249, 250, 299, 306, 319, 327, 361, 370, 382, 400, 412, 420, 422, 423, 430, 445, 453, 454, 459, 460, 472, 481, 492, 512, 515
hero, 13, 32, 40, 46, 49, 63, 64, 86, 97, 267
hiking, 103, 106
hindrance, 264
hiring, 504, 512

Index 553

history, 5, 13, 33, 38, 56, 62, 64, 65, 93, 94, 97, 109, 119, 129, 225, 227, 240–242, 247, 254, 267, 335, 358, 379, 385, 426, 427, 435, 436, 443, 455
hold, 9, 29, 33, 57–59, 145, 280, 302, 308, 324, 331, 335, 343, 365, 372, 383, 424, 452, 468, 478, 496
holder, 135, 177
homage, 436
home, 8, 106, 315, 455, 508
honor, 64, 83, 268, 349, 387, 427, 428, 437, 465, 482, 492
hope, 48, 86, 292, 304, 313, 408, 409, 417, 438
horizon, 357
host, 116
household, 7, 295
human, 6, 11, 27, 28, 44, 50, 52, 57, 61, 62, 69, 72, 80, 83, 92, 95, 111, 117, 146, 166, 174, 175, 180, 181, 198, 227, 235, 270, 276, 277, 280, 289, 290, 298, 312, 323, 338, 344, 345, 347–349, 361, 372–375, 382, 385, 386, 388, 403, 404, 409, 410, 412, 413, 416, 429, 431–433, 442, 445, 457, 459, 462, 464, 466, 475, 479, 480, 483, 484, 486, 495, 496, 503, 525
humility, 112
humor, 103, 110–112
hunger, 111
hunt, 43, 53

hurdle, 215, 261
hygiene, 515

idea, 2, 5, 7, 9, 39, 57, 218, 253, 313, 323, 343, 389, 461, 472, 475
ideal, 9, 115, 176, 479
identification, 303, 327, 515, 518
identify, 21, 79, 89, 161, 186, 207, 240, 241, 253, 269, 342, 347, 364, 374, 382, 400, 459, 469, 503, 512, 518
identity, 132, 134, 135, 137, 177, 192, 216, 240, 243, 247, 257, 272, 281, 305, 309, 314, 328, 330, 338, 345, 363, 405, 443, 454–457, 477, 498, 503, 511, 512
ideology, 200
imagination, 391
imagine, 115
imbalance, 98, 243, 254, 260, 478
immutability, 144, 208
impact, 3, 6, 10, 19, 21, 24–26, 31, 32, 37, 40, 41, 46, 48, 49, 52, 55, 60, 62–66, 68, 71, 73–76, 82, 83, 85, 86, 90–92, 99, 102, 106, 109–112, 115–117, 119, 122, 129, 130, 152–156, 158, 161–163, 166, 167, 170, 174, 175, 179–181, 185, 188, 190–193, 199, 200, 205, 211–213, 216–219, 225–229, 234, 235, 241, 252–254, 260, 268, 279–281, 289, 291, 294, 304, 310, 311, 313, 314, 316, 322, 340, 344,

347–349, 352, 357, 358,
362, 365, 368, 369, 371,
373–376, 378, 379, 384,
385, 387, 390, 391,
394–398, 400, 401, 406,
408, 409, 414–416, 418,
420–422, 425–429,
431–433, 436–438, 441,
445, 451, 461–464, 466,
468, 469, 471, 476, 477,
479, 483, 484, 491, 492,
500, 502, 504, 513, 516
imperative, 197, 259, 272, 273, 287,
349, 410, 441, 445, 465
impersonation, 160, 338, 342
implementation, 11, 88, 89, 129,
137, 138, 140, 142, 162,
165, 194, 221, 264, 269,
272, 277, 296, 342, 379,
391, 448, 459, 460, 486,
492, 494, 506
importance, 2, 3, 6, 8, 10–12, 15, 18,
20, 21, 24, 25, 27, 31, 34,
38, 41–44, 46–48, 53, 56,
57, 60, 63–65, 69, 72–74,
77, 82–85, 89–92, 94, 97,
98, 101–103, 105–109,
111, 113–115, 117, 122,
130, 140, 152, 153, 155,
156, 158, 159, 161, 164,
165, 167–170, 187, 189,
199, 203, 211, 214, 216,
221, 222, 224, 226–229,
235, 239, 245, 246, 250,
251, 254, 257–259, 262,
267, 268, 272, 275, 277,
287, 288, 291–295, 297,
301, 304, 307, 310–315,
319, 322, 323, 331, 333,
335, 338–342, 346,
348–350, 356–360, 362,
371–375, 377–379, 382,
384, 385, 387–392,
398–400, 402–404,
406–411, 413–415,
418–420, 424–433,
452–454, 459–464, 466,
467, 469, 473–478, 480,
481, 484, 486, 489, 491,
496, 514, 520
impression, 405
imprint, 181
imprisonment, 165
improvement, 64, 109, 135, 161,
173, 181, 211, 212, 301,
304, 356, 371, 392, 393,
396, 414, 429
inception, 415
incident, 7, 34, 80, 241, 246, 251,
261, 263, 305, 347
inclusion, 50, 52, 82, 224, 291, 421,
432, 433
inconvenience, 122, 183, 364
increase, 41, 65, 73, 176, 206, 208,
299, 315, 369, 381, 486
independence, 298
India, 197
individual, 14, 18, 27, 28, 31–35,
38–42, 46–48, 50, 52, 54,
57, 58, 60–62, 70, 72, 73,
75, 76, 81–83, 85, 87, 89,
91, 92, 94, 97, 100, 101,
103–105, 107, 110–112,
117, 138, 146, 148, 149,
153, 163, 178, 180,
197–200, 202, 205, 213,
216, 224, 228, 235, 236,
240, 242, 246, 247, 249,

252, 254, 260, 265, 267–270, 275, 281, 282, 285, 286, 288–292, 298, 304, 309, 311–313, 315, 319, 321–323, 327, 329, 334, 335, 339, 344, 347, 349, 375, 376, 378, 382, 385, 386, 388, 389, 396, 399–401, 406, 408, 410, 413, 415, 417, 420, 424–427, 429–431, 436, 438, 440, 443, 445, 451–454, 462, 465, 467, 468, 476–479, 481, 485, 490–492, 496, 509, 516–518, 522, 526
individuality, 412, 525
industry, 2, 5, 10, 20, 23–25, 29, 35, 41, 43, 44, 47, 95, 101, 109, 116, 117, 160, 196, 223, 228, 241, 255, 268, 294, 300, 303, 304, 313, 318, 322, 364–367, 370, 371, 382, 385, 391, 395–397, 408, 414, 415, 419, 421, 424, 426, 445, 446, 461, 463, 484, 486, 491, 502, 510
infancy, 94, 376
influence, 13, 58, 60, 84, 85, 106, 109, 112, 116, 162, 163, 174, 179–181, 211–213, 216, 226, 227, 237, 239, 241–244, 247, 254, 263, 268, 291, 292, 294, 309–311, 313, 314, 319, 322, 323, 343, 344, 357, 358, 367, 376–380, 385, 386, 393, 394, 414, 418, 419, 426, 433, 439, 440, 442, 445–447, 451, 457, 461, 463, 465, 466, 475–477, 494, 516, 517, 523
infographic, 469
information, 5, 7, 9, 13–20, 23, 25–27, 29, 33, 34, 40, 44, 45, 47–50, 54, 56–58, 61–63, 65, 72, 74, 75, 77, 78, 80, 81, 84, 88, 91, 101, 111, 119, 121–124, 126, 127, 130, 133, 134, 136–138, 140, 142, 144, 146–149, 152, 153, 156, 157, 164, 166, 169, 170, 172, 175–178, 183, 188–191, 193–200, 204, 212, 216–218, 221, 223, 225, 228–231, 234, 237, 238, 240–254, 257–264, 267–270, 272, 273, 276, 277, 280–283, 285–288, 290, 292, 293, 296, 298–305, 307–309, 312, 315–317, 320, 322, 323, 327–329, 332, 333, 335–340, 343–346, 364, 368, 374, 375, 378, 381–386, 388, 389, 395, 400, 403–406, 409–411, 413, 415, 423, 424, 427–432, 436, 439–444, 446–457, 461, 462, 466–468, 472, 473, 475, 477, 480, 482, 486–488, 490, 491, 493, 496–499, 503, 508–511, 513–517, 520–525

infrastructure, 69, 79, 207, 209, 304, 367, 369, 402, 420, 434
infringe, 50, 166, 269, 321, 336, 490
infringement, 90, 180, 312, 410
ingenuity, 163, 434
initiative, 366, 377, 384, 386, 419, 423, 433, 435
innovation, 21, 29, 43, 44, 48, 49, 55, 58, 71, 76, 81, 84, 92, 102, 105, 107, 142, 145, 152, 157, 158, 164, 179, 181, 203, 211, 218, 220, 222, 233, 241, 244, 286, 290, 292, 310, 316, 317, 319, 320, 323, 335, 342, 355–358, 361, 365, 367, 371–373, 376, 379, 382, 383, 385, 386, 393, 395, 405, 407, 409, 410, 412–414, 419, 421, 422, 426, 429, 430, 435, 443, 445–447, 453, 458, 463, 466, 474, 481, 489–492, 495, 510, 511, 513–516, 522, 525
input, 43, 102, 124, 125, 414, 479, 518
insider, 65
insight, 242, 330, 500
inspiration, 21, 40, 60, 86, 92, 98, 105, 108, 268, 312, 335, 343, 344, 372, 375, 391, 408, 416, 419, 425, 428, 430, 434, 438, 466, 468
instance, 83, 122, 251, 281, 314, 346, 449, 468
instrument, 106
insurance, 241, 346
integration, 55, 101, 153, 160, 161, 163, 170, 174, 187, 207–209, 211, 214, 215, 222, 224, 233, 262, 287, 365, 393, 394, 486, 490
integrity, 17–19, 34, 57, 58, 108, 120, 122, 124, 126, 134, 136, 138, 139, 142, 144, 149, 160, 162, 165, 167, 174, 176–178, 193, 205, 207, 208, 221, 225, 226, 234, 247, 258, 277, 291, 323, 328, 431, 474, 476, 481, 488, 492
intellect, 108
intelligence, 27, 31, 35, 45, 50, 54, 93, 116, 152, 183, 193, 194, 207, 218, 255, 258, 261, 269, 279, 280, 282, 317, 321, 325, 336, 345, 362, 365, 377, 379, 394, 395, 410, 446, 447, 449, 467, 499, 503, 505, 514
intensity, 103
intent, 4
interaction, 227
intercept, 35, 226, 238, 249, 277
interception, 57, 78, 124, 126, 138, 152, 183, 190, 234, 257–259, 276, 281, 293, 294, 302, 364, 366, 452, 478
interconnectedness, 293, 440, 468
interest, 1, 20, 29, 70, 85, 86, 98, 108, 169, 280, 281, 306, 383, 475
interface, 71, 122, 138, 153, 154, 159, 161, 163, 168, 173, 185–187, 207, 214, 215, 222, 301, 303, 367, 391,

464
interference, 54, 344, 473
internet, 7, 26, 29, 42, 62, 65, 91, 94, 109, 174, 198, 199, 219, 254, 261, 262, 285, 293, 299, 305, 312, 335, 337, 345, 376, 377, 382, 402, 432, 442, 448, 449, 468, 481, 498, 506, 511, 520, 522
interoperability, 207, 208, 210–213, 216, 393, 460
interplay, 3, 337
intersection, 57, 367, 483
intersectionality, 479
intimacy, 514
intimidation, 338
introduction, 3, 33, 86, 109, 129, 130, 213, 228, 295, 342, 384, 498
introspection, 477
intrusion, 16, 23, 54, 108, 140, 269, 335, 344, 364, 375, 410, 439, 443, 464, 514
invasion, 25, 449, 515
investigation, 33, 267, 283, 434
investment, 240, 364
involvement, 63, 303, 342, 348, 366, 367, 377, 395, 461
issue, 62, 72, 81, 82, 87, 132, 146, 148, 159, 196, 197, 237, 245, 246, 250, 254, 263, 268, 269, 282, 283, 285, 299, 310, 315, 316, 336, 375, 379, 439, 444, 447, 465, 475, 485, 487, 488, 498, 513, 523, 525
iteration, 293

Jacob Appelbaum, 57, 61
jam, 107
James H. Dempsey, 480
jargon, 303
Jeramie Scott, 480
John Lennon's, 314
Jon Callas, 157
Jonathan Katz, 130
journalism, 108, 235
journalist, 24, 25, 101, 108, 167, 170, 186, 494
journey, 7–9, 16, 19, 21–24, 28, 29, 32, 38, 64, 85, 93, 99, 100, 102, 111, 114, 117, 123, 154, 155, 157, 158, 173, 220–222, 229, 233, 235, 267, 294, 295, 329, 357, 365, 383, 391, 392, 397, 408, 416, 417, 419–422, 434, 471, 489, 492
joy, 98, 103, 107
judgment, 25, 410, 477, 514
Julia Horwitz, 480
Julian Assange, 57, 61
jurisdiction, 377, 450, 454
justice, 60, 108, 294, 479, 480
justification, 449
Jérémie Zimmermann, 57, 61

key, 14, 16–19, 21, 25, 33, 36, 37, 39, 45, 50, 54, 58, 60, 66, 74, 78, 86, 95, 96, 100, 107, 113, 119, 120, 123, 124, 127, 128, 130–137, 139, 140, 142, 144, 149, 151–155, 157, 158, 160–162, 165, 167, 169, 172, 174, 176–178, 180, 182, 184–190, 194, 199,

201, 203, 205–215, 217, 222–225, 227, 229, 234, 235, 243, 245, 249, 251, 257, 264, 269, 270, 272, 285, 293, 294, 296, 300, 302, 308, 310, 320, 322, 329, 341, 343–345, 349, 351, 356, 362, 365, 366, 368, 373, 376, 381, 383, 388, 391, 395, 396, 398, 400, 401, 414, 416, 420, 434, 448, 450, 458, 464, 465, 467, 469, 470, 472, 475, 483, 487, 489, 492, 494, 495, 504, 507, 512, 514–516, 520, 525
keyring, 186
kid, 8, 16, 85, 93, 267, 383, 390
kind, 4, 454
knack, 4, 7, 9, 85, 104, 116
knowledge, 2, 4, 5, 7–10, 14–16, 20–22, 42, 43, 59, 73, 80, 89, 93, 94, 100, 102, 103, 106, 108, 111, 115, 125, 152, 156–158, 163, 165, 167, 168, 174, 207, 211, 221, 230, 231, 233, 238, 242, 252, 269, 270, 278, 296, 298, 302, 305, 309, 321, 329, 332–334, 337, 339, 340, 343, 348, 353, 356, 361, 365, 369, 371, 382, 385, 395, 396, 398, 399, 401, 407, 418, 432, 434, 435, 437, 449, 453, 454, 461, 465, 468, 474, 478, 481, 484, 488, 495, 496, 515, 525
Kogan, 250

label, 186
labor, 293
lack, 72, 243, 251–254, 278, 449, 450, 453, 459, 488, 499, 504, 512, 515, 523
landmark, 12, 53, 335, 429
landscape, 2, 5, 19, 25, 27, 28, 32, 37, 38, 42, 44, 46–49, 52, 54, 58, 63, 65, 68, 72, 75–77, 82, 84–86, 90, 91, 106, 110, 115, 135, 148, 149, 152, 154, 157, 162, 170, 178–181, 189, 193, 203, 205, 208, 211, 217, 219, 220, 226, 229, 230, 235, 241, 246, 247, 249, 253, 255, 265, 268, 273, 287, 292, 300, 302, 307, 310, 316, 317, 319, 327, 329, 331, 332, 334, 337, 340–343, 355, 361, 364, 367, 370, 373, 375, 376, 381–383, 394, 395, 397, 401, 403, 408, 409, 412, 413, 415, 416, 418, 420, 427, 430, 437, 445, 454, 458, 460, 466, 472, 473, 478, 486, 487, 489, 491, 493, 494, 496, 499, 512, 513, 522
language, 93, 161, 173, 174, 186, 490, 517
latency, 488
lattice, 143, 210, 223, 231, 271, 357
Laura, 108
Laura Poitras, 494
Laura Poitras, 494
Laura Thompson, 108
law, 6, 11, 18, 30, 33–35, 39, 42, 45,

46, 48, 50, 52, 56, 58, 59, 87, 96, 97, 166, 178, 181, 183, 196–199, 213, 221, 238, 246, 258, 259, 261–264, 277, 278, 282, 283, 285, 302, 321, 328, 331, 334, 335, 343, 376, 391, 399, 435, 440, 443, 448, 449, 451, 452, 459, 472, 475, 492, 515

lawsuit, 283

layer, 44, 96, 115, 119, 153, 182, 183, 188, 194, 196, 207, 224, 272, 303, 342, 459

lead, 3, 8, 27, 87, 89, 103, 132, 154, 159, 165, 243, 254, 272, 279, 283, 328, 343, 372, 399, 400, 442, 498, 503, 511, 512

leader, 91, 421

leadership, 362, 397

leak, 166

leakage, 178

learning, 1, 2, 4, 5, 9, 21, 28, 29, 43, 44, 94, 105, 122, 143, 173, 187, 192, 206, 207, 253, 269, 287, 327–329, 339, 345, 371, 372, 383, 420, 467, 481, 503, 522

ledger, 144

legacy, 13, 16, 24, 25, 27, 34, 35, 38, 40, 41, 46, 48, 55, 60–64, 74, 76, 82, 84, 86, 90–92, 102, 116, 157, 181, 200, 213, 214, 216, 226, 227, 230, 235, 236, 250, 268, 292, 312, 313, 322, 343, 348–350, 355, 358, 373, 375, 376, 378, 384–387, 390–392, 403, 406, 409, 415, 416, 419, 422, 425–427, 430, 432, 433, 436–438, 442, 461, 463–466, 470, 471, 476, 480, 484, 486, 492, 497

legality, 220

legend, 436, 438

legislation, 64, 66, 73, 83, 197, 200, 217, 246, 288, 310, 311, 331, 342, 344, 361, 401, 423, 426, 437, 440, 462, 467, 476, 487, 489, 494, 495, 498

legitimacy, 205, 258

length, 120, 131, 132, 136

lens, 285

lesson, 220–222, 397, 414, 435

level, 9, 10, 50, 60, 79, 98, 120, 131, 137, 138, 140, 152, 201, 212, 215, 223, 226, 238, 247, 258, 270, 271, 298, 303, 333, 343, 345, 365, 369, 375, 478, 483, 514

leverage, 21, 70, 116, 120, 194, 223, 254, 313, 315, 359, 372, 400, 446

liberty, 313

lie, 287, 332, 362, 469, 486, 495

life, 2, 6, 7, 9–12, 43, 48, 49, 56, 82, 98, 99, 103–105, 107, 112, 115, 175, 188, 200, 217, 219, 228, 230, 232, 286, 296, 297, 347, 398, 400, 420, 429, 432, 433, 436, 437, 443, 454, 480, 511

lifecycle, 195, 287, 304

lifeline, 44, 166, 431, 462

lifestyle, 112, 241

light, 40, 56, 57, 61, 76, 101, 117, 238, 249, 251, 254, 262, 263, 279, 314, 342, 349, 379, 391, 405, 426, 434, 439, 442, 457, 465, 494
limit, 11, 58, 208, 246, 299, 327, 338, 440, 455
limitation, 128, 177, 214
linchpin, 120
line, 93, 208, 269, 286, 293, 439, 525
link, 523
Linux, 160
literacy, 59, 106, 148, 231, 288, 305, 332, 402, 444, 463, 478, 518, 522
literature, 313–316
lobby, 246, 440, 466
lobbying, 200, 310, 357
localization, 157, 161, 163, 173, 174
location, 43, 247, 254, 263, 361, 374, 443, 511, 520
logarithm, 368, 486
logic, 9
longevity, 163
look, 62, 105, 123, 125, 185, 241, 310, 318, 349, 352, 359, 415, 421, 426, 427, 430, 461, 494
loop, 162
loss, 65, 87, 242, 261, 272, 277, 314, 387, 424, 443, 456, 512
Louis Brandeis, 335
love, 1, 7, 28, 106, 107, 293
loyalty, 395, 396, 498
luxury, 69, 95, 230, 296, 333, 344, 388, 455, 483, 496, 517

machine, 122, 143, 207, 269, 287, 327, 328, 345, 467, 481, 503, 522
machinery, 506
mailing, 163, 165
mainstream, 55, 63, 101, 112, 168, 220, 267, 284, 293–295, 423, 464
maintenance, 71
making, 8, 10, 18, 25, 29, 45, 50, 55, 57, 59, 85, 87, 98–100, 104, 111, 112, 120, 123, 131, 140, 142, 155, 157–159, 161–163, 169, 173, 176, 179, 180, 183, 186, 189, 190, 193, 196, 199, 207, 209, 212, 213, 215, 216, 220, 224, 226, 230–232, 249, 252, 254, 261, 264, 270, 276, 280, 282, 289, 293, 301, 303, 309, 314, 317, 318, 337, 342, 345, 357, 362, 364, 367, 370, 373, 380, 383–385, 392–395, 413, 450, 455, 459, 471, 473, 477, 488, 499, 502, 503, 506, 512, 518, 523
malware, 154, 337, 454, 455
man, 8, 103, 110, 125, 132, 177, 355, 438
management, 19, 132, 133, 135, 137, 142, 154, 159–161, 173, 174, 177, 186, 187, 194, 196, 207–209, 211, 224, 272, 341, 343, 344, 363, 434, 488
managing, 133, 177, 209
manipulation, 26, 58, 124, 126, 170, 243, 247, 263, 338, 344,

Index 561

443, 446, 451, 514
manner, 297, 345, 363, 435, 509
Manning, 280
mantle, 63, 385, 416, 419, 495
Maria, 108
Maria Sanchez, 108
Mark, 108
mark, 14, 16, 49, 84, 90, 116, 157,
    229, 236, 298, 343, 367,
    375, 409, 416, 466
Mark Sullivan, 108
market, 316–318, 395, 442, 456,
    513
marketing, 102, 169, 170, 240
mass, 23, 26, 38, 74, 88, 92, 101,
    218, 228, 267, 268, 273,
    275, 276, 279, 283, 285,
    286, 290–292, 299, 310,
    321, 322, 343, 345, 384,
    408, 460, 480, 483, 486
master, 296, 464
mastermind, 152
match, 9
material, 112, 435
math, 271
mathematician, 108
matter, 20, 53, 55, 375, 377, 437,
    445
meal, 103
meaning, 197, 215, 285
means, 11, 17, 25, 26, 43, 48, 54, 98,
    126, 131, 143, 146, 194,
    195, 219, 262, 277, 293,
    302, 304, 314, 323, 333,
    350, 353, 359, 368, 375,
    389, 405, 443, 456, 474,
    475, 480, 485, 492, 493,
    498, 511, 525
measure, 55

mechanism, 34, 137
media, 27, 58, 61, 74, 101, 146, 148,
    168, 169, 175, 238,
    240–242, 246–254, 263,
    264, 286, 299, 305, 314,
    323, 338, 347, 403, 440,
    442, 450, 451, 454–457,
    467, 468, 481, 493, 498,
    499, 511, 514, 517, 522,
    523
meeting, 71, 300
melody, 106
member, 400, 449
membership, 343
memoir, 57
memory, 428, 487
mentor, 348, 421
mentorship, 5, 15, 20–22, 55, 86,
    106, 348, 357, 383, 386,
    408, 420, 421
message, 17, 21, 33, 41, 47, 73, 122,
    124, 126–128, 131–134,
    167, 168, 182, 186, 188,
    190, 194, 199, 205, 212,
    216, 249, 252, 297, 302,
    313, 342, 360, 461, 495,
    496
messaging, 56, 121, 126, 153, 156,
    168, 189, 197, 207, 209,
    213–215, 249, 252, 259,
    281, 294, 299, 300, 302,
    320, 359, 362, 366, 373,
    394, 423, 434, 441, 468,
    475, 488, 517
metadata, 190, 210, 279, 360
method, 17, 23, 33, 124, 128, 165,
    194, 200, 215, 283, 443
middle, 11, 125, 132, 177, 197, 238,
    248

migration, 223
milestone, 39
million, 272
mind, 1, 7, 94, 104, 105, 110, 252, 298, 355, 366, 422, 434
mindful, 244, 382, 383, 411, 454, 456, 467
mindfulness, 382
mindset, 226, 388, 397, 413, 414, 491
minimization, 286, 288, 327, 467, 525
mining, 381
mirror, 107, 316
mischief, 9
misconception, 73, 112, 516
mishandling, 187
misinformation, 58, 315
mission, 38, 62, 64, 70, 74, 75, 95, 112, 114, 267, 296, 298, 311, 313, 367
misuse, 45, 65, 87, 148, 208, 240, 242, 245, 246, 250, 257, 260, 262, 269, 276, 286, 287, 289, 290, 305, 308, 334, 410, 424, 439, 443, 447, 452, 473, 481, 484, 498, 509, 511, 513–515, 517, 524
mix, 46
mobilization, 58, 375
model, 28, 71, 98, 135, 214, 241, 242, 263, 393, 414, 418, 455, 461
moment, 6, 11, 35, 38, 49, 96, 116, 232, 335, 391, 426, 436, 445, 446
momentum, 92, 115, 226, 307, 349
Monero, 423

monetization, 254, 410, 498
money, 258
monitoring, 47, 79, 87, 242, 269, 273, 279, 345, 356, 442, 458
monopoly, 33
motif, 107
motion, 228, 282
motivation, 60
mouse, 202, 203
move, 23, 33, 85, 115, 158, 168, 197, 222, 260, 299, 370, 430, 433, 437, 460, 463, 489, 492, 495, 498, 508
movement, 23, 25, 31, 32, 41, 45, 49, 60, 65–68, 82, 83, 90, 92, 97, 110, 163, 175, 200, 218, 220, 226, 289, 302, 311, 348, 349, 384, 388, 389, 391, 401–403, 408, 414, 415, 437, 463, 471
movie, 314
Moxie Marlinspike, 394
multimedia, 435
multivariate, 143, 210, 271
music, 106, 107, 313–316

name, 7, 49, 97, 134, 240, 245, 248, 295, 389, 410, 436, 454, 498
narrative, 66, 112, 389, 407, 478, 486
nation, 50, 193
nature, 1, 3, 4, 7, 8, 94, 103, 104, 106, 111, 112, 123, 158, 162, 165, 168, 194, 208, 212, 220, 221, 225, 235, 261, 281, 285, 291, 339, 342, 377, 392, 394, 398,

Index 563

407, 410, 414, 423, 429, 442, 449, 451, 488, 516
Neal Stephenson, 109
necessity, 87, 90, 155, 294, 388, 460, 496
need, 5, 8, 12, 15, 17, 21, 23, 26, 28, 29, 39, 42, 44, 54–56, 62, 71, 73, 75–78, 81, 85–88, 90, 101, 105, 113, 115, 121, 123, 124, 127, 136, 138, 142, 143, 148, 149, 152, 153, 156, 157, 160, 164–169, 176, 179–181, 186, 187, 189, 193–195, 198, 203, 207–209, 211–214, 220–223, 225, 228–232, 241, 242, 245, 246, 249, 251–253, 258, 260–262, 267, 269, 270, 272, 273, 276, 280, 281, 286, 288, 290, 291, 293, 294, 296, 298, 303, 305, 307, 311–316, 321, 324, 327, 329, 332, 335–337, 339, 342, 343, 349, 356–360, 362, 363, 365–367, 374, 376, 384, 387, 388, 390, 394, 395, 400–402, 405, 406, 413, 416, 424, 430, 431, 439, 440, 444, 446–448, 450, 453, 454, 457, 458, 462, 465, 472, 481, 486, 489, 493, 495–497, 507, 508, 511, 514, 516, 518, 520
network, 2, 14, 17, 21, 70, 73, 75, 100, 104, 109, 113, 114, 177, 214, 276, 364, 371, 420, 459, 468, 506

New Jersey, 1, 3
newfound, 2, 10, 14, 112, 391
news, 23, 44, 130, 305, 382, 446
niche, 170, 187, 293, 295, 318, 403
Niels Ferguson, 129, 400
Nigel Marsh, 99
Nina, 455
noise, 106, 287, 309, 327, 523
non, 42, 64, 74, 153, 174, 187, 189, 194, 209, 224, 227, 295, 314, 360, 374, 449, 459, 464, 481
nonprofit, 373, 399
norm, 436
North Africa, 61
note, 190, 277
notice, 12, 95, 347
notification, 513
notion, 335, 343, 388–390, 393, 413
novel, 109, 163, 215, 344, 362, 481
novice, 159, 168
number, 120, 128, 131, 176, 225, 240, 300, 385, 461

obscurity, 267
observation, 106, 332
obstacle, 434, 488, 517
obtain, 33, 131, 308, 336, 448, 512, 525
occasion, 229
occurrence, 298
ocean, 106
off, 12, 38, 85, 128, 146, 148, 263, 270, 286, 446
offer, 27, 70, 116, 128, 148, 189, 207, 210, 215, 216, 234, 238, 260, 263, 271, 298, 299, 309, 310, 318, 328,

334, 434–436, 444, 474, 525
offering, 71, 109, 122, 175, 299, 301, 303, 308, 310, 316, 319, 343, 393, 397
official, 154
Oliver Stone, 314
omnipresence, 181
on, 1–6, 8–12, 14–16, 18–33, 35, 37–43, 46, 48, 49, 52–66, 68, 69, 73, 75, 76, 79, 80, 83–86, 89–92, 96–99, 101, 103–106, 108–113, 115–117, 119, 120, 123, 125–128, 130, 131, 137, 140, 143, 144, 152–158, 160–163, 165–170, 172–176, 178–183, 185, 186, 188, 190–194, 196–200, 203, 205, 206, 209, 211–219, 223–227, 229–232, 234–238, 240–243, 245–247, 250–254, 258, 260, 262–264, 268–271, 273, 275, 276, 278–281, 283, 285, 287, 288, 290, 292–294, 296, 298, 299, 301, 302, 304, 305, 307–316, 321, 322, 327–336, 338, 340–345, 347–349, 352, 355–371, 373–380, 382, 384–387, 389, 390, 392–395, 398, 400–403, 405, 406, 408, 410, 415, 416, 418–421, 423–429, 431–434, 436–446, 454–464, 466–469, 472, 474–480, 482–486, 488–491, 493–495, 497, 498, 503, 504, 512, 513, 515, 516, 518, 520, 522, 523, 525
one, 1, 4, 8, 10, 13, 15, 24, 31, 41, 42, 46, 48, 49, 52, 55, 87, 92, 93, 96, 98, 110, 113, 115, 125, 131, 140, 146, 157, 173, 176, 179, 196–198, 213, 216, 239, 245, 250, 258, 268, 272, 282, 283, 286, 302, 312–314, 341, 342, 355, 358–360, 365, 366, 368, 374, 385, 392, 416, 421, 427, 434, 436–438, 443, 453, 455–457, 461, 468, 469, 479, 493, 511, 513, 514, 516
online, 12–14, 17, 18, 20, 27, 34, 42, 56, 57, 61, 62, 64–66, 69, 70, 75–80, 83–87, 91, 106, 121, 123, 130, 137, 146, 147, 165, 168, 169, 173, 189, 199, 217, 221, 222, 230, 237, 241, 242, 244–247, 249, 252–254, 257–259, 263, 269, 277, 279, 286, 288, 293–295, 298, 299, 301, 305, 306, 309, 316, 317, 319, 320, 323, 330, 333, 334, 337–339, 344, 347, 349, 359, 361, 362, 373–376, 382, 384, 386, 388, 399, 402, 410, 411, 421, 424, 435, 439, 441, 443, 449–451, 453–456, 463, 467–469, 493, 498, 509,

514, 516, 518, 520, 521
opacity, 523
openness, 57, 157, 163, 394, 407
operating, 160, 163, 212, 301, 373, 469
opinion, 42, 46, 55, 74, 96, 110, 241, 243, 244, 252, 253, 295, 310, 313, 342, 358, 440, 446, 518
opponent, 38, 475
opportunity, 9, 20, 29, 107, 113, 296, 419, 420, 435, 490
opposition, 30, 31, 36, 39, 45, 49, 166, 167, 292, 342, 391, 429, 464
optimization, 161
option, 49, 215, 262, 330
orchestra, 106
order, 16, 87, 167, 197, 198, 209, 237, 283, 350, 376, 448, 480
organization, 75, 281, 373, 468
organizing, 61, 107, 296
other, 17, 23, 27, 42, 43, 45, 48, 50, 52, 54, 82, 87, 91, 100, 108, 113, 120, 128, 131, 133, 137, 140, 146, 147, 156, 157, 174, 176, 177, 179, 189, 190, 194, 195, 197, 198, 200, 211–214, 216, 219, 223, 229, 234, 238, 240, 241, 243, 245, 246, 249, 252, 258, 260, 262, 263, 269, 275, 276, 279, 282, 286, 293, 295, 304, 307, 312, 314, 319, 324, 334, 335, 341–343, 345, 361, 363, 366, 371, 374, 379, 387, 393, 396, 403, 421, 426, 429, 446, 450, 454, 459, 465, 472, 503, 506, 509, 511–513
out, 2, 4, 5, 8, 9, 11, 15, 20, 22, 39, 41, 42, 72, 73, 94, 99, 100, 105, 143, 155, 157, 170, 196, 267, 277, 279, 293, 306, 318, 366, 373, 386, 391, 398, 399, 414, 421, 431, 449, 525
outbox, 186
outdoors, 107
outdoorsman, 103
outlet, 106
outline, 303, 336, 514
outlook, 104
output, 124, 125, 459
outreach, 298
outset, 288, 308
outsourcing, 143
overexposure, 493
overhead, 140, 142, 160, 161
overreach, 32, 48, 60, 84, 101, 218, 285, 321, 386
oversight, 88, 251, 269, 276, 283, 303, 310, 448, 450, 478
owner, 131, 133, 134, 188
ownership, 132, 238, 254, 328, 414, 463, 493, 506, 513

pace, 55, 231, 261, 264, 270, 292, 331, 376, 377, 449, 466, 484, 514, 522
package, 122, 123, 152, 429
pair, 120, 127, 130, 131, 133, 160, 167, 176, 185, 188, 194, 212
panel, 64, 380
paradigm, 175, 386, 490

parallel, 368
parallelism, 271
parameter, 127
Parmy Olson, 62
part, 34, 42, 106, 116, 156, 168, 209, 221, 222, 232, 233, 235, 247, 269, 332, 377, 394, 411, 421, 464, 466, 511
participant, 107
participation, 392, 476, 522
partner, 70, 205, 232, 449
partnership, 100, 101, 158, 366, 406
party, 125, 145, 175, 228, 251, 303, 341, 421, 457, 459, 460, 474, 492, 521, 525
passing, 85
passion, 2–5, 7–11, 13, 14, 16, 19, 20, 23, 24, 28, 29, 42, 43, 60, 84, 85, 94, 98, 100, 104, 106, 108, 109, 111, 112, 267, 293, 297, 348, 353, 358, 377, 383, 398, 419, 436, 437
passphrase, 186, 187
password, 126, 299, 488
past, 173, 286, 421
path, 2, 4, 8, 29, 94, 100, 249
patient, 347, 458
pattern, 107, 503
payment, 151
peace, 106, 298, 366
peer, 194, 215, 220, 225, 235, 371, 382, 392, 395, 407, 481, 490
penchant, 7
people, 12, 23, 38, 41, 44, 47–49, 97, 114, 146, 167, 209, 225, 228, 240, 241, 253, 263, 294–296, 298, 299, 305, 311, 374, 386, 388, 398, 429, 437, 454, 457, 477, 478, 509, 516, 518
perception, 45, 169, 230, 291, 294, 295, 313, 314, 388–390, 407, 413, 426, 473, 516–519
perfection, 111
performance, 106, 129, 160, 161, 224, 369, 486, 488, 503
period, 32, 61, 86, 134, 267
permutation, 120
persecution, 25, 217, 312, 431, 462
perseverance, 13, 391, 419
persistence, 112
person, 13, 24, 30, 41, 48, 103, 113, 131, 157, 343, 416, 427, 437, 461
personality, 104, 107, 110, 112, 250, 253, 437
perspective, 3, 5, 15, 25, 99, 105, 107, 108, 196, 285, 374, 479
pervasiveness, 269, 451, 478
phase, 85, 224
phenomenon, 368
Phil, 3–16, 19–21, 28, 38–41, 49, 82–85, 90–92, 94–96, 98, 103–117, 436, 437, 492
Phil Dunkelberger, 101
Phil Zimmerman, 94
Phil Zimmermann, 1, 3, 6, 8, 13–16, 21, 23–25, 28, 32, 38–41, 43, 46, 49, 53, 57, 58, 62–64, 68, 69, 75, 80, 82, 84, 85, 90, 91, 93, 95–100, 103–107, 110–112, 115, 116, 119, 123, 126, 152, 154, 155,

157, 159, 167, 170, 172,
179, 196, 198, 199, 211,
216, 221, 228, 229, 236,
237, 255, 290, 291, 294,
296, 310, 322, 332, 337,
339, 350, 355, 359, 365,
367, 370, 373, 375, 376,
386, 387, 392, 395–400,
407, 413, 419, 422,
427–429, 431, 436–438,
442, 463, 466, 468, 470,
477, 483, 486, 492, 526
Phil Zimmermann's, 6–8, 16, 18,
19, 21, 25, 27, 35, 39–41,
44, 49, 59, 62–64, 72, 74,
76, 82–86, 90–93, 95–98,
102, 105, 107–112,
114–117, 122, 123, 175,
214, 225, 236, 239, 267,
268, 290, 292, 293, 298,
313, 322, 329, 332, 335,
340, 343, 344, 348, 350,
352, 353, 357–359, 362,
372–376, 378, 379,
384–387, 390, 392,
395–397, 401, 403, 404,
406–409, 413–416, 418,
419, 423, 425, 427, 429,
430, 433, 436–438, 442,
460–463, 465, 466, 471,
476, 480, 482, 484, 493,
496
philanthropic, 69, 82, 84, 85, 106,
115, 116, 268, 349, 357,
373–376
philanthropist, 84–86, 91, 311, 384
philanthropy, 69, 72, 76, 82–85,
106, 107, 357, 373–376
philosophy, 60, 104, 342, 344, 371,
372
phishing, 288, 337, 339, 411, 454
phone, 240, 365, 454
physics, 223
piece, 357, 370
pillar, 287, 408
pioneer, 16, 28, 94, 102, 105, 107,
427, 442, 480
place, 11, 61, 98, 226, 227, 280, 358,
362, 385, 427, 493, 513,
525
plaintext, 125, 140, 149, 270
plan, 58, 513
platform, 102, 105, 113, 163, 186,
199, 213, 215, 296, 301,
302, 316, 328, 366, 436,
466, 489, 511
play, 28, 58, 63, 64, 70–72, 88, 100,
115, 128, 132, 136, 140,
142, 198, 225, 229, 231,
242, 244, 246, 248, 249,
259, 260, 267, 279, 281,
288, 304, 307, 309, 317,
321, 334, 336, 355, 382,
401, 402, 411, 424, 430,
437, 440, 444, 445,
447–450, 454, 459, 478,
480, 488, 489, 491–493,
499, 506, 509, 515, 518,
522, 523
player, 106, 304
playing, 10, 60, 333, 483
point, 12, 31, 32, 48, 196, 225, 228,
246, 294, 452
polarization, 243
policy, 38, 42, 66, 68, 74, 91, 115,
116, 180, 181, 198, 200,
229, 235, 279, 307,
309–311, 313, 314, 319,

342, 343, 355, 358,
    376–380, 386, 401, 406,
    421, 426, 433, 440, 462,
    471, 473, 475–477, 481,
    482, 494, 521, 522
policymaker, 198
policymaking, 460
pool, 71, 162, 382
popularity, 33, 44, 122, 156, 169,
    173, 199, 215, 225, 252,
    258, 298–302, 384, 394,
    423, 441, 464
population, 54, 167, 293
portrayal, 313, 314
position, 44, 86, 169, 198, 218, 485
possession, 363
post, 18, 19, 28, 115, 135, 143, 145,
    210, 223, 224, 271, 273,
    299, 356, 357, 369, 370,
    439, 442, 458, 466, 473,
    486, 487, 489–492, 514
poster, 469
posture, 364, 459
potential, 2, 4–7, 10, 14, 17, 23, 25,
    26, 28, 29, 31, 42, 45, 47,
    52, 54–56, 58–62, 64, 65,
    72, 77, 84, 85, 87–90, 94,
    95, 110, 111, 115, 116,
    119, 130, 132, 143, 146,
    148, 153, 156, 169, 170,
    173, 177, 195–198, 200,
    203–205, 207, 208, 218,
    221, 223, 230, 231, 233,
    240, 241, 243–246,
    250–254, 262–264, 269,
    271, 273, 280, 281, 283,
    285, 287–290, 300, 303,
    305, 311, 314, 315, 318,
    320, 321, 323, 325, 328,
    334–338, 342, 343, 345,
    347, 349, 356–358, 360,
    362–365, 367, 368, 370,
    379, 383, 384, 388, 400,
    410, 421, 424, 429, 439,
    441, 443, 449, 450,
    452–456, 458, 459, 461,
    465, 467–469, 472, 473,
    475, 476, 480, 483, 484,
    486, 489, 490, 492, 498,
    499, 503, 504, 507,
    513–515, 517, 518, 520,
    522
power, 4, 5, 9–11, 13, 14, 21, 23–25,
    27, 29, 31, 32, 39–42, 47,
    48, 52, 54, 57–61, 63, 72,
    74, 85–87, 89, 92, 94, 96,
    97, 100, 103, 107, 114,
    115, 117, 143, 154, 155,
    157, 162, 166, 167, 176,
    177, 183, 195, 220, 221,
    229, 231, 237, 239–243,
    245, 246, 254, 260, 267,
    275, 276, 280, 283, 285,
    290, 291, 295, 313, 314,
    321, 328, 334, 335, 341,
    348, 355–358, 360, 361,
    367, 372, 373, 378, 385,
    387, 389, 391, 392,
    396–399, 404–406, 410,
    413, 414, 416–418, 423,
    427, 429, 431, 438, 440,
    441, 446, 451, 458, 462,
    468, 473, 477, 478, 481,
    483, 486, 487, 489, 496,
    514, 518, 523
practicality, 195
practice, 9, 78, 90, 127, 162, 176,
    220, 225, 250, 254, 273,

Index   569

389, 451
precedent, 32, 283, 423, 430, 468
prediction, 331
premium, 71, 241
presence, 143, 186, 338
present, 98, 238, 271, 310, 314, 336,
    362, 367, 413, 423, 440,
    445, 450, 461, 479
presentation, 53, 64
preservation, 27, 68, 88, 181, 270,
    287, 310, 342, 388, 433,
    477, 481, 482, 496
press, 40, 108, 170, 276, 294, 405,
    432
pressure, 113, 238, 248, 263, 424,
    426
prevalence, 253, 317, 403
prevention, 87, 268, 276
prey, 338
price, 388, 443, 514
principle, 57, 302, 336, 376, 378,
    392, 468, 480, 494, 523,
    525
priority, 334, 341, 455, 464, 526
privacy, 2–6, 8, 10–19, 21, 23–35,
    37–60, 62–77, 80–92,
    94–97, 100–105,
    107–117, 122–124, 127,
    130, 136, 138–140,
    142–149, 152–158,
    161–164, 166–170,
    172–175, 178–181, 183,
    187, 189–191, 193,
    195–201, 204–206,
    208–222, 224–265,
    267–270, 273, 275–325,
    327–353, 355–368,
    370–499, 502–511,
    513–526

privatization, 439–441
privilege, 29, 331, 335, 409, 456,
    483, 496
problem, 4, 9, 21, 28, 43, 75, 105,
    108, 186, 225, 368, 434,
    486, 503, 523
process, 10, 50, 107, 119, 127, 130,
    135, 153, 159, 160, 168,
    177, 185–187, 194, 207,
    209, 215, 217, 230, 238,
    249, 253, 257, 269, 270,
    276, 281, 282, 304, 308,
    341, 363, 368, 372, 392,
    420, 434, 448, 451, 472,
    499, 503, 506, 518
processing, 142, 143, 183, 261, 336,
    458, 488, 490, 493, 511,
    515, 520, 523
product, 128, 154, 155, 157, 262,
    304, 366, 396, 455, 456
productivity, 99, 146
profession, 98
professional, 99, 103, 109, 110, 193,
    280, 281, 397
professor, 237
profile, 30, 140, 240, 246, 247, 263,
    294, 300, 359, 456, 473,
    498, 517
profiling, 89, 247, 253, 269, 442, 465
profit, 69, 70, 242, 243, 247, 252,
    254, 263, 324, 415, 424,
    440, 443, 449–451, 457,
    464, 481, 525
program, 35–37, 57, 162, 217, 240,
    293, 384, 386, 405,
    419–421
programmer, 5, 13, 14, 16, 21, 28,
    33, 64, 85, 93, 94, 97, 98,
    100, 102, 103, 105,

107–112, 115, 126, 157, 198, 228, 296, 310, 322, 359, 370, 383, 395, 398, 427, 436, 470
programming, 2, 4, 5, 7, 20, 22, 29, 82, 85, 94, 97, 98, 100, 108, 111, 370–373, 383, 418
progress, 40, 371, 400, 421, 478, 491, 510, 514, 517
project, 36, 64, 71, 72, 163, 359, 360, 365, 370, 400, 429
proliferation, 27, 58, 164, 175, 222, 268, 286, 345, 385, 399, 401, 448, 455, 466, 481, 488, 490, 514, 522
prominence, 224, 246, 294, 443
promise, 145, 208, 343, 383, 460, 489
promotion, 63, 82, 373, 376, 394, 402
proof, 134, 194, 210, 360, 365, 397
proofing, 357
propaganda, 58
property, 218, 368, 376, 487
proponent, 69
proportionality, 87
proposal, 34, 35, 39, 41, 58, 96, 377, 379, 403, 464
prosecution, 31, 45
protection, 12, 18, 24, 65, 68, 74, 75, 81, 82, 88, 90, 100, 108, 109, 122, 123, 146, 164, 170, 180, 181, 188, 198, 199, 208, 211, 234, 240–242, 244–246, 252, 253, 255, 256, 260, 262, 269–272, 277, 280, 286, 288, 289, 292, 298, 300, 301, 305, 308, 310, 322, 336, 339, 343, 344, 355, 365, 376–378, 382, 390, 394, 402, 403, 407, 411, 421, 423, 429–431, 441, 443, 445, 448, 449, 452, 457, 464, 481, 487, 490, 491, 493–495, 498, 506, 509, 510, 514, 522, 524, 525
protocol, 309, 366, 368, 394
prototype, 123, 154, 155, 157
provider, 143
provision, 449
prowess, 10, 14, 60
pseudonymity, 330
pseudorandom, 120
psychology, 338, 400
public, 3, 12, 17–19, 23, 27, 30, 31, 33, 39, 42, 44–48, 54, 56–59, 74, 82, 85–91, 96, 97, 101, 102, 110, 113, 120, 123, 124, 127, 128, 130–134, 152–154, 160, 162, 163, 169, 170, 173, 174, 176–184, 186–190, 194, 197–199, 205, 212–214, 217, 224, 225, 228, 234, 241, 243, 244, 246, 248, 249, 252, 253, 261, 267–269, 273, 275, 276, 279–281, 286, 293–295, 297, 305, 307, 308, 310–315, 321, 328, 329, 338, 341, 342, 365, 372, 374, 375, 377, 379, 384, 387–389, 391, 395, 397–400, 403, 405–407, 413, 420, 426, 428, 429,

434, 440, 441, 446, 447,
449, 451, 454, 461,
464–467, 469, 472, 478,
479, 484, 496, 499,
516–519
punishment, 7
purchase, 18, 254, 258
purchasing, 241, 455
purpose, 20, 60, 71, 131, 196, 259,
288, 303, 323, 472, 525
pursuit, 4, 7, 21, 49, 52, 104, 108,
157, 224, 291, 292, 342,
358, 367, 408, 416, 417,
422, 430, 461, 479
push, 2, 5, 8, 9, 22, 49, 53, 54, 85,
93, 94, 108, 163, 248, 261,
294, 320, 344, 355, 372,
375, 377, 384, 393, 400,
427, 472, 494
pushback, 117

quality, 98, 301
quantum, 17–19, 54, 55, 115, 135,
143, 145, 178, 181, 183,
207, 208, 210, 211, 223,
224, 229, 231, 233, 271,
273, 355–357, 360, 362,
363, 367–370, 441, 458,
473, 474, 486, 487, 489,
492, 522
qubit, 368
query, 514
quest, 4, 152, 496
question, 1, 5, 7, 10, 20, 58, 64, 85,
111, 282, 285, 341, 409,
437, 496, 513
quiz, 250
quo, 1, 5, 7, 9, 10, 20, 23, 24, 32, 60,
94, 117, 229, 250, 335,
384, 418, 427, 433, 441,
477, 496

race, 140, 179, 323, 356, 381–383,
394
rally, 38, 47, 374, 414
rallying, 42, 60, 386
randomness, 309
range, 80, 103–105, 162, 214, 222,
312, 317, 318, 361, 362,
373, 376, 386, 458, 493,
496, 506, 521
ransom, 151
rate, 55, 302
Ray Bradbury's, 314
reach, 56, 73, 83, 102, 159, 167, 169,
173, 254, 302, 311, 365,
374, 403, 431, 447, 464
reader, 104
reality, 4, 62, 230, 277, 289, 322,
370, 447, 460, 465, 479
realization, 29, 85, 293, 323, 386
realm, 4, 13, 19, 26, 50, 72, 83, 85,
93, 103, 106, 107, 122,
170, 172, 180, 226, 229,
234, 244, 270, 277, 279,
294, 298, 323, 344, 349,
358, 375, 377, 386, 388,
396, 398, 408, 420, 426,
429, 431, 436, 440, 456,
462, 473, 493, 516
reasoning, 434
reassessment, 337
reassurance, 298
rebellion, 7
receiver, 17, 124, 127, 225
recipient, 18, 19, 124, 127, 128, 131,
132, 134, 152, 153, 176,
177, 182, 186, 188–190,

197, 212, 216, 217, 224,
231, 249, 252, 270, 302,
342, 360, 405, 443, 461
recognition, 49, 72, 74, 87, 89, 92,
105, 112–114, 148, 156,
261, 286, 335, 336, 345,
375, 377, 378, 394, 421,
446, 466, 469, 475, 490,
503, 515, 518
recommendation, 198, 523
record, 347
recording, 328
recovery, 209
redefinition, 285, 286, 292
reevaluation, 305
referendum, 250
refinement, 161, 224
refuge, 322
refusal, 4, 419, 426
regime, 24, 314
region, 52, 401, 449
regulation, 6, 58, 231, 253, 276, 288,
290, 325, 426, 445, 491,
492, 513, 518, 524
reidentification, 309
reign, 245
rejection, 74
relation, 490, 514
relationship, 37, 49, 65, 396, 457
release, 6, 10, 24, 53, 95, 151, 226,
314, 414
relevance, 154, 172, 181, 193, 211,
226, 408, 454, 462, 463
reliability, 156, 173, 221, 429
reliance, 209, 214, 246, 270, 444
reminder, 24, 26, 27, 35, 41, 55, 61,
77, 92, 108, 214, 229, 235,
236, 262, 268, 295, 298,
312, 313, 349, 358, 367,

378, 385, 387, 390, 392,
406, 408, 415, 419, 427,
430, 432, 433, 437, 438,
453, 463, 476, 486, 496
report, 161, 303, 403
reporting, 101, 165, 272, 280
repository, 435
representation, 315
representative, 328, 512, 518
reprisal, 57, 97, 280, 410, 431, 432,
462, 477, 483
reputation, 102, 111, 113, 116, 156,
297, 394, 512
request, 448, 473
research, 6, 64, 69, 70, 83, 160, 178,
215, 226, 277, 310, 311,
327, 328, 343, 356, 357,
364, 365, 373, 374, 379,
384, 386, 397, 419–421,
435, 442, 469, 488, 489,
491, 494
researcher, 42, 250
resilience, 8, 94, 112, 135, 174, 271,
364, 385, 428, 432
resistance, 23, 34, 44, 156, 160, 180,
200, 210, 218, 219, 228,
235, 358, 384, 426, 430,
472
resolution, 303
resolve, 12, 109, 161
resource, 20, 56, 91, 223, 469, 488
respect, 8, 41, 159, 256, 378, 382,
402, 494, 506, 516
response, 35, 65, 80, 211, 223, 224,
264, 276, 316, 335, 337,
341, 342, 344, 369, 444,
483, 487, 522
responsibility, 8, 53, 111, 114, 239,
251, 252, 259, 265, 289,

298, 334, 350, 370, 372, 390, 396, 406, 411, 413, 414, 424, 433, 440, 445, 447, 449, 455, 457, 466, 467, 469, 474, 479, 482, 484, 496, 497, 502, 506, 516
rest, 12, 25, 78, 97, 136, 137, 140, 153, 178, 215, 223, 272, 304, 359, 525
result, 237, 261, 286, 301, 302, 443, 455, 498, 512
retaliation, 166, 170, 279, 280
retention, 303, 304, 308, 451, 462, 525
retirement, 466
retribution, 57
retrieve, 119, 137
return, 240
revelation, 241
revenue, 69, 71, 263
review, 162, 194, 220, 225, 235, 371, 382, 392, 394, 395, 407, 481
revocation, 135, 209
revolution, 23, 119, 123, 170, 172, 214, 229, 336, 390, 446
ride, 13
riff, 106
rift, 33
right, 3, 6, 10–13, 15, 16, 23–25, 27–32, 34, 35, 38, 40, 45, 49, 50, 53–55, 57–60, 62, 64, 69, 72, 74–76, 80, 83–85, 87, 92, 95, 97, 109, 111, 112, 117, 122, 140, 146, 178, 181, 198, 206, 214, 224, 228, 235, 236, 245, 246, 250, 259, 267, 268, 270, 275–278, 281, 283, 286, 289–292, 296, 306, 308, 312, 313, 320–325, 331–337, 344, 345, 347–349, 353, 360, 361, 364, 374–378, 384–386, 388, 390, 392, 397, 401, 403, 404, 407, 409, 410, 412, 413, 416, 425, 426, 429, 431–434, 436–438, 441, 442, 444, 445, 447, 457, 460, 462, 464, 466, 471, 473–475, 477, 479, 480, 482–484, 486, 487, 491, 495, 496, 510, 511, 513, 514, 517, 525
rise, 26, 33, 35, 44, 54, 58, 60, 70, 75, 81, 115, 146, 175, 214, 223, 229, 234, 237, 238, 242, 243, 245, 262, 263, 269, 271, 273, 286, 293, 294, 299, 305, 316, 320, 335, 337, 367, 401, 432, 439, 442, 445, 446, 458, 465, 481, 489, 493, 498, 508, 522
risk, 5, 58, 65, 96, 115, 140, 143, 160, 165, 174, 194, 196, 240, 243, 272, 277, 279, 283, 286, 296, 321, 338, 347, 360, 364, 378, 405, 447, 450, 452–454, 465, 466, 503, 522, 524
roadblock, 282
roadmap, 425
robustness, 169
rock, 106
Roland Huesca, 480

role, 11, 12, 17–19, 21, 28, 33, 39, 40, 42, 44, 48, 57, 58, 61–64, 68, 70–72, 74, 78, 80, 84–88, 90, 97, 98, 100, 101, 108–110, 115, 123, 126, 128–130, 132, 133, 136–138, 140, 142, 144, 149, 153, 154, 157, 158, 161, 163–165, 168, 169, 174, 175, 179, 187, 189, 193, 195, 198, 200, 212, 216–218, 220–222, 225, 229, 231, 232, 234, 238, 244–246, 248, 249, 257–260, 264, 267, 268, 276, 277, 279, 281, 282, 285, 288, 293, 295, 298, 303–305, 307, 309, 310, 312, 314, 317, 320–323, 330, 332, 334, 336, 339, 342, 344, 348, 355, 361, 365, 367, 373, 376, 382, 383, 388–391, 398, 399, 401, 402, 405–407, 411, 414, 418, 424, 429–432, 437, 439–441, 444, 446–450, 454, 458, 459, 461–463, 472, 473, 475, 477, 478, 480, 481, 484–486, 488, 489, 491–493, 495, 496, 499, 506, 509, 513, 515–520, 522, 523
room, 103, 362
root, 135
rotation, 272
route, 520
rule, 52, 100
rush, 105

sacrifice, 323
safeguard, 14, 17, 23, 25, 27, 29, 49, 59, 63, 73, 83, 88, 146, 154, 156, 180, 195, 207, 218, 224, 225, 239, 244, 248, 258, 259, 262, 273, 280, 285, 286, 289, 293, 295, 298, 304, 307, 312, 316, 333, 334, 345, 349, 353, 374, 378, 383, 384, 389, 391, 401, 409, 413, 422, 429, 430, 448, 467, 474, 479, 480, 496, 523
safeguarding, 5, 11, 32, 33, 35, 40, 44, 48, 52, 57, 71, 74, 78, 82, 94, 101, 108, 113, 115, 140, 142, 145, 148, 149, 152, 164, 168, 172, 173, 175, 181, 195, 197, 204, 216, 221, 225, 229, 230, 244, 245, 251, 252, 258, 260, 264, 267, 268, 276, 288, 296, 298, 302, 307, 309, 320, 327, 332, 336, 345, 348, 376, 378, 388, 402, 403, 405, 408, 411, 415, 416, 428, 431, 432, 441, 456–458, 460, 461, 467, 472, 490, 493, 499, 509, 520, 522, 525
safety, 12, 27, 50, 86, 87, 165, 167, 170, 178, 193, 197, 198, 246, 248, 249, 268, 269, 273, 275, 276, 281, 310, 312, 328, 329, 405, 451, 462, 472, 496, 516, 518, 524
sailing, 7, 103
sake, 31, 55, 323, 342

Samuel Warren, 335
San Bernardino, 196, 283
sanctuary, 322–325, 433
Sarah, 421
satisfaction, 396
say, 243, 323
saying, 456
scalability, 135, 223, 357
scale, 83, 109, 137, 250, 474
scandal, 238, 241, 244–246,
    250–253, 261, 262, 305,
    452, 457, 498
scavenger, 43
scenario, 17, 43, 89, 198, 257, 347
scene, 60
schedule, 99
Schneier, 379
scholar, 247
school, 1, 2, 4, 7–9, 14, 28, 29, 85,
    94, 108, 211, 315, 383,
    496, 518
science, 1, 4, 5, 13, 14, 16, 19, 20, 29,
    94, 97, 98, 104, 123,
    127–129, 136, 176, 216,
    225–227, 229, 236, 358,
    371, 383, 385, 390, 399,
    400, 419, 426, 427, 435,
    437, 491, 495
scientist, 21, 250
scope, 88
screen, 103, 105
scrutiny, 6, 12, 31, 58, 87, 89, 113,
    155, 156, 165, 169, 215,
    220, 247, 269, 303, 311,
    342, 370, 384, 394, 424,
    426, 472
scuba, 106
search, 18, 65, 242, 335, 443, 446,
    499, 514, 521, 523

seclusion, 477
secrecy, 9
secret, 17, 18, 78, 94, 109, 119, 123,
    124, 127, 130, 131, 133,
    153, 176, 180, 190, 194,
    285, 327, 363
section, 3, 7, 13, 21, 32, 38, 41, 44,
    46, 53, 57, 65, 72, 75, 77,
    82, 87, 93, 100, 103, 110,
    112, 115, 116, 123, 126,
    130, 142, 146, 149, 154,
    162, 164, 167, 170, 175,
    179, 185, 188, 200, 211,
    230, 253, 260, 262, 276,
    279, 287, 298, 302, 307,
    313, 316, 322, 327, 329,
    332, 335, 337, 341, 344,
    350, 359, 362, 365, 367,
    370, 373, 395, 398, 400,
    410, 418, 422, 435, 436,
    448, 450, 455, 458, 463,
    477, 483, 486, 493, 516,
    520, 522
sector, 260, 346
secure, 2, 4, 5, 10, 11, 15–20, 23, 24,
    26, 29, 33, 35, 38, 40,
    43–45, 49, 54, 57, 58,
    60–62, 64, 70, 73, 75, 76,
    78, 80, 82, 83, 88, 91, 92,
    111, 112, 120–124,
    126–128, 130–137, 140,
    142, 143, 145, 146, 148,
    152–154, 156, 158, 160,
    164, 166–170, 173,
    176–181, 183, 184, 188,
    189, 193, 195, 196, 199,
    200, 202–204, 206–219,
    223, 225, 226, 228, 230,
    233, 234, 238, 247, 249,

252, 258, 264, 267, 270–272, 276, 277, 281, 282, 290, 293–295, 298–302, 304, 306, 310, 312, 317, 320, 322, 323, 325, 333, 338, 341, 343, 347, 349, 356–363, 365, 366, 370–374, 376, 381, 384, 385, 388, 391, 394, 395, 402, 405, 406, 415–418, 420, 423, 424, 427–429, 432–434, 441, 443, 453, 458–460, 463, 467, 473–475, 478, 480, 488–490, 492, 496, 499, 508, 514, 520, 524, 525
security, 2, 8, 9, 11, 12, 17–19, 23, 27, 29, 31–35, 38–40, 42–46, 48, 50–56, 58, 59, 63, 64, 70, 75–81, 83–92, 94, 95, 97, 100–102, 106, 108, 110–112, 119, 120, 122, 123, 125, 127, 128, 130, 131, 133, 135–137, 140, 142, 145, 147, 149–157, 160, 162–167, 169, 170, 172–175, 177–179, 181–183, 187, 189, 190, 192–201, 205–208, 210–215, 217–226, 228, 230–236, 238, 240, 243–246, 248, 249, 252, 257–259, 263, 264, 267–273, 275–278, 280, 282–286, 291–296, 298–303, 308, 310–312, 315, 321, 323, 325, 328, 329, 332, 334, 336–340, 342, 343, 347, 349, 356, 357, 359–361, 363–371, 373–379, 383, 384, 386, 389, 390, 392–394, 396–398, 400–402, 406–408, 410, 411, 413–416, 418, 423, 426, 429, 430, 434, 436, 440–442, 448, 449, 451–455, 459–463, 465–469, 472, 474–478, 480, 481, 483, 486–488, 490–493, 496–499, 508, 512–519, 521, 524
seizure, 335
self, 86, 208, 216, 263, 269, 314, 328, 344, 410, 445, 478, 514
send, 15, 17, 131, 133, 184, 186, 190, 212, 228, 241, 257, 384
sender, 17, 124, 126, 127, 132, 134, 153, 176, 182, 188, 190, 197, 205, 224, 225, 249, 252, 302, 360, 443
sense, 8, 12, 20, 39, 55, 60, 75, 87, 102, 103, 106, 108, 110, 112, 146, 165, 298, 327, 392, 394, 399, 410, 414, 436, 442, 456, 479, 517
sensitivity, 140
sentiment, 466
series, 61, 167, 314, 348, 426, 520
serve, 58, 148, 279, 308, 335, 378, 391, 401, 408, 418, 434–436, 438, 453
server, 186
service, 143, 213, 215, 228, 262, 294, 315, 366, 411, 463, 515
session, 107, 188

Index 577

set, 2, 4, 5, 8, 15, 28, 29, 32, 86, 98, 140, 144, 155, 163, 165, 167, 176, 189, 212, 213, 215, 223, 228, 294, 304, 308, 335, 366, 391, 395, 423, 430, 449, 468
setting, 9, 38, 98, 165, 174, 179, 263, 514
shape, 3, 5, 7, 11, 19, 24, 26, 28, 32, 38, 40, 42, 46, 68, 83, 86, 92, 94, 112, 114, 115, 117, 152, 155, 164, 169, 178, 181, 197, 224, 226, 229, 235, 237, 239, 241, 246, 262, 264, 265, 268, 287, 292, 295, 310, 311, 313, 319, 320, 322, 335, 342, 343, 355, 358, 362, 365, 367, 370, 373, 377, 378, 383, 384, 386, 387, 390, 391, 397, 399, 402, 406, 415, 416, 418, 419, 426, 430, 433, 440, 446, 447, 451, 458, 463, 465, 474, 476, 478, 489, 510, 514, 516, 522
share, 24, 25, 62, 64, 73, 75, 81, 99, 104, 111, 116, 148, 153, 158, 166, 170, 189, 194, 218, 225, 234, 238, 247, 252, 257, 263, 281, 299, 346, 347, 360, 374, 380, 382, 398, 399, 401, 411, 419, 420, 431, 432, 439, 451, 454, 460, 462, 477, 490, 495, 497, 498, 509, 514
sharing, 5, 18, 73, 98, 103, 148, 156, 158, 163, 165, 174, 188, 203, 214, 215, 217, 241, 263, 281, 287, 289, 299, 303, 305, 309, 311, 316, 320, 337, 338, 361, 363, 371, 382, 385, 396, 398, 399, 401, 414, 418, 441, 444, 449, 451, 454–456, 467, 468, 488, 494, 512, 514, 515, 518
shield, 48, 54, 57, 149, 179, 199, 217, 460
shift, 24, 85, 173, 175, 305, 306, 375, 386, 388, 389, 407, 413, 466, 479
shopping, 146, 237, 241, 253, 258, 286, 305, 455
Shor, 368
Shoshana Zuboff, 237, 247, 296
Shoshana Zuboff - An, 469
shoulder, 413
show, 523
side, 103, 105, 110, 146, 147, 177, 196, 200, 204, 250, 381, 400, 490
sign, 184, 188
Signal Messenger, 300
signature, 134, 184
significance, 21, 33, 71, 74, 101, 119, 154, 195, 235, 260, 279, 297, 337, 360, 410, 415, 426, 429, 461, 463, 466, 477
signing, 17, 39
silence, 106
Simon Singh, 56, 62, 109, 129, 219, 279, 295
Simon Singh - An, 65
simple, 8, 125, 154, 186, 295, 424
simplicity, 104, 153, 168

Siri, 446
situation, 39, 485
size, 47, 98, 124, 140
sketchbook, 106
sketching, 106
sky, 105
skydiving, 105, 106
slope, 472
smartphone, 366
Snowden, 101, 279, 291, 294, 431
society, 5, 6, 13, 16, 24, 27, 31, 39, 42, 46, 53, 56, 59, 61–63, 65, 76, 81, 85, 87, 88, 111, 119, 122, 130, 146, 170, 175, 179, 185, 189, 200, 202, 205, 216, 217, 236, 239, 241, 243, 250, 260, 262, 268, 270, 276, 277, 279–283, 285, 287, 296, 310, 313–316, 319, 320, 332, 334, 340, 347, 358, 365, 371, 378, 385, 387, 388, 396, 406, 408, 410, 412, 413, 415, 418, 420, 427, 440, 442, 445, 447, 449, 453, 460, 465, 474, 476–479, 484, 489, 493, 506, 510, 511, 513, 514, 517, 526
socio, 374, 402
sociology, 399, 435
software, 2, 8, 10, 15, 23, 26, 30, 31, 33, 44, 63, 91, 102, 108, 111, 122, 123, 126, 152, 154–158, 160–163, 165, 168, 173, 175, 178, 179, 183, 187, 188, 198, 200, 205, 207, 211, 212, 217, 220, 221, 225, 226, 228, 267, 271, 293, 296, 303, 311, 312, 323, 338, 342, 361, 366, 370, 371, 384, 388, 391–395, 398, 405, 413, 414, 425, 426, 429, 434, 454, 455, 460–462, 464, 466, 469, 474, 481, 506
Soghoian, 57
solace, 85, 103, 105, 106
solidarity, 165, 479
solution, 20, 25, 35, 44, 50, 98, 122, 138, 140, 153, 155, 156, 161, 165, 175, 193, 194, 269, 271, 295, 300, 301, 327, 343, 400, 413, 421, 479, 492, 515
solving, 4, 9, 28, 105, 108, 271, 363, 408, 434, 435, 458, 486, 503
sophistication, 323, 489, 522
soul, 98, 103, 106
sound, 106
source, 100, 108, 155, 156, 158, 162–165, 167, 169, 173, 181, 194, 210, 212, 213, 215, 220, 225–227, 229, 235, 268, 291, 300, 303, 304, 311, 342–344, 357, 361, 362, 366, 370–372, 382, 385, 389, 392–395, 397–399, 405–407, 413, 414, 418–420, 423, 426, 429, 430, 435, 466, 481, 488, 494
sourcing, 155, 418
sovereignty, 82, 193, 393
space, 25, 91, 348, 349, 373, 399, 410, 431, 477

Index 579

speaker, 297
speaking, 42, 74, 116, 169, 173, 277, 279, 297, 311, 374, 388, 397, 398, 406, 421
spectrum, 472
speech, 40, 57–60, 84, 91, 97, 101, 166, 217, 246, 276, 283, 294, 312, 345, 410, 431, 498, 503
speed, 146, 160, 362, 367
spending, 106
sphere, 80, 377
spirit, 8, 9, 41, 62, 94, 105, 107, 163, 229, 366, 392, 398, 399, 407, 408, 413, 414, 419
spotlight, 105, 114, 250, 307
spread, 23, 31, 39, 42–44, 47, 58, 59, 156, 159, 246, 259, 446, 481
stage, 4, 8, 9, 19, 28, 29, 38, 75, 179, 197, 442, 477
stake, 50, 246, 283
stance, 34, 53, 198, 291, 315, 383, 483, 485
stand, 4, 12, 64, 82, 174, 175, 291, 301, 384, 409, 415, 416, 418, 426, 437, 464, 465
standard, 1, 78, 84, 91, 158, 208, 210, 212, 213, 215, 216, 223, 234, 294, 304, 308, 366, 389
standardization, 207
staple, 419
startup, 421
state, 26, 64, 70, 87, 106, 137, 149, 161, 222, 270, 273, 291, 368, 381, 420, 472, 481, 489, 498, 499, 522
statement, 343

status, 1, 5, 7, 9, 10, 20, 23, 24, 32, 60, 94, 117, 229, 250, 325, 335, 384, 418, 427, 433, 441, 477, 496
step, 49, 125, 127, 132, 313, 314, 355, 358, 360, 362, 369, 384, 441, 453, 493, 495
Stephen M. Kohn, 282
Steven Levy, 62, 379
stigmatization, 269
stir, 14, 23, 391
stone, 111
storage, 137, 146, 186, 188, 195, 215, 243, 270, 271, 299, 341, 441, 445, 448, 488, 514, 520, 524
store, 126, 186, 252, 262, 304, 368
storing, 123, 126, 132, 137, 259, 363, 474, 515, 521
story, 13, 24, 32, 41, 46, 48, 98, 105, 167, 186, 222, 229, 236, 314, 408, 417, 418, 421, 427, 437, 438, 461
strain, 98
strategy, 42
streak, 1, 4, 7, 28, 365
street, 269
strength, 104, 120, 136, 160, 176, 187, 313, 408
stress, 245, 321, 364
stricter, 251, 305, 307
string, 127
struggle, 15, 47, 71, 97, 98, 149, 152, 235, 246, 261, 263, 412, 428, 437, 451, 513
student, 4, 28
study, 2, 119, 225, 347
style, 297

subject, 5, 20, 57, 60, 87, 269, 276, 360, 377, 448, 478
substitution, 120
success, 48, 100, 102, 103, 157, 158, 213, 220–222, 226, 227, 235, 294, 366, 379, 389, 393–396, 398, 399, 415, 421, 423, 468
suite, 366
superposition, 363, 368
support, 12, 21, 31, 37, 39, 41, 42, 44–47, 60, 69–72, 75, 83, 86, 96, 98, 101, 109, 113, 114, 160–162, 165–167, 169, 174, 189, 194, 217, 239, 246, 267, 277, 280, 293, 295, 311, 313, 357, 373–375, 384, 386, 389, 398, 414, 419–421, 424, 429, 464, 465, 473, 485, 496, 499, 515
supporter, 311, 349, 461
suppression, 432, 477
surge, 473
surveillance, 5, 11, 13, 16, 18, 23, 25–29, 31–33, 37–39, 42–44, 47, 50, 56, 57, 60, 61, 65, 74–76, 81, 82, 84–92, 95, 96, 101, 108–110, 115–117, 146, 148, 153, 156, 165, 170, 174, 180, 181, 189, 190, 196, 200, 201, 210, 211, 218–220, 223, 228, 235, 237, 240, 242–245, 247–250, 254, 260, 262, 263, 267–270, 273, 275, 276, 279, 283–287, 290–295, 297–299, 301–303, 305, 310, 314, 315, 319–322, 324, 333, 335, 337, 343–345, 347–349, 360, 366, 372, 375, 377, 379, 381, 384, 386, 388, 389, 400, 401, 403–405, 408, 410, 411, 415, 418, 424, 426, 428–432, 436, 439, 440, 442–446, 448–451, 454, 456, 458, 460, 462–465, 467, 473, 475–480, 483–486, 490, 493, 495, 496, 498, 514, 516, 522
suspect, 263
suspicion, 166, 391
sustainability, 71, 372
Switzerland, 197
symbol, 12, 23, 34, 47, 180, 196, 200, 213, 218, 219, 228, 235, 384, 426, 430
system, 7, 23, 33, 46, 57, 58, 89, 98, 126, 130–132, 136, 151, 157–159, 162, 168, 170, 177, 186, 194, 196, 208, 210, 214, 222, 237, 247, 262, 282, 283, 369, 384, 429, 434, 464, 468, 508

table, 421
Tadayoshi Kohno, 129, 400
tale, 8, 245, 252, 314, 427
talent, 28, 85, 106, 422
talk, 57, 64
tamper, 194, 328
tampering, 17, 78, 123, 125, 132, 138, 160, 188, 190, 193, 208

target, 222, 237, 238, 240, 241, 250, 252, 254, 262, 317, 440, 498
task, 21, 59, 128, 140, 196–198, 391, 394, 400, 412, 503
teaching, 1, 288, 296, 333, 338, 383, 435, 493, 518
team, 45, 109, 155–157, 159–161, 168, 169, 241, 296, 359, 394, 400
teamwork, 103
tech, 11, 24, 31, 34, 35, 39–47, 49, 81, 86, 95, 96, 103, 109, 116, 117, 196–198, 210, 220, 228, 238, 239, 245–256, 263, 264, 267, 268, 276, 282, 283, 286, 295, 300, 302–304, 312, 316–320, 322, 331, 334, 337, 342, 355, 358, 365, 367, 370, 375–380, 384, 385, 389–392, 395–397, 399, 401, 405, 407, 408, 411, 413–416, 421, 423, 426, 429, 432, 439, 440, 446, 451–453, 459–465, 467, 473, 474, 476, 483–486, 491, 493–495, 517
technique, 21, 124, 143, 225, 287, 302
technologist, 494
technology, 3, 4, 6, 7, 9, 13, 14, 17–19, 21, 22, 24–28, 31–34, 37, 38, 40, 42, 44–46, 49, 54, 55, 57–60, 63, 65, 69, 72, 74, 80–86, 88, 90–92, 94, 98, 102, 107, 108, 111, 115–117, 119, 123, 139, 140, 143–145, 149, 154, 162, 164, 170, 173, 175, 178–181, 183, 189, 195–197, 199, 200, 203, 208–210, 216, 217, 220, 222, 225, 228–230, 234, 236, 239, 241, 245, 246, 249, 251, 252, 259–262, 264, 267, 269, 270, 272, 276, 277, 282, 283, 285, 287, 292, 294, 295, 302, 305, 307, 309–315, 320, 324, 325, 327–329, 331, 335–337, 340, 347, 348, 351, 352, 355–358, 360–365, 367, 369–374, 376, 381, 383, 385–393, 396–398, 400, 401, 405, 406, 408–410, 412, 415, 418, 423, 424, 426, 429, 431, 433, 436, 437, 439, 441, 442, 445–448, 450, 453, 455, 457–460, 466–469, 474–477, 479–481, 483–486, 488–490, 493, 496, 498, 508, 510, 513, 515, 517, 518, 520–523, 525, 526
Telecomix, 61
tenacity, 19
tendency, 7
tension, 27, 58, 76, 81, 146, 178, 217, 224, 246, 263, 269, 281, 328, 440, 492
term, 71, 210, 237, 247, 370, 396, 481
terrain, 276
territory, 14

terrorism, 18, 27, 50, 87, 183, 196, 197, 258, 269, 275, 277, 282, 444, 472, 492
terrorist, 283
Terry, 108
Terry Walker, 108
test, 94, 413, 432
testament, 13, 32, 41, 47, 97, 154, 157, 175, 295, 365, 367, 392, 421, 428, 434, 463
testing, 79, 168, 169, 176, 364
text, 50, 126, 127, 136, 186, 187, 190, 215
textbook, 130
the Middle East, 61
the United Kingdom, 197
the United States, 33, 173, 197, 260, 335, 374, 415, 440, 464, 498
the United States Constitution, 335
theft, 128, 216, 240, 243, 247, 257, 272, 305, 314, 338, 345, 443, 454–457, 498, 503, 511, 512
theme, 226, 313, 314
theory, 176
thermostats, 506, 508
think, 9, 10, 20, 24, 42, 90, 92, 100, 108, 109, 111, 211, 245, 295, 347, 371, 390, 392, 407, 426, 427, 438
thinker, 5
thinking, 1, 4, 5, 20, 95, 100, 104, 108, 111, 112, 285, 295, 316, 340, 343, 358, 362, 365, 366, 370, 399
thirst, 8, 9, 20, 93
thought, 25, 64, 91, 112, 397, 434
threat, 23, 33, 45, 47, 60, 64, 77, 81, 89, 125, 151, 174, 178, 183, 207, 210, 231, 271, 273, 291, 327, 345, 362, 367–370, 384, 401, 408, 410, 440, 451, 458, 473, 478, 486, 496, 522, 523
thrill, 4, 8, 14
thrive, 69, 343, 361, 373, 376, 394, 516
tightrope, 71
time, 2, 5, 9, 10, 14, 15, 21, 25, 39, 60, 94, 98, 103, 105, 106, 113, 125, 155, 160, 162, 176, 183, 209, 211, 214, 222, 250, 254, 259, 341, 357, 363, 371, 413, 414, 416, 426, 436, 437, 458, 472, 482, 503, 525
timing, 241
today, 17, 19, 25–27, 40, 54, 55, 61, 77, 80, 81, 85, 87, 112, 136, 140, 148, 149, 152, 162, 175, 193, 218, 235, 237, 239, 247, 253, 257, 262, 268, 270, 273, 276, 285, 290, 298, 302, 305, 307, 316, 320, 322, 335, 338, 341, 370, 377, 381, 390, 394, 400, 408, 410, 414, 415, 430, 434, 442, 445, 447, 450, 455, 481, 486, 498, 499, 512, 516, 517, 520
tool, 10, 11, 16, 23, 24, 26, 30, 34, 40, 45, 47, 54, 58, 60, 62, 74, 87, 95, 100, 102, 121, 128, 136, 140, 142, 152, 156–158, 161, 162, 164, 169, 174, 177–180, 183,

Index 583

    189, 192, 193, 204,
    206–208, 211, 215, 218,
    222, 228–230, 249, 268,
    270, 276, 277, 291,
    293–295, 320, 327, 372,
    377, 378, 391, 399, 407,
    415, 431, 452, 464, 472,
    474, 496, 521
topic, 64, 281, 283, 287, 312, 313, 315, 332, 338, 470, 498, 505
torch, 13, 28, 35, 55, 73, 250, 268, 325, 335, 349, 350, 353, 358, 387, 430, 433, 437, 442, 468, 497
touchstone, 200, 229
tour, 42
town, 19
tracker, 382
tracking, 81, 269, 299, 344, 498, 521
traction, 12, 44, 47, 71, 144, 157, 159, 293, 335
trade, 59, 85, 87, 128, 146, 148, 193, 263, 270, 277, 286, 347, 446, 487
trademark, 10
traffic, 459, 520
trafficking, 282
trail, 65, 333, 522
trailblazer, 391
trailblazing, 116
training, 106, 122, 165, 167, 194, 280, 309, 369, 503, 504, 513, 518
trajectory, 102, 414
tranquility, 106
transact, 146
transaction, 18, 65, 514
transfer, 234, 258

transit, 17, 25, 78, 121, 136–138, 140, 153, 177, 178, 215, 223, 272, 304
transition, 173, 369
translation, 173
transmission, 121, 184, 194, 271, 281, 480, 508, 520
transparency, 27, 57, 64, 71, 87, 89, 101, 144, 155, 162, 164, 169, 173, 194, 220, 226, 239, 242, 243, 251, 253, 270, 279–281, 285, 288, 291, 300, 303, 304, 308, 310–312, 317, 320, 321, 323, 337, 342, 371, 378, 382, 387, 389, 392–395, 409–411, 414, 443, 445, 447, 450, 460, 462, 466, 467, 481, 484–486, 494, 495, 499–502, 504, 506, 509, 511, 512, 515, 517, 523, 525, 526
treasure, 157, 440
treatment, 315, 512
trend, 262, 301
triumph, 46, 48, 49, 96, 267
troop, 258
trouble, 1, 4, 7–9, 14, 28, 85, 94, 383
troubleshooting, 165
trove, 440
trust, 19, 52, 71, 88, 102, 134, 135, 146, 162, 165, 169, 174, 193, 203, 208, 214, 215, 217, 221, 228, 243, 261, 269, 270, 275, 277, 285, 300, 302, 303, 308, 309, 317, 320, 346, 362, 366, 389, 392, 394, 395, 411, 444, 445, 460, 478, 488,

489, 500, 509, 511, 512, 517
trustworthiness, 481
truth, 108, 294, 343
tuning, 155, 159–161
turn, 4, 314, 446
turning, 12, 31, 32, 48, 225, 228, 247, 294, 451, 499
tutelage, 20
type, 125

U.S., 3, 15, 30, 31, 33–35, 38, 47, 58, 95, 173, 241, 250, 267, 342, 384, 391, 426, 427, 434
understanding, 2–4, 6, 8–10, 19–21, 25, 29, 56, 59, 89, 93, 94, 101, 107, 108, 111, 115, 122, 126, 152, 157, 163, 167, 185, 193, 197, 198, 227, 228, 238, 244, 252, 267, 269, 273, 286, 288, 303, 307, 315, 316, 329, 332, 337, 357, 360, 365, 369, 371, 383, 395, 396, 402, 413, 426, 427, 435, 445, 451, 453, 454, 456, 457, 459, 482, 488, 491, 492, 496, 498, 503, 511, 512, 518, 519, 523
United States, 10, 35, 46, 244
unity, 414
update, 183, 338, 455
urgency, 60
US, 238, 260, 452
usability, 43, 129, 135, 155, 157, 163, 168, 206, 208, 214, 222, 227, 343, 344, 359, 371, 400, 444, 480, 488

usage, 166, 167, 189, 201, 206, 231, 293, 325, 376, 442, 444, 445, 452, 493, 494, 522
use, 3, 6, 8, 11, 12, 16, 17, 24, 32, 33, 40, 47, 61, 62, 65, 85, 87, 88, 90, 95, 100, 101, 116, 122, 126, 127, 130–132, 137, 140, 144, 148, 152–155, 161, 165–168, 173, 174, 176, 177, 179, 180, 182–185, 188, 189, 194, 196, 200, 201, 204, 208, 209, 212, 215, 217, 218, 221–225, 229, 231–234, 240–242, 244, 246–249, 251–254, 260, 262, 264, 267, 272, 283, 285, 286, 291, 294, 295, 301, 304, 310, 312, 314, 315, 320, 323, 333, 336–338, 340, 347, 348, 357, 364–366, 368, 372, 376–378, 382, 393, 394, 406, 410, 413, 419, 426, 429, 431, 432, 442, 443, 447, 448, 454, 455, 459, 460, 468, 469, 472, 473, 480, 481, 488, 491, 494, 498, 499, 503, 513–515, 517, 518, 521
user, 10, 17, 24, 26, 44, 55, 58, 70, 71, 80, 88, 102, 112, 122, 126, 129–131, 138, 140, 144, 148, 153–156, 159–161, 163–165, 167–170, 173–175, 179, 186, 187, 189, 192, 194, 195, 197–199, 203, 204, 206, 207, 209, 211,

Index 585

213–216, 220–222, 224, 226–231, 234, 235, 237, 238, 241–248, 251–256, 262, 263, 277, 283, 288, 289, 293–295, 300–304, 306–312, 316, 317, 319, 320, 322–324, 327, 332, 337–341, 343, 356, 359, 360, 364, 367, 370–372, 382, 384, 388, 389, 391, 394–397, 400, 405–407, 410, 411, 423–426, 428–430, 433, 434, 439–441, 443, 445–447, 451–455, 457, 460–464, 467–469, 475, 476, 480, 488, 489, 493, 494, 506, 508, 512, 514, 520–522, 524

validation, 18, 44, 132, 160
validity, 134, 343
value, 1, 38, 96, 98, 140, 146, 154, 194, 211, 226, 238, 300, 314, 322, 343, 349, 357, 372, 391, 395, 413, 441, 456, 457, 467, 482
variety, 301, 451
venture, 4, 69
verification, 18, 19, 135, 160, 207, 209, 214, 215, 309, 343
viability, 71
victim, 151, 337, 453–455, 488
victory, 12, 31, 32, 34, 37, 39–41, 47–49, 53, 86, 96, 267, 429, 434
video, 215, 300, 508
view, 162, 264, 279, 429, 516

vigilance, 77, 166, 220, 229, 249, 313, 412, 463, 471, 515
violation, 269, 321, 347
visibility, 494
vision, 3, 5, 10, 15, 24–27, 31, 42, 49, 54, 60, 63, 72, 73, 75, 83, 91, 93, 101, 113, 116, 117, 158, 175, 228, 268, 293, 298, 316, 322–325, 330, 340, 349–353, 357, 365, 373, 384–386, 391, 392, 399, 407–409, 416, 418, 419, 427, 429, 430, 433, 436–438, 442, 461, 462, 465, 466, 476, 477, 480–482, 485, 492, 496
visionary, 3, 5, 16, 45, 68, 100, 115, 119, 126, 198, 295, 310, 329, 355, 362, 370, 387, 390–392, 398, 401, 407, 413, 436
voice, 12, 38, 39, 116, 189, 214, 215, 289, 300, 365, 375, 377, 378, 446, 466, 508, 518
volunteering, 20, 425
voter, 457
vulnerability, 5, 155, 196, 217, 263, 282, 305, 355, 366, 452, 472, 475, 498

wake, 115, 214, 245, 253, 405, 445, 452
walk, 71
war, 15, 280, 474
warrant, 351, 448
water, 7
wave, 44, 92, 228, 405, 418, 426, 461, 466

way, 9, 13, 16, 29, 34, 35, 42–44, 48, 58, 59, 63, 64, 71, 72, 83, 91, 92, 106, 107, 111, 117, 122, 126, 127, 140, 145, 146, 148, 152, 161, 162, 164, 167, 168, 170, 174, 175, 188–190, 193, 196, 199, 200, 209, 211, 213, 220, 234, 238, 241, 245, 250, 252, 255, 263, 276, 281, 282, 291–294, 302, 311, 329, 336, 339, 341, 343, 344, 348, 360, 362, 363, 365, 368, 370, 384–386, 390–394, 398, 399, 411, 414, 416, 426, 427, 429, 438, 440, 446, 447, 451, 453, 454, 457, 463, 468, 470, 476, 477, 480, 482, 483, 492, 499, 514, 516, 522, 526
weakening, 205, 277, 321, 465, 475
weakness, 472
wealth, 112, 166, 247, 337, 395
weapon, 60, 62, 474
wearable, 337
web, 174, 214, 215, 306, 440, 521
website, 379
week, 99
weight, 44
well, 7, 25, 27, 41, 44, 50, 87, 99, 103, 107, 108, 123, 142, 169, 187, 200, 216, 224, 238, 253, 264, 269, 281, 303, 315, 329, 335, 346, 350, 390, 396, 397, 402, 465, 468, 469
whirlwind, 103
whistle, 281

whistleblower, 279–281, 314, 321
whistleblowing, 280, 485
Whitfield Diffie, 42
whole, 50, 130, 241, 285, 332, 347, 410, 415, 418, 419, 440, 442, 445, 477, 506
wife, 98
will, 7, 25, 27, 28, 44, 46, 53, 57, 62, 63, 65, 72, 75, 76, 82, 85, 87, 90, 92, 93, 97, 112, 115–117, 123, 130, 142, 146, 152, 162, 164, 170, 175, 178, 179, 181, 184, 186, 188, 189, 195, 197, 200, 208, 211, 216, 224, 225, 227, 229–233, 239, 241, 246, 247, 249, 253, 260–262, 264, 276, 279, 283, 287, 292, 298, 302, 304, 307, 316, 322, 327, 329, 332, 335, 337, 341, 346, 349, 350, 355, 356, 358, 359, 362, 364, 365, 367, 370, 383, 387, 394, 395, 410, 418, 419, 422, 430, 437, 445, 447, 448, 450, 455, 458, 460, 465, 474, 477, 483, 486–489, 491, 493, 494, 512, 520–522, 525
willingness, 5, 99, 111, 399, 401, 414, 418
win, 45, 48
wind, 10
window, 434
wisdom, 20, 158, 213, 370, 372, 373, 419
witness, 399
wizard, 160

Index 587

word, 42, 159, 293
work, 6, 9, 13, 15, 16, 18, 20, 25, 26, 28, 29, 32, 40, 44, 48, 49, 53, 60, 61, 63–65, 68, 70, 72, 74–76, 80, 82–86, 90–95, 97–100, 102, 103, 107–116, 122, 130, 146, 152, 158, 165–167, 173, 218, 228, 229, 247, 255, 267, 268, 287, 289–292, 298, 307, 310–313, 316, 322, 332, 336, 340, 342–344, 347–350, 356, 358, 359, 366, 367, 370–374, 377–379, 384–390, 392, 393, 396–398, 400–402, 405, 406, 408, 409, 413–416, 418, 419, 422, 424, 426–428, 430–433, 435–438, 442, 445–447, 450, 457, 460–464, 466–468, 470, 475–477, 479–486, 491, 492, 494, 495, 514, 519, 522, 523
workflow, 98
working, 24, 42, 71, 74, 83, 101, 145, 155, 157, 166, 167, 179, 186, 223, 237, 319, 355, 356, 359, 361, 362, 370, 371, 378, 398–400, 403, 406, 418, 447, 464, 496, 515
workshop, 380
world, 1, 2, 4–16, 18–20, 22, 24, 26–29, 31, 32, 34, 43, 46, 48, 49, 51, 52, 54, 56, 57, 60, 62–64, 68, 72, 73, 75, 77, 80–87, 90–94, 97, 100, 101, 103–109, 111, 112, 115–117, 122, 123, 125–127, 129, 130, 132, 133, 140, 142, 145, 146, 148, 149, 152, 154, 156–158, 161, 162, 165–167, 169, 170, 172, 173, 175, 179, 181, 189, 192, 193, 195, 196, 200, 204, 211, 214, 216, 217, 220, 222, 224, 228, 229, 232, 233, 235, 237–239, 245, 248–250, 260, 262, 265, 267, 268, 272, 278, 282, 285–298, 300, 302, 307, 309, 310, 312, 314, 316, 318, 320, 322, 323, 325, 327, 329, 331, 332, 337, 339–344, 348–350, 355, 358, 362, 365, 367, 370–375, 379, 383–389, 391, 392, 398–403, 406, 408–411, 415, 416, 418, 420–422, 426–430, 433, 435–438, 440–442, 446, 450, 452–455, 457, 461–466, 468, 473, 474, 476, 477, 481, 487, 489, 493–496, 499, 505, 508, 515, 517, 519, 520, 522, 523, 525, 526
writing, 39, 94, 228, 293, 297, 399
wrongdoing, 170, 279, 280, 321

Yasha Levine, 109
Yasha Levine - A, 65
Yehuda Lindell, 130
yourself, 13
youth, 8

zest, 103
Zimmerman, 102
Zimmermann, 1–3, 17, 23–31, 33, 34, 41–49, 54, 55, 60–62, 69, 72–76, 82, 85, 86, 100–102, 119, 122, 155–159, 162, 167–169, 179, 180, 199, 200, 211, 212, 218, 228, 250, 267, 268, 291–293, 296–298, 310–313, 322–325, 329–332, 340–344, 348, 349, 355–362, 365–367, 370–379, 383–391, 395, 396, 398, 399, 401, 405–409, 413–416, 418, 419, 426–435, 461–466, 471, 475, 476, 480, 481, 483–485, 495–497

Milton Keynes UK
Ingram Content Group UK Ltd.
UKHW020313021124
450424UK00013B/1216